WineTrails
OF OREGON
A guide for uncorking your memorable wine tour

South Slope Productions

by Steve Roberts

MORE WINE ▶

WINETRAILS NW

WineTrails of Oregon
A guide for uncorking your memorable wine tour

Published by
South Slope Productions
9311 SE 36th Street, Suite 108, Mercer Island, WA 98040

© 2009 South Slope Productions

Library of Congress Cataloging in Publication Data available.

 WineTrails Northwest logo by Beth Hayes,
King Salmon Creative Designs

Edited by Sunny Parsons and Seattle Publishing, Inc.

Cover and interior design by Lisa J. Pettit, Lisa Pettit Designs

Photos by Steve Roberts, South Slope Productions, except where otherwise indicated

Plum Hill Vineyards' description by Alexander S. Roberts

Layout and production by Seattle Publishing, Inc.

First Edition
ISBN 13 - 978-0-9792698-1-3
ISBN 10 - 0-9792698-1-3

Printed in China by C&C Offset Printing Co., Ltd.

Acknowledgements & Dedication

To the hundreds of wine industry personnel working the tasting rooms of Oregon I am hugely indebted. Not only did they pour me generous samples of wine, they welcomed me with friendly salutations. Lest you think it is easy pouring wine all day while maintaining a welcoming grin, think again. It takes a certain fortitude and patience. Imagine satisfying the thirsty needs of folks poodling up to the bar all day and then having to be friendly to a geeky guy with a "Wineaux" hat toting a camera and notebook in hand. To this collective group of tasting room personnel (which includes a large number of winemakers themselves) I am forever grateful.

I know it is a cliché, but it does take a village to create a guidebook of this magnitude. It starts with the design of the book. To that end, I am eternally grateful to Seattle-based Lisa J. Pettit, artist extraordinaire. Lisa designed the cover as well as the interior layout. She has the rare talent of fusing pure art with color and iconic schemes to make the book easy to navigate. However, when it comes to another type of talent, I'd be sunk without the amazing gift of my chief editor, Sunny Parsons. She took my choppy prose and made it fluid. She must have a big supply of red ink pens.

The actual production of the book is the work of a very talented team of professionals at Seattle Publishing. They are like an exquisite Bordeaux blend, bringing together top-notch technologists, editors, designers and production management staff. Aside from professional expertise, however, they bring another key ingredient… they care. When it comes to a book of this size and scope, you need sticklers for detail. Seattle Publishing brought all that and more. For post-production needs, I wish to give special mention to Oregon-based Bob Smith, of the BookPrinters Network. He is my go-to guy with the printer of this book, C&C Offset Printing in China. All my concerns about language barriers and time zone changes, melted away under his guidance.

My kids, Alex and Meg Roberts, were lovingly supportive throughout the process. When I couldn't get to Plum Hill Vineyards in Gaston, I turned to Alex to be my eyes and ears and capture the essence of this new winery. His write-up highlights his wonderful writing skills. Meg, thanks for listening to your father go on and on about "the book." Your patience serves you well.

Finally, I wish to dedicate *Wine Trails of Oregon* to my soul mate and life partner, Kathleen von Reumont. Her encouragement and belief in me makes this book a reality for you to enjoy. Quite simply, I'm a lucky guy.

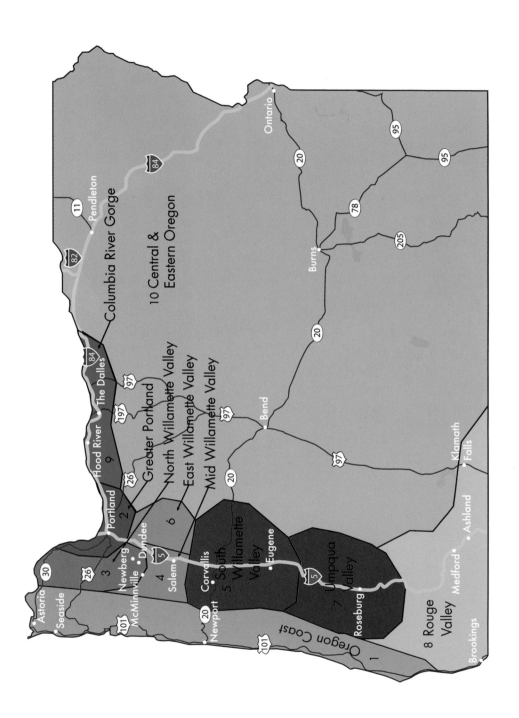

Contents at a Glance

Detailed Table of Contents

Mid Willamette Valley Wine Country

South Willamette Valley Wine Country

East Willamette Valley Wine Country

Umpqua Valley Wine Country

Heading West – Oregon's WineTrails

Angie Clarno cradled a bottle of their jug wine and I snapped a picture. I wanted to capture a photo of the Old Bridge Winery's unusual jug-bottled wine, but the image also revealed the care she took just holding the bottle, and a certain glee in her eye. That special caring passion struck me.

Angie Clarno, Old Bridge Winery

Old Bridge Winery was the 186th winery I had visited in Oregon, and I thought I had seen everything. I had been all over, from tasting rooms in chateaus to renovated banks, to create the ultimate, most comprehensive guidebook on Oregon wineries. However, here I was in a doublewide in Remote, Oregon, halfway between Roseburg and the Pacific Ocean, tasting sparkling cranberry wine. Despite the fact that diversity rules in Oregon, it struck me that there is a common denominator — winemakers all have great zeal for making wine. It doesn't matter what the location of the winery is, what varietals are produced, or what type of bottle, be it soft-shoulder Burgundy bottles or moonshine jugs. Oregon winemakers have unbridled enthusiasm for their product, and it's little wonder that year after year they receive high praise and accolades from wine critics around the world.

I must admit that I was feeling a little nutso while driving to Remote. I was thinking what the heck was I doing driving to the middle of nowhere to experience Old Bridge Winery. After all, I had already visited plenty of exquisite wineries throughout Oregon, and adding a winery known in large part for their fruit wine might distract. I understood the chances that Old Bridge Winery would be featured in *Sunset Magazine* were … well, remote. As I pulled up to the weathered structure, my suspicions were confirmed. But had I not gone to Old Bridge Winery, I would have violated a cardinal rule of this book — to feature all Oregon wineries having regular tasting room hours. You see, *WineTrails of Oregon* is not about rating the wines. Rather, it's about capturing the story behind each winery and giving you, dear reader, the information you need to get out there and explore for yourself. So, with that thought, I entered Old Bridge Winery and ended up surprising myself. I was the accidental wine tourist who stumbled on a good time and met some amazing people.

For those open to discovering new wines and going beyond million-dollar tasting rooms, your world just got easier. *WineTrails of Oregon* makes it trouble-free and fun to experience the many tasting rooms throughout the state. From Hood River to the Rogue River Valley, the book provides detailed maps, driving directions, contact information, tasting room hours, fee information and more. *WineTrails of Oregon* groups wineries into 24 incredible WineTrails, most of which can be experienced in a day or two. You'll also find practical information for planning your wine tour getaway to Oregon, including online resources for where to stay and where to eat, wine-related festivals, and tips for

LaVelle Vineyards

traveling with children and pets. There's advice for tasting wine as well as a section on tasting room etiquette. To cyclists out there (and I know that many WineTrail trekkers like to combine wine touring with spinning): you won't be disappointed. Some of the WineTrails featured in the book are specially noted as ideal for biking.

Are you planning a wedding and need a vineyard to host a wedding? Are you looking for an ideal place to picnic? Alternatively, do you need a perfect holiday or birthday gift for a "wineau" friend? You've come to the right place. In the "Favorites" section of this book, you'll find my best-of-the-best with respect to winery lodging, dining, retail shopping, viewing dramatic scenery, and hosting the ideal wedding.

I wrote this book to make it easy for you to get out there and explore Oregon wines. I made a boatload of mistakes along the way, getting lost and forgetting to bring cash for tasting fees. Now you don't need to make those same blunders. Take along *WineTrails of Oregon* and read aloud as you taste your way through Oregon's splendid WineTrails. Cheers!

Oregon's Amazing Wine Country Regions

To understand Oregon wine country, visitors need to know that there are four different viticultural areas: Willamette Valley, Umpqua Valley, Rogue River Valley, and the Columbia Gorge. Each area offers distinct climates and soils; consequently each wine country is hugely different. If your visit to Oregon wine country only includes the Willamette Valley, it's like Europeans visiting New York City and saying they've seen America. Sure, Oregon enjoys a reputation for great pinot noir, but visits to the warmer climes of Southern Oregon and the Columbia Gorge provide visitors with a richer picture of Oregon's wine-growing diversity.

For the most part, *WineTrails of Oregon* mirrors the wine growing regions of Oregon — but not quite. For example, I've taken an editorial liberty in creating Oregon Coast Wine Country, even though you won't find vineyards there! However, you will find select wineries and a paradise playground for tourists. In addition, I have lumped together Oregon's side of the Walla Walla viticultural area and central Oregon under the name Central and Eastern Oregon Wine Country. I know Bend is a long way from Milton-Freewater, but a guidebook devoid of this outdoor wonderland and its splendid wineries would have me tarred and feathered. For the cork dorks out there that have serious trouble with my wine country region definitions, it will be OK: trust me.

For planning purposes, see **Appendix B — Wine Tour Planning**. There you will discover a plethora of resources to aid you in planning your wine tour getaway, including a month-to-month listing of key events around the state.

Without diving into descriptions of the soil composition, grape clones, or average annual rainfall (which I am sure you were eager to read), here's a brief overview of these four wine country regions.

Willamette Valley Viticultural Area

Spanning 150 miles long and 60 miles wide, the Willamette Valley is home to over 200 wineries and 10,000 acres of grapes. It is Oregon's largest federally designated American Viticultural Area, or AVA. Within the Willamette Valley AVA, there are six sub-appellations, including Chehalem Mountains, Dundee Hills, Eola–Amity Hills, McMinnville, Ribbon Ridge, and Yamhill Carlton.

Erath Vineyards

There is significant variation in topography and climate from one area to another. The pronounced hills in the northern reaches of the Willamette Valley make way for the relatively flat area around Corvallis and further south to Eugene. Consequently, the Willamette isn't just for "pinotphiles"; there is plenty of riesling, gewürztraminer, cabernet sauvignon, merlot, and syrah to taste, using grapes either grown in the Willamette Valley or sourced from southern Oregon or Washington's Columbia Valley.

Fourteen of the twenty-four WineTrails featured in this book are in the Willamette Valley. Attacking all fourteen WineTrails can easily consume summer weekends and spill into the fall. I know. I did it. And, yes, visitors will have their fill of pinot noir, pinot gris, and chardonnay, but get ready for some wonderful surprises. For example, pinot noir tastes different from one appellation to another. The pinot noir from the McMinnville sub-appellation is darker and more full-bodied than the lighter, silkier pinots of the Dundee Hills. Soil and climate have a way of doing that. I learned that historic places such as Newberg, Dundee, McMinnville, Carlton, and Salem sport amazing restaurants that satisfy even the hard-to-please foodies. There are many places to stay that include cottages and delightful bed-and-breakfast inns. Bring a camera for this region with plenty of digital storage space… you'll need it.

Umpqua Valley Viticultural Area

There's a reason they call this area the Hundred Valleys of the Umpqua. Pack your GPS for this wine country region and be prepared for sudden stops to take pictures of covered bridges, mountain ranges, and fly fishermen at dusk. But don't dawdle too long admiring the scenery; there are wines aplenty for tasting. Here you will discover the oldest extant Oregon winery, Hillcrest Vineyards, founded by Richard Sommers in 1961. You will also enjoy a variety of wines

Brandborg Winery's tasting room

due to the diversity of climate and soils. Near the northern reach of the Umpqua, the town of Elkton boasts four wineries known for their cool weather grape varietals — after all, from this point the Pacific Ocean is a mere forty miles to the west. Further south, as you get closer to Roseburg, Bordeaux-style grapes take over in the warmer climes. The Umpqua

Valley receives 40% less rainfall than the Willamette Valley. However, many a WineTrail trekker makes an annual pilgrimage to stock up on baco noir. And, for fans of tempranillo, your heaven-on-earth place has arrived.

Once you've satisfied the wine tasting bug, make sure to plan plenty of time for whatever "floats your boat" — literally. The Umpqua is America's playground for white-water rafting, tubing, and fishing. With Crater Lake National Park and Diamond Lake easy day trips, there are wonders galore to sample. It's also the location of the historic Steamboat Inn on the North Umpqua River, known for its evening dinners featuring great fare and Oregon wines. The city of Roseburg offers a variety of hotels and restaurants to satisfy discriminating tourists. Bring walking shoes and throw your bike and golf clubs in the car — Roseburg boasts a number of parks, hiking and riding paths, and golf courses to get you moving.

Rogue Valley Viticultural Area

For wine touring, the Rogue Valley Appellation has it all. Take equal parts history, Shakespearian theater, charming inns and delightful restaurants and mix in spectacular wines and you have a getaway vacation sure to create grand memories. Historically, the renowned pioneer, Peter Britt, launched a winery in Jacksonville in 1852. The Britt Music Festival honors his memory for his many accomplishments. However, in the 1920s Prohibition did a lot to end the fledgling wine industry. Vines were yanked in favor of orchards. For farmers, their cash crop was in the form of pears and apples. Can you say, "Harry and David"?

In recent years, fruit orchards have receded in favor of premium wine grapes. As visitors will discover, the vineyards are confined to the three major tributaries

Paschal Winery

of the Rogue River — Bear Creek, Applegate River, and the Illinois River. Not surprisingly, the valleys are where the wineries reside and comprise our WineTrails. Each river valley has unique soils and microclimates and produce different grape varieties. For example, visitors are surprised to learn that the Illinois Valley gets 60 inches of rain per year, whereas Bear Creek Valley only receives 20 inches. The Illinois Valley is closest to the Pacific Ocean and high in elevation, making it ideal for riesling and pinot noir. Further inland, Bear Creek and Applegate valleys showcase Bordeaux-style grapes much like their vineyard neighbors to the south in California. Visitors with a penchant for merlot and cabernet sauvignon need to plan their sipping adventures around these WineTrails.

In between plays, fabulous restaurants, and serious wine tasting, visitors can work off calories biking, hiking, skiing, golfing, rafting, or perhaps parasailing off Woodrat Mountain. There are also plenty of boutique shops and art galleries to explore in Ashland and Jacksonville for those needing retail therapy.

For information related to the Oregon Shakespeare Festival in Ashland, visit www.osfashland.org or contact 541-482-4331 or boxoffice@oshashland.org. See www.brittfest.org to plan a trip around Jacksonville's Britt Music Festival in August.

Columbia Gorge Viticultural Area

My understanding is that Lewis and Clark didn't try windsurfing when they cruised through the Columbia Gorge in 1805. Too bad. They could have kicked back and had a good time exploring this awe-inspiring region. By the end of the 1800s, Italian immigrants planted zinfandel vines and established the Columbia Gorge as a winegrowing region before Prohibition put the kibosh on such activities. Nevertheless, on both the Washington and Oregon sides of the Columbia River, premium grape production evolved. In 2004 the federal government approved the Columbia Gorge as an official American Viticultural Area. Today visitors can sample a host of varieties, including chardonnay, pinot noir, syrah, cabernet sauvignon, gewürztraminer, riesling, pinot gris, merlot, sangiovese, and zinfandel.

For wine tourists, the Columbia Gorge is ideal for several reasons. The area is relatively compact, encompassing a 40-mile stretch along the Washington and Oregon banks of the Columbia. On the Oregon side, visitors typically make the friendly confines of Hood River their base camp for wine exploration, eating and sleeping. Hood River is a food lover's mecca, with chef-owned restaurants, bistros, microbrewers, and historic hotels and quaint inns. In fact, with four separate tasting rooms to visit in downtown Hood River, plenty of shopping, and abundant coffee shops and galleries, it is easy to spend an entire day in the town's core. However, for the more adventurous, Mount Hood is nearby for hiking and skiing, and of course the Columbia River beckons windsurfers and kite boarders alike.

Choosing the Wineries to Include in the Book

I chose 200 wineries to include in *Wine Trails of Oregon*. This represents less than two-thirds of the wineries in the state! So the first question that might pop into your head is why I would leave out a third of the state's wineries. The answer is simple: *Wine Trails of Oregon* focuses only on those wineries that have tasting rooms open to the public with regular tasting hours. The remaining wineries are open by appointment only or not open at all. I encourage you to visit the appointment-only wineries as well (see **Appendix B** for contact information). Often a visit to the by-appointment-only wineries will give you the opportunity to talk one-on-one with the winemaker. Many of Oregon's renowned wineries are not open to the public and require calling in advance to set up an appointment. Examples include Owen Roe, Beaux Frères, Ken Wright Cellars, Beran Vineyards, Cameron Winery, and Ayoub Vineyard. However, not to worry my fellow Wine Trail enthusiasts: many of the publicly accessible wineries are the best of the best. Unless you are obsessive-compulsive (like a certain Wine Trails Guy), visiting the wineries featured in this book will consume years.

How to Use This Guidebook

I've organized this book into ten "Wine Country Regions," from the Oregon Coast to Central and Eastern Oregon. Within these regions, I've organized wineries into geographic clusters called Wine Trails. There are 24 distinct

WineTrails to explore throughout Oregon representing 200 wineries. The wineries featured in this book are open to the public and have regular tasting room hours. There was no fee paid to WineTrails Northwest to be a part of this book. Please note that wineries are included in this book because they have regular tasting room hours — it has nothing to do with the quality of their wine. I leave that up to you, dear reader, to discover on your own!

Use this guidebook and its companion website, www.winetrailsnw.com, to plan your wine tour. Decide where you want to go and when — please be mindful that some wineries are open daily and others limited to the weekends. Some wineries are open year-round and others vary their hours by the season. Even if they have posted regular tasting room hours, it's a good idea to call ahead to verify that they are open. Also, many WineTrail trekkers like to plan their visit during events and wine release parties. Consult www.winetrailsnw.com for event information as well as contacting the winery in advance to learn about winery-sponsored events.

Ready, Set, Swirl!

Prior to drinking my way through Oregon, I had the notion that my love of big red wines would preclude my enjoying pinot noir. I stared at the map of the

Willamette Valley, saw the hundred-plus wineries on my agenda, and realized each one offered excellent pinot noir. I was nervous that I would miss the tannin-laden reds most familiar to me — the big Walla Wallas, the spicy syrahs, the zesty zins. The huge fruit bombs. However, a funny thing happened while tasting my way from the outskirts of Portland to Eugene. I fell in love with pinot noir. I leaned to slow down, concentrate, and really taste this amazing varietal, with its bright cherry notes, its silky feel in the mouth, and every once in awhile a special mid-palate sensation that made me exclaim, "Damn, that's good."

As my research continued (tough duty, I know, but someone had to do it), I discovered that pinot noir differs from one appellation to another. Just try a pinot from lower Yamhill County next to a pinot from the Dundee Hills. It's almost like two different varietals. I also discovered Oregon's other great varietals, including pinot gris, pinot blanc, tempranillo, and relatively unknown varieties, like baco noir and grüner veltliner, that make me wonder why we don't see more of them.

But more than learning about the wines of Oregon, I learned something about myself. I learned the important lesson that wine is simply a complement to life's pleasures. Don't get me wrong, I love a glass of wine by itself. However, I saw many folks gathered at a picnic table enjoying a bottle; I sampled many hard

Maragas Winery

cheeses and chocolates that paired wonderfully with wine; I learned that pinot noir and Pacific Northwest seafood were born for each other; and at one winery in the Rogue, the background opera music helped me swirl to the sound.

My travels also reinforced five key to-do's before venturing out on a wine tour: (1) bring cash for tasting fees; (2) take along a cooler in hot weather; (3) bring water; (4) take along a GPS device if you have one; and (5) call ahead to verify that they are open. On that "call ahead" note, I have traveled to wineries that were out of wine, wineries closed because someone was at the hospital having a baby, and wineries that were open but had no one around.

Harvest in the Columbia Gorge

It's also a good idea to designate a driver ahead of time. Pace yourself. Those ounces add up. It's fine to spit. Drink responsibly. Drive responsibly.

The number one thing to remember is to take along this book and read aloud as you sip and swirl your way through wine country. It has maps and driving directions to aid you, hours that the tasting rooms are open, and WineTrail tips sprinkled throughout. By the way, ask the winemaker for his or her autograph. Winemakers love being asked, and they take great pleasure in autographing their page in the book.

Happy WineTrails!

Steve Roberts, the WineTrails Guy

Favorites

As the "WineTrails Guy," I'm often asked about my favorite wineries to visit. While I duck questions about which wines I like the best, I'm not shy when it comes to questions about wineries with the best views, where to host a wedding or what wineries offer overnight lodging and eats. It's true that I should have a bumper sticker that reads, "I brake for all wineries." However, it's not fair for me to be mute when it comes to wineries exceptional for their views, food, lodging and wedding venues. Without further ado, here are my favorites:

Favorite Wineries for Lodging

Visitors to Oregon's wine country regions have choices galore in terms of hotels, motels, and bed-and-breakfast cottages. Included in Appendix B is a listing of wine country resources readers can use to plan a wine vacation getaway. However, imagine a stay at a vacation rental nestled amongst the vineyards — a place where you don't need to go more than a short walk to get a bottle of wine and throw a stick to the winery dog along the way. Often WineTrail trekkers wish to combine wine tasting with other activities such as hiking, white water rafting, skiing, shopping and, around the Columbia Gorge, windsurfing. They need a place to call home for a short stay — a place to kick back and sip wine at the end of the day. Fortunately, for them there are a number of winery-owned and -managed guest cottages to rent. Here are my favorites:

1. **Wine Country Farm Cellars** (Dayton) — The address says Dayton but the quaint villa drips with Oregon wine country charm on the top of the Dundee Hills. Proprietor Joan Davenport serves up fine wine, spectacular views, and white picket fences that corral her prized Arabian horses. It's decidedly Dundee.
2. **Weisinger's of Ashland** (Ashland) — Features a "Vineyard Cottage" complete with kitchen and private bath. Those on a romantic getaway will enjoy the hot tub, not to mention the fine wines of Weisinger's.
3. **Cherry Hill Winery** (Rickreall) — The Cherry Hill Dude Ranch provides a romantic getaway or a wonderful spot for a corporate retreat in the heart of wine country. Guests have the difficult task of choosing among relaxing with a book, riding a bike, or learning about winemaking. Just remember: if you drink no noir, you pinot noir.
4. **Edgefield Winery - McMenamins** (various locations in Troutdale, McMinnville, Portland and Forest Grove) — Featuring McMenamins' funky charm, full-service restaurants, and Edgefield wines; guests at McMenamins may forget to check out. A fusion of exceptional lodging, food, and wine under one roof.
5. **Pheasant Valley Winery** (Hood River) — Visitors to the Columbia Gorge in need of a base camp to host a family retreat or a weekend getaway just got

lucky. The spacious guesthouse comes complete with a spectacular view of Mount Hood and the wines of Pheasant Valley Winery a short walk away.

6. **Bridgeview Vineyards & Winery** (Kerby) — If visiting the Illinois Valley, consider staying at the Kerbyville Inn, owned by Robert and Lelo Kerivan of Bridgeview Vineyards & Winery fame. With four wine-themed suites, two with spas, and a guest room, all with private entrances and bathrooms, you have a base of operations from which to explore Nature's playground just north of the California border.

7. **Chateau Bianca Winery** (Dallas) — Wine tourists can spend a romantic getaway in the heart of wine country. Incredible views, a king size bed, a private bath and a gourmet breakfast await visitors at an affordable rate.

Favorite Wineries for Eats

From menus that offer a full-course dinner to chalkboards listing appetizer specials, select wineries provide the perfect atmosphere to enjoy wine with Northwest cuisine. Some wineries serve al fresco, weather permitting, so don't drop by in February and expect to eat. But whether the dining space is inside or outside, if you're hitting the WineTrails and your tummy begins to rumble, check out these wineries for mouth-watering chow:

Pfeiffer Vineyards

1. **King Estate Winery** (Eugene) — Excellent lunch and dinner fare served on the patio in nice weather. For dinner, the menu will dazzle with such entrees as Soy Glazed Mahi Mahi and Knee Deep Filet of Beef Tenderloin. Organic greens and herbs come right from their garden.

2. **Cana's Feast Winery** (Carlton) — Cana's Feast features great Italian food and wine. Get ready to pair Cana's Feast wines with *antipasti*, *zuppe* and *insalate*, *primi*, *secondi*, *formaggi*, and *dolci*. Local produce assures fresh ingredients.

3. **Edgefield Winery - McMenamins** (Troutdale) — The fun atmosphere of McMenamins provides an inviting space for breakfast, lunch and dinner. Visit the downstairs winery to sample wine beforehand and then order a bottle of Edgefield wine to go with your meal. Other friendly McMenamins are located in Portland, Forest Grove and McMinnville in the heart of wine country.

4. **Pfeiffer Vineyards** (Junction City) — Proprietors Robin and Danuta Pfeiffer created Villa Evenings to provide high-end multi-course dinner packages to groups up to 12. Reservations required well in advance. Added bonus has Robin educating guests in wine tasting at their intimate downstairs cellar. Unforgettable experience fused with silky wines and extraordinary food. See www.villaevenings.com for details.

5. **Orchard Heights Winery** (Salem) — Orchard Heights Winery's Sunday brunch serves up farm-fresh food with a wide assortment of wine. The friendly waitstaff make each visitor feel special.

6. **Erin Glenn Winery** (The Dalles) — Tim and Erin Schechtel serve up wine country fare, remarkable wine, and live music Friday nights. Think grilled panini sandwiches and Bordeaux-style blends with foot-tapping music in a historic building and you have a memorable treat for the senses.

Erin Glenn Winery

7. **R. Stuart & Co.** (McMinnville) — Located in downtown McMinnville's historic district, this red brick space serves up delectable food to pair with wine for that midday hunger. Try the savory Asiago cookies with their Rosé d'Or sparkling wine. Delish!

8. **Evergreen Vineyards** (McMinnville) — Two cafés are located at the Evergreen Aviation & Space Museum to satisfy vistors' hunger. Lest you think this is standard cafeteria food under heat lamps, consider this menu offering: Berry brie salad and seared Alaska line-caught salmon. Add pinot noir, and you're ready for the on-site IMAX theatre.

9. **Flying Dutchman Winery** (Otter Rock) — The funky old-time red and white truck outside the tasting room is the place to stock up on snacks, ice cream, and espresso before hitting the beach. Please note that it is fine to have chocolate ice cream with pinot noir.

10. **LongSword Vineyard** (Jacksonville) — Boxed lunches never tasted so good. Hard cheeses, sausage, and savory crackers served on the outside patio pair wonderfully with LongSword Chardonnay. In between nibbles, don't miss the hang gliders soaring above Woodrat Mountain.

Although they don't qualify as restaurants per se, I would be derelict if I didn't mention the appetizers served at two Umpqua-based wineries: Sienna Ridge Estate and Reustle-Prayer Rock Vineyards. Visitors can nosh on specially prepared *hors d'oeuvres* and gourmet spreads. Come for the wine, but enjoy the treats!

Favorite Winery Views

Oregon is the land of diverse views, from ocean beaches to the rolling wheat fields of Eastern Oregon. However, for wine tourists who enjoy sights of undulating vineyards mixed in with mountains in the background and alpacas, hazelnut orchards, covered bridges and white picnic tables dotting the landscape, you can't beat Oregon. There's a reason why the Umpqua is called the "Land of 100 Valleys," and there's a reason why a place like Bend has exploded in growth — it's drop dead gorgeous. For the million-plus visitors that hit the Willamette Valley each year, the views will also keep them coming back and not just the pinot. I could easily tick off fifty wineries that get my vote for top views, but if forced to choose my top ten winery views, here are my favorites:

1. **Flying Dutchman Winery** (Otter Rock) — I'm an unabashed fan of the Oregon Coast, and crashing waves, rocky cliffs, and an occasional seagull thrown in give the Flying Dutchman Winery my top vote for views.

2. **Dundee Hills WineTrail North and Dundee Hills WineTrail South** (Willamette Valley) — Yep, all the wineries included in these two WineTrails get my vote for spectacular views. Whether you are visiting Lange Estate Winery & Vineyards or Domaine Drouhin Oregon, there's no way that one winery's view is better than another. Flip a coin.

3. **Elk Cove Vineyards** (Gaston) — From the patio looking down at the rows of pruned vineyards it's easy to imagine a herd of Roosevelt elk coming over the hillside.

4. **WillaKenzie Estate** (Yamhill) — 360-degree views from the tasting room may keep you there all day. Breathtaking!

5. **Van Duzer Vineyards** (Dallas) — Looking westward, visitors see the magnificent Coast Range beckoning them to reach for their cameras.

Elk Cove Vineyards

6. **Tie — King Estate Winery and Sweet Cheeks Winery** (Lane County WineTrail) — Both wineries did one smart thing ... they built spacious patios to relax with a glass (or two) of wine and view the amazing valleys below.

7. **Maragas Winery** (Bend) — Looking west toward the Cascade Mountain Range the eyes will delight in dancing from the Three Sisters to Mount Bachelor. With a glass of Maragas' Legal Zin in hand, be prepared to swivel your head north to south as your view the volcanic peaks of the Cascades.

8. **Bethel Heights Vineyard** (Salem) — Nestled in the Eola Hills with panoramic views of the valley below and Mount Jefferson in the distance, it doesn't get much better than this! Be prepared to extend your visit here an hour.

9. **Pheasant Valley Winery** (Hood River) — Straight-on views of Mount Hood in the distance include rows of gewürztraminer and perhaps a couple of

pheasants flying by. There's a reason why the porch is super-sized... pack picnic and camera for this winery.

10. **Tie — Troon Vineyard, Applegate Red Winery, LongSword Vineyard, Valley View Winery** (Applegate Valley WineTrail) — Your visit here will have you thinking about pulling up stakes and moving here. It offers year-round rural splendor and a river valley full of vineyards.

The following wineries fall into the "honorable mention" bucket, and could just as easily be in the top 10. Get ready for fantastic views at these wineries:

- Willamette Valley Vineyards (Turner)
- Abacela Vineyards & Winery (Roseburg)
- Ankeny Vineyard (Salem)
- Airlie Winery (Monmouth)
- MarshAnne Landing (Oakland)
- Patton Valley Vineyard (Gaston)
- Trium (Talent)
- Weisinger's of Ashland (Ashland)
- Del Rio Vineyards and Winery (Gold Hill)
- Penner-Ash Wine Cellars (Newberg)
- Adelsheim Vineyard (Newberg)
- Sineann Cellars at Medici Vineyards (Newberg)
- Lenné Estate (Yamhill)

Incidentally, of the 200 wineries visited for this book, 181 of them offer a place to picnic. All the above "best in view" wineries offer picnic benches or outdoor furniture to enjoy a picnic and open a bottle of wine.

Favorite Winery Gift Shops

In terms of retail, Oregon wineries run the gamut from bare-bones logo wear to a wealth of merchandise. If you are looking for a wine-related gift for a loved

Melrose Vineyard

one or a friend, it might be just down the street at your local winery. Yes, we often venture to the winery to purchase wine, but now consumers augment the wine purchases with Riedel stemware, elegant wine country clothing, and $65 wine bottle openers. Beyond picnic supplies and T-shirts, take along your Visa to these select wineries:

1. **RoxyAnn Winery** (Medford) — Wine, picnic supplies and wine gear under one roof... all in good taste. Fashionable goods, artfully presented, greet visitors.
2. **Melrose Vineyard** (Roseburg) — With so much merchandise to mull over, getting to the tasting bar may take a while.
3. **Valley View Winery** (Jacksonville) — Applegate Valley's best wine-related merchandise, bar none.
4. **Edgefield Winery — McMenamins** (Troutdale) — With lodging and restaurant all under one roof, guests need a generous gift shop for last-minute shopping.
5. **Coelho Winery of Amity** (Amity) — A surprise find in the town of Amity; a cornucopia of choice.
6. **Tyrus Evan** (Carlton) — Someone with a Nordstrom-like eye is the buyer for this winery.
7. **Flying Dutchman Winery** (Otter Rock) — A mix of wine-related and nautical gifts make this one of the most unusual gift shops.
8. **Duck Pond Cellars** (Dundee) — Merchandise galore, only limited by the size of the tasting room.
9. **Eola Hills Wine Cellars** (Rickreall) — Dazzling wine-related produce.
10. **Pheasant Valley Winery** (Hood River) — Quality over quantity is the mantra.

Favorite Wineries for Weddings

Here's a news bulletin. I'm not a wedding planner. Consequently, I won't attempt to give my top ten places to wed. After all, I went to the wineries to check out the wine and experience the ambience. I didn't visit them to see if the winery has floor-to-ceiling mirrors in the women's changing room, or whether or not the guy's room has flat-screen TVs and video games. There's a myriad of issues for would-be nuptials — everything from catering to ordering the flowers to arranging the transportation. Many wineries have established relationships with these vendors and can suggest what vendors to use. Nevertheless, each winery is different, so check with them to determine who does what.

EdenVale Winery

In addition, weddings are an individual thing. What you think is the perfect venue for a wedding might be too garish in my book or vice versa. Are you looking for an intimate setting for 20 people or do you need space for 200? Do you want indoors or outside? What's your budget? and more.

Nearly a quarter of the wineries highlighted in *WineTrails of Oregon* host weddings. Below we've listed those wineries (by wine country region) that accommodate weddings. We're sure they would be happy to include some wine in the deal!

Oregon Coast Wine Country: Nehalem Bay Wine Co.

Rose City Wine Country: Edgefield Winery - McMenamins, Helvetia Vineyards, Oak Knoll Winery, Ponzi Vineyard, Urban Wineworks/Bishop Creek Cellars

North Willamette Valley Wine Country: David Hill Vineyard and Winery, Elk Cove Vineyards, Kramer Vineyards, Laurel Ridge Winery, Rex Hill Vineyards, SakéOne, Shafer Vineyard Cellars, Vista Hills Vineyard & Winery, Wine Country Farm Cellars

Mid Willamette Valley Wine Country:
Airlie Winery, Cubanisimo Vineyards, Eola Hills Wine Cellars, Kathken Vineyards, Namasté Vineyards, Orchard Heights Winery, St. Innocent Winery, Stangeland Vineyards & Winery

South Willamette Valley Wine Country: Chateau Lorane, King Estate Winery, Secret House Winery, Silvan Ridge-Hinman Vineyards, Sweet Cheeks Winery, Tyee Wine Cellars

East Willamette Valley Wine Country: Alexeli Vineyard & Winery, St. Josef's Winery, Silver Falls Vineyards,

Umpqua Valley Wine Country: Bradley Vineyards, Melrose Vineyard

Rogue Valley Wine Country: Del Rio Vineyards and Winery, EdenVale Winery, Jacksonville Vineyards, John Michael Champagne Cellars, Paschal Winery, RoxyAnn Winery, Schmidt Family Vineyards, Valley View Winery

Columbia Gorge Wine Country: Cathedral Ridge Winery, Naked Winery, Pheasant Valley Winery, Wheatridge in the Nook, Wy'East Vineyards

There you have it... my favorite destination wineries for lodging, views, eats, and shopping. However, don't just take my word for it; please explore and discover for yourself your likes and dislikes. Your opinion matters. Please let me know what you think are the best of the best — it gives me an incentive to revisit the wine country regions of Oregon repeatedly. As if I needed an excuse to get out there and explore!

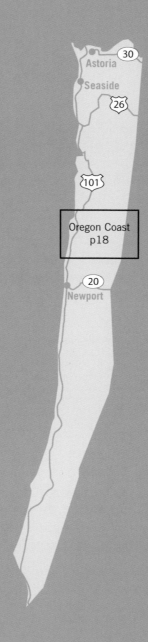

Astoria

30

Seaside

26

101

Oregon Coast
p18

20

Newport

Oregon Coast
WINE COUNTRY

Oregon Coast
Wine Trail

View from Flying Dutchman Winery

From Astoria in the north to Brookings in the south, the Oregon Coast Wine Trail offers a number of remarkable wine stops to experience. Over this great distance marked by unbelievable beauty, WineTrail trekkers can swirl and sample unforgettable brandies, Bordeaux reds, Burgundian pinots, and unusual whey-based chocolate wines. Whether you are driving by car or the family RV or doing that once-in-a-lifetime Oregon Coast bicycle trip, the tasting rooms of the Oregon Coast will leave an indelible mark. Budget plenty of time to visit these wineries — it's beyond a weekend jaunt. More likely, you will visit these over several forays to the Oregon Coast. In the end, you will truly understand why seafood and wine go together like Frisbees and tail-wagging dogs. Salud!

Oregon Coast WineTrail
1 Shallon Winery   3 Nehalem Bay Wine Co.   5 Brandy Peak Distillery
2 Laurel Hood   4 Flying Dutchman Winery

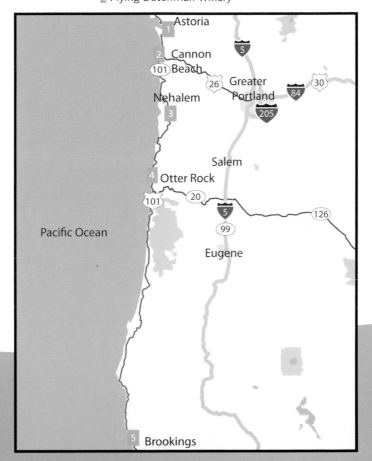

Region:	**Oregon Coast Wine Country**
# of tasting rooms on tour:	**5**
# of satellite tasting rooms:	**1**
Estimate # of days for tour:	**3 to 5**
Getting around:	**Car**
Key Events:	❏ **In February, Newport's Seafood & Wine Festival –**
	call 541-265-8801.
	❏ **In April, Astoria-Warrenton's Crab and Seafood Festival –**
	call 800-875-6807, or visit www.oldoregon.com.
	❏ **In May, Seaside's Downtown Wine Walk –**
	call 503-717-1914.
Tips:	❏ **See Appendix B – Wine Tour Planning, for planning**
	your visit.
Best:	❏ **Eats, views and weddings: Flying Dutchman Winery.**

Shallon Winery

He's given the spiel a thousand times before, but somehow Paul van der Veldt keeps it fresh. He usually waits until a critical mass of at least a half-dozen folks arrive at his tasting room/winery at the corner of Duane and 16th streets in Astoria. While in a holding pattern, Paul peppers visitors with questions about their jobs and where they come from. He's not trying to put you on the spot — he just happens to be burdened with a powerfully inquisitive mind, and it's his way of gaining knowledge. This little preamble is a clue that you are about to experience a wine tour like no other.

The tour begins with pours of Paul's concoctions, and because he produces such small quantities of wine, this writer can't say with certainty what wines you would sample. However, if you are here for Bordeaux blends or Burgundian-style wines, you will need to flush that notion. At Shallon Winery, Paul's potions are primarily fruit wines, and your taste buds will experience flavors such as lemon, blackberry, blueberry, and cranberry. However, the *pièce de résistance* is Paul's chocolate wine, made from real chocolate, orange, and whey. As Paul notes on the Shallon Winery website, "This [chocolate wine] is the ultimate creation of my older years; anything I create after this will be a total anticlimax. I know of nothing like this on the face of the earth; if you find something, tell me." He's right. Move over, Ghirardelli, this stuff is "whey" better than a chocolate bar.

Unlike other tasting-room experiences, at Shallon, Paul leads the group beyond the tasting room on a tour of his production facility, his spotless beaker-filled laboratory and his office. While explaining his winemaking process and tools, Paul fields a myriad of questions, not just about wine, but about life in general. He's got opinions about local restaurants, Astoria history, flying machines and local architecture. It's at this point you realize that Paul is blessed with a rich and varied background and that winemaking came to him later in life.

Named after the winemaker's favorite local wild plant — salal (*Gaultheria shallon*) — Shallon Winery is a memorable stop along the Oregon Coast WineTrail. After visiting 20 wineries in the Willamette Valley that all profess to make the very best pinot noir, chances are you would eventually forget each winery's distinctive features. However, you won't forget your visit to Shallon Winery and Paul van der Veldt, its one-of-a-kind winemaker and host.

SHALLON WINERY
opened: 1978
winemaker(s): Paul van der Veldt
location: 1598 Duane Street, Astoria, OR 97103
phone: 503-325-5978
web: www.shallon.com
e-mail: paul@shallon.com
tours: Yes
fee: Complimentary wine tasting
hours: Daily 1–6

Paul van der Veldt

DIRECTIONS: From US-30 [Lower Columbia River Hwy] entering Astoria from the east or west, go (south) onto 16th St. Arrive at 1598 Duane St. on the right. Shallon Winery is one block from the Maritime Museum.

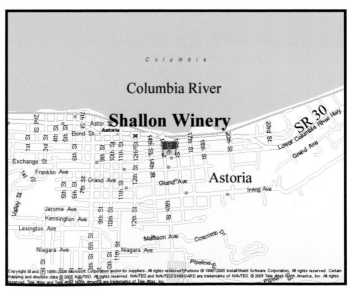

Laurel Hood 2

If you've been to Cannon Beach and had the pleasure of eating at Bistro Restaurant and Wine Bar on Hemlock Street, chances are you walked right by a tasting room and didn't even realize it. That's because the tasting room is cloaked inside a wine shop — Laurel Hood's Wine Shop to be exact. Laurel Hood herself is usually at the shop, working the cash register and helping people with wine-pairing questions, most often those of the seafood or picnic-on-the-beach variety. While a fount of information for such inquiries, Laurel doesn't seem as forthcoming about the fact that she is also pouring samples of her own label, Laurel Hood Wines, for a mere $1 per pour.

Laurel Hood

Why? Because Laurel Hood has that "unassuming" gene common among people in the Pacific Northwest. She would never push her own wines on visitors to her wine shop. It's not in her nature. But if you do inquire about her own creations — perhaps a pinot gris or a pinot noir — she lights up. Even after 20 years of making wine, Laurel still has that drive and passion in her eyes. When she pours a sample of her wine, you know that she's pouring her heart and soul into the waiting glass.

When not managing the wine shop, Laurel is managing her vineyard on the western edge of the Chehalem Mountain viticultural area. Her goal is to make the fruit itself shine through to the taste buds. Thus, she relies on a "judicious" use of oak for her small-lot productions of wine. In addition to pinot noir and pinot gris, she makes tempranillo and a unique clone of tempranillo dubbed Tinto del Pais. She's after "age worthy" wines that can lie down for years. However, our sampling discovered wine ready to be enjoyed that day.

If you are going to the Bistro Restaurant and Wine Bar, let me suggest you make a quick stop at Laurel Hood's wine shop to pick up a bottle of her pinot noir to pair with the bouillabaisse or salmon. The corkage fee is nominal. A Burgundian wine paired with Northwest seafood always makes a great marriage to a great day on the beach.

Laurel Hood

LAUREL HOOD
winemaker(s): Laurel Hood
location: 263 N Hemlock Street,
Cannon Beach, OR 97110
phone: 503-436-1666
web: None
gift shop: Yes
fee: $1 refundable with purchase
hours: Call for hours

DIRECTIONS: **Heading south or north on US-101** [Oregon Coast Hwy] take second Cannon Beach exit proceed .1 miles. Bear left (west) onto E 2nd St. for .2 miles. Turn right (north) onto N Hemlock St. and arrive at 263 N Hemlock St.

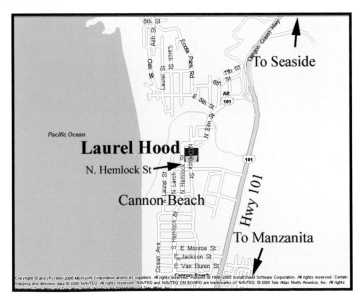

Nehalem Bay Wine Co. ③

Throughout *Wine Trails of Oregon*, about 400 words are devoted to a winery's story. But 400 words don't begin to tell the Nehalem Bay Winery story — they only scratch the surface. The reason lies not so much in the wines that it produces but in the energy,

vision, and life's adventures of Nehalem Bay Winery's owner, Ray Shackelford.

Ray's patchwork background includes sales, the military, real estate and world travel. His winery is a résumé of those experiences, and you discover Ray's indelible touches throughout the winery. For example, take time to check out the colorful handbags from Cambodia in the winery's gift shop. It was Ray's tour of duty in Vietnam that compelled him to return to southeast Asia and establish a sewing project for ethnic minorities in Chheneng, Cambodia, in 2005. Today, Ray's program provides much needed revenue to the impoverished Cambodian village. As we discovered, the handbags also proved useful for toting a bottle a wine or two from the winery.

Speaking of wine, Nehalem Bay Winery produces about 4,000 cases annually and offers a full line-up of reds and whites as well as fruit wines, including Ray's traditional blackberry wine. Although many a wine tourist might argue that his portfolio is too ambitious, the fact is, everyone has their likes and dislikes. If your palate goes for the Burgundy-style wines, you can focus on the winery's pinot noir. Alternatively, if your Aunt Zelda only likes sweet wines, she would enjoy his mead (honey wine).

Now in his sixties, Ray continues to travel throughout the world helping people. The winemaking duties have been turned over to a Salem-based vintner. Chances are, Ray won't be at the winery when you visit. However, a stop at Nehalem Bay Winery will introduce you to his well-trained and gracious staff, and the winery's cool stone floors and weathered brick walls. But more than that, the experience will take you to other parts of the world and perhaps touch a kid's life half a world away.

NEHALEM BAY WINE CO.
winemaker(s): Ray Shackelford et al.
location: 34965 Highway 53, Nehalem, OR 97131
phone: 503-368-9463
web: www.nehalembaywinery.com
e-mail: nbwines@hotmail.com
picnic area: Yes
weddings: Yes
gift shop: Yes
fee: Complimentary wine tasting
hours: Daily 9–6

DIRECTIONS: **Coming west from Portland on Hwy 26**, take SR-53 (left off 26) to Nehalem. The winery is 1 mile before SR-53 ends at Hwy 101 [Oregon Coast Highway].

Coming from the north on Highway 101, turn left at the junction of SR-53 and Hwy 101 (between Wheeler and Nehalem). The winery is 1 mile east on your left in Mohler.

Coming from the south, turn right at the junction of SR-53 and Hwy 101.

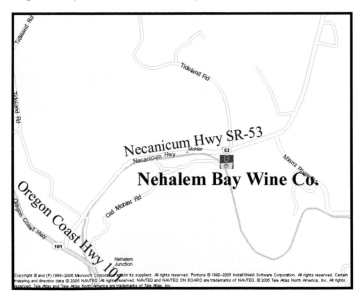

Flying Dutchman Winery

Borrowing a phrase from the 1970s the owner and winemaker of the Flying Dutchman Winery, Richard Cutler, likes to say, "We will sell no wine before its time." Richard is referring to each step of the winemaking process. For example, Richard points out that his "cold-soak" process allows freshly harvested and de-stemmed grapes to sit outside soaking in the salt air for seven to 10 days before the fermentation process begins. Other wineries allow the grapes only three days to cold soak. He could also be referring to the fact that once barreled; the wine matures for 10 to 36 months, before bottling. Once bottled, many of his wines lay sideways for at least 12 months. Goodbye bottle-shock.

Richard often lauds the salt air spray of the Oregon coast in slowing down the process and allowing the cold soak and fermentation processes to takes their sweet time. He's coined the phrase "salt air fermentation" to make the case perfectly clear. But to really appreciate what Richard is saying WineTrail adventures need to visit the Flying Dutchman Winery

in Otter Rock. When you step outside your car and your lungs fill with the salt air you know that the grape juice is in good hands.

Don't look for vineyards when visiting the Flying Dutchman Winery. Richard gets his grapes from a variety of vineyards in the central and southern portions of Oregon. Don't look for the Flying Dutchman ship either. After all, legend has it that the Flying Dutchman never reached port. Rather walk around awhile and check out the amazing views and the spectacular picnic grounds. The tasting room and gift shop resides on the Devil's Punchbowl State Park and the famous 'Devil's Punchbowl' cauldron. Speaking of the gift shop, imagine a fusion of winery and nautical items and you get the most unusual wine retail shop in Oregon and certainly wins our top honors. Great views, great picnic area, and great gift shop. But it's the wines of the Flying Dutchman that matters.

By the way, before you hike down to visit the Otter Crest tide pools and explore Beverly Beach, you might want to pick up some ice cream, snacks and espresso from his concession stand located in a 1934 Dodge Truck outside the Flying Dutchman Winery. Even a latte pairs nicely in this salt air.

Richard Cutler

FLYING DUTCHMAN WINERY
opened: 1997
winemaker(s): Richard Cutler
location: 915 First Street, Otter Rock, OR 97369
phone: 541-765-2553
web: www.dutchmanwinery.com
e-mail: cmi@harborside.com
picnic area: Yes
gift shop: Yes
fee: Complimentary wine tasting
hours: Daily 11–6 June through September; Daily 11–5 October through May; Closed Christmas Day

★ BEST Eats, views and gift shop

DIRECTIONS: **From Portland** follow I-5 south to exit 260A near Salem. This exit is to the Salem Parkway, which will take you through town to Hwy 22 where you will see a sign 'to the ocean beaches'. Follow Hwy 22 through the countryside to Hwy 18 then stay on 18 through the Coastal Mountain Range until it merges into Hwy 101 just north of Lincoln City. Travel south on 101 through Lincoln City then 15 miles to Otter rock. The travel time from Portland is about 3 hours.

If you are arriving from the south on I-5, take the Hwy 34 exit near Albany and follow this highway until it merges with Hwy 20. Stay westbound on Hwy 20 through Corvallis and the Coastal Mountain Range to Newport and Hwy 101. Otter Rock is 8 miles north of Newport. The travel time from Corvallis is about 2 hours.

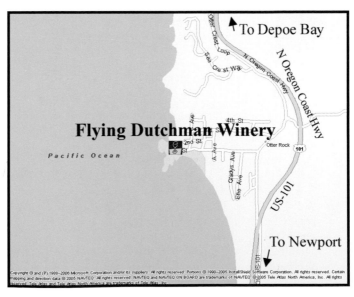

Brandy Peak Distillery 5

Do you remember the joy of being a kid and going on a field trip? Well, a visit to Brandy Peak Distillery is the grown-ups' version of a field trip.

David R. Nowlin

There are only a handful of distilleries in the United States that start out with premium wine grapes and distill them into brandy. We're not talking spirits in the sense of vodka, whiskey, or gin. Those spirits rely on grains to produce high-octane booze. No, we're talking brandy made from grapes or other fruits.

In France, this drink is referred to as Cognac, so named for the region where it is produced. Here in the United States, it goes by its generic name, brandy, and our field trip today takes us to Brandy Peak Distillery. The distillery is located outside the beach town of Brookings, near the California border. Ironically, there really is a mountain in the area with the name Brandy Peak, so it was only natural to call this "winery" Brandy Peak Distillery.

David Nowlin, Brandy Peak's distillery guru, leads tours through the facility, explaining the brandy-making process. He shows the wood-fired pots developed by his gifted father, R.L. Nowlin, and demonstrates how a small percentage of the original liquid is condensed and captured as a distillate. Fortunately for us, some dude in the Middle Ages figured out that alcohol has a much lower boiling point than water. Therefore, there's no need to heat the "mash" to boiling before the alcohol vents off. But for brandy, a whole lot more fruit is required than for traditional wine. Tons more.

The tour continues from the outside wood-fired pots to the inside barrel room, where the brandy is aged in oak for varying lengths of time. The color of the brandy is dependent upon barrel aging, with the more golden-colored "marc" brandies aged longer. The product is usually sold in 375 ml bottles. In the tasting room, visitors can sample pinot noir, muscat, gewürztraminer, riesling, and sauvignon blanc brandies. In addition, Brandy Peak's popular pear brandy, made from 100 percent Bartlett pears, is a wonderful surprise — layers of flavor, subtle pear notes, and a great finish. David is quick to point out that Brandy Peak Distillery uses no artificial flavors or colorings for its brandies. He also makes a liqueur that we were told does involve the addition of a natural flavoring. Can you say "blackberry liqueur"? Yup. Don't end your field trip without a taste of Brandy Peak's blackberry liqueur. Yummy.

BRANDY PEAK DISTILLERY
opened: 1994
winemaker(s): David R. Nowlin
location: 18526 Tetley Road, Brookings, OR 97415
phone: 541-469-0194
web: www.brandypeak.com
e-mail: distiller@brandypeak.com
picnic area: Yes
fee: Small tasting fee may apply
hours: Tuesday through Saturday 1–5 March through the first week of January, or by appointment

DIRECTIONS: **From Gold Beach** take US-101 [S Ellensburg Ave.] south for 20.8 miles. Turn left (east) onto Martinranch Rd and go 2.4 miles. Turn right (south) onto Carpenter Rd and go .4 miles. Turn left to stay on Capenterville Rd and continue for 1.3 miles. Turn left onto Tetley Rd and arrive at Brandy Peak Distillery.

From Brookings take US-101 west for 2.1 miles. Turn right (northeast) onto Carpenterville Rd and go 4.1 miles. Turn right (east) onto Tetley Rd and look for Brandy Peak Distillery on your right.

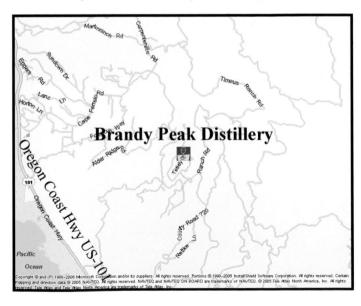

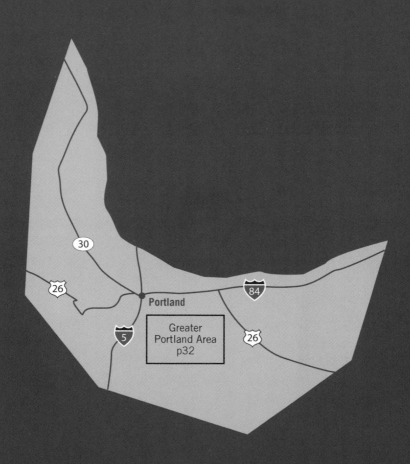

Portland

Greater
Portland Area
p32

Rose City
WINE COUNTRY

Greater Portland
WineTrail

Ponzi Vineyard

Folks in Portland (and visitors alike) have reason to cheer. With wineries abounding in their own backyard, there's no reason to race down to Umpqua or McMinnville to experience great wine. The Greater Portland WineTrail will take you from urban neighborhoods to rich farmlands, all within striking distance of each other. Surprisingly, wineries in and around Portland are often overlooked by WineTrail trekkers dashing off to the Dundee Hills. However, they are missing out on some of the "crown jewels" of Oregon's short but rich wine history. With names like Ponzi Vineyard, Oak Knoll Winery, Helvetia Vineyards, and Cooper Mountain Vineyards, this WineTrail is a who's-who of established wineries. But there are new kids on the block as well for your taste buds to experience. Hip Chicks Do Wine and Oswego Hills immediately pop to mind for new wines to experience. What's more, the Greater Portland WineTrail lets you do more than taste — at Urban Wineworks you can create your own blend of Bordeaux-style wine and slap your personalized label on the bottle. When you're done there, head on over to Clear Creek Distillery and discover how they get the ripened pear in the bottle.

Greater Portland WineTrail

1. Clear Creek Distillery
2. Urban Wineworks/
   Bishop Creek Cellars
3. Helvetia Vineyards
4. Oak Knoll Winery
5. Cooper Mountain Vineyards
6. Ponzi Vineyard
7. Oswego Hills
8. Hip Chicks Do Wine
9. Wasson Brothers Winery
10. Edgefield Winery -
    McMenamins

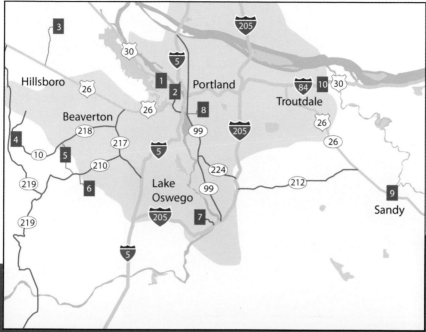

Region:	**Rose City Wine Country**
# of tasting rooms on tour:	**10**
Estimate # of days for tour:	**3**
Getting around:	**Car**
Key Events:	☐ **Memorial Weekend in Wine Country – Willamette Valley – visit www.willamettewines.com.**
	☐ **In July, McMinnville's International Pinot Noir Celebration – call 800-775-4762 or visit www.ipnc.org.**
	☐ **In November, Portland's ¡Salud! Oregon's Pinot Noir Auction – call 503-681-1850 or go online to www.saludauction.org.**
	☐ **In November, Portland's NW Food and Wine Festival – call 800-422-0251 or visit www.nwfoodandwinefestival.com**
	☐ **Wine Country Thanksgiving – Willamette Valley – call 503-646-2985 or visit www.willamettewines.com.**
Tips:	☐ **Consider using a limousine service (e.g., Grape Escape Winery Tours 503-283-3380, grrrrape@GrapeEscapeTours.com, www.grapeescapetours.com and My Chauffeur Wine Tours also serving Columbia River Gorge, 877-692-4283, winetour@winetouroregon.com, www.winetouroregon.com, are some of the many services to contact).**

 Best: ☐ **Lodging, eats, and gift shop: Edgefield Winery - McMenamins.**

Clear Creek Distillery 1

Stephen McCarthy's specialized line of libation gives him great job security. Hobbyists can simply purchase kits to make wine or beer in their basement or garage. That's relatively cheap. But Stephen relies on traditional German pot stills to make his fermented drink — fruit brandy, also known as *eau-de-vie*. The equipment needed to produce *eau-de-vie* from local fruit requires relatively deep pockets. The necessary equipment and facilities are costly, and the fruit required also demands a sizable bank account. Twenty-eight pounds

of pears are needed to make just one bottle of Stephen's signature pear brandy! Small wonder that there are just a handful of artisan brandy producers on the West Coast.

In his earlier days, Stephen spent considerable time in Europe. It was there, on a bike ride through the countryside of France, that he noticed bottles tied to the branches of pear and apple trees. The fruit itself was growing inside the bottles. Being from an Oregon family with 100 years of orchard experience, Stephen immediately knew its purpose — brandy.

For more than 20 years, Clear Creek Distillery has been evolving its product line of fruit brandies, grappas (made from leftover fruit skins and seeds), liqueurs, and single-malt whiskeys. In addition to pear and apple brandies, visitors can also sample Clear Creek's cherry, raspberry, plum, and, in what has to be a first, Douglas fir brandies. (Just for the experience, you should try the Douglas fir brandy, a true tree spirit made with an infusion of springtime Douglas fir buds.) Clear Creek also features a full lineup of fruit-flavored liqueurs made from local fruit, including blackberry, loganberry, cassis, cherry, pear, and raspberry. However, ever since getting great press in the 2004 edition of *The Whiskey Bible*, it's Stephen's Oregon Single Malt Whiskey that has been the big hit, particularly among whiskey aficionados.

Still, it's the *eaux-de-vie* that are Stephen's main love and his focus, especially the pear brandy made from local Bartlett pears. Each year, the staff of Clear Creek Distillery hangs bottles on the branches of pear and apple trees, manages their growth, harvests and cleans the bottles, and finally fills and labels them. Phew! The resulting Pear-in-the-Bottle is Clear Creek Distillery's signature beverage, and we have Stephen to thank for taking that bicycle trip in the French countryside in his younger days.

CLEAR CREEK DISTILLERY
opened: 1985
winemaker(s): Stephen McCarthy
location: 1430 NW 23rd Avenue,
Portland, OR 97210
phone: 503-248-9470
web: www.clearcreekdistillery.com
e-mail: steve@clearcreekdistillery.com
wheelchair access: Yes
tours: Yes
fee: Complimentary wine tasting
hours: Weekdays 9–5, Saturday 12–5; Closed major
holidays; call in advance recommended

Stephen McCarthy

DIRECTIONS: In Portland on I-405 heading north or south take exit 3 toward US-30 / NW Industrial Area. Take ramp onto Columbia River Hwy [US-30W] and go .3 miles. Turn right onto NW 23rd Ave. and take the first left on 24th Ave. Clear Creek Distillery will be ahead one block on the right hand side at 2389 NW Wilson Ave.

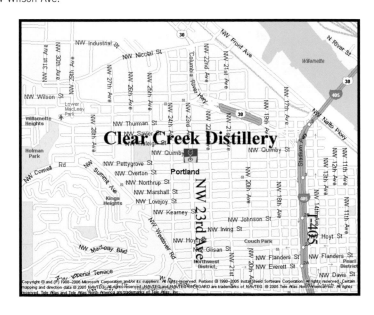

Urban Wineworks/Bishop Creek Cellars

## 2

Portland's Urban Wineworks/Bishop Creek Cellars is different. It's different because it's wonderfully educational. Where else are you given the ingredients and tools to blend your own wine? It's different because it celebrates other wineries and not just its own. How often do you see "guest wineries" on a wine-tasting menu? And it's different because it mixes local art with wine. The first Thursday of each month, Urban Wineworks is a

featured stop along the community art walk. Check out its renowned barrel art at the tasting room — it's like visiting the Portland Art Museum with one huge advantage: You can swirl and sip while taking in the art.

Urban Wineworks at NW 16th Avenue in the Pearl District is the name of the tasting room; Bishop Creek Cellars is the name of the winery. And the UW/BCC motto, "Wine country without the drive," says it all. In addition, there's another tasting-room locations in Newberg (614 E First Street).

How empowering (and cool) is creating your own cuvée from singular Bordeaux varietals, including cabernet sauvignon, cabernet franc, and merlot? For a price tag of less than $25, Urban Wineworks provides you with the tools — including a beaker, a syringe, and a blending placemat — to create your own personal red blend. There's also an add-on feature that allows you to create your own label.

Speaking of empowerment, Urban Wineworks/Bishop Creek Cellars offers a full program that gives students hands-on experience, from harvest through bottling, to learn how to create their own winery. This approach stems from the UW/BCC philosophy of "we're in this thing together."

Winemaker Marcus Goodfellow collaborates with vineyard manager Jeremy Saville to create pinot gris and pinot noir under the Bishop Creek Cellars label. These guys are on a mission, and as they state on their website, "We want to make the best damn pinot noir, or die trying." Now that's passion! However, what's refreshing is that they don't take a myopic view of wines. They feature other wines on a monthly rotation: One month might highlight wines of South Africa; another month, California zinfandels; and the next month, acclaimed women winemakers. Urban Wineworks is also ground zero for May's Indie Wine Month, which celebrates "guerillas, garagistes, and gung-ho winemakers" and their small-lot productions.

Different? Unabashedly so. Thanks to Urban Wineworks/Bishop Creek Cellars, WineTrail trekkers have a way to experience wine country without the long drive.

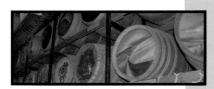

URBAN WINEWORKS/BISHOP CREEK CELLARS
opened: 2000
winemaker(s): Marcus Goodfellow
location: 407 NW 16th, Portland, OR 97209
phone: 503-226-9797
web: www.urbanwineworks.com
e-mail: info@urbanwineworks.com
picnic area: Yes
wheelchair access: Yes
weddings: Yes
tours: Yes
fee: Tasting fees vary – $9 average
hours: Monday through Saturday 12–8:30;
Sundays 12–6

DIRECTIONS: Heading southbound on I-5 toward downtown Portland, take exit 302B (right) onto I-405 [Stadium Fwy] and go 1.6 miles. Take exit 2B toward Everett St. and keep straight onto NW 16th Ave. and arrive at 407 NW 16th Ave.

Heading northbound on I-5 toward Portland take exit 299B left toward I-405 / US-26W. At exit 1A, take ramp (right) onto I-405 [Stadium Fwy] for 1.9 miles. At exit 2B, take ramp (right) onto NW 14th Ave. for .3 miles. Turn left (west) onto NW Gilsan St. followed by another left (south) onto NW 16th Ave. and arrive at the winery at 407 NW 16th Ave.

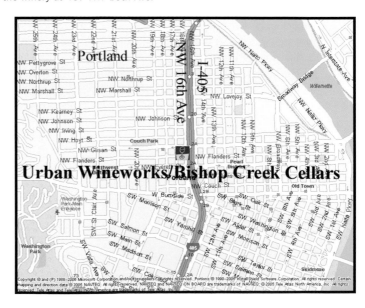

Helvetia Vineyards 🯄

"Welcome! Are you here for the wine tasting?" the guy with the purple shirt and baseball cap asked from the porch of the old farm house. Thus began my introduction to John Platt, co-owner (along with his wife, Elizabeth Furse) of Helvetia Vineyard & Winery in the rural beauty of Helvetia. The charm of the old house (built in 1906) was trumped by John's welcoming smile as he guided us into the parlor room that serves as the tasting area. Following brief introductions to his dogs — Cocoa, Jake (the one with the gooey tennis ball in his mouth), and Sushi — John proceeded to share the story of Helvetia Vineyard & Winery.

John Platt

Turns out the area was settled in the late 1800s by families from Switzerland and Germany. In fact, for you linguist fans out there, "Helvetia" is the term Italians used to refer to people living north of Italy in present-day Switzerland. Gracing the walls of the tasting room are framed photographs of the original settlers of Helvetia, including pictures of the family that built the original farmhouse.

John poured from an impressive array of estate wines made by winemaker John Derthick. Beginning with whites (pinot gris and chardonnay), John wove stories of the community, the dogs, the vineyards, and the characters who shaped the winery. He doesn't feed your head with many adjectives about the wine. He leaves that to you to experience. Moving through the reds (including his pride and joy pinot noir), John ended with a delightful rosé. I already had been won over, but I was blown away by John's "pinot noir training plate." During our visit, two women visitors exclaimed that they only liked whites. Working fast, John prepared a plate of smoked salmon and crackers, and invited the women to try a little taste of the pinot noir with the salmon. "Oooooh, that's good," remarked one of the new converts. Nice touch.

Helvetia Vineyard & Winery is a required stop along the Greater Portland WineTrail. Experience the wine. Stay for the bucolic beauty. Soak in the history. And before leaving, check out the quotation on the wildflower-adorned wine labels, from the property's original owner, Jacob Yungen: "The north wind howls here every time it frosts. However, the grapes often ripen full and wonderful." He wrote this to his Swiss relatives in 1917 — a true harbinger for what was to come for John Platt and Elizabeth Furse.

HELVETIA VINEYARDS
opened: 1996
winemaker(s): John Derthick
location: 22485 NW Yungen Road,
Hillsboro, OR 97124
phone: 503-647-5169
web: www.helvetiawinery.com
e-mail: info@helvetiawinery.com
picnic area: Yes
wheelchair access: Yes
weddings: Yes
fee: $2 tasting fee refundable with purchase
hours: Weekends 12–5 or by appointment

DIRECTIONS: From Portland heading west on US-26 [Sunset Hwy] for about 13.5 miles. Take exit 61 and turn right (north) onto NW Helvetia Rd and go 3.1 miles. Turn right (north) onto NW Bishop Rd and go .6 miles. Turn right (east) onto NW Yungen Rd and go .5 miles. Arrive at 22485 NW Yungen Rd on the right and follow signs to the tasting room.

From Hillsboro, go north on N 1st Ave. for .8 miles. Road name changes to NW Glencoe Rd. Continue for 1.2 miles. Turn right (east) onto NW Evergreen Rd and go 3.4 miles. Turn left (north) onto NW Shute Rd and go 1 mile. Road name changes to NW Helvetia Rd. Continue 3.1 miles. Turn right (north) onto NW Bishop Rd and proceed .6 miles. Turn right (east) onto NW Yungen Rd and go .5 miles and look for winery on the right.

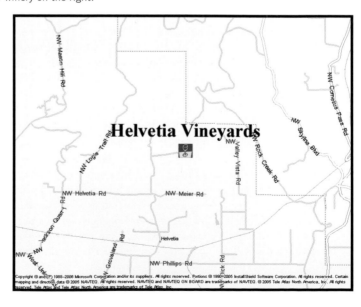

Oak Knoll Winery 4

WineTrail trekkers living in and around Portland have a jewel of a winery in their own backyard. Located west of Portland in Hillsboro (where high tech meets family-run farms), Oak Knoll Winery sits ensconced in rural splendor. An über-lawn that would make John Deer nervous invites would-be picnickers and bocce enthusiasts alike to relax

with a glass of wine and enjoy the setting. Yes, those are the Chehalem Mountains in the distance — Oregon's newest designated American Viticultural Area.

Founded in 1970 by Ron and Marj Vuylsteke, Oak Knoll Winery is Oregon's third-oldest winery. It was an abundance of blackberries that led Ron, an Oregon native, to break out an old family recipe and create a blackberry wine that friends and family came to relish. This gave birth to Oak Knoll Winery. One in three bottles of wine sold in Oregon in the late '70s had the Oak Knoll label. Oak Knoll Winery is a survivor. If there were a reality TV series featuring wineries, Oak Knoll Winery would be a finalist.

Fast-forward nearly 40 years. Although Ron is no longer in the picture, Marj still works the tasting room on a part-time basis. She still has that passion in her eyes when it comes to Oak Knoll's portfolio of wines and to the success of her six children. With good reason, she happily remarks that all five sons are in the wine business up and down the West Coast.

Oak Knoll's winemaker, Jeff Herinckx, cranks out a full array of wines, including an assortment of Burgundian pinots, chardonnay, and other cool-climate varietals, such as Müller-Thurgau, as well as raspberry wine. (**WineTrail note:** A full pound of raspberries goes into the production of each 375 ml bottle of Oak Knoll's Frambrosia raspberry wine.) As Marj notes, "From the beginning our motto was 'Make a wine for every palate, taste and occasion.'" For a mere $5, visitors can sample as many as 12 wines, from bone dry to semi-sweet pours. Better yet, purchase a glass of wine as I did and retreat to a picnic table on the manicured lawn. The hustle and bustle of nearby Portland is but a distant memory.

OAK KNOLL WINERY
opened: 1970
winemaker(s): Jeff Herinckx
location: 29700 SW Burkhalter Road,
Hillsboro, OR 97123
phone: 503-648-8198
web: www.oakknollwinery.com
e-mail: Info@oakknollwinery.com
picnic area: Yes
wheelchair access: Yes
gift shop: Yes
weddings: Yes
tours: Yes
fee: $5 tasting fee
hours: Monday through Friday 11–6; Saturday and
Sunday 11–5 during spring and summer;
Daily 11–5 fall and winter

DIRECTIONS: From Portland take US-26 west about 5 miles to exit 69A. Take ramp onto SR-217 [Beaverton-Tigard Hwy] for 1.7 miles. At exit 2A, turn right onto ramp and proceed west on SR-8 [SW Canyon Rd] for 8.4 miles. Turn left (south) onto SE Minter Bridge Rd and go 1 mile. Bear left (south) onto Minter Bridge Rd and continue 2.5 miles. Keep straight onto SW Burkhalter Rd for .2 miles and arrive at winery on your right.

If traveling from the Hillsboro town center, go south on S 1st Ave. .2 miles. Road name changes to SR-219 [S 1st Ave.]. Continue .5 miles. Keep straight onto SR-219 [SW Hillsboro Hwy] and proceed 3.3 miles. Turn left (east) onto SW Burkhalter Rd and go .6 miles and arrive at the winery at 29700 SW Burkhalter Rd.

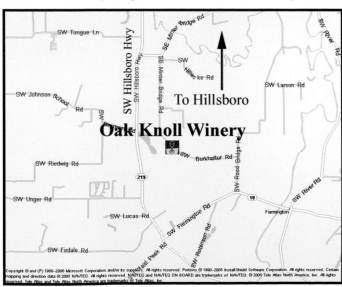

Cooper Mountain Vineyards 5

Is it possible for a winery to leave no carbon footprint? Can you be greener than green? It is if your name is Cooper Mountain Vineyards and your motto is "Where less is more."

At the heart of Cooper Mountain Vineyards is its founder and visionary, Dr. Robert Gross. Dr. Gross, whose background includes psychiatric, homeopathic, and

acupuncturist practices, rejected the use of pesticides and other non-organic methods for growing grapes. He adopted this approach back in the early 1990s, and consequently, Cooper Mountain Vineyards became the second certified organic vineyard in Oregon.

But being certified organic was not enough. Dr. Gross also embraced biodynamic practices developed by Austrian Rudolf Steiner in the early 1900s. One Wikipedia definition of biodynamic farming states, "Biodynamic agriculture is a method of organic farming that has its basis in a spiritual world-view, ... treats farms as unified and individual organisms, emphasizing balancing the holistic development and interrelationship of the soil, plants, animals as a closed, self-nourishing system. Regarded by some proponents as the first modern ecological farming system, biodynamic farming includes organic agriculture's emphasis on manures and composts and exclusion of the use of artificial chemicals on soil and plants."

Phew! This WineTrail trekker only knows that the results taste pretty darned good.

Producing 16,000 cases of estate wine per year is no small task. It takes leadership, deep pockets, and a winemaker with extensive experience. Enter French-born and Bordeaux-trained Gilles de Domingo. Gilles (pronounced "Jeel") worked his way around the world — New Zealand, Australia, South Africa, to name a few stops — on various wine stints before arriving in Oregon. He chose to work at Cooper Mountain Vineyards in large part because of the opportunity to work with a proven team of viticulturists and to make organic wines that truly express the tastes associated with Cooper Mountain's *terroir*.

Nestled in the hills of Beaverton, Cooper Mountain Vineyards is just 30 minutes from downtown Portland. The tasting room provides an inviting sanctuary in which to taste Cooper Mountain's lineup of pinot gris, chardonnay, and pinot noir. However, it is the patio outside, with its refined deck furniture (of which Martha Stewart would even approve), that holds our attention. Uncorking a bottle of Cooper Mountain Vineyards in this setting gets a nod of approval from Mother Nature herself.

Winemaker Gilles de Domingo

COOPER MOUNTAIN VINEYARDS
opened: 1987
winemaker(s): Gilles de Domingo
location: 9480 SW Grabhorn Road,
Beaverton, OR 97007
phone: 503-649-0027
web: www.coopermountainwine.com
e-mail: sales@coopermountainwine.com
picnic area: Yes
wheelchair access: Yes
fee: $8 tasting fee
hours: Daily 12–5 or by appointment;
Closed January

DIRECTIONS: From Portland drive west on Hwy 26 for about 8 miles and take the 185th St. exit. Travel south approximately 4.5 miles on 185th St. to Farmington Rd. Turn right onto Farmington Rd and drive about 1.2 miles until the Grabhorn Rd junction. Turn left onto Grabhorn Rd and travel south for another 1.2 miles and Cooper Mountain Vineyards is on the left.

From Salem travel north on I-5 for about 40 miles until the Hwy 217 junction. Take Hwy 217, exit 292, and follow Highway 217 northwest for about 3 miles until the Scholls Ferry Road exit. Follow Scholls Ferry Rd to the west for just over 4.7 miles until the junction of Tile Flat Rd. Turn right onto Tile Front Rd, and follow it for about 1 mile until the Grabhorn Road junction. Turn right onto Grabhorn Rd and 1.7 miles north is Cooper Mountain Vineyards on the right.

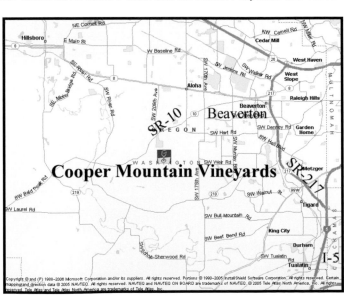

Ponzi Vineyard ⑥

WineTrail trekkers with a modicum of Oregon wine history know the name Ponzi. Just hearing the name conjures up images of pioneers, industry leaders, land stewards and family. Dick and Nancy Ponzi moved to the northern end of the Willamette Valley in the 1960s with the express purpose of growing cool-weather Burgundian grapes and other varietals. Although many observers in the wine world would have considered them a little crazy, they proved otherwise and showed the world that pinots and chardonnays would do

just fine in the rich earth found between the Oregon Coast Range and the Cascade Mountains.

Visitors to the Ponzi Vineyards estate in Beaverton are advised to budget extra time for this winery. It's a field trip. First off, the well-manicured grounds and indigenous gardens, populated with amazing sculpture, will hold your attention even if landscaping isn't your thing. Weather permitting, you will likely see people playing bocce, sharing a picnic, or strolling about. Once inside, your eyes will lock on the pictures and storyboards sprinkled on the walls. The image of little Luisa Ponzi in the vineyard with her blond hair foretells her future role as Ponzi's second-generation winemaker. By now, you look at your watch and realize that a full half-hour has slipped by and you haven't had your first swirl and sip!

The eager-to-please pouring staff paces you through a tasting bonanza of reds and whites, including Italian dolcetto and an unusual arneis varietal. Of course, center stage is pinot noir served in Riedel stemware designed especially for savoring this Burgundian varietal. (Try it. It works! You will taste a difference.)

For those wishing to spend extra time learning more about Ponzi Vineyards, including technical winemaking information, groups of five or more can arrange a customized tour of the winery. Call 503-628-1227 to arrange a private tour.

If your wine-tasting weekend only allows a quick getaway to Dundee, check out the Ponzi Wine Bar at 100 SW Seventh Street. The wine bar features select wines from Oregon's top vintners, microbrews, Italian coffee, and a selection of appetizers and local gourmet foods. (Dick and Nancy Ponzi also founded Oregon's oldest microbrewery, BridgePort Brewing Company in Portland.) This is your opportunity to address the burning issue of which pairs best with pinot noir: cheese or chocolate?

PONZI VINEYARD
opened: 1974
winemaker(s): Luisa Ponzi
location: 14665 SW Winery Lane,
Beaverton, OR 97007
phone: 503-628-1227
web: www.ponziwines.com
e-mail: info@ponziwines.com
picnic area: Yes
wheelchair access: Yes
weddings: Yes
gift shop: Yes
tours: Yes
fee: Tasting fee varies – complimentary tasting for
select wines; $10 for white and red wine flights
hours: Daily 11–5; Closed Easter Sunday,
Christmas Day, Thanksgiving Day and New Year's Day

DIRECTIONS: From Portland, take I-5 south to exit 292 turning right onto Highway 217. Take the Scholls Ferry/Progress exit to Scholls Ferry Road and turn left. Follow Scholls Ferry Road until you see the Ponzi Vineyards Winery highway sign on your right, and turn left onto Vandermost Road. This will take you to Winery Lane and the Ponzi winery.

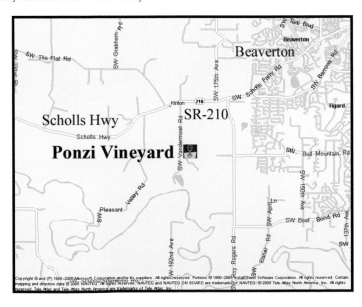

Oswego Hills 7

This is the story of two people who bought the farm. Literally.

Jerry and Lesley Marshall lived near a horse farm in this bucolic section halfway between the town centers of West Linn and Lake Oswego. For years, they witnessed the farm property fall into disrepair and were saddened by its plight. Early photos of the property showed a magnificent equestrian center of gleaming white buildings, fences, and barns. They understood its potential. After all, this was the place where Roy Rogers brought

Trigger and Buttercup for boarding when he came to Portland during the years he was the grand marshall for the Rose Parade!

In 1996 following Jerry's retirement as a senior pilot for American Airlines, the Marshalls acquired the property, complete with overgrown blackberry canes and dilapidated buildings. But they had a vision of a vineyard and working winery, and knew that beneath the neglected outer shells of the buildings existed a strong skeleton of posts and beams. They cleared the land (no small task in itself) and planted pinot noir, pinot gris, and Marechal Foch, an unusual varietal to the Pacific Northwest.

To say this was a labor of love is an understatement. It was a rehab of giant proportions that included huge amounts of blood, sweat and lots of white paint. But in 2003 the winery opened, thanks in large part to the assistance of the Marshalls' three daughters and their spouses. In fact, one of the daughters' husbands, Derek Lawrence, became the winemaker for Oswego Hills Winery. When he's not managing the winemaking process, Derek is a hospital pharmacist at Legacy Emanuel Hospital's ICU.

Oswego Hill's tasting room resides in the former horse barn, which drips with country elegance. When asked about the fact that they don't charge a tasting fee, Lesley notes that they want to be good neighbors. They sell most of their annual production of 3,000 cases to people in the community. Having a tasting fee just wouldn't be neighborly. What's more, they sell their wine in a handy six-pack (you can mix and match the wines you want), and when you come to refill your empty six-pack, you get a free glass of wine. Nice touch. When tasting, be sure to experience the Marechal Foch paired with Moonstruck chocolate. Portland-based Moonstruck is the chocolatier that Oprah Winfrey gushes over. The folks at Moonstruck were so inspired by Oswego Hill's Marechal Foch that they created a special chocolate to pair with the wine. Forget the calories — indulge!

OSWEGO HILLS
opened: 2003
winemaker(s): Derek Lawrence
location: 450 S Rosemont Road,
West Linn, OR 97068
phone: 503-655-2599
web: www.oswegohills.com
e-mail: help@oswegohills.com
picnic area: Yes
tours: Yes
fee: Complimentary wine tasting
hours: Sundays 12–5

Derek Lawrence

DIRECTIONS: From Portland take US-26 [SW Arthur St.] .2 miles. Turn left (east) onto SW Hood Ave. and go .2 miles toward I-5 S/OR-43/Salem/Lake Oswego. Road name changes to SR-43 [SW Hood Ave.]. Continue 6.5 miles. Bear right onto McVey Ave. and go .7 miles. Road name changes to Stafford Rd. Continue 1.1 miles. At the roundabout, go left (east) onto Rosemont Rd and go .9 miles. Arrive at 450 Rosemont Rd in West Linn.

Heading northbound on I-5 toward Portland take exit 288 onto I-205 [Veterans Memorial Hwy]. At exit 3 turn right heading toward Stafford Rd/Lake Oswego. Turn left (north) onto SW Stafford Rd and go 1.9 miles. Turn right (east) onto Rosemont Rd at the roundabout and go .9 miles.

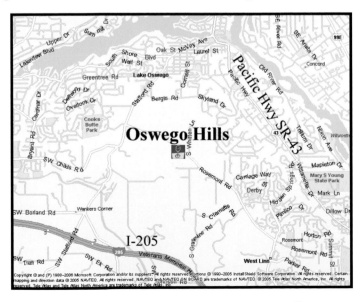

Hip Chicks Do Wine 🔳

If you answer "yes" to any of following questions, you're a good candidate to visit Hip Chicks Do Wine:

- You live in the Portland area and don't have time to go to Willamette Valley for wine tasting, but you have a hankering for liquid enjoyment.
- Friends from out of town are visiting and you need something to do, something that's fun and flavorful.
- You're bored with manicured lawns and logo-wearing pouring staff, and long for some industrial edginess.

If you replied in the affirmative to any of the questions above, you should head to southeast Portland, near Reed College, and taste nectar of the gods (or rather, *goddesses*). Hip Chicks Do Wine is nestled in an old industrial park on SE 23rd — imagine concrete and rebar meets wine barrel and stemware.

Laurie Lewis and Renee Neely found joy in the Willamette Valley in the mid-'90s while touring wineries and decided that they, too, wanted to be part of the wine scene — in a big way. Rather than planting a vineyard on a south slope in the Dundee Hills, the two women opted to open an urban winery in the heart of Portland. By doing so, they have the advantage of selecting grapes from top growers in Washington and Oregon. They offer a variety of white and red wines, from chardonnay and pinot gris to cabernet sauvignon and pinot noir. Plus, with their urban location, they can draw in Portland wine lovers who seek a day trip or a spot for a family get-together or corporate event.

After considerable study and hard work, Hip Chicks Do Wine opened in 2001 and has been satisfying taste buds ever since to the tune of 3,000 cases per year. Laurie and Renee distribute their wines themselves, primarily through the tasting room in Portland and their newer satellite tasting room in Newberg. Their product is especially appealing to women; nearly 70 percent of their clientele are women who like the chic industrial feel, the labeling of the bottles, and the art that adorns the walls. But it's the wine that knows no gender boundaries and appeals to both sexes. After all, Laurie and Renee may have packaged a winery in a fun motif, but they are quite serious about their wines.

HIP CHICKS DO WINE
opened: 2001
winemaker(s): Laurie Lewis and Renee Neely
location: 4510 SE 23rd Avenue,
Portland, OR 97202
phone: 503-234-3790
web: www.hipchicksdowine.com
e-mail: winegoddess@hipchicksdowine.com
wheelchair access: Yes
tours: Yes
fee: 3 complimentary wine samples; 4 wines at $5
tasting fee
hours: Daily 11–6

DIRECTIONS: From downtown Portland, head east over Hawthorne Bridge. Take ramp (right) onto
SR-99E [SE Martin Luther King Blvd] and go 1.5 miles south. Keep right onto local road for .1
mile. Road name changes to SE Holgate Blvd. Continue for .6 miles. Turn right (south) onto SE
26th Ave., then turn right on SE Schiller followed by a left (west) onto SE Pardee St. Turn right
(north) onto SE 23rd Ave. Winery is on the right.

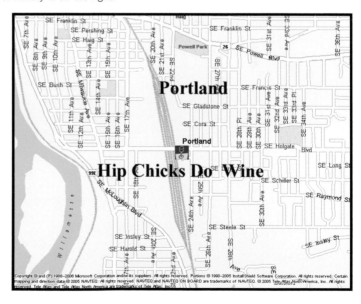

Wasson Brothers Winery 9

Who says you can't please all the people all the time?

In the case of Wasson Brothers Winery, both the enthusiasts of fruit and berry wines as well as the folks who like "pinot" in the name of their wines are satisfied. Production at

the winery is split about 50/50 between fruit and berry wines and varietal grape wines. Anecdotal evidence finds that local folks prefer the tasty loganberry, blackberry, and rhubarb wines, and the city folks like the pinot. It shouldn't come as a surprise that Wasson Brothers specializes in berry cane wines. After all, in this part of Oregon, you have miles of berry fields in any given direction. It would be a shame not to take advantage of all that fruit!

WineTrail trivia: Oregon's Tri-County area (Clackamas, Marion, and Multnomah counties) is one of the leading producers of nursery stock in the world. Driving to Wasson Brothers Winery, you'll pass mile after mile of nurseries.

Wasson Brothers winery is located in Sandy, Oregon, right off Highway 26 on the road leading to Mount Hood. Owners John and Jim Wasson have pursued their winemaking passion for several decades. When they're not making wine, they are often involved with their other infatuation — flying. The Wasson brothers are identical twins, though there is a slight difference in their heights; a couple of knee surgeries are responsible for John being slightly shorter than Jim.

Their number-one selling wine is Niagara, the white-wine cousin of Concord grape wine. A big chunk of their annual production of 3,500 cases is this sweet wine. But they also produce a fair amount of pinot noir, riesling, and chardonnay. And you can't beat their prices. Most Wasson Brothers wines cost between $11 and $16. It's also the place where locals purchase their beer and winemaking supplies. If Prohibition revisits us, the folks of Sandy and other nearby burgs are sitting pretty.

Now in their sixties, the Wasson brothers are thinking about life beyond the winery. At the time of this writing, their winery was up for sale. If you pluck down $260,000, the winery — including the business, its loyal following, as well as the equipment — is yours. Although inventory is extra, you're going to need some bottles to celebrate.

WASSON BROTHERS WINERY
opened: 1982
winemaker(s): Jim and John Wasson
location: 17020 Ruben Lane Highway 26,
Sandy, OR 97055
phone: 503-668-3124
web: None
e-mail: wassonbw@teleport.com
gift shop: Yes
fee: Complimentary wine tasting
hours: Daily 9–5

DIRECTIONS: Heading east on I-84 take exit 13 toward 181st Ave./Gresham. Turn right (south) onto NE 181st Ave. and go 1.3 miles. Turn left (east) onto E Burnside St. and go 4.1 miles. Keep straight onto US-26 [Mt. Hood Hwy] and go 10.2 miles to Sandy. Wasson Brothers Winery is located right off US-26 on the right at 17020 Ruben Lane across from the Safeway.

From I-205 heading north take exit 12 toward OR-212/OR-224/Mt. Hood. Turn right (east) onto SR-212 [SR-224] and go 11.5 miles. Bear right (southeast) onto Mt. Hood Hwy [US-26 E] and go 4.7 miles toward Sandy. Wasson Brothers Winery is located across from the Safeway.

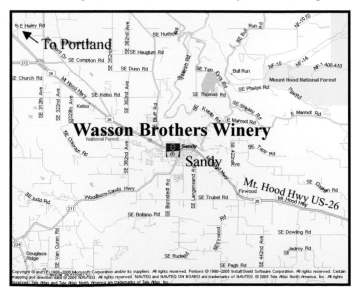

Edgefield Winery - McMenamins 🔟

This is a "winery" that you can visit and not leave for a week. With 38 acres of property, highlighted by The Edgefield Manor and its whimsical Art Nouveau motif, guests can eat, sleep, enjoy spa treatments, golf, and drink without worrying about global warming or the price of gas (the absence of TVs and phones in the bedrooms are just part of this inn's charm). It's a mere 30-minute drive from downtown Portland to Troutdale's Edgefield Manor, but it might as well be a world away. When you see the small vineyard in front of

Halsey Street you know you've arrived. Once parked, resist the urge to get comfortable in one of the veranda's rocking chairs and follow the signs to the tasting room, which is strategically located in the basement.

There, for a nominal tasting fee, you will find a full line-up of wines to choose from. You know you are in Oregon when the wine list includes pinot gris and pinot noir, but you also have the option to choose from Columbia Gorge varietals such as chardonnay, cabernet sauvignon, syrah, merlot, and others.

Indeed, this is winemaker Davis Palmer's playground. He's not confined to one or two varieties. Rather, he has a full portfolio of premium grapes to choose from. One of the most popular wines is called Black Rabbit Red, which features a blend of cabernet sauvignon, merlot, cabernet franc, zinfandel, and grenache, and sells for around $15. That's a good value.

Edgefield Winery had its first crush in 1990 and later added the downstairs tasting room. After you've worked your way through a flight of wines, make sure you budget time to stroll the grounds of this old "poor farm" and check out the gardens, hidden pubs, classic pool hall, and well-stocked gift shop. By then, you may have worked up an appetite and be ready to experience one of Edgefield Manor's many pubs. To neutralize your tummy's grumblings, check out the Black Rabbit Restaurant & Bar. If you do, you might want to ask your server to uncork that fresh bottle of Black Rabbit Red you just purchased. ¡Salud!

EDGEFIELD WINERY - MCMENAMINS
opened: 1990
winemaker(s): Davis Palmer
location: 2126 SW Halsey Street,
Troutdale, OR 97060
phone: 503-665-2992
web: www.mcmenamins.com
e-mail: winery@mcmenamins.com
picnic area: Yes
wheelchair access: Yes
weddings: Yes
fee: Wine flights from $3 to $5
hours: Daily 12–10

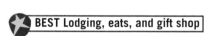

BEST Lodging, eats, and gift shop

DIRECTIONS: From Portland heading east on I-84 go about 13.5 miles and take exit 16. Turn right (south) onto NE 238th Dr. and go .2 miles. Turn left (east) onto Birch Ave. and go .2 miles. Turn right (east) onto Halsey St. and travel .4 miles. Look for winery at 2126 SW Halsey St.

If traveling westbound on I-84 toward Portland take exit 16. Turn left (south) onto NE 238th Dr. and go .2 miles. Turn left (east) onto Birch Ave. and go .2 miles. Turn right (east) onto Halsey St. and travel .4 miles.

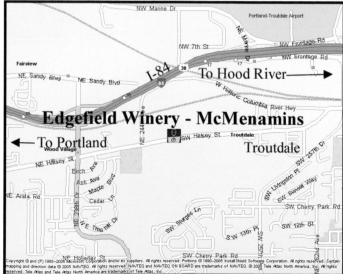

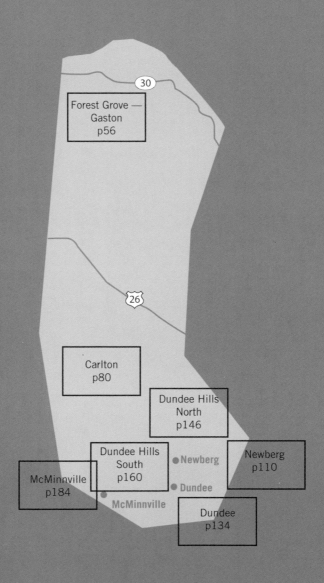

30

Forest Grove —
Gaston
p56

26

Carlton
p80

Dundee Hills
North
p146

Dundee Hills
South
p160

● Newberg

Newberg
p110

McMinnville
p184

● Dundee

McMinnville

Dundee
p134

North Willamette Valley
WINE COUNTRY

Forest Grove – Gaston
WineTrail

David Hill Vineyard & Winery

Often referred to as the Sip 47 wine tour, member wineries of the Forest Grove – Gaston WineTrail dot the landscape along Highway 47 that connects these towns. Within an hour's drive from downtown Portland, the Forest Grove – Gaston WineTrail is an easy romp for day trippers. WineTrail trekkers particularly like the fact that most of these wineries are surrounded by their own vineyards. From Elk Cove to Tualatin Estate Vineyards wine tourists can swirl, sniff, taste, and spit with rows of wine grapes in the background. There is one big exception however — SakéOne. Their saké wines depend upon high grade rice for production, and you won't find rice paddies in Oregon. But you will find friendly tasting staff throughout this northern part of the Willamette Valley eager to pour you a sample of Oregon's best.

Forest Grove – Gaston WineTrail

1. Tualatin Estate Vineyards
2. Apolloni Vineyards
3. Purple Cow Vineyards
4. Shafer Vineyard Cellars
5. David Hill Vineyard and Winery
6. SakéOne
7. Montinore Estate
8. Plumb Hill Vineyards
9. Patton Valley Vineyard
10. Elk Cove Vineyards
11. Kramer Vineyards

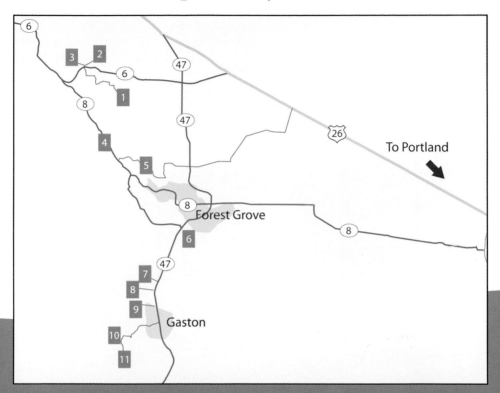

Region:	**North Willamette Valley Wine Country**
# of tasting rooms on tour:	**11**
# of satellite tasting rooms:	**1**
Estimate # of days for tour:	**2**
Getting around:	**Car and bike**
Key Events:	❑ **Memorial Weekend in Wine Country – Willamette Valley – visit www.willamettewines.com.**
	❑ **Wine Country Thanksgiving – Willamette Valley – call 503-646-2985 or visit www.willamettewines.com.**
Tips:	❑ **Need a place to stay? Consider McMenamin's Grand Lodge in Forest Grove.**
	❑ **See Appendix B, Wine Tour Planning, for planning your visit.**
Best:	❑ **Gift shop: Kramer Vineyards.**
	❑ **Views: David Hill Vineyard and Winery, Patton Valley Vineyard, Elk Cove Vineyards.**

Tualatin Estate Vineyards 🔲

Someone had warned me that Tualatin Estate Vineyards was off the beaten path. As I made turn after turn on the rural roads outside Forest Grove, I began to understand. Where the heck is this place, I wondered (only with more colorful language). Fortunately,

blue roadside signs eventually led me to the winery. And as I drove into the parking lot, my suspicions were confirmed — I was the only car there. That, my fellow WineTrail trekker, is a good thing.

A winery devoid of tour buses and crowds bellying up to the wine bar is fine by me. I love it when you have the time to chat with the wine-pouring staff and get a sense of the place and, of course, the wines. Quite often, wineries that lack visitors don't have bad wine to blame; rather, it's often their location off the beaten path that's responsible. Such is the case with Tualatin Estate Vineyards, despite the fact that it's just 30 miles west of Portland.

Tualatin Estate Vineyards' tasting room reflects its age. Founded in 1973, the tasting room itself feels like one of those buildings you see in a B Western. I thought for sure a cowboy would ride up and park his horse. But don't let the outer shell of a tasting room fool you. There's a reason Tualatin's motto is "Old vines — new vision." Perhaps that new vision coincided the 1997 merging of Tualatin Estate Vineyards with Willamette Valley Vineyards.

Opening the door, two tasting-room pourers greeted me with a friendly "Welcome to Tualatin Estate. Are you here for some tasting?" I knew I was at the right place — especially when they brought out the Riedel stemware and gave me a generous pour of the pinot gris. From there, I sampled my way through their estate chardonnay, pinot noir, syrah, and a semi-sparkling muscat (wonderful in that July day's heat). Riedel glasses. Generous pours. Friendly staff. What's not to love?

Yes, I enjoyed Tualatin Estate Vineyards wines big time; I can well understand why it has collected a number of awards and accolades over the years. However, the number-one impression I took away from this winery was its relaxed atmosphere and the friendly demeanor of its staff. Here's a bit of related **WineTrail trivia:** The word "tualatin," derived from the language of the indigenous people, means "gentle and easy flowing." Perfect.

TUALATIN ESTATE VINEYARDS
opened: 1973
winemaker(s): Forrest Klaffke and Don Crank III
location: 10850 NW Seavey Road,
Forest Grove, OR 97116
phone: 503-357-5005
web: www.tualatinestate.com
e-mail: info@wvv.com
picnic area: Yes
wheelchair access: Yes
fee: Complimentary wine tasting
hours: Weekends 12–5 March through December;
closed January and February

DIRECTIONS: From Portland follow Hwy 26 west to Hwy 6 west. Begin looking for blue highway information signs. Follow Hwy 6 to Hwy 47. Travel south on Hwy 47 approximately 1 mile to Greenwood Rd. Turn right. Follow to first stop sign at Kansas City Rd. Turn left. Take first right onto Clapshaw Hill Rd. Follow until road forks. Take the right fork (Seavey Rd) and follow for approximately .5 mile. Tualatin Estate Vineyards will be on your right-hand side.

From Forest Grove travel west on SR-8 for 1.3 miles. The road name changes to Gales Creek Rd. Bear right (north) onto NW Thatcher Rd and go 2.7 miles. Road name changes to NW Kansas City Rd. Continue 2.1 miles. Turn left (west) onto NW Clapshaw Hill Rd and go 1 mile. Keep straight onto NW Seavey Rd and go about .5 miles. Arrive at Tualatin Estate Vineyards on your right.

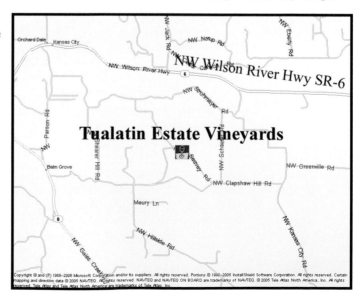

Apolloni Vineyards ²

At Apolloni Vineyards, our wine-tour guide, John, brought us a tray of nibbles and placed them on the wine bar. My partner, Kathleen, and I were first-time visitors to Apolloni

Vineyards, and the salami, nuts, olives, and cheeses made me think I shouldn't have had that extra waffle for breakfast. It was our first wine-tour foray into the famed Willamette Valley, and we made the smart choice of choosing Grape Escape as our chauffeur and tour company. Turns out, our Grape Escape tour guide (John) had considerable experience in Europe managing U.S. military-dependent schools in places like Germany and Spain before returning to America. While there, John experienced the ultimate wine 101 training venturing to Bordeaux and Burgundy. We realized early on that John did the tour gig not because he had to, but because he wanted to.

As I munched on almonds, John noted that the wine label I was staring at was the Apolloni family coat of arms. He remarked that the distinctive label reflects owner/winemaker Alfredo Apolloni's core values: family, tradition, and legacy. The black eagle emblazoned on the label got my attention and had me thinking of how cool it would be on a baseball cap. It is definitely an emblem of strength. John broke my musing with a comment that the family's winemaking tradition goes back 150 years.

Apolloni Vineyards' estate wines rely on fruit from 45 acres of pinot noir, pinot blanc, and pinot gris from their Forest Grove location. The vineyard is certified by LIVE and Salmon Safe. Although Alfredo learned his winemaking technique growing up in Italy, he has had to adapt to Oregon's climate and growing conditions. The result is Oregon/Italian-style wines with fresh, crisp, fruit-forward taste. (His whites don't touch oak and don't go through malolactic fermentation.) Still, the bottle he uses has the big shoulders used in Italy rather than the slender-shouldered Burgundian-style bottle you would find containing other Oregon pinot gris.

Just when I thought my food foraging was done, the pourer gave me a generous sample of Apolloni Vineyards' estate pinot noir. Thank goodness there was plenty of white cheddar to pair with this offering. As I savored this combo and listened to the talk around me, I learned that one of Alfredo's children is named after his winemaking father, Adolfo. I knew then that Apolloni Vineyards is well set for the next generation.

APOLLONI VINEYARDS
opened: 1999
winemaker(s): Alfredo Apolloni
location: 14135 NW Timmerman Road,
Forest Grove, OR 97116
phone: 503-330-5946
web: www.apolloni.com
e-mail: info@apolloni.com
picnic area: Yes
wheelchair access: Yes
tours: Yes
fee: $5 tasting fee refundable with purchase
hours: Friday through Sunday 12–5

DIRECTIONS: From Portland head west on US-26 [Sunset Hwy] toward Ocean Beaches. Keep left onto SR-6 [NW Wilson River Hwy] for 7.7 miles. At milepost 44, turn right (north) onto NW Timmerman Rd and arrive at the winery in .2 miles on your left.

From Forest Grove go west onto SR-8 [Pacific Ave.] then immediately turn right (north) onto Main St for .3 miles. Turn right (east) onto University Ave for .1 miles. Bear left (northeast) onto Sunset Dr. and go .9 miles. Turn left (northwest) onto SR-47 [Nehalem Hwy] and travel 5.3 miles. Take ramp (right) onto SR-6 [NW Wilson River Hwy] and go 5.5 miles. At milepost 44, turn right (north) onto NW Timmerman Rd and look for winery on your left in .2 miles.

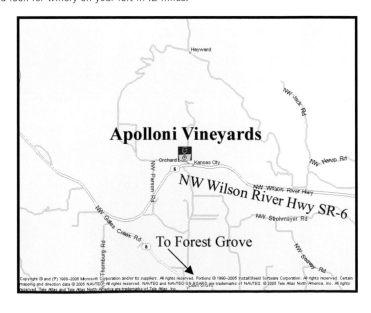

Purple Cow Vineyards 3

Jon and Wendy Armstrong were in another room one day when they overheard then-18-month-old daughter Sophie, who was taking a bath, exclaim, "It's a purple cow!" At the time, Sophie's language skills were minimal, so this observation got Jon and Wendy's attention and they decided it wasn't just a random occurrence. Thus, Purple Cow Vineyards was named.

Jon and Wendy Armstrong with Quincy

What distinguishes Purple Cow Vineyards from the pack is Jon Armstrong's willingness and desire to grow tempranillo grapes. You simply don't find this variety in the Willamette Valley. To track it down, you need to venture more than 100 miles south to Umpqua Valley's Abacela Vineyards & Winery. Tempranillo in the cool climes of Willamette Valley is unheard of. Yet thinking of tempranillo as a warm-weather grape is misguided. Tempranillo is the main noble grape variety in Spain's northern region of La Rioja, where it thrives in the cool climate. This dark, almost black, noble grape ripens early and is great by itself as a single varietal wine or blended with other grapes. The Armstrongs have nearly 7 acres of grapes planted on the slopes of their clay Melbourne soil. In addition to tempranillo, the Armstrongs grow pinot noir, Muscat, and Maréchal Foch.

By day, Jon works at a nearby high-tech company; at night and on weekends, he satisfies his passion for making wine. Wendy is the business brains behind Purple Cow Vineyards; she manages the books, pours wine, updates the website and works as a full-time mom for the couple's two daughters. Their Australian shepherd, Quincy, stays busy herding visitors and looking adorable. Although their tasting room is currently located within their home, that arrangement will change with the construction of a new winery and tasting room in 2009. Jon notes that the plans are ready to build the new winery on the hill above their home. No doubt, the views will be exceptional. Listening to their dreams and the excitement in their voices, it's easy to imagine the whole family involved in the new facility, with Quincy running circles around them, a gleam in his eye.

PURPLE COW VINEYARDS
winemaker(s): Jon Armstrong
location: 52720 NW Wilson School Road,
Forest Grove, OR 97116
phone: 503-701-1294
web: www.purplecowvineyards.com
e-mail: jon@purplecowvineyards.com
picnic area: Yes
fee: $5 tasting fee refundable with purchase
hours: Saturday 11–5 year round; Friday 12–5
July through September

DIRECTIONS: From Portland take US-26 [Sunset Hwy] about 20 miles west. Keep left onto SR-6 [NW Wilson River Hwy] and go 7.7 miles. Turn right (north) onto NW Timmerman Rd and travel a short distance to the winery.

From Forest Grove head west on SR-8 [Pacific Ave.], then immediately turn right (north) onto Main St. Go .3 miles and Turn right (east) onto University Ave. and go .1 miles. Bear left (northeast) onto Sunset Dr. and go .9 miles. Turn left (northwest) onto SR-47 [Nehalem Hwy] and travel 5.3 miles. Take ramp (right) onto SR-6 [NW Wilson River Hwy] and continue 5.1 miles. Turn left (west) onto NW Wilson School Rd only .1 miles to the Purple Cow Vineyards.

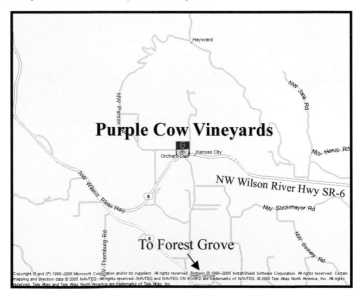

Shafer Vineyard Cellars 4

Do you need to pick up some European glass Christmas ornaments with your pinot noir?

Welcome to one of the most unusual wineries in Oregon, where visitors can experience a collection of northern Willamette estate wines along with a Christmas shop that would make Costco envious. Here, WineTrail trekkers can answer that age-old question: Does riesling pair with German nutcrackers?

Owners Harvey and Miki Shafer planted their vineyards in the foothills of Gales Creek Valley, west of Forest Grove, in 1973. Their goal was simple — to grow grapes. However, within a few years, that goal morphed when Harvey began making wine from their estate fruit. Friends and neighbors encouraged them to produce wine. That was 1978. Now as Harvey works the vineyard, he's producing pinot noir, pinot gris, chardonnay, fumé blanc, riesling, Müller-Thurgau, gewürztraminer, and dessert wines from their 70-acre property. WineTrail visitors can experience their complimentary wines and then purchase a bottle without breaking the bank. For example, a bottle of their pinot gris sells for around $15. Even their pinot noir reserve won't dent your wallet, selling for $28. The tasting room, and Miki's Christmas Shop, is decidedly Northwest in look and feel. Made of cedar, it makes a relaxed setting to chat with Miki and enjoy fine wines.

If you do snap up a bottle of their estate wine, you might want to check out their über picnic ground. In the midst of vineyards and stately oaks, the 2-acre picnic ground offers a great place to unwind. Let the kids run around the gazebo, admire your just purchased Christmas ornament, and uncork a bottle of Shafer Vineyard Cellars' Miki's Blush (assuming it isn't sold out). *Prost!*

SHAFER VINEYARD CELLARS
opened: 1981
winemaker(s): Harvey Shafer
location: 6200 NW Gales Creek Road,
Forest Grove, OR 97116
phone: 503-357-6604
web: www.shafervineyardcellars.com
e-mail: MikiShafer@msn.com
picnic area: Yes
wheelchair access: Yes
gift shop: Yes
weddings: Yes
fee: Complimentary wine tasting
hours: Daily 11–5 except Wednesdays; Closed on Easter, Thanksgiving and Christmas

DIRECTIONS: Shafer Vineyard Cellars is located approximately 35 miles west of Portland and 4.5 miles west of the town of Forest Grove, on SR-8 at 6200 NW Gales Creek Rd.

From Forest Grove, take SR-8 [Pacific Ave.] going west .5 miles. The road name changes to E St. Continue .5 miles. Go straight on SR-8 [Gales Creek Rd] 1.1 miles. Bear left (west) onto SR-8 [NW Gales Creek Rd] 3.8 miles and arrive at destination.

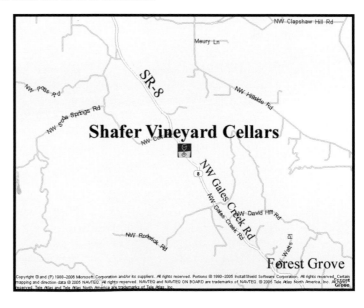

David Hill Vineyard and Winery ⑤

History buffs unite!

David Hill Vineyard & Winery is a field trip into Oregon history taking visitors to a place first homesteaded in 1883. The name itself, David Hill, pays homage to two Oregon pioneers: A David Hill who served on the committee overseeing the Oregon territorial government, and Frederick David, from whom the hill gets its name. The owners of the property, Milan and Jean Stoyanov, restored the building and grounds, beginning in 1992 when they purchased the property. Choosing to preserve the exterior was smart, but renovating the interior to give it a nice flow and a contemporary feel was brilliant. It's no accident that all the "touch points" of the winery reinforce its branding. From the color of the exterior to the labels on the bottles, the distinctive yellow, white and black colors remind you of the place and its wines.

Today, the property is on the Washington County Historical Register. David Hill Vineyard & Winery has the look and feel of a Southern plantation, only Pacific Northwest style. While visiting, stroll the grounds, perhaps uncork a bottle, and, weather permitting, break out the picnic basket. The farm itself is an expansive 140 acres, with 40 acres planted in pinot noir, pinot gris, riesling, chardonnay, gewürztraminer, pinot blanc, semillon, sylvaner, and muscat. Half the vineyard is planted in pinot noir.

If someone in the family is getting married and needs an idyllic setting for exchanging vows, you may have just stumbled on it. Or if your boss is asking if you know of a great place for the next corporate meeting, you just scored some points. To celebrate your find, you might just want to spring for a bottle of the estate pinot noir. Then go outside and enjoy the wine while soaking in the views of the Coast Range in the distance. It's the same view the pioneers enjoyed in the 1800s. (**WineTrail history note:** Those same pioneers planted wine grapes throughout the Willamette Valley. Unfortunately, Prohibition came along in 1913 and the vineyards disappeared.)

DAVID HILL VINEYARD AND WINERY
opened: 2000
winemaker(s): Pascal Valadier
location: 46350 NW David Hill Road,
Forest Grove, OR 97116
phone: 503-992-8545
web: www.davidhillwinery.com
e-mail: davidhill.winery@verizon.net
picnic area: Yes
weddings: Yes
wheelchair access: Yes
tours: Yes
fee: Complimentary wine tasting
hours: Daily 12–5

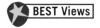 BEST Views

DIRECTIONS: From Portland, head west on US-26 [Sunset Hwy] for about 16 miles. At exit 57, keep right onto ramp. Turn left (south) onto NW Glencoe Rd and proceed 1.3 miles. Turn right (west) onto NW Zion Church Rd and go 2 miles. The road name changes to NW Cornelius Schefflin Rd; continue 1.6 miles. At the roundabout, take the first exit onto NW Verboort Rd and go 2.1 miles. The road name changes to NW Purdin Rd. Turn left (south) onto NW Thatcher Rd and continue .8 miles. Turn right (west) onto NW David Hill Rd and go 1.8 miles to reach destination.

From Forest Grove, head west on SR-8 [Pacific Ave.] .5 miles. Continue straight on SR-8 for .5 miles. Keep straight onto SR-8 [Gales Creek Rd] for .3 miles. Bear right (north) onto Thatcher Rd for .8 miles. Turn left (west) onto NW David Hill Rd and go 1.8 miles. Look for signs to the winery.

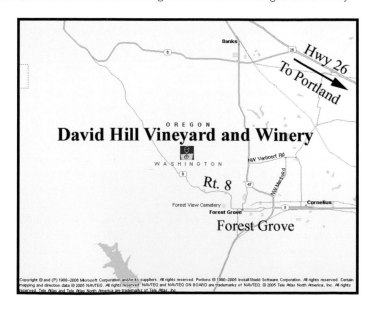

SakéOne

"It is kind to my head, stomach, and nose, lifts my spirits without causing inebriation, and never leaves me hung over. I think this must be due to its purity…"
— Dr. Andrew Weil, foreword of *Saké Pure and Simple*

I had to give it a try. Sure, I've had saké before on numerous occasions. However, I mistakenly thought it would be me and a few wayward Japanese tourists when I visited the SakéOne tasting room in Forest Grove. Au contraire, my fellow wine trekkers. The place was buzzing with visitors four deep trying to get the attention of the lone server. But I was not to be deterred. I was there for the true saké experience – not just the heated stuff you get at Benihana.

At SakéOne, the pouring of saké for your tasting pleasure is accompanied by much pouring of saké knowledge into your head. Although you won't be set to crank up the saké home brewing kit, you will impress your boss the next time you're at a fancy restaurant and ask what sakés the proprietors feature. You learn about the importance of fresh, clean water; the milling of rice to get at the starchy center; and the use of *koji* to make it easy for yeast to break down the starch. What's more, like grape wine, saké can be bone dry or sweet. And, as you will discover, it doesn't need to be served warm.

Wineries have their winemakers, and *kuras* (saké breweries) have their saké masters. In the case of SakéOne, it is fortunate to have Greg Lorenz as its saké master. He is the *only* American saké master, and as such, has extensive training and years of experience handcrafting award-winning saké. At SakéOne you can experience and purchase a variety of Greg's sakés, including traditional saké under the Momokawa label, with names such as Silver, Diamond, Ruby and Pearl, each with their own unique flavor profile. In addition, check out SakéOne's Moonstone brand, which uses natural fruit flavors such as pear and (my favorite) raspberry to create fruit- infused saké. There's also G-labeled saké with some sleek packaging. G is short for genshu, which is described as an "ultra-premium super-sexy" saké that checks in at 18 percent alcohol. A taste of this and you're likely to decide that this is a truly special junmai ginjo genshu saké experience!

SAKÉONE
opened: 1998
winemaker(s): Greg Lorenz
location: 820 Elm Street,
Forest Grove, OR 97116
phone: 503-357-7056
web: www.sakeone.com
e-mail: info@sakeone.com
picnic area: Yes
weddings: Yes
tours: Yes
fee: $3 initial tasting fee, $5 premium flight, and
$10 food pairing flight
hours: Daily 11–5

DIRECTIONS: From downtown Portland, head west on US-26 [Sunset Hwy] about 17 miles. At exit 57, keep right onto ramp. Turn left (south) onto NW Glencoe Rd and go 1.3 miles. Turn right (west) onto NW Zion Church Rd and proceed 2 miles. The road name changes to NW Cornelius Schefflin Rd. Go 1.6 miles. At roundabout, take the first exit onto NW Verboort Rd and proceed .4 miles. At roundabout, take the third exit onto NW Martin Rd and proceed 1.9 miles. Turn left (south) onto SR-47 [Nehalem Hwy] and go 1.7 miles. Turn left onto Elm St. and go .1 mile to the winery.

From Hillsboro, head west on SR-8 [SW Baseline St.] 4 miles. Turn left (south) onto SR-47 [Tualatin Valley Hwy] and go 1.3 miles. Turn left (south) onto Elm St. and go .1 mile.

From Gaston, travel north on SR-47 [Front St.] for 5.7 miles. Turn right (south) onto Elm St. and go .1 mile to the winery.

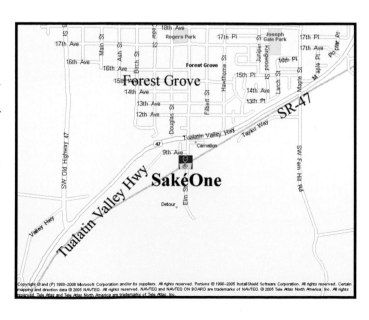

Montinore Estate 7

Consider making Montinore Estate a day trip. Yes, you can dash in and enjoy samples of their estate wines and jet to the next winery, but you would be missing out. How often do you get a chance to indulge your palate, check out local art and hear live music? Not too often.

The name Montinore is a hybrid coined by the original owner of the property, John Forbis. He moved from Montana in 1905, following a career as an attorney for Anaconda Copper Company. He took the phrase "Montana in Oregon" and came up with "Montinore." Besides having a creative streak, John Forbis also must have had a penchant for style, given the oversized Sears Craftsman-style house located next door to the Montinore Estate winery.

Montinore Estate prides itself on producing premium-quality wines from its own grapes. Winemaker John Lundy and his team craft pinot gris, gewürztraminer, riesling, pinot noir, Müller-Thurgau, and dessert wines from varietals that thrive in the relatively cool and protected Willamette Valley. Of course, when it comes to this viticultural area, one thinks "pinot," and sure enough, Montinore Estate is known for its pinot noir estate wines — including many single-vineyard labels.

The tasting room doubles as a venue for local artists to showcase their talents. Here, artwork is displayed on a rotating basis, changing monthly. Lucky visitors to the winery on Sundays will also enjoy live music in the tasting room (from noon to 4 p.m.).

Rudy Marchesi, the owner of Montinore Estate, draws on a rich heritage of Italian-Americans to produce fine wines. However, he recognizes that it all starts in the vineyard. And it's Montinore's vineyards that draw your attention. Actually, "rivet" might be a more accurate verb. Whether you take a stroll before or after your wine tasting, it is a required wine-trekking exercise to check out the grounds of Montinore and marvel at the biodynamically farmed vineyards, the beautifully maintained gardens, and the wide-open grounds that would give the most energetic Frisbee-chasing dog a run for his kibble. (**WineTrail tip:** Pack a picnic.)

It's the land that matters. Terra, terra, terra. Why? Because "land is the only thing worth fighting for, worth dying for and the only thing that lasts," to paraphrase a line from *Gone with the Wind*.

MONTINORE ESTATE
opened: 1987
winemaker(s): John Lundy
location: 3663 SW Dilley Road,
Forest Grove, OR 97116
phone: 503-359-5012
web: www.montinore.com
e-mail: info@montinore.com
picnic area: Yes
wheelchair access: Yes
fee: $5 tasting fee refundable with case purchase
hours: Daily 11–5 June through December; Weekends 11–5 January through May; Store open daily 8–5 year round

DIRECTIONS: From Portland follow Sunset Hwy (US 26) westbound to North Plains exit 57. Exit to right, then cross over freeway. Proceed south on Glencoe Rd for 1.3 miles. At the light, turn right on Zion Church Rd (becomes Cornelius-Schefflin Rd) and continue about 3.6 miles to stop sign. Turn right on Verboort Rd and go .5 mile. Turn left on Martin Rd. Continue to Hwy 47, turn left onto Quince St., as you enter Forest Grove. Cross the tracks and go straight at the light. Continue for 3 miles to Dilley and turn right on Dudney St. Go past the school and nursery. Turn into Montinore at main gate.

From locations south of Portland, follow Beaverton-Hillsdale Hwy (Oregon 8) westbound through Hillsboro, Cornelius and into Forest Grove. At the intersection with Hwy. 47 turn left (following signs to McMinnville.) Continue for 3 miles to Dilley and turn right on Dudney St. Go past the school and nursery. Turn into Montinore at main gate.

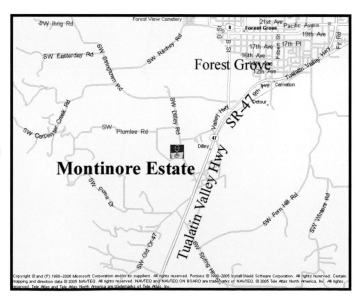

Plum Hill Vineyards 🎱

Both photos courtesy of Plum Hill Vineyards

RJ and Juanita Lint found a second life in their hobby vineyard behind their home on Plum Hill Lane in Forest Grove. With the experience they gained from volunteering with Kramer Vineyards, the former California techies discovered they made a great glass of pinot. When a dilapidated dairy farm down the road in Gaston came on the market, they found the setting for their new lives as vintners.

The dairy sits atop a knob overlooking the Scoggins Valley. When I visited in mid-autumn, glowing deciduous trees sprawled in all directions, broken up by neighboring vineyards. Look to the north on a clear day for the snow-capped volcanoes of Mount St. Helens and Mount Adams. RJ and Juanita are keeping the old farm buildings intact, giving this winery classic agrarian character. The old barn now houses the wine barrels. When you're looking around, try not to disturb "Hoot," the resident barn owl.

Come inside the warm tasting room in the old ranch house. Parts of the beautifully woodworked bar come from the old Mothersheds restaurant in Forest Grove. However, it was RJ himself who invested a solid two months in building the foundation and framework for the "U"-shaped bar. Be sure to look over the beautiful works of local glass artist Dave Johnson that are on display. One of Juanita's passions is local gifts and crafts, making Plum Hill Vineyards an ideal place to get a souvenir from "Wine Country."

Now, with glass of wine in hand, enjoy yourself next to the fire on the back patio or under the oak grove out front. Cheers!

PLUM HILL VINEYARDS
opened: 2008
winemaker(s): RJ Lint
location: 6505 SW Old Highway 47,
Gaston, OR 97119
phone: 503-359-4706
web: www.plumhillwine.com
e-mail: juanita@plumhillwine.com
picnic area: Yes
wheelchair access: Yes
weddings: Yes
retail sales: Yes
fee: Complimentary wine tasting
hours: Daily 11–7; Closed Christmas Day
and Thanksgiving

DIRECTIONS: From Portland, take highway 26 west to exit 57. Take a left on Glencoe Road for about a mile. Stay right at the light onto Zion Church Road. At the first roundabout, take the first exit onto Verboot Road, which brings you to another roundabout. Take the third exit onto Martin Road. Head down Martin for two miles until you meet highway 47. Turn left on this country highway and drive 5 miles. Watch for the uniform blue winery sign for "Plum Hill Winery in 1/4 mile." Take a right onto "Old" Highway 47 and angle left, up the hill until you find the Plum Hill Winery sign on your right.

From McMinville, get on highway 99 north to 47 north for 13 miles. Turn left onto Seghers Road and go up to "Old" Highway 47. Hang a right for a minute and keep your eyes peeled for the Plum Hill sign on your left.

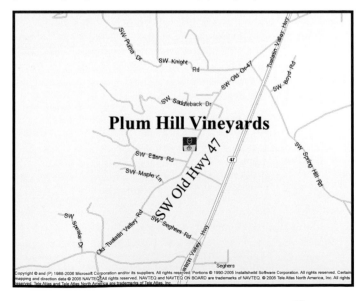

Patton Valley Vineyard 🄰

One of the joys of being the WineTrail guy is discovering a winery that you didn't have on your radar. Before venturing out to wine country, I invest hours in planning the trip and getting to know each winery intimately in advance — well at least as far as the Internet allows me. But as often happens, I will stumble on a winery that I didn't know existed or that had made the conversion from "by appointment only" to now open to the public.

Such was my first-time experience with Patton Valley Vineyard.

There I was bebopping down Highway 47 near Gaston, intent on the next winery on my list, when the blue sign jumped out on the side of the road announcing Patton Valley Vineyard. Going from 60 mph to 10 mph and executing a hard right would earn my mother's admonishment, but this becomes standard practice on the WineTrails of Oregon.

The owners of 72-acre Patton Valley Vineyard, Dave Chen and Monte Pitt, were told that they couldn't grow good pinot noir west of Highway 47, but they were out to prove people wrong. With a score of 94 from *Wine Spectator* for their Willamette Valley Pinot Noir Lorna-Marie Cuvée 2005, evidently they've succeeded. Dave and Monte appreciate that it all begins in the vineyard and from the beginning, these two Chicago transplants (they met in business school in the early 1980s) have strived to make pinot noir that is true to the vineyard's unique personality. To this end, they have the winemaking expertise of Jerry Murray. Using the finest French oak, aging on the lees, using indigenous yeast, and producing nonfiltered wines are just some of the techniques Jerry implements to produce wines of distinction.

As stewards of the land, the Chens and the Pitts rely on sustainable and organic techniques. Patton Valley Vineyard is LIVE certified for its low-input viticultural and enological practices. For example, rather than using traditional methods to reduce the rodent population, they have installed owl boxes to keep the rodent population in check.

While at the tasting room, take time to get the camera from the car. The views from the bluff are nothing short of spectacular. On a clear day, you can see Mount Adams and Mount St. Helens to the east. Below you is Highway 47 snaking through the rich agricultural land that defines the Willamette Valley. Great views and wonderful wine blend to make a wonderful experience.

PATTON VALLEY VINEYARD
opened: 1999
winemaker(s): Jerry Murray
location: 9449 SW Old Hwy 47, Gaston, OR 97119
phone: 503-985-3445
web: www.pattonvalley.com
e-mail: info@pattonvalley.com
picnic area: Yes
fee: Complimentary wine tasting
hours: Thursday through Sunday 11–5

 BEST Views

DIRECTIONS: From Portland take Hwy 26 West, toward Beaverton. After approximately 18 miles, exit to Hwy 6, Tillamook (a left exit). Follow Hwy 6 for about one mile, and exit at Hwy 47, Banks/ Forest Grove. Go south (right) on 47, through Forest Grove. Approximately 6 miles south of Forest Grove, look for the Patton Valley/Cherry Grove sign and turn right at the sign. Travel about .3 miles and bear right at the sharp right-hand turn (Old Hwy 47; follow the sign to Hagg Lake). Look for Patton Valley Vineyard sign on the left side of the road. Turn left into the driveway and follow it .5 miles up the hill to the vineyard.

From McMinnville, take 99W north. Turn left at the Hwy 47 junction just outside of McMinnville. Stay on 47 through Carlton and Yamhill, proceeding north to Gaston. Once through Gaston, 1 mile north of town is a left-hand turn marked with a yellow traffic control sign (no street sign posted). Turn left, proceed .3 miles and bear right at the sharp right-hand turn (Old Hwy 47; follow the sign to Hagg Lake). After about 1,000 feet, look for Patton Valley Vineyard sign on the left side of the road. Turn left into the driveway and follow it .5 miles up the hill to the vineyard.

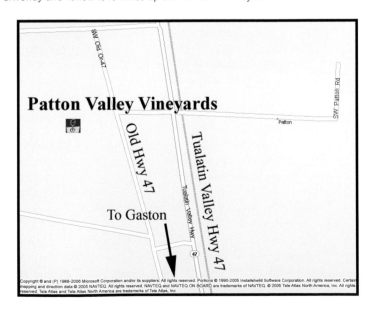

Elk Cove Vineyards 🔟

One of Elk Cove's single-vineyard pinot noirs is called Five Mountain Pinot Noir. It's aptly named: From Five Mountain Vineyard, you can spot the peaks of five Cascade mountains. Can you guess which five?

As you drive through Elk Cove's entrance, you can well imagine the winery's namesake Roosevelt elk roaming the rolling hills where vineyards now grow. The tasting room itself

sits on top of the hill and offers one of those Kodak-moment panoramas. None other than Robert Parker of *The Wine Advocate* notes, "For the pure beauty of its setting, no winery in Oregon can match the breathtaking views from Elk Cove's splendid wine-tasting room." Exacto mundo, Robert.

As I parked my car, two cyclists were wiping their brows, looking back at the hill they had just climbed. This is heart-pounding terrain to cycle, but I made a mental note that I would like to come back here soon with my own bike to experience the wineries of Gaston.

The center of attention in the light and airy tasting room is an elk head mounted on the wall above the tasting bar. It wouldn't look good in my living room, but it works here. Once you get past the staring elk, you're ready to experience the fantastic wines of Adam Campbell. His portfolio of pinot noir, pinot gris, pinot blanc, riesling, and dessert wine (trademarked as Ultima) is nothing short of amazing. So much for a rumor started by "people in the know" that you can't grow good pinot west of Hwy. 47!

Since 1974, Elk Cove Vineyards has been making award-winning wines. In 2007, *Wine Press Northwest* awarded Elk Cove Vineyard the prestigious title of Pacific Northwest Winery of the Year. Although there are many reasons why this winery got this award, one of the key reasons is its devotion to producing single-vineyard pinot noirs. How's this for a line-up: La Bohème Pinot Noir; Windhill Pinot Noir; Roosevelt Pinot Noir; Mt. Richmond Pinot Noir; and Five Mountain Pinot Noir. However, before you launch into the reds, first sample its award-winning pinot gris; if it's a hot summer day, take a glass of it out to the deck!

Did you happen to guess the five Cascade peaks you can see from Five Mountain Vineyard? If you said Mount Rainier, Mount St. Helens, Mount Adams, Mount Hood, and Mount Jefferson, you can go to the head of the class (or better yet, the cellar room).

ELK COVE VINEYARDS
opened: 1977
winemaker(s): Adam Godlee Campbell
location: 27751 NW Olson Road, Gaston, OR 97119
phone: 503-985-7760
web: www.elkcove.com
e-mail: info@elkcove.com
picnic area: Yes
weddings: Yes
wheelchair access: Yes
fee: $5 tasting fee refundable with purchase
hours: Daily 10–5; Closed Christmas Eve Day, Christmas Day, New Year's Day, and Thanksgiving Day

 BEST Views

DIRECTIONS: From Gaston, take SR-47 [Front St.] (south) for .2 miles. Turn right (west) onto NW Olson Rd, go 2.6 miles, and look for signs to the winery on your right.

From Yamhill, depart on SR-47 [S Maple St.] going north for about 11 miles. Turn left onto NW Olson Rd at the south end of Gaston and proceed 2.6 miles. Arrive at 27751 NW Olson Rd.

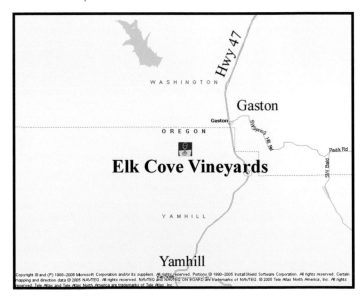

Kramer Vineyards 11

Your black canine escorts are named Cassie (short for the constellation Cassiopeia) and Cosmo. Cassie is the older dog, and Cosmo is the winery dog in training. Together they make sure that you're greeted, led to the tasting room, and given ample opportunity

to rub their bellies. Their job is to make you feel at ease, and to this end they succeed.

In a real sense the dogs are a symbol of what's in store when you visit Kramer Vineyards. There's no pretense here; owners/winemakers Keith and Trudy Kramer see to that. From the warmth of the tasting room staff to the comfy outdoor furniture, they invite you to relax and experience their wines. The Kramers have succeeded in winning converts for nearly 20 years, with retail sales from the tasting room accounting for 85 percent of their revenue. With estate pinot noir starting at $18 and pinot gris going for $15, everyone wins!

The most important thing I took away from Kramer Vineyards was the true meaning of the word "estate." OK, we know "estate" means the juice in the bottle comes from the vineyards you own. However, when the tasting room staff talks about removing grape leaves and stink bugs from freshly harvested grapes, you appreciate their intimacy with the fruit. Or when Trudy Kramer takes time to train a few unruly grape vines during a hot June day, you really understand the devotion and attention that goes into each bottle. Year after year, the Kramers continue to tweak varietal plantings on their 23 acres. Being close to the *terroir*, they appreciate what varietals grows best in specific locations. It's this attention to detail — call it passion or call it love — that characterizes Kramer Vineyards.

The Kramers now find time to visit other wine-growing regions of the world. Exhibit A is a 2008 trip to Australia, where they visited wineries in various locations. They learned of the Aussies' extensive use of netting to protect the grapes from pesky birds, wallabies and kangaroos. Although Oregon doesn't have too many kangaroos, the state does have its share of grape-devouring birds as well as other animals that treat a vineyard like a Sunday buffet. Now, if you source your fruit from other vineyards, all that is the supplier's problem. But to the Kramers, their relationship to the land keeps their focus sharp, from bud break to bottling and ultimately, to you the customer.

KRAMER VINEYARDS
opened: 1990
winemaker(s): Trudy Kramer
location: 26830 NW Olson Road, Gaston, OR 97119
phone: 503-662-4545
web: www.kramerwine.com
e-mail: info@kramerwine.com
picnic area: Yes
gift shop: Yes
weddings: Yes
tours: Yes
fee: Complimentary wine tasting (except small charge during special events)
hours: Daily 12–5 April through October; Friday, Saturday and Sunday 12–5 November through December; Closed January and Easter; Weekends February and March

Trudy Kramer

BEST Gift shop

DIRECTIONS: From Portland, take Hwy 26 to Banks. Go South to Forest Grove on SR-47. Gaston is 7 miles south of Forest Grove. Olson Road is by the Post Office. Turn right and go 3.5 miles to Kramer Vineyards on the left.

From Newberg take Hwy 240 West toward Yamhill. About six miles out turn right onto Ribbon Ridge Rd. Cross the valley and go to the left to follow the base of a ridge. About 6 miles, you come to a left turn that is Flett Road which you follow across the valley. The road ends at a stop sign at Hwy 47. Turn right and go 2 miles into Gaston. Turn left at the post office. Follow the blue signs from there.

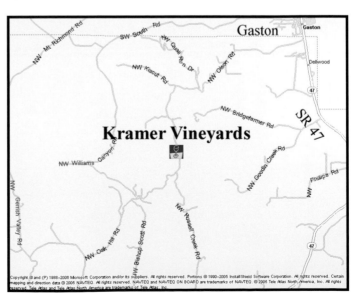

Carlton
WineTrail

Looking for a WineTrail where you can park your car and walk to most of the wineries? We've got one, and it's only about an hour from Portland. The Carlton WineTrail features a huge range of wines within blocks of each other. Here you can experience "hot weather" wines made from grapes from the Rogue Valley and Columbia Valley as well as wines made from the cool climes of the Willamette Valley. It clearly defines the Northwest wine scene and is guaranteed to satisfy Uncle Bill's penchant for big reds and Aunt Beth's love of Alsatian whites. Imagine if all 14 wineries of the Carlton WineTrail featured only pinot noir. That would be like a small town only offering Italian food! Don't get me wrong, I love pinot, but a steady diet of nothing but pinot noir would get boring.

With plenty of restaurants to choose from, lots of interesting shops and art galleries, Carlton is a destination for WineTrail lovers. Come early. Stay late. Just remember where you parked your car!

Carlton WineTrail

1. Carlton Winemakers Studio
2. Cana's Feast Winery
3. Dornaine Coteau
4. Zenas Wines
5. Terra Vina Wines
6. Cliff Creek Cellars
7. Barking Frog Winery
8. Folin Cellars
9. Soléna Cellars
10. Scott Paul Wines
11. EIEIO & Company
12. Tyrus Evan
13. Carlo & Julian Winery
14. Laurel Ridge Winery

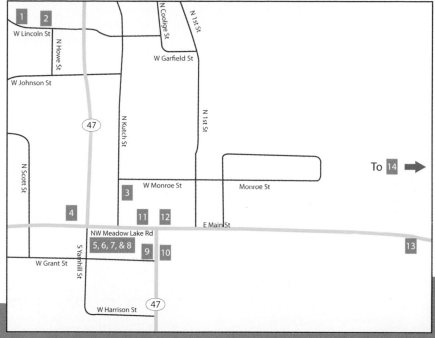

Region:	**North Willamette Valley Wine Country**
# of tasting rooms on tour:	**14**
Estimate # of days for tour:	**2 to 3**
Getting around:	**Car and foot**
Key Events:	❑ **In March, McMinnville's Wine & Food Classic –** **call 503-472-4033 or visit www.macwfc.org for event schedule and ticketing.**
	❑ **Memorial Weekend in Wine Country – Willamette Valley – visit www.willamettewines.com.**
	❑ **In August, Carlton's Walk in the Park – call 503-852-6572 or visit www.carltonswalkinthepark.com.**
	❑ **Wine Country Thanksgiving – Willamette Valley call 503-646-2985 or visit www.willamettewines.com.**
Tips:	❑ **Eat at Cuvee's Restaurant in Carlton; or grab a sandwich at the Filling Station Deli.**
	❑ **Need a place to stay? Check out the The Carlton Inn at www.thecarltoninn.com.**
	❑ **See Appendix B, Wine Tour Planning, for planning your visit.**

 Best: ❑ **Eats: Cana's Feast Winery.**
  ❑ **Gift shop: Tyrus Evan.**

Carlton Winemakers Studio 🔳

How's this for a concept: one-stop - wine-tasting. That's what you find at the innovative Carlton Winemakers Studio. The studio of wineries became a reality in 2002 through a partnership between Eric Hamacher and others, including his wife and winemaker of Ponzi Vineyards, Luisa Ponzi. Carlton Winemakers Studio's slogan is "Liquid Synergy," and that pretty much says it all.

Carlton's contemporary facility is incredible and well worth the trip. True to Oregon's winemaking spirit, the studio has gone "green" with a building that is sustainable and

designed to meet LEED (Leadership in Energy and Environmental Design) Green Building Rating System. The 15,000-square-foot facility is energy efficient and makes use of recycled materials. There's enough space to comfortably fit 10 resident winemakers and their individual staffs. Although the roster of wineries changes over time, during my visit, the following artisanal wineries were present: Hamacher Wines, Andrew Rich Vintner, Lazy River Vineyard, Boedecker Cellars, Bryce Vineyard, Domaine Meriwether, Dominio IV Wines, J.Daan Wine Cellars, Resonance Vineyard, Ribbon Ridge Vineyard and Wahle Vineyards and Cellars. Given this all-star lineup, it's little wonder that *Food & Wine* magazine gushed, "The Carlton Winemakers Studio is just plain cool."

And it's right, especially when it comes to wine tasting.

Whether you choose to do your sampling inside or out on the patio, WineTrail trekkers can taste the creations of each winemaker via tasting flights that range in price from $8 to $14. For example, the day I visited, I sprung for the white-wine flight and had the Carlton Winemakers Studio Pinot Gris, a Dominio IV Viognier "Still Life," and an Andrew Rich Wines Roussanne.

Individual tastes and glasses of wine are also available for purchase. Visitors can purchase gourmet cheeses and other seasonal offerings to pair with the wine. Nearly 40 different wines produced by 10 winemakers are available to sample and purchase. Be sure to budget plenty of time; you might be here for the afternoon.

Of special note is Carlton's Wednesday Night Dinners from 6 to 7:30 p.m., available for as many as 20 people. Guest chefs prepare a three-course meal to pair with select wines. For example, Wednesday Night Dinners have paired Andrew Rich Wines with chef Michael Uhnak of MiNGO; Hamacher Wines with chef Chloe of Eat Your Heart Out Catering; and J. Daan Wine Cellars with Lauro Kitchen Restaurant. To reserve a spot, call 503-852-6100.

CARLTON WINEMAKERS STUDIO
opened: 2002
winemaker(s): Various winemakers
location: 801 N Scott Street, Carlton, OR 97111
phone: 503-852-6100
web: www.winemakersstudio.com
e-mail: info@winemakersstudio.com
picnic area: Yes
wheelchair access: Yes
tours: Yes
fee: Tasting fee varies from $8 to $14 for flight tastings
hours: Daily 11–5; Thursday through Sunday during January and February

DIRECTIONS: **From Newberg**, head north on SR-240 [N Main St.] 11.4 miles. Turn left (south) onto SR-47 [S Maple St.] and travel 3.2 miles. Turn right (west) onto W Johnson St. and arrive at 801 N Scott St.

From McMinnville head north on SR-99W [NE Baker St.] 3 miles. Bear left (northeast) onto local road. The road name changes to SR-47 [Tualatin Valley Hwy] and continue for 4.4 miles. Turn left (west) onto SR-47 [W Main St.] and proceed .1 miles. Turn right (north) onto SR-47 [Tualatin Valley Hwy] for .1 of a mile. Turn left (northwest) onto local road and arrive at Carlton Winemakers Studio.

Cana's Feast Winery 2

The smell of the baking focaccia bread greeted me. I had walked by the bocce court and entered through the patio door into the barrel-lined tasting room. A small crowd of tasters were listening to the pourer explain the winery's special focus on Italian wines, including nebbiolo, sangiovese, and barbera. My initial thought was that I needed an emergency glass of sangiovese to go with the focaccia. My second thought centered on the fact that I

had stumbled into a special winery and a terrific tasting room with the auspicious name of Enoteca, which is Italian for wine cellar.

It was at a wedding feast in Cana that Jesus performed his first miracle. All reports indicate that a good time was had by all, especially when Jesus turned water into wine. The parable was Gino Cuneo's inspiration in naming his winery Cana's Feast, which also offers a feast of great Italian food with its wine. I glimpsed at the menu and noted traditional Italian headers: "Antipasti," "Zuppa," "Insalata," "Primi," and "Secondi." I rehearsed saying, "I'd like your raviolo with whole-milk ricotta, morel mushrooms and fresh farm egg with a bottle of your Bricco Sangiovese." On the bottom of the menu, I read the sentence, "Menu subject to change due to availability and inspiration from the garden." I found this curious at best, but later when I meandered by the well-tended garden, I got it: Everything on the menu is both fresh and local.

Within this world of fine food and wine, winemaker Patrick Taylor produces 6,000 cases of wine annually, one small batch at a time. His collection of red wines include blends with the names Bricco Rosato, Bricco Two Rivers Bordeaux Style, Bricco Sangiovese, Cana's Feast "Cuvée G" Pinot Noir, and Cuneo Syrah.

I joined a group of other tasters and eventually, armed with a glass of Bricco Rosato, retreated to the stone-paved patio to take in the spectacular views of the Coast Range and the aroma of that baking focaccia. The winery's Mediterranean-inspired stucco colors perfectly complement the nearby cypresses. To my left, a group of four visitors played bocce, juggling the bocce ball in one hand with a glass of wine in the other. I wondered if they knew that the Romans had refined the game centuries after its debut in ancient Egypt. Funny how food, wine, and games go together just as well today as they did in times long past.

Gino Cuneo and Patrick Taylor

CANA'S FEAST WINERY
winemaker(s): Patrick Taylor
location: 750 West Lincoln Street,
Carlton, OR 97111
phone: 503-852-0002
web: www.canasfeastwinery.com
e-mail: laura@canasfeastwinery.com
picnic area: Yes
wheelchair access: Yes
fee: $5 refundable with purchase
hours: Daily 11–5

 BEST Eats

DIRECTIONS: From Portland take I-5 South to 99W exit, towards McMinnville and Newberg. Follow 99W through Tigard, Sherwood, Newberg, Dundee and Lafayette. Outside of Lafayette, turn right onto Route 47, towards Carlton and Gaston. Follow 47 into Carlton. Take a left onto the main street of the town. At stop sign, turn right and continue on Route 47 for about 6 blocks. You will see Cana's Feast Winery on the left side. Turn left onto West Lincoln to access the parking lot.

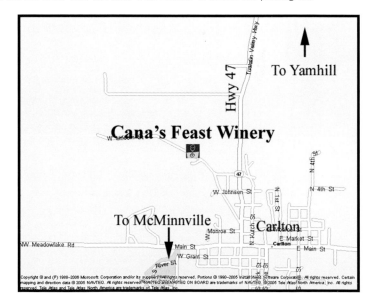

Domaine Coteau

## 3

True confession time: I never made it inside the Domaine Coteau tasting room. I tried. In fact, I went back twice, but in each instance, it was closed.

That's the problem when you get stellar reviews by none other than the *Wine Enthusiast* (90 points), a gold medal from the Los Angeles International Wine and Spirits, the critics gold award at the Critics Challenge International Wine Competition, and a silver medal at the Pacific Rim International Wine Competition. As stated on its web site, the goal of Domaine Coteau is "To gain and maintain recognition as one of Oregon's best pinot noir producers." I suppose you can say that it nailed that one.

When you get awards and accolades like these, you have a good problem — your wine sells like hotcakes. At least that was what a couple of the locals in Carlton reported. That might explain why the winery's doors were closed the day that I sampled my way through Carlton.

Fellow WineTrail enthusiasts, I ask for your help. Please share your pictures and experience if you are fortunate enough to visit Domaine Coteau. I promise to post it at www.winetrailsnw.com/wineries/domaine_coteau.

DOMAINE COTEAU
winemaker(s): Dean Sandifer
location: 258 N Kutch Street,
Carlton Wine Bar, Carlton, OR 97111
phone: 503-697-7319
web: www.domainecoteau.com
e-mail: dean.sandifer@comcast.net
fee: $5 tasting fee
hours: Saturday and Sunday 12–5

DIRECTIONS: From Yamhill, depart Yamhill on SR-47 [S Maple St.] south for 3.3 miles. Turn left (east) onto W Monroe St. and arrive at 258 N Kutch St.

From McMinnville head north on SR-99W [NE Baker St.] 3 miles. Bear left onto SR-47 [Tualatin Valley Hwy] and proceed 4.4 miles. Turn left (west) onto SR-47 [W Main St.] followed by turning right (north) onto N Kutch St. and arrive at 258 N Kutch St.

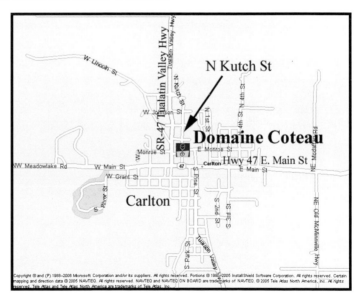

Zenas Wines 4

Zenas (pronounced "zen-aws") Wines honors the Howard family's great-great-great-great-great grandfather Zenas Howard. He and some other brave souls risked life and limb when they hit the Oregon Trail and moved out west in 1856. A picture of Zenas hangs on the wall in the winery's tasting room. He's the guy with the long, white beard. Zenas, who probably imbibed some hard cider in his day, would be surprised to learn that his grandson five generations removed, Kevin Howard, crafts premium wines in his native Oregon.

Kevin's calling is to make single-vineyard wines. Many of his wines are created from the fruit of Del Rio Vineyards far to the south in Rogue Valley. The grapes for his claret, cabernet franc, and merlot all came from this warm-weather region. Zenas' riesling originates in a vineyard much closer to home — Montinore Vineyard in Willamette Valley. Essentially, Zenas Wines is a celebration of all things Oregon and can rightfully claim its wines as "made in Oregon."

Kevin's Bordeaux-style reds reflect the *terroir* of the vineyard's soil and climate. He takes special care to produce tannin-tamed wines with minimal interference. These are fruit-forward, food-friendly wines, with that last trait touted by the winery with such food-pairing suggestions as braised leg of lamb and Zenas Claret (a blend of cabernet franc and merlot), or Zenas Merlot and roasted duck. De-lish!

WineTrail Tip: If hunger strikes, check out The Filling Station Deli near Zenas Wines. It offers great fare at won't-break-the-bank prices. May we suggest a Reuben to pair with that bottle of Zenas Cabernet Franc you just purchased?

ZENAS WINES
opened: 2008
winemaker(s): Kevin Howard
location: 407 W Main #7, Carlton, OR 97111
phone: 503-852-3000
web: www.zenaswines.com
e-mail: info@zenaswines.com
fee: $10 tasting fee – keep the stemware
hours: Saturday 12–5

DIRECTIONS: From southbound I-5 (south of Portland) take exit 294 towards OR-99W/Tigard/ Newberg. Continue for .3 miles. Drive straight on SW Pacific Hwy for 24 miles. Turn right onto Hwy 47 north to Carlton. Drive for 5 miles. Follow Hwy 47 north and go left onto Carlton Main St. Drive for .1 miles to the corner of Hwy 47 and W Main St.

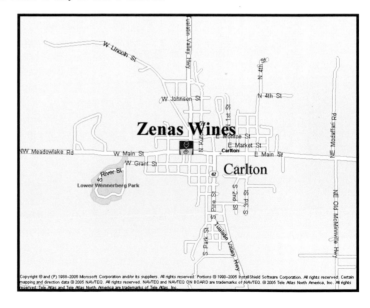

Terra Vina Wines ⑤

Formerly Dalla Vina Wines, Terra Vina Wines is the creation of Carole and Karl Dinger. During my visit on a hot July day, the cool tasting room was a welcome oasis. Even more welcoming was the broad array of wines available for tasting for a nominal fee. At Terra Vina, you can experience Karl's line-up of Burgundian-, Italian-, Bordeaux-, and Rhône-style wines. It's a veritable tour of Old World classic wines: chardonnay, pinot noir,

sangiovese, cabernet franc, cabernet sauvignon, and syrah are some of the wines to taste in this smorgasbord.

Although many followers of Terra Vina Wines know it by its former name, the name change was prompted because of a California-based winery with a similar moniker. However, a wine by any other name would taste as sweet, to paraphrase a certain English playwright. While waiting for their Wilsonville-based vineyard to come into production, the Dingers source most of their grapes from vineyards in Washington state and eastern Oregon. As a member of the tasting room staff noted, the wines are ready to be enjoyed today, but also can be stored in the cellar for many years, awaiting that special moment (it's got to be 5 p.m. somewhere).

Karl must be doing something right. Although new to the Oregon wine scene, this former garagiste has received a treasure trove of awards and accolades, including gold, silver, and bronze awards from some prestigious Oregon wine competitions. For example, at the 2008 McMinnville Food & Wine Classic, his 2006 Syrah took home the gold.

WineTrail tip: Purchase a bottle of Terra Vina Wines to accompany your dinner at Cuvée restaurant. Located next to Terra Vina Wines, Cuvée gets our vote for the best French restaurant in Oregon wine country. I believe it waived the corkage fee when we produced the Terra Vina Syrah for uncorking. Nice touch. It was a perfect way to end the day, even though it was still early — 5 p.m.

TERRA VINA WINES
winemaker(s): Karl Dinger
location: 128 W Main Street,
Carlton, OR 97111
phone: 503-925-0712
web: www.terravinawines.com
e-mail: tvw@terravinawines.com
picnic area: Yes
fee: $5 tasting fee for about 9 wines
hours: Saturday and Sunday 12–5, or by appointment

DIRECTIONS: From Yamhill, take SR-47 [S Maple St.] 3.4 miles to Carlton. Go left (east) onto SR-47 [W Main St.] for .1 miles. Arrive at 128 W Main St. where the tasting room is located.

From McMinnville, go north on SR-99W [NE Baker St.] for 3 miles. Bear left (northeast) on SR-47 [Tualatin Valley Hwy] and proceed 4.4 miles to Carlton. Arrive at 128 W Main St. where the tasting room is located.

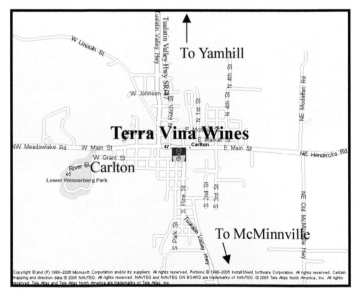

Cliff Creek Cellars 6

Even in the Willamette Valley, it's possible to find a pinot-free winery. That winery is Cliff Creek Cellars. Once you understand that the winery's fruit comes from its southern Oregon vineyard — Sam's Vineyard outside Gold Hill — you'll suspect that your visit will entail big reds, and you'd be right. Get ready for Bordeaux wines and syrah.

The wine is the culmination of a partnership between the proprietors of Cliff Creek Cellars, the Garvin family, and their winemaker, Joe Dobbes, Jr. The winery's foundation, of course, is 60-acre Sam's Vineyard, owned and managed by Vern and Dorothy Garvin. Amazingly only one and a half tons of grapes grow per acre. That's only half of a typical harvest. The surviving fruit translates into red wines that can easily take on a grilled T-bone steak. A nominal tasting fee grants WineTrail trekkers access to syrah, cabernet sauvignon, cabernet franc, merlot, and a Bordeaux-blend claret. To put your adventure into perspective, the *San Francisco Chronicle* rates Cliff Creek's 2004 syrah as no. 1 of the Top 100 Wines of 2007. Small tasting room, big wines.

Another Garvin, Ruth Garvin, lives near Carlton and manages the operation. Her résumé includes ownership of Portland-based Papaccino's Coffeehouse. However, Ruth gives credit for Cliff Creek Cellars' success to the entire Garvin family. Their website and brochure literature uses an analogy to describe their family-owned and -managed winery. It notes, "Much like a family, each grape is growing individually in a cluster of grapes.... And, of course, you cannot make a great wine with just one grape, it is the cluster you need, with each unique and individual grape full of flavor and sweetness." From planting, harvesting, marketing, and tasting, three generations of the Garvin family have played vital roles in Cliff Creek Cellars' amazing story.

CLIFF CREEK CELLARS
opened: 2008
winemaker(s): Joe Dobbes, Jr.
location: 130 W Main Street, Carlton, OR 97111
phone: 503-852-0089
web: www.cliffcreek.com
e-mail: info@cliffcreek.com
picnic area: Yes
fee: $5 tasting fee refundable with purchase
hours: Thursday through Monday 11–6;
Friday and Saturday 11–7;
Closed Tuesday and Wednesday

DIRECTIONS: Heading south from Gaston on Hwy 47 enter the town of Carlton. Turn left (east) on W Main St. and go about .1 mile to the tasting room on the right.

From McMinnville take SR-99W 3 miles to the north. Bear left (northeast) onto SR-47 [Tualatin Valley Hwy] and proceed 4.4 miles. In Carlton turn left on W Main St. and look for winery's tasting room on the left a short distance.

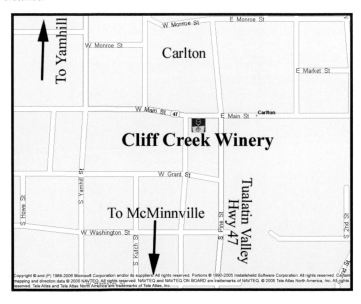

Barking Frog Winery 🄋

While you are in Carlton, be sure to hop in to the Barking Frog Winery's diminutive tasting room. According to Native American lore, the barking frog is a symbol of prosperity as it is said he signals to humankind that all is well with the environment. I leaped at the chance to experience this winery.

Cindy and Ron Helbig

To understand Barking Frog Winery is to know Ron Helbig. First, you need to know his background. He came out of California's Silicon Valley during the heyday of the computer and aerospace phase. In the early '90s, he made his way north to Oregon and became a college instructor. However, it wasn't long before Ron's amateur passion for winemaking steered him to assisting noted winemaker Laurent Montalieu in creating fine wines. While keeping his day job as a college professor, Ron took classes himself at Chemeketa College's winemaking program in Salem. It wasn't long before Ron launched his own winery under the label Barking Frog.

However, in Oregon the challenge for winemakers is to differentiate their product. To distinguish Barking Frog, Ron focused on a combination of warm- and cool-weather grapes. He sources his warm-weather grapes — including syrah, cabernet sauvignon, and sangiovese — from small vineyards in Washington state, and his pinot noir from Blakeslee Vineyard Estate in Chehalem. He chooses to work with small vineyards because he feels they pay more attention and take more care in growing premium grapes. Another distinction is his bottling, which relies on a revolutionary glass-closure technique called Vino-Seal. There ain't no taint, because there ain't no cork.

He must be doing something right. In 2008 alone, he garnered 24 ribbons for his wines. That's a definite sign of prosperity for Barking Frog Winery.

BARKING FROG WINERY
opened: 2005
winemaker(s): Ron Helbig
location: 128 W Main Street, Carlton, OR 97111
phone: 503-702-5029
web: www.barkingfrogwinery.com
e-mail: touchsto@hevanet.com
picnic area: Yes
fee: $5 tasting fee
hours: Friday through Sunday 11-5

DIRECTIONS: Heading south from Gaston on Hwy 47 enter the town of Carlton. Turn left (east) on W Main St. and go about .1 mile to the tasting room on the right.

From McMinnville take SR-99W 3 miles to the north. Bear left (northeast) onto SR-47 [Tualatin Valley Hwy] and proceed 4.4 miles. In Carlton turn left on W Main St. and look for winery's tasting room on the left a short distance.

Folin Cellars 8

Thirty-something Rob Folin is the winemaker, tasting room manager, and chief bottle washer for the Folin Cellars winery. Following graduation from Oregon State University, Rob cut his winemaking teeth at Domaine Serene for seven years. Rob's parents, Scott and Loraine Folin, are proprietors of both winery and vineyard and reside at the family's Sams Valley vineyard location in Rogue Valley, where Scott manages the 25 acres of vineyards. The grapes in these vineyards — viognier, syrah, tempranillo, petite syrah, mourvèdre, and grenache — thrive on the region's hot summer days.

For the grape geeks among us, here is the vineyard data straight from FolinCellars.com:

- 25 acres planted
- VSP trellis
- 8-by-4 spacing
- Small-block irrigation
- Approximately 2.5 tons/acre
- Elevation: 1,300 to 1,450 feet
- Slopes 10° to 20° (Average 11°)
- Site aspect: southerly to westerly (150° to 270°)
- Average: southwest (216°)
- Average growing degree days: 2,583
- Soils: clay loam to sandy clay loam with gravel

What does all this data mean? I don't have a clue, but I can testify that the 8-by-4 spacing and small-block irrigation translated into a truly remarkable viognier showcasing the long finish and combination of citrus and floral notes that only viognier delivers.

At the tasting room in Carlton, visitors find Rob pouring wine from Folin's current releases, including the aforementioned viognier, as well as tempranillo, syrah, and a refreshing grenache rosé. You might notice that the winery uses the Vino-Seal glass closure, just like its next-door neighbor, Barking Frog Winery. As Rob points out, "No cork. No worries."

At the time of this writing, the Folins are busy readying their new tasting room, located at their winery in Sams Valley, near Gold Hill. They anticipate opening the tasting room in the fall of 2009. Even with the opening of the new tasting room, they intend to maintain the tasting room in Carlton. Check out WineTrailsnw.com for updates, or if you're planning a visit to Rogue Valley, call the winery to get the latest scoop.

Rob Folin

FOLIN CELLARS
winemaker(s): Rob Folin
location: 118 W Main Street, Carlton, OR 97111
phone: 503-805-9735
web: www.folincellars.com
e-mail: info@folincellars.com
picnic area: Yes
fee: Complimentary wine tasting
hours: Saturday and Sunday, or by appointment

DIRECTIONS: Heading south from Gaston on Hwy 47 enter the town of Carlton. Turn left (east) on W Main St. and go about .1 mile to the tasting room on the right.

From McMinnville take SR-99W 3 miles to the north. Bear left (northeast) onto SR-47 [Tualatin Valley Hwy] and proceed 4.4 miles. In Carlton turn left on W Main St. and look for winery's tasting room on the left a short distance.

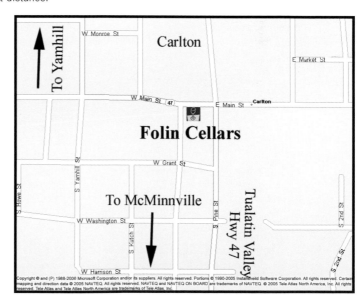

Soléna Cellars 🄰

Just for curiosity's sake, try Googling the name "Laurent Montalieu." The result is page after page of references to his body of work as a winemaker for 25 wineries, a key partner of NW Wine Company, and the co-owner and winemaker for Soléna Cellars. We find

Photo courtesy of Soléna Cellars

Laurent's signature throughout the Oregon wine industry and most importantly in the wines we enjoy. He is truly a master artisan.

The Carlton WineTrail includes a stop at Soléna Cellars, the creation of Laurent and his winemaking wife, Danielle Andrus Montalieu, and named for their daughter Solena. The name is a hybrid of two words that mean the sun and the moon, respectively. Outside the Montalieus' Pine Street tasting room location, WineTrail trekkers will find their distinctive "S" sandwich board informing you that you've arrived at wine central! Here, you can sample Laurent's Willamette Valley–derived pinot noirs and pinot gris, along with wines made from the harvest of warm-weather vineyards in Washington and southern Oregon. Prepare to experience merlot, zinfandel, and cabernet sauvignon, in addition to pinot gris and estate pinot noir. The list is a who's who of Northwest vineyards with names like Klipsun, Del Rio, Shea, Wooldridge, and perhaps most important, the Montalieus' own Willamette Valley 80-acre Estate Domaine Danielle Laurent Vineyard.

As you swirl and sip Soléna Cellars' offerings, keep in mind that Laurent went through a lifetime of experience to get to this point. Imagine this: He grew up on the Caribbean island of Guadeloupe, but spent summers in his family's homeland of Bordeaux. He immersed himself in his family's love of making wine, which led to a degree from the renowned Institute of Oenology of Bordeaux. Following a circuitous route that eventually landed him as the chief winemaker for Bridgeview Vineyards in Cave Junction, Laurent began the Oregon chapter of his life. That stint led to a partnership and winemaking position with WillaKenzie Estate. Finally, in 2003, he left WillaKenzie to launch Soléna Cellars. Phew!

WineTrail tip: While in McMinnville, check out the NW Wine Bar at 326 NE Davis St. An offshoot of Laurent's NW Wine Company (a state-of-the-art custom winemaking facility in McMinnville), the NW Wine Bar features wines from more than 25 different Oregon-based wineries. Here, you can experience wine by the sip, glass, flight, bottle, or case.

SOLÉNA CELLARS
opened: 2002
winemaker(s): Laurent Montalieu
location: 213 S Pine Street, Carlton, OR 97111
phone: 503-852-0082
web: www.solenacellars.com
e-mail: info@solenacellars.com
wheelchair access: Yes
fee: Complimentary wine tasting
hours: Thursday through Sunday 12–5
or by appointment

DIRECTIONS: **Heading south on SR-47 from Gaston** go 11.6 miles. In Carlton go left (east) onto SR-47 [W Main St.] and proceed .1 miles. Turn right (south) onto SR-47 [S Pine St.] and look for Soléna Cellars on right.

From McMinnville, go north on SR-99W [NE Baker St.] 3 miles. Bear left onto SR-47 [Tualatin Valley Hwy] and proceed 4.7 miles. Arrive at 213 S Pine St. on left.

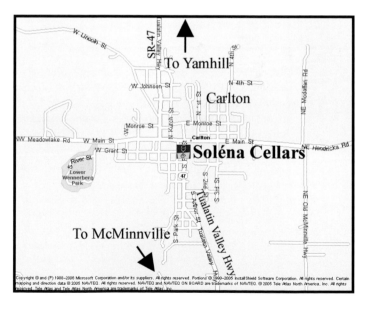

Scott Paul Wines 🔟

Do you ever have dyslexic moments? I was having a major problem transposing the words in this winery's name; was it "Paul Scott Wines" or "Scott Paul Wines"? Fortunately, my oldest sister Carole has two sons named Scott and Paul, and Scott was born first. Using this mnemonic device was the only way I could finally get it straight!

As you visit this winery's remodeled tasting room in Carlton, note the rabbit motif. Turns out this is intentional, and there's actually an interesting story behind it. Prior to launching Scott Paul Wines, Scott Paul Wright was living in southern California with his wife and future co-proprietor, Martha Wright. Scott was ready to leave his entertainment

gig, but his partners convinced him to remain with their booming business. Due to stress (or an undiagnosed bug), Scott became very ill and was bedridden with a high fever for weeks. About that time, Martha discovered a 6-foot-tall painting of a bound rabbit looking skyward, trapped and looking to free his soul. They bought the painting. That was in 1998, and the painting was the catalyst that spurred them to leave southern California and eventually start a winery. That same remarkable painting hangs in their Carlton tasting room. In many ways, the rabbit painting has come home. You see, the artist who painted it is Oregon-based Cody Bustamante, the head of the art department at Southern Oregon University.

Scott Paul Wines has discovered a way to differentiate itself from a crowded field of wineries devoted to pinot noir. Scott has developed close working relationships with select vintners in Burgundy. Like him, these artisan vintners practice "minimal" intervention to produce pinot noirs that reflect their *terroir*. Their love of pinot noir led to the creation of Scott Paul Selections, an import business that works with 15 French vintners to import wine to America. It's Old World meets New World, permitting tasting-room visitors to taste select French-made pinot noirs alongside Oregon-based Scott Paul pinots.

I admit I have one regret regarding this winery, and it will require a return trip to make right. In retrospect, I wish I had purchased both a Scott Paul Wine pinot noir and a bottle of one of the French pinots. I wanted to take them home and do the same side-by-side comparison at the next bash I hosted for friends and family. I could have used that recipe for *lapin en cocotte* I found in an airline magazine.

SCOTT PAUL WINES
opened: 2001
winemaker(s): Kelley Fox
location: 128 S Pine Street, Carlton, OR 97111
phone: 503-852-7300
web: www.scottpaul.com
e-mail: scott@scottpaul.com
wheelchair access: Yes
fee: $5 tasting fee refundable with purchase
hours: Wednesday through Sunday 11–4

DIRECTIONS: From Yamhill, take SR-47 [S Maple St.] 3.4 miles heading south. Turn left (east) onto SR-47 [W Main St.] and go .1 mile to arrive at the winery at 128 S Pine St.

From McMinnville, go north on SR-99W [NE Baker St.] 3 miles. Bear left onto SR-47 [Tualatin Valley Hwy] and proceed 4.7 miles. Arrive at 128 S Pine St.

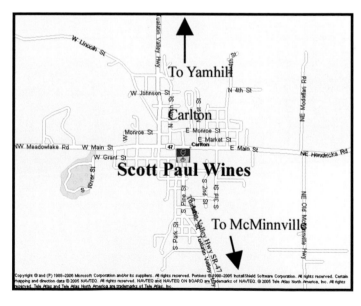

EIEIO & Company [11]

Old McDonald had a farm, EIEIO…

The brainchild of owner Jay McDonald, EIEIO & Company opened its doors at The Tasting Room in Carlton in 1995. Located in a stately red-brick corner building in Carlton, The Tasting Room is on the site previously occupied by the Carlton Bank. It was

the first tasting room in Carlton. Today it's a safe haven for Jay's wine deposits under the label EIEIO. Other winemakers (& company) also showcase their wares in this location.

With regard to his own wines, Jay is a consummate négociant, meaning that he purchases existing wines from various vineyards and then blends them to create pinot noir cuvées and single-vineyard labels. This practice goes way back in Burgundy, where négociants are highly regarded. We of normal palates can only gawk in awe at Jay's ability to create great wines at down-to-earth prices.

There's a reason The Tasting Room has adopted as its slogan "A serious wine shop for serious wine buyers." It's here that you can purchase wine from hard-to-find artisan wineries with such names as Belle Pente, Bergstrom, Brick House, Dominio IV, Evesham Wood, Patricia Green Cellars, Soter, and Beaux Freres. You might recognize the name Beaux Freres; Mike Etzel, Beaux Freres' winemaker, is the brother-in-law of none other than Robert Parker.

The Tasting Room's tasting fee is a little steep at $20, but you get a full flight of top-notch wines to sample, and, if you break out your Visa for a case of wine, the tasting fee is refundable. With glass of wine in hand, wander around The Tasting Room and check out the inventory — especially in the vault. There's some special wines deposited there, collecting serious interest.

EIEIO & COMPANY
opened: 1995
winemaker(s): Jay McDonald
location: 105 W Main Street, Carlton, OR 97111
phone: 503-852-6733
web: www.onhisfarm.com
e-mail: Info@OnHisFarm.com
wine shop: Yes
fee: $10 to $20 tasting fee
hours: Thursday through Monday 11–5

DIRECTIONS: From Yamhill take SR-47 [S Maple St.] 3.4 miles heading south. Turn left (east) onto SR-47 [W Main St.] .1 miles and arrive at 105 W Main St.

From McMinnville go north on SR-99W [NE Baker St.] for 3 miles. Bear left onto SR-47 [Tualatin Valley Hwy] and go 4.4 miles. Arrive at 105 W Main St.

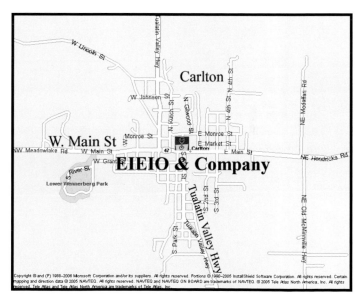

Tyrus Evan

I noticed the term "genius loci" printed on Tyrus Evan brochures while visiting the winery in Carlton, but in my haste to capture the essence of the place, I forgot to ask the tasting-room personnel what the Latin term meant. Genius forgetful.

Ken Wright, owner/winemaker of Ken Wright Cellars as well as Tyrus Evan, is intimately familiar with cool-weather grapes. He ought to be; Ken was instrumental in the development of subappellations in the Willamette Valley AVA. Ken Wright Cellars is synonymous with pinot noir, yet with Tyrus Evan Ken has done a 180, focusing exclusively on warm-weather grapes. With great appreciation for his vineyard partners, Ken sources grapes from three distinctive grape-growing vineyards: Washington Red Mountain's Ciel du Cheval; Walla Walla's Pepper Bridge and Seven Hills vineyards; and southern Oregon's Del Rio Vineyard. Tyrus Evan production includes a claret and syrah from each region, and a cabernet franc and Malbec from Del Rio Vineyard. These are complex wines, intensely fruit-forward with lingering finish — polar opposites of pinot noir. Without a doubt, Tyrus Evan adds to Ken's overall winemaking résumé and rich portfolio of product.

Tyrus Evan is located at The Depot, which, for many years, served as the train depot for Carlton. Ken purchased The Depot in 2001 and, following a complete overhaul, opened the renovated space in 2003, christening it Tyrus Evan, a combination of his two sons' middle names. I haven't a clue what the "before" picture of this place looked like, but I can testify that the "after" picture is beautiful. In addition to offering a variety of "warm-weather" wines to experience, WineTrail visitors can also splurge in one of the more tasteful gift shops in the Northwest. Here, you can buy specialty and gourmet foods, along with books, picnic supplies, gifts, and collectibles. Outside the tasting room, you'll find plenty of table space to seat you and 20 of your best friends for an afternoon picnic, with no shortage of wine.

By the way, according to Wikipedia, in contemporary usage, "genius loci" most commonly refers to a location's distinctive atmosphere, or a "spirit of place." Now I get it.

TYRUS EVAN
opened: 2003
winemaker(s): Ken Wright
location: 120 N Pine Street, The Depot,
Carlton, OR 97111
phone: 503-852-7010
web: www.tyrusevan.com
e-mail: tyrusevan@embarqmail.com
picnic area: Yes
wheelchair access: Yes
gift shop: Yes
fee: $10 tasting fee
hours: Daily 11–6 in summer; daily 11–5 in winter

BEST Gift shop

DIRECTIONS: From Yamhill take SR-47 [S Maple St.] 3.4 miles south. Turn left (east) onto SR-47 [W Main St.] and go .1 miles to The Carlton Depot/Tyrus Evan.

From McMinnville go north on SR-99W [NE Baker St.] for 3 miles. Road name changes to SR-47. Continue 4.4 miles. Arrive at The Carlton Depot/Tyrus Evan.

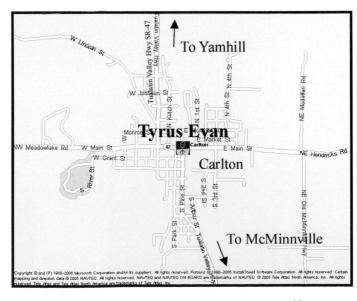

Carlo & Julian Winery 13

I drove into the parking area of Carlo & Julian Winery and spotted a man walking toward me. It was Felix Madrid, owner/winemaker of Carlo & Julian Winery. It was a Sunday, and he politely informed me that the winery was open to the public only on Saturdays. I must have had that "I've driven for hours to get to your winery" look on my face, because he took sympathy. He explained he had an appointment to get to in town, but he would

be happy to give me a quick tour. With camera in hand, I jumped at the opportunity.

I thought I would get a big download of information about the winery, but such was not the case. Instead, Felix led me to his pride and joy — his organic garden. I managed to snap some pictures in the midday sun

and crossed my fingers that I had captured his great smile and engaging eyes. In the background was an undulating vineyard and beyond the vineyard, a flock of sheep. There were several farm cats running around. It was picture-perfect idyllic.

Felix noted that he focuses on tempranillo, nebbiolo, and pinot noir, representing Spain, Italy, and France respectively. When he was 5 years old, his family moved to the U.S. from Argentina. Wine was always an important part of his family's life while he was growing up. Little wonder that he went on to study winemaking in the enology graduate program at University of California, Davis, where he studied weather and soil. His first crush was in 1996 and it netted 600 gallons of pinot noir. That coincided with the launch of his winery, which he named after his two sons, Carlo and Julian.

He reminded me that he needed to scoot, but he allowed me to hang around by myself in the tasting room and encouraged me to walk around and check out the vineyard. The open bottles of wine in the tasting room beckoned me, but I showed amazing restraint in not sneaking a sample. I meandered around a bit and visited with the vineyard workers while they cut the bottom shoots off the vines. As I returned to my car, I thought to myself that Felix Madrid has created a truly remarkable setting to celebrate life.

Felix Madrid

CARLO & JULIAN WINERY
opened: 1996
winemaker(s): Felix Madrid
location: 1000 E Main Street, Carlton, OR 97111
phone: 503-852-7432
web: None
e-mail: carlojulwine@yahoo.com
fee: Complimentary wine tasting
hours: Saturdays 12–5

DIRECTIONS: Located in Carlton. Take Highway 47 north from McMinnville. Take Highway 240 west from Newberg.

From southbound I-5 (south of Portland) take exit number 294 towards OR-99W/Tigard/Newberg. Continue for .3 miles. Drive straight on SW Pacific Hwy for 24 miles. Turn right onto Hwy 47 north to Carlton. Drive for 5 miles. Follow Hwy 47 North and go right onto Carlton Main Street. Go to 1000 E Main St. — the home of Carlo & Julian Winery.

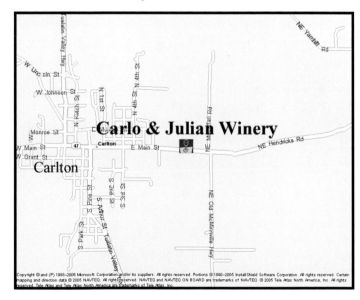

Laurel Ridge Winery 14

Order in the court! A word of caution before you park your car in that space reserved for handicapped vehicles. By day, the owner of Laurel Ridge Winery, Susan E. Teppola, is an administrative law judge for the state of Oregon. She is also happens to be one of the nicest people you'll ever meet.

In fact, Laurel Ridge Winery gets one of my top 10 "congeniality" awards for Oregon wineries. As you enter the new, state-of-the-art winery, staff members make you feel welcome in a special way.

Perhaps because they offer a full portfolio of wines, including white blends, chardonnay, sauvignon blanc, pinot gris, gewürztraminer, riesling, pinot noir, and a unique pinot port, they have the confidence to ask you, "What would you like to try?" Their friendliness may also have something to do with the pleasing appointment of the tasting room itself — it has a spacious design and plenty of windows that provide a spectacular view of their Finn Hill Vineyard and the surrounding hills of the Chehalem Valley. Here, visitors can have fun and not be intimated to ask questions like, "Where do you grow your wine?" While tasting the wine, you may notice your hand being licked by one of the two winery dogs, Bailey or Kaiser. They're just part of the charm of Laurel Ridge Winery.

However, I suspect the pooches' demeanor is a reflection of their human, Susan, whose attitude seems to radiate from the top down to her staff. She's been a part of the Oregon wine scene for many years, co-owning and managing a winery in Washington County before moving south to the Finn Hill Vineyard with her late husband, David Teppola. I suspect those experiences, coupled with an appreciation for the finer things in life (like good wine), make her a good listener and attentive to visitors' needs.

By the way, if you are in need of a special place to get married, Laurel Ridge Winery fits the bill. Beautiful grounds, lovely views, plenty of parking, and generous space to change clothes make this a perfect spot for getting hitched. In addition to its regular still wines, Laurel Ridge Winery uses the methode champenoise process for producing premium sparkling wine that pairs perfectly with white lace and promises. Now, to find a judge to do the honors….

LAUREL RIDGE WINERY
opened: 1986
winemaker(s): Chris Berg
location: 13301 NE Kuehne Road, Carlton, OR 97111
phone: 503-852-7050
web: www.laurelridgewinery.com
e-mail: staff@laurelridgewinery.com
picnic area: Yes
weddings: Yes
fee: $5 for 6 wines
hours: Daily 11–5

DIRECTIONS: From Newberg, take Hwy 240 toward Yamhill about 6 miles to Kuehne Rd. Take a left at Kuehne Rd (also takes you to Carlton) and look for the winery on the right. Follow the blue highway signs.

From Carlton depart on E Main St. heading east. The road name changes to NE Hendricks Rd. Continue for 3.2 miles. Keep left onto NE Kuehne Rd and travel 1.1 miles to arrive at the winery.

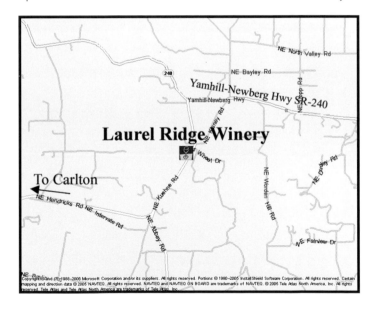

Newberg
WineTrail

Chehalem Mountains Viticulture area

"Hey WineTrail Guy, what's your favorite WineTrail in Oregon?"

Good question, and I am often asked this. Most often I manage to disappoint my listeners because I tick off a bunch of WineTrails that are my favorite. After all, for me it's a little like naming my favorite child — I love them all equally. However, I must confess that inevitably I include the Newberg WineTrail in my list of favorites. Here's why.

My taste buds go bonkers at these wineries. I could spend a day at each of these wineries and help them close at night. It's a pairing of Newberg WineTrail flavor profiles and my palate. Then too, the views of rolling hills with their rows of vineyards are stunning in this section of the north Willamette Valley. Pack a picnic for sure. But sans picnic, there are plenty of restaurants and bistros to sample. In fact, my tip for fellow WineTrail trekkers is to make a reservation at the Painted Lady Restaurant for the end of the day munching and imbibing. It simply solidifies why wine is a perfect complement to Northwest cuisine. Cheers!

Newberg WineTrail

1 August Cellars
2 Rex Hill Vineyards
3 Sineann Cellars
  at Medici Vineyards
4 Adelsheim Vineyard

5 ArborBrook Vineyards
6 Aramenta Cellars
7 Penner-Ash Wine Cellars
8 WillaKenzie Estate

9 Lenné Estate
10 Chehalem
11 VX (Vercingetorix)
   Willamette Farms

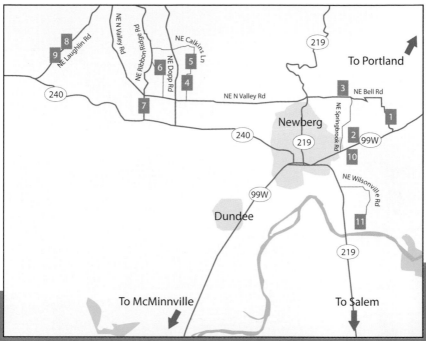

Region:	**North Willamette Valley Wine Country**
# of tasting rooms on tour:	**11**
# of satellite tasting rooms:	**3**
Estimate # of days for tour:	**2**
Getting around:	**Car**
Key Events:	❑ **In March, McMinnville's Wine & Food Classic – call 503-472-4033 or visit www.macwfc.org for event schedule and ticketing.**
	❑ **Memorial Weekend in Wine Country – Willamette Valley – visit www.willamettewines.com.**
	❑ **Wine Country Thanksgiving – Willamette Valley – call 503-646-2985 or visit www.willamettewines.com.**
Tips:	❑ **Sample Medici Vineyards wine and other local wines at Dark Horse Wine Bar in Newberg.**
	❑ **Newberg's downtown boasts satellite tasting room – check out Bishop's Creek and Hip Chicks do Wine.**
	❑ **For hunger pains, eat at Painted Lady Restaurant.**
Best:	❑ **Views: Sineann Cellars at Medici Vineyards, Adelsheim Vineyard, Penner-Ash Wine Cellars, WillaKenzie Estate, Lenné Estate.**

August Cellars

Your trek along the Newberg WineTrail begins with a visit to August Cellars (assuming you're heading from the Portland area). Given that August Cellars actually houses multiple wineries under one roof, your wine-touring field trip might begin and end at August Cellars! Here you will find a variety of wines to sample — from light to full-bodied — from about a half-dozen wineries. This could mean some serious swirling.

Although the line-up of participating wineries changes over time, during my visit, the wineries included Et Fille, Toluca Lane, WildAire, Crowley Wines, Artisanal Wine Cellars, Laura Volkman Cellars, and, of course, August Cellars. Given the high start-up cost associated with launching a winery, the idea of being a tenant winemaker makes buku sense. August Cellars is a cooperative of sorts with participating wineries sharing equipment, a tasting room, cellar storage and the winery dog (just kidding). The contemporary building has a definite Northwest style and feel, with a generous use of glass and wood, and a landscape to match. One-third of the building houses August Cellars with the other two-thirds reserved for tenant wineries. Tasting-room offerings are rotated among the wineries, so it is a bit of a crapshoot as to which wines will be available during your visit. Don't come expecting to sample everyone's wines, but do expect to experience a nice variety, including gewürztraminer, riesling, rosé, pinot noir, Maréchal Foch, and port.

August Cellars is a family-owned winery created in 2002 by the Clarence Schaad family. Located on Chehalem Mountain, the winery is named in honor of the Schaads' ancestor August Schaad, who immigrated to Oregon in the 1890s. The Schaads' unabashed goals are twofold: First, to produce affordable table wines, and second, to keep their family farm operating. The farm is quintessential Willamette Valley, populated by prunes, walnuts, and pinot noir. Today, brothers Jim and Tom Schaad oversee August Cellars. Jim is the winemaker and head of the company, and Tom is the facility manager coordinating all of the daily activities at the winery.

Whatever the month, be sure to plan an August visit.

AUGUST CELLARS
opened: 2002
winemaker(s): Jim Schaad and others
location: 14000 NE Quarry Road,
Newberg, OR 97132
phone: 503-554-6766
web: www.augustcellars.com
e-mail: sales@augustcellars.com
picnic area: Yes
wheelchair access: Yes
tours: Yes
fee: Complimentary wine tasting
hours: Daily 11–5 from May until the middle of
October; open Friday through Sunday year round

DIRECTIONS: Heading southbound on I-5 from Portland, take exit 294 toward OR-99W/Tigard/
Newberg. Go 13 miles and turn right (north) onto NE Quarry Rd and arrive at August Cellars.

From Newberg, head east on SR-99W and continue on SR-219 [SR-99W] for about 3 miles. Turn
left (north) onto NE Quarry Rd for .1 of a mile. Arrive at 14000 NE Quarry Rd.

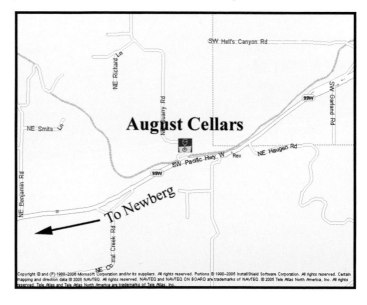

Rex Hill Vineyards 2

When you show up unannounced at a winery armed with a camera and writer's notebook, you often need serendipity to capture the story. Sometimes you luck out and stumble on a treasure trove of information. Such was the case when we visited Rex Hill Vineyards on a hot July day. Following the usual "I'm writing a guidebook," introductions, we shook Rick Toyota's hand. He left the wine bar to give us a quick tour of the tasting room. Turns out

that Rick knew volumes about the Willamette Valley, and its many appellations and subappellations. I wrote furiously, trying to capture soil types, climate, clones, specific appellations and subappellations.

I finally stopped Rick to ask, "Are you an educator by background?" Not surprisingly, we learned that Rick is the director of wine education for Rex Hill. He teaches in-depth classes that take your palate on a world tour of wine regions. If you really want to cure that newly acquired wine bug or if you have an upcoming trip to France, this is just what the doctor ordered.

Paul Hart and his wife Jan Jacobsen fell in love with this property in 1982 when they saw its potential for growing grapes on the hillside, and so they converted this former nut-drying facility into a winery. Success followed hard work, and eventually they were managing more than 250 acres of vineyards in the Willamette Valley, and in the process, positioning Rex Hill Vineyards as a leader in the fledging Oregon wine industry.

The tasting room itself features engaging art and antiques, and visitors can still see remnants of its nut-drying origins. Outside, the landscaping is nothing short of spectacular. The gardens and amphitheater beckon all to relax and enjoy the scenery.

In 2007, A to Z Wineworks acquired Rex Hill Vineyards with the intention of keeping the label and operations separate from A to Z. The wines offered for tasting at Rex Hill Vineyards focus on its Burgundian offerings: chardonnay, pinot gris, and pinot noir. It is refreshing to find a winery that concentrates on a few varietals. After all, you're in the heart of the Willamette Valley's Yamhill County; you might as well enjoy what the land has to offer. Evidently *Wine & Spirits* magazine did. In 2001, 2002, 2003, and 2006, *Wine & Spirits* chose Rex Hill Vineyards as "Winery of the Year." 'Nuff said.

REX HILL VINEYARDS
opened: 1982
winemaker(s): Michael Davies, Sam Tannahill, and Cheryl Francis
location: 30835 N Highway 99W, Newberg, OR 97132
phone: 503-538-0666
web: www.rexhill.com
e-mail: info@rexhill.com
gift shop: Yes
picnic area: Yes
wheelchair access: Yes
fee: $10 tasting fee
hours: Daily 10–5 in summer; Daily 11–5 after Thanksgiving weekend until Memorial weekend

DIRECTIONS: **From Portland** take exit I-5 south. Take exit 99W McMinnville (exit number 294) and continue on 99W 13.4 miles. Arrive at 30835 N Hwy 99W.

From Newberg, go east on SR-99W [E 1st St.] for .2 miles. Keep straight onto SR-219 SR-99W] for .5 miles. Keep straight on SR-99W [Pacific Hwy W] for 2.3 miles. Arrive at 30835 N Hwy 99W.

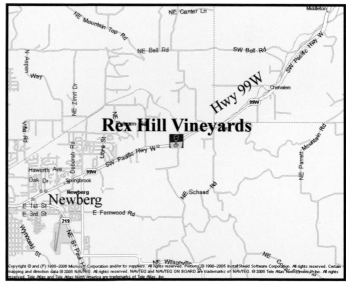

Sineann Cellars at Medici Vineyards 3

Bear with me, because this is a little confusing. In order to taste Sineann Cellars wines, you need to venture to Medici Vineyards. However, if you also want to sample Medici Vineyards wines, you need to go to the Dark Horse Wine Bar in Newberg. On

Thanksgiving or Memorial Day weekends, you're in luck. During those weekends, you can experience both Medici Vineyards and Sineann Cellars wines at Medici. Phew!

Many visitors are surprised to learn that Sineann Cellars lacks its own tasting room. However, you won't be disappointed when you venture to the hillside location of Medici Vineyards, with its commanding view of the Willamette Valley, its rows of premium grapes, and the purple fields of lavender growing behind the rustic white barn. In fact, you will be delighted to sample Peter Rosback's Sineann Cellars wines amongst row upon row of French oak barrels bearing that aromatic smell so redolent of premium wine.

Sineann Cellars proudly sources its fruit from well-known vineyards throughout the Pacific Northwest. Paying homage to the grape growers, Peter often uses a vineyard designation to name his wines. For example, his Wy'East Pinot is produced with grapes from the Hood River vineyard of the same name, and Medici Riesling hails from… you guessed it. Visitors can sample their way through several pinot noirs, pinot gris, cabernet sauvignons, merlots, gewürztraminers, chardonnays, and zinfandels (with grapes from Old World zinfandel vines grown in Hood River). At the end of this wine bonanza, be sure to sample Peter's zinfandel ice wine, called Sweet Sydney. Named after his daughter Sydney, Sweet Sydney contains 58 percent residual sugar and is the perfect accompaniment to pound cake or drunk just by itself.

Peter is also the winemaker for Trium in the Rogue River Valley, The Pines in Hood River, and Medici Vineyards. As previously mentioned, you can taste Medici Vineyards' wines at the Dark Horse Wine Bar in Newberg at 1505 Portland Road (99W). The wine bar is open 11 a.m. to 5 p.m. Thursday through Saturday, and it serves Ferraro wines in addition to its Medici and Sineann offerings. A special treat is in store for visitors if they happen to run into Hal Medici while visiting the Dark Horse or Medici Vineyards. No doubt, his youthful mind and quick wit have contributed to the long history of Medici Vineyards and his other enterprises.

SINEANN CELLARS AT MEDICI VINEYARDS
opened: 1994
winemaker(s): Peter Rosback
location: 28005 NE Bell Road,
Newberg, OR 97132
phone: 503-341-2698
web: www.sineann.com
e-mail: peterr@sineann.com
fee: Complimentary wine tasting
hours: Saturday 11-5

 **BEST Views**

DIRECTIONS: From Portland, take I-5 south about 6 miles to exit 294. Take ramp onto SR-99W and proceed 11 miles. Turn right onto local road followed by an immediate left onto Bell Road. Go 2.5 miles and arrive at the winery (Medici Vineyards) at 28005 NE Bell Road on the right.

From downtown Newberg, take SR-99W [E 1st St.] heading east for .2 miles. Turn left (north) onto SR-219 [N College St.] and proceed 2.3 miles. Turn right (east) onto NE Bell Road and go 1 mile. Arrive at Medici Vineyards on the left (the location of Sineann winery's tasting room).

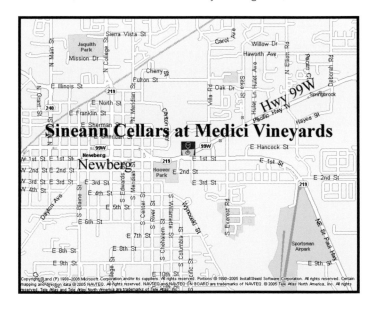

Adelsheim Vineyard

Founded in 1971, Adelsheim Vineyard is one of the oldest and most respected wineries in Oregon. Following a trip to Europe, David and Ginny Adelsheim planted the vineyard in the northern Willamette Valley with the express purpose of growing pinot noir and other cool-weather grapes. Today, they source most of the fruit for their wines from nine separate estate vineyards in the Chehalem Mountains.

Their winery and tasting room offers visitors a chance to experience elegance and lovely wines under one roof — or under the sky on the patio overlooking their Calkins Lane Vineyard.

Unbeknownst to tasting-room visitors, constructed caves below their feet are the resting place for barrel upon barrel of aging pinot noir and other varieties, all under the watchful direction of chief winemaker Dave Paige. Speaking of elegance, I'm a sucker for the pen-and-ink drawings adorning the wine labels for their Willamette Valley pinot noir, pinot gris, and chardonnay vintages. I refuse to open my bottle of 2006 Adelsheim Willamette Valley Pinot Noir because I see it as an art piece in my fledging cellar!

Interestingly, Dave Paige works with the usual assortment of Willamette Valley grapes (e.g., pinot noir, pinot gris, pinot blanc, and chardonnay) as well as some unusual varieties, such as Auxerrois and Tocai Friulano. A rare Alsatian variety, Auxerrois is a cross between pinot noir and gouais blanc (say that 10 times) and produces a "bright straw" taste, according to Stephen Tanzer's *International Wine Cellar*. The white wine Tocai Friulano is from northern Italy and part of the sauvignon family of grapes. Don't leave the tasting room without tasting these two varieties — you won't find them at other WineTrail locations.

Approaching its 40th anniversary, Adelsheim Vineyard is not just a founding member of the Oregon wine industry, but a vibrant and leading winery well worth a visit by even the most experienced wine tourist. **WineTrail tip:** If time permits, take the hour-and-a-half tour of the winemaking facility and get a first-hand look at its "hands-off" winemaking style.

ADELSHEIM VINEYARD
opened: 1971
winemaker(s): David Paige
location: 16800 NE Calkins Lane,
Newberg, OR 97132
phone: 503-538-3652
web: www.adelsheim.com
e-mail: info@adelsheim.com
picnic area: Yes
wheelchair access: Yes
tours: Yes
fee: $15 tasting fee
hours: Wednesday through Sunday 11–4

BEST Views

DIRECTIONS: Heading southbound on I-5 from Portland take exit 294 toward 99W/Tigard/Newberg. Go 16.3 miles to Newberg and turn right onto Hwy 240 (Main St.) where a green highway sign points to Chehalem Valley and Yamhill. Follow Hwy 240 west as it curves left out of town for 1.5 miles until you reach Tangen Rd. Turn right and follow Tangen Rd for 1 mile to its intersection with North Valley Rd. Turn left on North Valley Rd. and proceed 2.3 miles to Calkins Ln., watching for a blue Adelsheim Vineyard sign on your left. Turn right on Calkins Ln. and drive .5 mile until you reach the far end of a white fence running along the right-hand side of the road. Turn right through the gate (marked 16800) into the driveway at Adelsheim Vineyard; the winery's main parking lot and entrance are to your left.

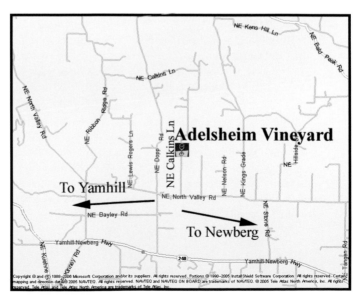

ArborBrook Vineyards 5

ArborBrook is the creation of Dave and Mary Hansen, both of whom dreamed of one day producing premium wines. Located near Adelsheim in the northern Willamette Valley in the foothills of the Chehalem Mountains, ArborBrook is the home for their pinot noir vines and Mary's Arabian horses. The property is also the site of the Hansens' charming 1910 farmhouse, as well as the 1940s-era walnut-drying barn, which now serves as ArborBrook's tasting room. Although Dave and Mary make pinot gris and semillon, make no mistake: Their focus is on producing excellent pinot noir. Dave keeps his day job as a banker, but invests his spare time in overseeing more than 11 acres of pinot noir (Dijon clones 777, 115 and Pommard). He understands that great wine can only come from superb grapes.

Like other artisanal producers of fine wine in the Willamette Valley, Dave and Mary turned to Laurent Montalieu as their consulting winemaker. In addition, they rely on the state-of-the-art production facilities of McMinnville-based NW Wine Company to make their wine. ArborBrook currently produces about 2,500 cases of wine annually.

Here's what Jay Miller of online guide *eRobertParker.com* had to say about the Hansens' 2005 ArborBrook Vineyards Pinot Noir Estate 777 Block: "It has a lovely perfume of damp earth, saddle leather, cherry cola, black raspberry, and blackberry liqueur. This leads to a velvety-textured wine with a solid core of sweet fruit with all components nicely integrated. The finish lasts for 45+ seconds. This fine example of the 2005 vintage may well evolve for 5-7 years, but why take a chance?" For a winery with such a short history, I'm sure Dave and Mary loved that review!

Dave Hansen

ARBORBROOK VINEYARDS
opened: 2006
winemaker(s): Dave Hansen and Laurent
Montalieu (Consultant)
location: 17770 NE Calkins Lane,
Newberg, OR 97132
phone: 503-538-0959
web: www.arborbrookwines.com
e-mail: mary@arborbrookwines.com
picnic area: Yes
wheelchair access: Yes
fee: Complimentary wine tasting
hours: Thursday through Sunday 11–3;
private tastings by appointment

DIRECTIONS: From Newberg go north on SR-240 [N Main St.] 4.3 miles. Turn right (north) onto NE Dopp Rd and go .9 miles. Turn right (east) onto NE North Valley Rd and go .4 miles. Turn left (north) onto NE Calkins Ln and proceed 1.3 miles to ArborBrook winery.

From Yamhill go east on SR-240 [E Main St.] 7.1 miles. Turn left (north) onto NE Dopp Rd and go .9 miles. Turn right (east) onto NE North Valley Rd and go .4 miles. Turn left (north) onto NE Calkins Ln and proceed 1.3 miles to ArborBrook winery.

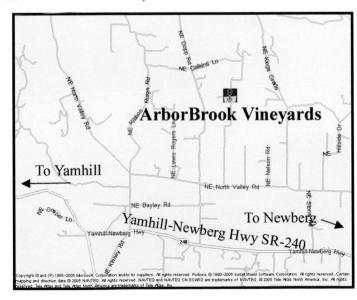

Aramenta Cellars 6

Named for Darlene Looney's aunt Ethel Aramenta Evans, Aramenta Cellars is located in Oregon's smallest appellation, Ribbon Ridge. At only five square miles, the Ribbon Ridge American Viticultural Area is a subappellation of the Willamette Valley AVA. Aramenta Cellars (love that name) is a jewel of a winery, but often gets overlooked with neighbors such as Penner-Ash Wine Cellars, WillaKenzie Estate and Adelsheim Vineyard. However,

if you seek a friendly winery devoid of crowds where you can relax with friends and enjoy outstanding wine, Aramenta Cellars fills the bill.

Ed Looney, Darlene's husband, began growing grapes at Looney Vineyard in 2000. Once a tool-and-die guy at Tektronix, Ed retired and turned full-time dirt guy at the family vineyard. With a long-term lease signed by Archery Summit for his pinot noir, he must have been doing something right. This is what Archery Summit has to say: "Planted in 2000, Looney Vineyard slopes gently to the south and southeast between 360 and 550 feet in elevation. On sedimentary soils, it produces an exciting new addition to our portfolio of Oregon Pinot Noirs." With these accolades, it is little wonder that Ed creates his own wines under the Aramenta Cellars label.

WineTrail enthusiasts with time on their hands should pack a picnic. Outside the tasting room is a small patio featuring splendid views of a large redwood tree planted in 1905, a springfed trout pond, the picturesque Looney Vineyard, and a grassy field big enough to accommodate tourists who arrive by helicopter (no kidding). Inside the tasting room, Ed greets visitors and pours several estate pinot noirs, chardonnay, as well as a Bordeaux-blend claret for folks who like bigger reds, including myself.

The atmosphere is relaxing and serene, and not designed for drive-by tastings. Here, "linger" is the operative word for experiencing Aramenta Cellars. Immerse yourself in it.

Ed Looney

ARAMENTA CELLARS
opened: 2002
winemaker(s): Ed Looney
location: 17979 NE Lewis Rogers Lane,
Newberg, OR 97132
phone: 503-538-5086
web: www.aramentacellars.com
e-mail: eddarloon@cs.com
picnic area: Yes
fee: $5 tasting fee for 5 wines
hours: Daily 10:30–5

DIRECTIONS: From Newberg go north on SR-240 [N Main St.] for 4.3 miles. Turn right (north) onto NE Dopp Rd and go .9 miles. Bear left (west) onto NE North Valley Rd and go .4 miles. Turn right (north) onto NE Lewis Rogers Ln and go .2 miles to Aramenta Cellars.

From Yamhill take SR-240 [E Main St.] east for 6.1 miles. Turn left (west) onto NE Ribbon Ridge Rd and go .8 miles. Turn right (east) onto NE North Valley Rd and go .6 miles. Turn left (north) onto NE Lewis Rogers Ln and go .2 miles to Aramenta Cellars.

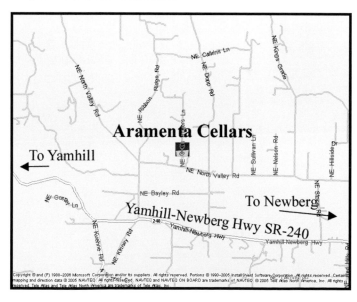

Penner-Ash Wine Cellars 7

Most people don't realize that winemaking involves hundreds of decisions: when to pick the grapes, what equipment to use, what strain of yeast to inoculate with, when to rack and when to bottle. From growing the grapes to marketing the product, it's more than a full-time job. And to do it well, you need a big dose of experience.

Exhibit A: Penner-Ash Wine Cellars.

Blessed with a penchant for science, winemaker Lynn Penner-Ash got her degree in enology from University of California–Davis, which is essentially the mecca of winemaking academe. She followed that up with various winemaking stints at California wineries, including Stag's Leap Wine Cellars. Eventually, she made her way north to become Rex Hills Winery's winemaker, president, and chief operating officer. At Rex Hills, she garnered awards and accolades, but more importantly, she gained the experience to take the next step. Together with her husband, Ron Penner-Ash (a self-described mature cellar rat), they dreamed of creating their own wines bearing the Penner-Ash label. That dream was to become a reality.

Collectively, all those years of experience were instrumental in the design of Penner-Ash Wine Cellars. Nestled between the Chehalem Mountains to the north and the Red Hills of Dundee to the south, the sustainable facility has an architectural layout that's nothing short of fabulous. As in making wine, myriad decisions went into the design of this three-story gravity-flow winery with its wrap-around clerestory windows. Nothing escaped this team's planning — from worker ergonomics to maximizing the surrounding views — as the foursome withdrew from their professional bank of knowledge.

The wines themselves — particularly Lynn's pinot noirs and syrahs — are wonderfully well balanced, complex, and packed with berry flavors. What's more, Penner-Ash wines are relatively affordable and accessible to savvy folks who appreciate Oregon wines. These wines are ready for tonight's barbecue or can be considered as candidates for the cellar to enjoy years from now. And, as you visit the tasting room and are suitably impressed by the surroundings and the great wine, just remember that this moment in time didn't happen overnight. It came together through years of collective experience, partnerships, and love.

PENNER-ASH WINE CELLARS
opened: 2005
winemaker(s): Lynn Penner-Ash
location: 15771 NE Ribbon Ridge Road,
Newberg, OR 97132
phone: 503-554-5545
web: www.pennerash.com
e-mail: sales@pennerash.com
picnic area: Yes
wheelchair access: Yes
fee: $5 refundable with purchase
hours: Thursday through Sunday 11–5;
Closed January

BEST Views

DIRECTIONS: **From Yamhill,** head east onto SR-240 [E Main St.] 6.1 miles. Turn left (west) onto NE Ribbon Ridge Rd and go .8 miles. Arrive at Penner-Ash Wine Cellars at 15771 NE Ribbon Ridge Rd.

From Newberg, go west onto SR-99W [E Hancock St.] .1 miles. Turn right (north) onto SR-240 [N Main St.] and proceed 5.4 miles. Keep right onto NE Ribbon Ridge Rd for .8 miles. Arrive at 15771 NE Ribbon Ridge Rd.

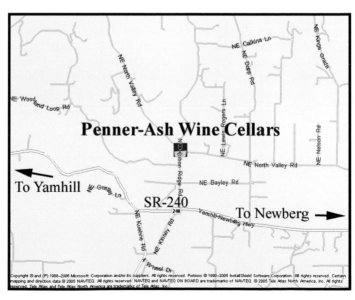

WillaKenzie Estate

Located in the Chehalem Mountains of Willamette Valley's northern region, WillaKenzie Estate is one of a handful of wineries that has it all. What is it? It's one part bucolic setting — the rolling hills, acres of north-south running vineyards, and the proverbial hawk circling in the blue sky; it's one part wonderful tasting room, complete with knowledgeable staff members who make you feel at home and plenty of space to roam. You can see first-hand the equipment and appreciate the term "gravity flow." Then add to the mix that indefinable Oregon sensibility involving an appreciation for the land and the people who work it; a mission of sustainability, an effort to safe salmon and a good

working environment (complete with health benefits for the vineyard crew) and it all adds up to WillaKenzie Estate.

Spurred by an ad in *Wine Spectator* in the early '90s, Bernard Lacroute purchased a 420-acre cattle ranch in Yamhill. It was a chance to return to his French roots à la U.S.A. He and his wife, Ronni Lacroute, proceeded to plant primarily pinot noir and eventually other Burgundian and Alsatian grapes on more than 100 acres of the property. They opted to preserve much of the land as it was, leaving blackberry patches, Douglas fir, and other native plants. The result is an ecosystem in keeping with the couple's biodynamic philosophy and sustainable approach to growing grapes. Even the natural watersheds on the property are preserved and classified as salmon-safe.

In the tasting room, you won't hear the sound of corks popping from the bottles. This is a corkscrew-free zone. The WillaKenzie Estate management team, including winemaker Thibaud Mandet, elected to shun the bottle corks in favor of twist-offs. Their reason was simple — less cork taint, or trichloranisole (TCA), a chemical that occasionally forms on natural cork. While sampling their marvelous pinot noirs, pinot gris, and other varietals, you can't help but be enthralled by the large mural above the tasting bar. It's easy to immerse yourself in this scene and imagine pouring the wine, tearing off a hunk of fresh bread to go with the Brie, and feeling the sun on your face. Then you're suddenly awakened from your fantasy with a tap on the shoulder. Your friends are handing you their Canon with that "Can you take our picture?" look. You're happy to oblige.

WILLAKENZIE ESTATE
opened: 1995
winemaker(s): Thibaud Mandet
location: 19143 NE Laughlin Road,
Yamhill, OR 97148
phone: 503-662-3280
web: www.willakenzie.com
e-mail: tastepinot@willakenzie.com
picnic area: Yes
fee: $10 to taste released wines and keep the 7-oz tasting glass or $15 to include barrel tasting and 25-oz burgundy glass
hours: Daily 12–5 May through December; Friday through Sunday 12–5 January through April, or by appointment

DIRECTIONS: From Portland take I-5 south to exit 294, Hwy 99W. Continue southwest on Highway 99W for 15 miles to Newberg. In Newberg, turn right on Main St., which is also Hwy 240W signed Chehalem Valley, Yamhill. Continue on Highway 240 about 10 miles to Laughlin Rd. Turn right on Laughlin Rd and continue about 1.5 miles. WillaKenzie Estate is on the left.

From Portland via Forest Grove. Take Hwy 26 (Sunset Highway) west about 20 miles to Highway 6, exiting to the left. Continue south on Highway 6 for about 2.5 miles to Highway 47. Continue south on Highway 47 for about 23 miles to the town of Yamhill. In Yamhill, turn left at the blinking yellow light onto Highway 240. Follow Highway 240 about 1.5 miles to Laughlin Rd. Turn left on Laughlin Rd and continue about 1.5 miles. WillaKenzie Estate is on the left.

From Salem take Hwy 22W about 10 miles to Hwy 99W. Follow Hwy 99W north about 22 miles through the town of McMinnville to Highway 47. Follow Hwy 47 north about 8 miles to the town of Yamhill. In Yamhill, turn right at the blinking yellow light onto Highway 240 and travel 1.5 miles to Laughlin Rd. Turn left on Laughlin Rd and continue about 1.5 miles. WillaKenzie Estate is on the left.

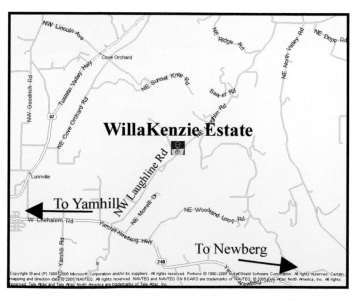

Lenné Estate 9

Principal owner Steve Lutz knew that the steep southerly slope and unfavorable soil (predominantly Peavine and Willakenzie soils) was a good sign. He understood that good wine comes from stressed grapes — grapes that don't get irrigated. The vines grow deep roots in search of water. As a result, the clusters that survive are packed with flavor. Steve and his wife, Karen, visited the prospective site in this part of Yamhill County in 2000 and knew its steep slope and summertime heat would conspire to create great pinot noir. After all, nearby vintners, including WillaKenzie Estate, Deux Vert, Soléna, Soter, and

Beau Frères, had established great reputations. The Lutzes and their partners took the plunge, bought the land, and planted pinot noir.

The name "Lenné" pays homage to Karen's dad, Len, who was a British chicken farmer. Len and the farm are now gone, but the love for him lives on in the name. It also lives in the vineyard where Steve and his partners have had to coax and nurture the vines, and become true dirt guys to make up for a high vine death rate. However, after many seasons, success is measured in bottle units with the production of their estate pinot noir.

Success is also measured by the creation of a charming tasting room. The stone façade of the new tasting room has a French country flavor, and somehow the giant rooster sculpture out front complements the property. The rolling-hill views of nearby vineyards are stunning. Within, the tasting room is an inviting space with its cool Mediterranean colors and light, airy feel. In addition to Lenné wines, WineTrail trekkers will be surprised to find other "guest" wines at the tasting room. For example, I swirled and sipped Owen Roe wine during my visit.

Are you interested in crossing over from being a mere spectator to a co-owner? For $15,000, you, too, can become a partner in a winery! Hey, that's got my attention. Check out www.lenneestate.com to learn more about this opportunity.

LENNÉ ESTATE
opened: 2007
winemaker(s): Steve Lutz
location: 18760 NE Laughlin Road,
Yamhill, OR 97148
phone: 503-956-2256
web: www.lenneestate.com
e-mail: steve@lenneestate.com
picnic area: Yes
fee: $5 tasting fee
hours: Thursday through Sunday 12–5

 BEST Views

DIRECTIONS: From Newberg take SR-240 west towards Yamhill. About 10 miles from Newberg you will come to Laughlin Rd (look for a blue highway directional sign to WillaKenzie Estate Winery) and go right. Just over a mile you will see our blue Lenné sign; take a right and proceed straight up the hill into the vineyard.

From Yamhill go east on SR-240 [E Main St.] for 1.8 miles. Turn left (northeast) onto NE Laughlin Rd for 1.2 miles. Arrive at 97148 NE Laughlin Rd.

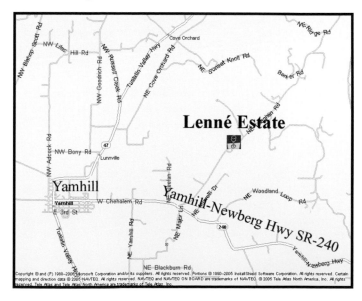

Chehalem 🔟

Make no mistake, the brains and drive behind the Chehalem winery is founder, partner and co-winemaker Harry Peterson-Nedry. In a world where the "art of winemaking" is a common refrain, Harry is Mr. Science. He's a chemist by profession, but he caught the

wine bug in the 1980s with the planting of his 37-acre Ridgecrest Vineyard. Yet there's no conflict between the two realms for Harry. As he stated in the spring 2008 Chehalem newsletter, "Innovation is the nexus of rational, scientific, left-brain thought and spontaneous, innovative, right-brain thought." Taking this approach, he tinkered with types of yeast, ripeness level, fermentation temperature and their appropriate levels, and other variables to quantify what makes better wine. That was during his formative wine years back in mid-'80s. Further trial and error found that whole-cluster pinot noir fermentations may be superior in dry years, but problematic in rainy years.

Interesting. I only know that the proof is in the pudding — or in this case, the pinot noir.

Joining Harry as Chehalem's other winemaker is Mike Eyres. This is what the Chehalem website notes about Mike, a transplant from New Zealand: "When he is not at the winery, Mike is likely careening along an Oregon waterway in his kayak, keeping up with the Portland restaurant scene, and drinking beer." Now, this is my kind of a guy! Together, Mike and Harry produce pinot noir, pinot blanc, chardonnay, riesling, and gamay noir. Of special note is their passion for riesling, which they view as the white wine of the future for Oregon. Chehalem has developed a cult following of loyal customers snapping up its riesling. Still, it's Chehalem's chardonnay wins my vote. Named "Inox" (French for "stainless"), Chehalem's brand of chardonnay is devoid of the oaky flavors that were popular years ago.

WineTrail enthusiasts will discover Chehalem's new tasting room located alongside Hwy. 99W in Newberg. Inside, the colors are a striking combination of parakeet green and lark blue — to match the colors of the "Inox" label. In essence, the warm colors of the tasting room and friendliness of the staff reflect the origin of the winery's name: Chehalem is a Native American word meaning "gentle land" or "valley of the flowers."

CHEHALEM
opened: 1990
winemaker(s): Harry Peterson-Nedry and Mike Eyres
location: 106 S Center Street, Newberg, OR 97132
phone: 503-538-4700
web: www.chehalemwines.com
e-mail: harrypn@chehalemwines.com
wheelchair access: Yes
fee: Core flight $5 for 3 wines; Reserve flight $10;
refundable with purchase
hours: Thursday through Monday 11–5

DIRECTIONS: From Portland heading south on I-5 take exit 294 toward OR-99W/Tigard/Newberg. Continue to Newberg about 16 miles. Turn left (south) onto Center St. and arrive at Chehalem's tasting room.

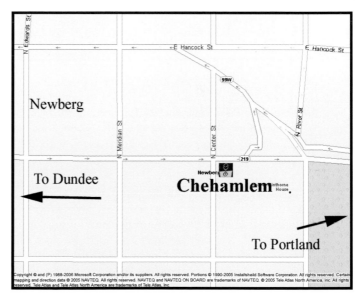

VX (Vercingetorix) Willamette Farms ⑪

OK, this winery's official name is not "VX," but like most folks who aren't fluent in the French language, I have a difficult time getting my mouth around "Vercingetorix" (pronounced "vûr-sin-jet-u-riks"). Vercingetorix was a Gallic hero who, more than 2,000 years ago, launched a quixotic rebellion against Caesar's Roman legions. He may have lost that battle, but he won the hearts of his fellow Gauls; visitors to Burgundy today can still find statues honoring him. Legend has it that Vercingetorix adopted a scorched-earth

policy to thwart the Roman conquerors, yet he spared the vineyards. He must have realized that under Roman rule, the locals would sorely need the solace of the grape.

As you approach VX Willamette Farms, you'll see signs reminiscent of the old Burma Shave ads, coaxing visitors to "KEEP GOING,"

"ALMOST THERE," and "YOU'RE CLOSE." Those signs are a necessity, because at this point, the paved Parrish Road is a receding object in your rearview mirror. From Parrish Road, you drive a good half-mile past fenced pastures to Willamette Farms, the site of "VX" winery. Once there, you discover a little slice of heaven on earth, with beautifully maintained pastures and a big old farmhouse at its center. Nearby are picnic tables, hiking trails, nature walks, horses, llamas, and scenic views of the Willamette River.

The person responsible for this rich tapestry of rural splendor is eighty-something Bruce Hall. He doesn't look or act his age, and that is meant as a compliment. His mind is as sharp as a tack, and with his engaging smile and eyes, he could easily pass for a young 60-year-old. Still, he's had a lifetime full of experiences, including a stint with the 10th Mountain Division of the U.S. Army during WWII. These soldiers wore solid white uniforms and fought the Germans on skis.

The VX winery features well-balanced pinot gris and silky pinot noirs from Hall's estate Willamette Farms vineyard. Visitors to the tasting room can purchase a glass or bottle and retreat to a nearby picnic table. **WineTrail note:** You can also purchase a bag of Willamette Farms hazelnuts to pair with your wine. (The dark-chocolate-covered variety is especially tasty.) And for just $9, you can also purchase a box lunch for two to go with that bottle of "VX" Pinot Noir; uncork as you commune with the horses and llamas.

Here's to Vercingetorix and his sparing of the grapes. *A votre santé!*

Bruce Hall

VX (VERCINGETORIX) WILLAMETTE FARMS
winemaker(s): Jason Silva
location: 8000 NE Parrish Road,
Newberg, OR 97132
phone: 503-538-9895
web: www.vxvineyard.com
e-mail: info@vxvineyard.com
picnic area: Yes
fee: $5 tasting fee
hours: Monday through Saturday 11–5 from April
through December, plus all holiday weekends

DIRECTIONS: **From Newberg** take SR-99W [E 1st St.] .2 miles east. Keep straight onto SR-219 [SR-99W] for 1.7 miles. Turn left (east) onto NE Wilsonville Rd and go 1.1 miles. Turn right (south) onto NE Parrish Rd and travel 1.2 miles to arrive at VX (Vercingetorix) Willamette Farms.

Coming from the south on SR-219 toward Newberg turn right (east) onto NE Wilsonville Rd and go 1 mile. Turn right (south) onto NE Parrish Rd and go 1.2 miles to arrive at 8000 NE Parrish Rd.

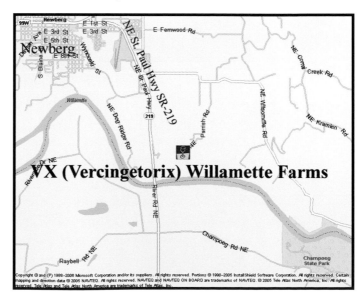

Dundee
WineTrail

I love the names: Duck Pond Cellars, The Four Graces, Dobbes Family Estate, Argyle Winery, and A to Z Wineworks. Each of them offers great pinot noir (and other wines) and yet they are unique and have their own story to tell. That story is found in the tasting rooms where you can relax and kibitz with knowledgeable tasting room personnel. Get ready for some surprises, too. From the elegance of the Craftsman-style bungalow of The Four Graces to the sparkling wines of Argyle, your visit won't disappoint. For sure, talk to the tasting room personnel at A to Z Wineworks to get an appreciation for their meteoric success story. Perhaps it is their tag line, "Aristocratic wines at democratic prices," that reveals their story, but it's more than that for sure. Sit out on their patio, unscrew a bottle and discover for yourself the art of blending.

Dundee WineTrail

1 Duck Pond Cellars
2 The Four Graces

3 Dobbes Family Estate
4 Argyle Winery

5 A to Z Wineworks

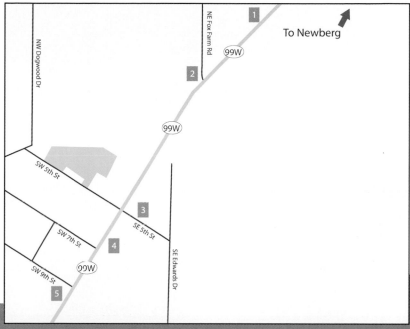

Region:	**North Willamette Valley Wine Country**
# of tasting rooms on tour:	**5**
# of satellite tasting rooms:	**1**
Estimate # of days for tour:	**1**
Getting around:	**Car and foot**
Key Events:	❑ **In March, McMinnville's Wine & Food Classic – call 503-472-4033 or visit www.macwfc.org for event schedule and ticketing.**
	❑ **In April, Dundee Hills Passport Weekend – call 800-582-6668.**
	❑ **Memorial Weekend in Wine Country – Willamette Valley – visit www.willamettewines.com.**
	❑ **Wine Country Thanksgiving – Willamette Valley – call 503-646-2985 or visit www.willamettewines.com.**
Tips:	❑ **Budget time for Ponzi tasting room and wine bar in Dundee.**
	❑ **The Black Walnut Inn & Vineyard's elegance is only matched by its great location. To make reservations call well in advance 1-866-429-4114.**
	❑ **Looking for fine dining in wine country? Consider The Painted Lady (Newberg), the Dundee Bistro, Tina's (Dundee) or the Joel Palmer House (Dayton).**

 Best: ❑ **Gift shop: Duck Pond Cellars.**

Duck Pond Cellars

I've had several people tell me that their wine tour of the Willamette Valley consists of going to one winery — Duck Pond Cellars. I had to wonder, with all the amazing wineries to visit, why would people go to just one winery. I had to discover for myself.

I got my first taste of Duck Pond Cellars' elegance when I turned into the entrance, conveniently located right off Highway 99W in Dundee, and beheld the beautiful tasting room beyond the decorative vineyard. The elongated patio wraps around the front of the building, beckoning visitors to relax and sip. I pulled my car into the generously sized parking lot and wondered what was in store for me inside.

I quickly learned that "tasting room" is a misnomer for Duck Pond Cellars' interior. Offering what has to be a "best in class" in wine-related retail, this shop meets the needs of would-be shoppers, from holiday gifts to a souvenir for that hard-to-buy-for mother-in-law. Whoever is the buyer for Duck Pond Cellars clearly has an eye for merchandise worthy of Nordstrom.

However, lest I forget Duck Pond's *raison d'être*, I was here for the wine tasting, and here I discovered its secret for success. Essentially, the winery offers a complete buffet-style line-up of white, red, dessert, port, and sparkling wines to meet everyone's palate. The reason for this wide selection of wines? How about 840 acres of premium wine grapes growing in the diverse climates of Washington's Columbia Valley and Oregon's Willamette Valley, owned by Doug and Jo Ann Fries. Since the late 1980s, Doug and Jo Ann have been building Duck Pond's vineyard and winery properties (including their newest grand winery in Prosser, Washington, named Desert Wind). With such a diverse mixture of wines — from Bordeaux to Burgundy, sweet to dry, and red to white — Duck Pond has it all.

Another reason that WineTrail trekkers make a beeline to Duck Pond is its low prices. I snapped up a bottle of its white blend Clos d'Pond for $10. A bottle of its pinot noir reduced my wallet by only $20. It's little wonder that Duck Pond Cellars enjoys an active wine club, with members who routinely share in wine tasting parties and other events.

Great value, family history, an amazing gift shop, splendid patio sitting: These attributes explain why many visitors simply go to one winery for their Willamette Valley getaway — Duck Pond Cellars.

DUCK POND CELLARS
opened: 1989
winemaker(s): Mark Chargin
location: 23145 Highway 99W, Dundee, OR 97115
phone: 503-538-3199
web: www.duckpondcellars.com
e-mail: dpinfo@duckpondcellars.com
picnic area: Yes
wheelchair access: Yes
gift shop: Yes
tours: Yes
fee: Complimentary wine tasting; small fee for select reserves
hours: Daily 10–5 May through September; October through April 11–5

BEST Gift shop

DIRECTIONS: From Portland take exit I-5 south. Take exit 99W McMinnville (exit number 294) and continue on 99W through Tigard, Sherwood, Newberg and Dundee. Arrive at 23145 Hwy 99W on your right in Dundee.

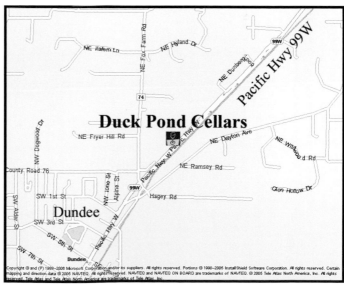

The Four Graces ②

Named in honor of owners Steve and Paula Black's four daughters — Alexis, Vanessa, Christiana, and Jillian — the Four Graces tasting room is located just off Hwy. 99W in Dundee. The white bungalow-style home exudes charm and refinement. Everything from the French doors leading to the outside patio, to the decorative molding and the tasteful artwork on the inside speaks of elegance. This sets the stage for what visitors have anticipated — fine wines.

It was Steve and Paula's vision to launch a winery as a legacy for their children. The Blacks have a ready source of premium wine grapes in their two organic and biodynamic estate vineyards, Black Family Estate Vineyard and Doe Ridge Estate. However, to turn fruit into fine wine, the Blacks rely on winemaker/consultant Laurent Montalieu. As would be expected in this northern Willamette Valley region, the Four Graces produces lots of pinot: Black Family Estate Pinot Noir, Dundee Hills Reserve Pinot Noir, Willamette Valley Pinot Noir, Dundee Hills Pinot Gris, and Dundee Hills Pinot Blanc. The end result is liquid elegance.

WineTrail note: Turns out the Black sisters have a brother named Nicholas. By no means forgotten, Nicholas is on the reserve wine labels as "Keeper of the Four Graces."

In welcoming visitors to their winery's website, Steve and Paula note, "Though it's not quite possible to invite the world to our table, The Four Graces is our family's way of sharing with you our passion for loving life and each other. So have a seat. Pour yourself a glass of one of our delightful pinots. And make a toast with us to this good life."

Sustainable viticulture meets sustainable elegance.

THE FOUR GRACES
winemaker(s): Steve Black and Laurent Montalieu (Consultant winemaker)
location: 9605 NE Fox Farm Road, Dundee, OR 97115
phone: 800-245-2150
web: www.thefourgraces.com
e-mail: steve@thefourgraces.com
picnic area: Yes
wheelchair access: Yes
fee: $10 tasting fee waived with purchase of 6 bottles or more
hours: Daily 10–5; Closed Christmas Day, New Year's Day, Easter Sunday, Thanksgiving; Early close Christmas Eve, New Year's Eve, 4th of July

DIRECTIONS: From Newberg go west onto SR-99W [E Hancock St.] and proceed 1.8 miles. Arrive at 9605 NE Fox Farm Rd.

From Dundee take SR-99W [Pacific Hwy W] north for .5 miles. Turn left (north) onto CR-74 [NE Fox Farm Rd] and arrive at the winery.

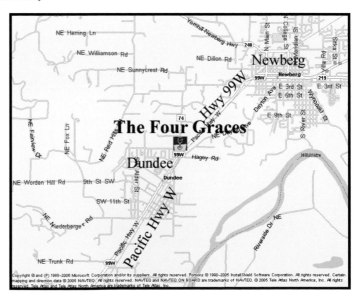

Dobbes Family Estate ③

"Of the earth comes the fruit of the vine, from the artistry of our hands and nature comes gratification, libation and our reward." — From Dobbesfamilyestate.com

Joe Dobbes, Jr. is a force among Oregon winemakers. His résumé reads like a short history of the Oregon wine industry with stints at Elk Cove Vineyards, Eola Hills Cellars, Hinman Vineyards, and Willamette Valley Vineyards. He's the winemaker for his own

labels: Wines by Joe, Jovino Pinot Noir and Dobbes Family Estate. In addition, Joe is the winemaker for Cliff Creek Cellars and Paschal Winery, and consults to others.

His exposure to other wineries based in the Rogue Valley has served him well and helps explain his production of syrah and viognier. In a sense, Joe is like a chef at a five-star restaurant combining the viniferous harvest of the relatively cool Willamette Valley and that of warm southern Oregon. Add to that recipe more than 20 years of winemaking and you have a rich banquet of red and white wines to experience.

Located just off Hwy. 99 west in Dundee, the new Dobbes Family Estate tasting room resides near their production and barrel-storage facilities. I arrived at an odd hour during the week and, along with three visitors from New York, got the 25-cent tour of the facilities. There's plenty of industrial-size space and equipment to position Dobbes Family Estate as one of the larger producer of wines in Oregon. During the tour, I learned that the Dobbes Family Estate label is an offshoot of parent label Wines by Joe. These are "wines without attitude" and priced to buy and enjoy the same evening. For example, the Wines by Joe Pinot Noir sells for around $19 and Joe's Pinot Gris is only $14.

Back in the tasting room, we sampled our way through Dobbes Family Estate pinot gris, viognier, pinot noir, and syrah. My senses were rocked by the switch from the crispness of the pinot gris to the velvety viognier. Then I experienced the light-bodied, fruit-forward pinot noir juxtaposed with the full-bodied syrah. Wow! As I smacked my lips and dapped drool, I couldn't decide which one appealed to me most. I did a mental "eeny, meeny, miny, moe" and opted for the Cuvée Noir Pinot Noir. I figured I could cellar this one for years before pairing it with a salmon yet to be hatched.

www.winetrailsnw.com/wineries/dobbes_family_estate

DOBBES FAMILY ESTATE
winemaker(s): Joe Dobbes, Jr.
location: 240 SE 5th Street, Dundee, OR 97115
phone: 503-538-1141
web: www.dobbesfamilyestate.com
picnic area: Yes
wheelchair access: Yes
fee: Wines by Joe complimentary; Tasting fee applies to Dobbes Family Estate Wines but refunded with $50 purchase or joining the wine club
hours: Daily 11–6

DIRECTIONS: **From Portland** heading south on I-5 take exit 294 toward OR-99W/Tigard/Newberg. Continue on SR-99W about 19 miles to Dundee. Turn left (east) onto SE 5th St. and arrive at Dobbes Family Estate on the left.

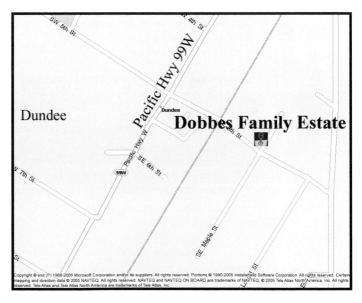

Argyle Winery 4

Unquestionably, Argyle Winery is a required stop along the Dundee WineTrail. Why, you ask? Because in a sea of pinot, Argyle Winery offers something different — sparkling wine, and lots of it.

Using the méthode champenoise, winemaker and general manager of Argyle Winery Rollin Soles ferments bubbly in a bottle — one bottle at a time. It's labor intensive and requires each bottle to age four to ten years. As you're sampling Argyle's mouthwatering

Blanc de Blancs, Knudsen Vineyard Brut, Black Brut, or Brut Rosé, just imagine what foods to pair with these sparkling wonders. I had a clear vision of a Thanksgiving turkey when I tasted the Brut Rosé.

In between sips, you might hear the tasting-room staff use vernacular particular to the méthode champenoise world. Terms such as "disgorgement" (removal of frozen yeast from the bottle's neck), "dosage" (the process of adding sweetened wine just prior to closure), or "riddling" (the rotating process used to get sediment into the bottles neck) may be mentioned as you watch the carbon dioxide bubbles float to the top of your flute glass.

Despite an annual production of 55,000 cases of sparkling and still wine, Argyle Winery's no. 1 seller is pinot noir. The winery makes four different pinot noirs, which bear the names Reserve Pinot Noir, Nuthouse Pinot Noir, Spirithouse Pinot Noir, and Willamette Valley Pinot Noir. The name Nuthouse pays homage to the fact that the production facility originally was a site for drying hazelnuts. However, most intriguing is the name "Spirithouse," which refers to the turn-of-the-century farmhouse that now serves as Argyle's tasting room. Here, in the early 1900s, 25-year-old Lena Elsie Imus took her life. Since then, various inhabitants of the building hear strange noises, smell unexplained flowery scents, and feel puffs of air ostensibly created by the ghost of Lena. She's a friendly ghost and a welcome presence in the tasting room. Amongst other relatives' tombstones, her Dundee gravestone reads, "Not Dead, But Gone Before." A little creepy, I would say.

If you like white wine, taste Argyle's chardonnay or riesling. For those with a sweet tooth, check out its dessert wine with a captivating name of Minus Five. Like their red wine brothers, the white wines come standard with a screw cap for easy opening and storage. No corkage here! If, however, you do notice a puff of air, your bottle cap removed, and some of your wine missing, it wasn't me, I swear.

ARGYLE WINERY
opened: 1987
winemaker(s): Rollin Soles
location: 691 Highway 99W, Dundee, OR 97115
phone: 503-538-8520
web: www.argylewinery.com
e-mail: tastingroom@argylewinery.com
picnic area: Yes
wheelchair access: Yes
fee: Red, white and bubbly flight $10; or $2.50 per taste
hours: Daily 11–5 except major holidays

DIRECTIONS: From Portland take exit I-5 south. Take exit 99W McMinnville (exit number 294) and continue on 99W through Tigard, Sherwood, Newberg and Dundee. Arrive at 691 Hwy 99W (Argyle Winery) on your left.

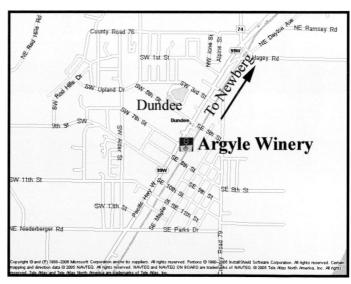

A to Z Wineworks ⑤

Meteoric – *adjective*, like a meteor; momentarily dazzling or brilliant, flashing, or swift

Founded in 2002, the A to Z Wineworks is Oregon's fastest-growing winery, in large part because it produces good wine at great prices. Its tagline, "Aristocratic wines at democratic prices," says it all. To keep their costs down, the founders of A to Z Wineworks follow that old and revered Burgundian practice in which they blend existing wines into a cuvée, or blended wine. With the right touch (and the requisite palate), these wine *négociants* exploded out of nowhere to become one of Oregon's top producers of wine. Exhibit A:

Their A to Z pinot noir, which sells for a mere $20, yet wins awards. Exhibit B: Their pinot gris, which goes for only $13.

To understand A to Z Wineworks' rise to fame is to appreciate the unique skills and experience that jump-started A to Z Wineworks. Bill Hatcher, Debra Hatcher, Sam Tannahill, and Cheryl Francis together brought acquisition, finance, marketing, and blending expertise to the mix. Collectively, they have many years in the Oregon wine industry, and know the best sources for acquiring wines to blend. Other partners with amazing backgrounds more recently have joined the A to Z Wineworks team, including one Gregg Popovich, the head coach of NBA champions the San Antonio Spurs.

I love the fact that the A to Z Wineworks tasting room is understated. It's in keeping with their philosophy of maintaining low costs to benefit consumers. I suspect that they could open their checkbook and provide a grand French chateau of a tasting room for those who desire such trappings, but they've opted not to. That experience can be found at their newly acquired Rex Hill winery in Newberg. There, you can swirl and sniff in a setting of lovely grounds and tasteful art. However, at the A to Z Wineworks tasting room in Dundee, you're there for the tasting. It's intimate. It's fun. And, weather permitting, you can retreat to the outside and enjoy your wine on the patio.

At A to Z Wineworks, you'll discover the essence of Oregon in a bottle.

A TO Z WINEWORKS
opened: 2002
winemaker(s): Various Oregon winemakers
from A to Z
location: 990 N Hwy 99W, Dundee, OR 97115
phone: 503-538-4881
web: www.atozwineworks.com
e-mail: info@atozwineworks.com
picnic area: Yes
wheelchair access: Yes
fee: $5 tasting fee
hours: Sunday through Thursday 11–5; Friday and
Saturday 11–6

DIRECTIONS: From Newberg take SR-99W [E Hancock St.] west for 2.6 miles. Arrive at 990 SR-99W on the right — home of A to Z Wineworks in Dundee.

From Dayton go northwest on SR-221 [SE 3rd St.] for .3 miles. Turn off onto ramp and go right onto SR-18 [SR-233] for 1.3 miles. Keep straight onto SR-99W [Pacific Hwy W] for 3.6 miles and arrive at 990 N. Hwy 99W in Dundee.

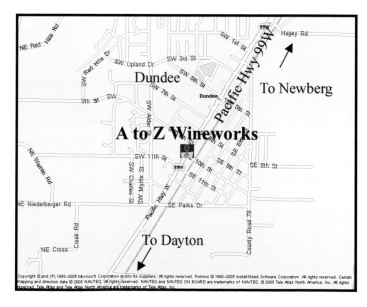

Dundee Hills North
Wine Trail

Torii Mor Vineyard and Winery

Make sure you have a cooler or two in the back of your car for the Dundee Hills WineTrail North. There's a reason that I also refer to this WineTrail as the "Frequent-Flyer-Mile WineTrail" because you are sure to use your credit card. Yes, the wines are first-rate but it might be hard to find wine such as Torii Mor, Bella Vida Vineyard, Maresh Red Barn, or Winderlea Vineyard and Winery in your neighborhood bottle shop. Thus, if you find a wine you like, think seriously of buying it.

The Dundee Hills WineTrail North also includes Erath Vineyards and Lange Estate Vineyards & Winery. To understand Oregon's wine history, a visit to these wineries is a must. Dick Erath is a pioneer for the Oregon wine industry, and the tasting room with photos adorning the wall reflects this history. Don Lange followed Dick Erath with his own brand of passion for making fine wine. I am like Pavlov's dog when I see his Blue Saturn dry fly on the wine label. My tail waggles.

Dundee Hills WineTrail North

1 Torii Mor Vineyard and Winery
2 Lange Estate Winery & Vineyards
3 Erath Vineyards
4 Bella Vida Vineyard
5 Maresh Red Barn
6 Winderlea Vineyard and Winery

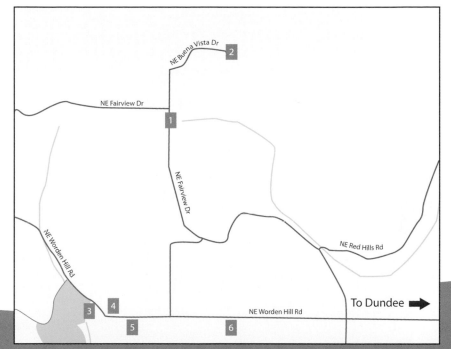

Region:	**North Willamette Valley Wine Country**
# of tasting rooms on tour:	**6**
Estimate # of days for tour:	**1 to 2**
Getting around:	**Car**
Key Events:	❏ **In April, Dundee Hills Passport Weekend – call 800-582-6668.**
	❏ **Memorial Weekend in Wine Country – Willamette Valley – visit www.willamettewines.com.**
	❏ **Wine Country Thanksgiving – Willamette Valley – call 503-646-2985 or visit www.willamettewines.com.**
Tips:	❏ **The Black Walnut Inn & Vineyard's elegance is only matched by its great location. To make reservations call well in advance 1-866-429-4114.**
	❏ **Budget time for Ponzi tasting room and wine bar in Dundee.**
	❏ **Looking for fine dining in wine country? Consider The Painted Lady (Newberg), the Dundee Bistro, Tina's (Dundee) or the Joel Palmer House (Dayton).**
Best:	❏ **Views: Torii Mor Vineyard and Winery, Lange Estate Winery & Vineyards, Erath Vineyards, Bella Vida Vineyard, Maresh Red Barn, Winderlea Vineyard and Winery.**

147

Torii Mor Vineyard and Winery 1

As you approach Torii Mor Vineyard and Winery, your eyes drink in the surrounding Olson Estate Vineyard and the Willamette Valley. Planted way back in 1972, Olson Estate Vineyard is one of the oldest vineyards in Yamhill County. You're smack dab in the heart

of Oregon's spectacular Dundee Hills viticultural area, and the panorama is breathtaking.

Founded in 1993 by Donald and Margie Olson, Torii Mor's wine production began as a modest initiative to showcase the fruit from Olson Estate Vineyard. The wine was a hit, and production has been climbing ever since,

with Torii Mor Vineyard and Winery releasing 10,000 to 12,000 cases annually. At the center of all this winemaking is Burgundian-born and -trained Jacque Tardy, whose job is to turn fruit into wine — chardonnay, pinot gris, gewürztraminer, and, of course, pinot noir.

Let's face it, like most visitors here, you've come for the pinot noir. Prepare to experience an assortment of vineyard-designated pinots, reserve pinots, and blended pinots. Even if you have a relatively undeveloped wine palate, you will discover the unique taste of pinot noirs made from Dundee Hills grapes. Dundee Hill pinots are lighter and fruitier than their pinot noir cousins in the lower elevations of the Willamette Valley.

As you enter the Torii Mor tasting room, the views of Japanese gardens and Northwest-style architecture come into focus. Next, you're struck by the friendliness of the tasting-room staff and the relaxed nature of the visitors. You figure that either they've just gotten a foot-to-head massage or they are well into a bottle of pinot noir.

Armed with a glass of wine, you saunter outside to the picnic gardens and notice visitors with delectable nibbles to pair with wine. Plates of hummus and pita bread and pulled pork on rolls got my attention. There just might be a lot of toasting and laughter going on.

Now about that name: The Olsons chose the name "Torii" because the elegance of their place conjures images of Japanese garden gateways; "mor" is the ancient Scandinavian term for "earth." The melded name of "Torii Mor" represents a fusion of East and West. It's also a fusion of great wine and stellar views.

www.winetrailsnw.com/wineries/torii_mor_vineyard_and_winery

TORII MOR VINEYARD AND WINERY
opened: 1993
winemaker(s): Jacques Tardy
location: 18325 NE Fairview Drive,
Dundee, OR 97115
phone: 503-554-0105
web: www.toriimorwinery.com
e-mail: info@toriimorwinery.com
picnic area: Yes
wheelchair access: Yes
fee: $10 tasting fee
hours: Daily 11–5

 BEST Views

DIRECTIONS: **From the north**, take I-5 south to 99W. Take 99W west through Tigard, Sherwood and Newberg and into Dundee. In Dundee, turn right onto 9th St. (9th St. turns into Worden Hill Rd). Travel approximately one mile and turn right onto NE Fairview Drive. The Torii Mor Tasting Room is approximately one mile on the right.

From the south, take I-5 north to 99W. Take 99W west through Newberg and into Dundee. In Dundee, turn right onto 9th St. (9th St. turns into Worden Hill Rd). Travel approximately one mile and turn right onto NE Fairview Drive. The Torii Mor Tasting Room is approximately one mile on the right.

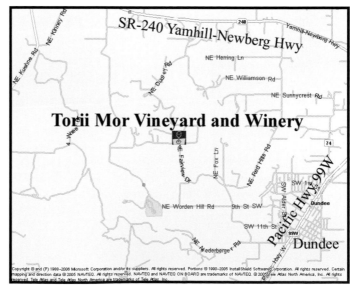

Lange Estate Winery & Vineyards ②

I've heard it said that the dry fly on many of the Lange Estate wine bottle labels is a Blue Saturn fly. It wasn't chosen simply because it's a nice image. Rather, it reflects an appreciation for the great outdoors that shapes the lifestyle of owners Don and Wendy Lange, as well as their approach to winemaking, I suspect. Although I am not a fly-

fisherman, I do appreciate the beauty of an accomplished angler's smooth cast and ability to hit the right spot — just like the wines of Lange Estate Vineyard & Winery.

Don and Wendy came north to Oregon from Santa Barbara in the mid-1980s. They cast their lot and hit a perfect spot: the red hills of Dundee. It didn't take long to get a bite, and soon they were producing handcrafted pinot gris, chardonnay, and pinot noir. That was in 1987. Since then, their production has steadily increased to an annual production of 16,000 cases, most of which comes from their own 45-acre estate vineyard. With the winemaking assistance of their son, Jesse, they create a number of pinot noirs bearing the names of their sources — Lange Estate Vineyard, Freedom Hill Vineyard, Yamhill Vineyards, and Three Hills Cuvée — and they continue to work the vintages year after year. Each year, however, presents new challenges brought by heat and rain, and requires constant vigilance and inventiveness (and, like fly-fishing, a little luck).

For the white wine lovers among us, Lange continues to produce two styles of pinot gris with distinctive flavor profiles. Don was the first to produce barrel-fermented pinot gris and offers this alongside their stainless steel variation. Their chardonnay releases also rely on a combination of barrel-fermented and stainless-steel-produced vintages. After sampling my way through many, many chardonnays, I've come to a point where I don't feel that one chardonnay is any better than another. Which chardonnay I choose to take home depends on what I am eating. For me, barrel-fermented goes nicely with a richer white fish or a seafood linguine, whereas I like the stainless-steel-produced chardonnay with ahi or Thai cuisine.

When you visit Lange Estate, be sure you take in the views of the Chehalem Valley below and the Cascade Mountains in the distance. This vista certainly ranks among the top 10 views for Oregon wineries, and the winery is the perfect spot to reel in one of life's great pleasures.

LANGE ESTATE WINERY & VINEYARDS
opened: 1987
winemaker(s): Don Lange and Jesse Lange
location: 18380 NE Buena Vista Drive,
Dundee, OR 97115
phone: 503-538-6476
web: www.langewinery.com
e-mail: tastingroom@langewinery.com
picnic area: Yes
wheelchair access: Yes
fee: $10 tasting fee
hours: Daily 11–5

BEST Views

DIRECTIONS: From Dundee, head southwest on SR-99W [Pacific Hwy W] and turn right (west) onto 9th St. SW Proceed 1 mile. Turn right (north) onto NE Fairview Dr. and go 1.5 miles. Turn right (east) onto NE Buena Vista Dr. and arrive at Lange Estate Winery & Vineyards.

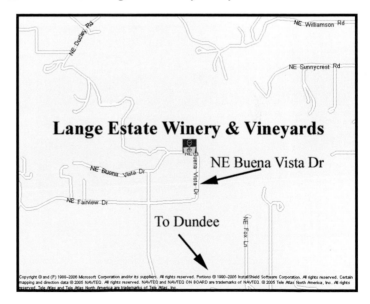

Erath Vineyards 3

The story of Erath Vineyards is the story of Dick Erath, an Oregon pioneer. No, Dick didn't climb down off the Conestoga and homestead after a long haul on the Oregon Trail. Rather, Dick's pioneering story is one that has filled the pages of *The Boys Up North — Dick Erath and the Early Oregon Winemakers* by Paul Pintarich. To appreciate this history, a timeline of key events is in order:

1968 – Dick Erath moves to Oregon from California and establishes his first vineyard.
1972 – Produces his first commercial vintage (216 cases) in his basement.
1975 – Partners with lumber magnate Cal Knudsen to create Knudsen-Erath label.
1976 – Launches first winery in the Dundee Hills.
1977 – Has a "defining moment" when he spends six weeks touring wineries in Europe.
1987 – Produces first 35,000 cases. Awards continue to mount up.
1988 – Buys out Cal Knudsen's interest to restore Erath Vineyards label.
1994 – Hires Rob Stuart to share title as winemaker with him.
1996 – Takes home the gold and best in show from L.A. County wine competition.
2002 – Hires Gary Horner as winemaker.
2006 – Sells Erath Vineyards to Ste. Michelle Wine Estates.
2008 – Is discovered by WineTrails guy (that's a joke).

The weathered tasting room is beginning to show its age, but that's a big part of its charm. Inside the room's wood-paneled walls you'll find photos depicting the Erath story; they're fun to look at and they add to the room's relaxed feel. It's purposefully designed for Northwest comfort and it's a great place to experience Erath's many affordable wines. Today, Erath Vineyards cultivates 118 acres of premium grapes and sources additional grapes from 130 acres throughout Oregon. At a case production of 65,000 annually, Erath Vineyards is in the upper echelon of Oregon wine producers. A full two-thirds of that production is pinot noir sold throughout the United States. Other wines include Oregon's finest: pinot gris, pinot blanc, riesling, Gewürztraminer, and dolcetto. In the summer, take advantage of the spacious patio, with its spectacular views of the surrounding vineyard and Cascade Mountains in the distance.

Scrabble aficionados, take note that the letters in Erath also spell "earth" and "heart." I know that's a non sequitur, but still, it's interesting. Yet, no matter how you spell it, an Erath wine by any other name would taste just as sweet.

ERATH VINEYARDS
winemaker(s): Gary Horner
location: 9409 NE Worden Hill Road,
Dundee, OR 97115
phone: 503-538-3318
web: www.erath.com
e-mail: info@erath.com
picnic area: Yes
wheelchair access: Yes
fee: Complimentary wine tasting for select wines;
Charge for winemaker's flights
hours: Daily 11–5; Closed for Easter, Thanksgiving
Day, Christmas Day, and New Year's Day

BEST Views

DIRECTIONS: From Dundee take SR-99W [Pacific Hwy W] heading southwest for .3 miles. Turn right (west) onto 9th St. SW and go 1 mile. Road name changes to NE Worden Hill Rd and continue 1.2 miles. Arrive at 9409 NE Worden Hill Rd.

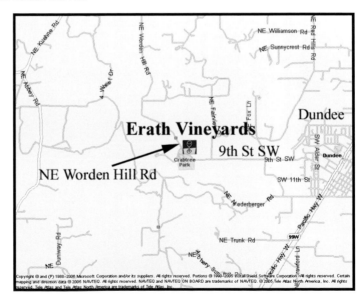

153

Bella Vida Vineyard 🄴

What to do? What to do? Imagine having 12 of the best acres of pinot noir in Oregon and yet neither of you have a winemaking background. What's more, you reside in Tucson, Arizona, and have full-time professional careers that preclude grape stomping, racking

wine and bottling. It's a dilemma that might force most of us to give up on the whole wine idea and put up the "For Sale" sign.

However, it's not a problem for Steven and Allison Whiteside, owners of Bella Vida ("Beautiful Life") Vineyard in the Dundee Hills, who split their time between Arizona and Oregon. Inside the spacious tasting room, with its commanding views of the surrounding vineyard, this very cute couple do the pouring honors. (Steve's title is "President of the Vines," and Allison's title is "President of the Wines.") As they pour, they let you in on the secret of their success and the solution to the lack of winemaking experience.

Essentially, they offer the same vintages and same vineyard grapes, but rely on different winemakers to produce distinct pinot noirs. They call this the Bella Vida Winemaker series, and each vintage displays the talent of one of three winemakers: Jacques Tardy, Jay Somers, or Brian O'Donnell. As visitors work their sampling way through these wines, bearing the labels Tardy, J. Christopher, or O'Donnell, they should keep in mind that each was made with the same grapes from the same harvest.

Feeling a little indecisive about which of the three to buy? No problem: You can purchase Bella Vida's "Party in a Box" and get all three for $80, a savings of more than $20. Now, that deal adds to an already beautiful life. By the way, if you're interested in white wine, check out their estate Gris-Ling blend of 80 percent pinot gris and 20 percent riesling.

Bella Vida's soil is red clay Jory soil, and the slope adds to the drainage. Here you have hot summer days, followed by cool nights with a breeze supplied by the Pacific. With its breathtaking views, it's truly an exquisite setting for growing that most noble of Burgundy grapes, pinot noir.

Your next stop along the Dundee Hills WineTrail North is Maresh Red Barn. Ironically, the friendship between the Whitesides and the Maresh family led Steve and Allison to purchase and create Bella Vida Vineyard.

Steven and Allison Whiteside

BELLA VIDA VINEYARD
opened: 2001
winemaker(s): Jacque Tardy, Jay Christopher Somers and Brian O'Donnell
location: 9380 NE Worden Hill Road, Dundee, OR 97115
phone: 503-538-9821
web: www.bellavida.com
e-mail: info@bellavida.com
picnic area: Yes
wheelchair access: Yes
tours: Yes
fee: $5 tasting fee
hours: Friday through Sunday 11–5, Memorial Day through Thanksgiving Weekend

DIRECTIONS: From Dundee, head southwest on SR-99W [Pacific Hwy W] for .3 miles. Turn right (west) onto 9th St. SW and continue for 1 mile. Road name changes to NE Worden Hill Rd. Proceed for 1.2 miles and arrive at 9380 NE Worden Hill Rd.

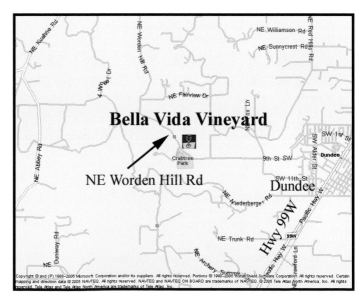

Maresh Red Barn ⑤

It was in the mid-'70s that Jim and Loie Maresh's neighbor Dick Erath suggested to them that they plant pinot noir on their farm. Erath Vineyards had proven that Oregon could produce outstanding pinot, and Dick knew that this farm on Worden Road, down the hill from his vineyard, would also produce excellent pinot noir. He was right.

What's interesting is that Jim and Loie didn't have a lick of farming experience when they acquired the property way back in 1959. However, the selling agent required that they

purchase all 27 acres and not just a portion of the land. I guess you could say they bought the farm.

Over the years they replaced orchards with pinot noir, pinot blanc, sauvignon blanc, riesling, and pinot gris grapes, and sold their annual harvest to Erath Vineyards. And, as their neighbors left

the area, they acquired more property for growing grapes. Eventually, they realized that they should retain a portion of the grapes for themselves and their own Maresh Red Barn label. Annual case production is small; only about 1,000 cases, and those are only sold at the Maresh Red Barn, a delightful stop along the Dundee Hills WineTrail North. The view from inside the tasting room is equal to the view of the red barn from the outside. Both are beautiful.

Today, following the passing of Loie, Jim and his offspring manage Maresh Red Barn Vineyard. The vineyard now consumes 60 acres of prime Dundee Hills real estate. Its roots go 15 to 18 feet deep into the Jory soil in search of water. The result is an earthy pinot noir with delicate flavors, garnet colors, and light cherry notes. It's the quintessential Oregon pinot noir. You can smell its very essence.

WineTrail Tip: Need a place to stay for a family reunion or corporate retreat? Check out the Maresh Red Hill Vineyard Retreat, nestled amongst vineyards with great views of the Cascades. Call Martha Maresh at 503-538-7034 for details.

MARESH RED BARN
winemaker(s): Jim Maresh
location: 9325 NE Worden Hill Road,
Dundee, OR 97115
phone: 503-537-1098
web: http://vineyardretreat.com
e-mail: HagMMM@aol.com
picnic area: Yes
fee: $5 tasting fee
hours: Wednesday through Sunday 11–5, March
through December

 BEST Views

DIRECTIONS: **From Dundee** to SR-99W [Pacific Hwy W] heading southwest .3 miles. Turn right (west) onto 9th St. SW and go 1 mile. The road name changes to NE Worden Hill Rd. Continue 1.1 miles to Maresh Red Barn winery.

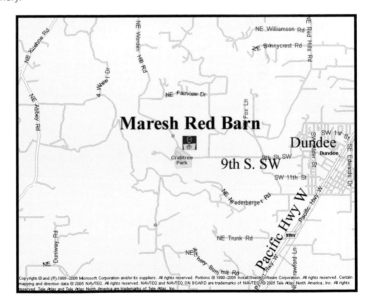

Winderlea Vineyard and Winery 6

Committed to creating a business together, fifty-something Bill Sweat and Donna Morris purchased the legendary 20-acre Goldschmidt Vineyard in the heart of the Dundee Hills in 2006. They left their professional lives behind to pursue a common passion — pinot noir. For years, they knew that pinot was their wine of choice, especially when they realized it influenced the restaurants they frequented and the food they cooked. When you have the pinot noir bug that bad, no amount of visiting Dijon or maintaining a robust cellar of pinot noir could satisfy the need to actually make it. They put "Oregon or Bust,"

metaphorically speaking, on the car and headed west to pursue their dream.

Bill and Donna brought a key component with them from New England — the name Winderlea. Also the name of their Vermont-based farm, the word is derived from German and loosely translates to "valley protected from the wind." When they began their enterprise, Bill and Donna had their estate grapes from Goldschmidt Vineyard, but they needed one more key ingredient to make the wine. Enter acclaimed winemaker Robert E. Brittan, formerly of Stags' Leap Winery, to make several vineyard-designated and reserve pinot noirs.

Winderlea's contemporary architecture is nothing short of spectacular. Drawn up by Ernest R. Munch, Architect & Urban Planner, LLC, of Portland, the design takes advantage of recycled materials and uses minimal amounts of electricity. Once inside, you can see why the electricity bill is low. One entire side of the tasting room is composed of glass, providing views of the Goldschmidt Vineyard and the Willamette Valley below. These glass walls open to the patio, where, on hot summer days, the division between indoors and outdoors evaporates. As your wine touring continues in and around Dundee, you likely will hear folks ask, "Have you been to Winderlea?" They're anxious to get your reaction and affirmation that Winderlea is truly a one-of-a-kind experience. Design matters.

WineTrail Tip: On Fridays during the summer, Winderlea hosts three-course lunches paired with Winderlea wines. (An offering made possible by a full-sized kitchen that was included in the winery's design.) Space is limited to 12 guests, and reservations are required. Call 503-554-5900.

WINDERLEA VINEYARD AND WINERY
opened: 2008
winemaker(s): Robert E. Brittan
location: 8905 Worden Hill Road,
Dundee, OR 97115
phone: 503-554-5900
web: www.winderlea.com
e-mail: info@winderlea.com
wheelchair access: Yes
fee: $10 tasting fee donated to Salud!
hours: Friday through Sunday 11–4, Memorial Day
weekend through Thanksgiving weekend

BEST Views

DIRECTIONS: From Dundee to SR-99W [Pacific Hwy W] heading southwest .3 miles. Turn right (west) onto 9th St. SW and go 1 mile. The road name changes to NE Worden Hill Rd. Continue about 1 mile to Winderlea Vineyard & Winery on the left.

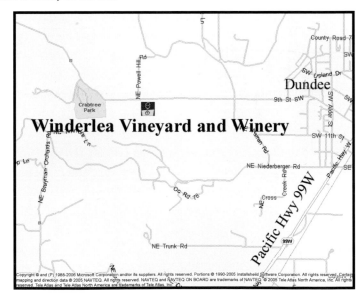

Dundee Hills South
WineTrail

Stoller Vineyard and Winery

No doubt Oregon wine lovers have their top 10 picks in terms of great wine. And, no doubt that the list would be heavily weighted toward wines of the pinot noir variety. Think Oregon wines; think pinot. Think pinot noir and you no doubt focus on the Dundee Hills, and more specifically the wineries of Dundee Hills WineTrail South. And why not? With names like Domaine Serene, Domaine Drouhin Oregon, Archery Summit, De Ponte Cellars, Sokol Blosser and others, your tasting room excursion is a guaranteed hit.

On this WineTrail you will discover that these pinot noirs differ remarkably from the pinots that you might have had down the road in McMinnville, using grapes from different viticulture areas. The culprit in this difference is the soil of the Dundee Hills, which results in wines that are lighter and fruitier than other meatier pinots. Someone above must have determined that a wine was needed to match perfectly with Northwest Seafood, summer salads, grilled chicken, and light pasta dishes. He succeeded with the creation of these pinot noirs from the Dundee Hills.

Dundee Hills WineTrail South

1. Sokol Blosser
2. Archery Summit
3. De Ponte Cellars
4. Domaine Drouhin Oregon
5. Wine Country Farm Cellars
6. Domaine Serene
7. Vista Hills Vineyard & Winery
8. Winter's Hill Vineyard
9. White Rose Wines
10. Stoller Vineyard and Winery
11. Anne Amie Vineyards

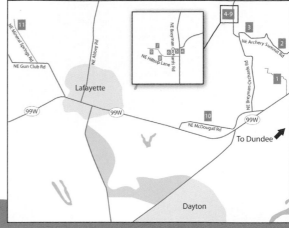

Region:	**North Willamette Valley Wine Country**
# of tasting rooms on tour:	**11**
Estimate # of days for tour:	**2 to 3**
Getting around:	**Car**
Key Events:	❑ **In March, McMinnville's Wine & Food Classic – call 503-472-4033 or visit www.macwfc.org for event schedule and ticketing.**
	❑ **In April, Dundee Hills Passport Weekend – call 800-582-6668.**
	❑ **Memorial Weekend in Wine Country – Willamette Valley – visit www.willamettewines.com.**
	❑ **Wine Country Thanksgiving – Willamette Valley – call 503-646-2985 or visit www.willamettewines.com.**
Tips:	❑ **Pack a picnic and a camera.**
	❑ **Make plans to eat/sleep in nearby Dundee, McMinnville, Dayton, or Carlton.**
	❑ **Sokol Blosser has a steady stream of special events – See www.sokolblosser.com for event information.**
	❑ **Budget time for Ponzi tasting room and wine bar in Dundee.**
	❑ **The Black Walnut Inn & Vineyard's elegance is only matched by its great location. To make reservations call well in advance 1-866-429-4114.**
	❑ **Looking for fine dining in wine country? Consider The Painted Lady (Newberg), the Dundee Bistro, Tina's (Dundee) or the Joel Palmer House (Dayton).**

 Best:
❑ **Lodging: Wine Country Farm Cellars.**
❑ **Views: Sokol Blosser, Archery Summit, De Ponte Cellars, Domaine Drouhin Oregon, Wine Country Farm Cellars, Domaine Serene, Vista Hills Vineyard & Winery, Winter's Hill Vineyard, White Rose Wines, Stoller Vineyard and Winery, and Anne Amie Vineyards.**

Sokol Blosser

The heart of the Sokol Blosser is its cofounder and leader Susan Sokol Blosser. From growing grapes, producing wines, going green, to marketing its product, to understand Sokol Blosser is to understand Susan. Her self-chronicled story, eloquently and candidly presented in *At Home in the Vineyard*, honestly weaves the highs and lows of being an Oregon wine pioneer (She started the winery in 1971.) Imagine keeping your wits and sense of humor in a male-dominated industry, raising children, nurturing and losing love, all while evolving her business to become a major Oregon winery. That's a legacy we can all aspire to.

As you drive onto the Sokol Blosser property, right off Highway 99W, you're struck by its well-maintained vineyard, the tasting room in the distance, and rows of solar cells positioned to capture the sun's best light. The set of solar panels is your first clue that you're about to enter an eco-friendly zone. Your tasting-room experience and facility tour (if time permits) expose you to a bunch of other environmentally sensitive initiatives Susan has engineered. Check out the LEED-certified underground barrel room with its living roof composed of the same wildflower crops you see growing in Sokol Blosser's organically certified vineyard. Many vintners in Oregon use organic practices, but just a few can boast that they have achieved LIVE (Low Input Viticulture and Enology), as Sokol Blosser has. Its vineyard tractors rely on biodiesel fuel, and even its paper products — from labels to bags — are unbleached. If you manage to finish a bottle at the winery, be assured, the bottle will be recycled.

At the core of Sokol Blosser's success story is its fine wines, particularly its pinot noir. Depending upon your taste preference and cash on hand, the tasting fee varies from $5 to $15. It would be a shame, however, to come all this way and not experience Sokol Blosser's renowned pinot noirs. I can taste the Dundee Hills earthiness in each sip. But a real crowd pleaser is the red blend named for a Roman goddess of wine — Meditrina — a blend of pinot noir, syrah, and zinfandel. Their white blend Evolution happens to be my favorite. With each sip, I mentally pair it with grilled mahi mahi tacos and mango salsa.

Vintage after vintage, the cycle continues at Sokol Blosser. Its approach is sustainable yet evolutionary, and at the core of this success is its leader and visionary, Susan Sokol Blosser.

SOKOL BLOSSER
opened: 1971
winemaker(s): Russ Rosner
location: 5000 Sokol Blosser Lane,
Dayton, OR 97114
phone: 503-864-2282
web: www.sokolblosser.com
e-mail: info@sokolblosser.com
picnic area: Yes
wheelchair access: Yes
tours: Yes
fee: $5 to $15 tasting fee
hours: Daily 10–4

BEST Views

DIRECTIONS: **From Portland** take I-5 south to exit 294 at Tigard. Turn right on Hwy 99W, go through Tigard and Newberg to Dundee. From Dundee, follow 99W another 2 miles to a blue sign reading Sokol Blosser Winery. Take a right at the sign, and drive a short distance to the winery.

From Eugene and points south take I-5 north to Exit 271 at Woodburn. Turn left onto Hwy 219 and follow it through St. Paul, across the Willamette River to Newberg. Turn left on Hwy 99W, go through Newberg to Dundee. From Dundee, follow 99W another 2 miles to a blue sign reading Sokol Blosser Winery. Take a right at the sign, and follow the lane to the winery.

If driving from the Oregon Coast, go east on Hwy 18, 5 miles north of Lincoln City. Stay on Hwy 18, following signs for Dayton/OR-18 E/Portland. Turn right onto Hwy 99W towards Portland. After one-half mile, turn left at a blue sign reading Sokol Blosser Winery. Follow the lane to the winery.

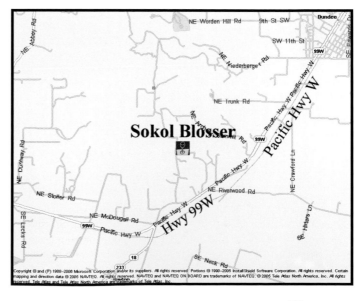

Archery Summit 2

"Archery Summit has established itself as the Rolls-Royce of Oregon Pinot Noir."
— Wine Spectator

For all you WineTrail trekkers planning a trip to Archery Summit, my one piece of advice is to take the tour. To understand Archery Summit one needs to go inside the bowels of its winemaking operation and learn the importance of gravity-fed winemaking. Modeled on the cellars of France's Côte d'Or, Archery Summit's design begins underground. It's in the caves where you can sample pinot noir from the barrel and understand why it

earned the "Rolls-Royce" label. **WineTrail note:** Daily tours begin at 10:30 a.m. and 2 p.m. And even though it may be 90 degrees outside, bring a jacket for the 55- to 59-degree constant temperatures in the caves. To reserve a spot, call the Guest Relations Department at 503-864-4300.

In scanning Archery Summit press reviews, I found certain words and phrases cropping up, such as "fine in texture," "round," "bright cherry and coffee flavors," "velvety," and my personal favorite, "cool and leafy." Clearly, 90 percent of the battle is working with the best-in-class fruit, but it's also Archery Summit's unique method of making wine in its gravity-fed winery. Guided by winemaker Anna Matzinger's technical background and intuitive palate, Archery Summit grapes are submitted to a time-tested treatment, which includes sorting clusters by hand, cold-soaking the clusters for five days, and using indigenous yeast.

At Archery Summit, blending is the rule rather than the exception. This age-old Burgundian practice is key in the production of the winery's Premier Cuvée Pinot Noir, a blend of its oldest Pommard and Dijon estate clones. It's a classic case of the whole being better than the sum of its parts. How about this description from Archery Summit to get your mouth watering? "Scarlet red in color, the Archery Summit Premier Cuvée opens with lifted aromas of black cherries, rose petal, vanilla and a hint of savory spice."

Membership has its privileges, and this is certainly true for members of Archery Summit's A-List. There is no cost to join the A-List, and members receive at least eight wines annually; many of them are vineyard-designated wines allocated only to A-List members. Members also have access to a unique resource: they can contact a dedicated Archery Summit concierge to plan their next Oregon wine-tour getaway. It's a classy touch representative of what you can expect from Archery Summit.

ARCHERY SUMMIT
opened: 1993
winemaker(s): Anna Matzinger
location: 18599 NE Archery Summit Road, Dayton, OR 97114
phone: 503-864-4300
web: www.archerysummit.com
e-mail: info@archerysummit.com
tours: Yes
fee: $15 tasting fee
hours: Daily 10–4; Tours at 10:30 and 2:30

 BEST Views

DIRECTIONS: From Portland take exit I-5 south. Take exit 99W McMinnville (exit number 294) and continue on 99W through Tigard, Sherwood, Newberg and Dundee. Approximately 1 mile south of Dundee, turn right on Archery Summit Rd. Follow gravel road .8 of a mile until you reach the Archery Summit gate.

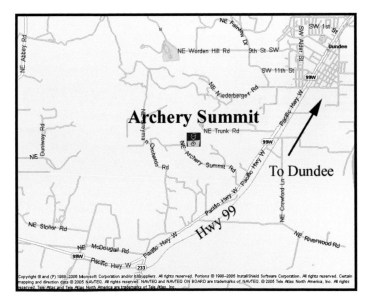

De Ponte Cellars ❸

Home to many things, the Dundee Hills are famous for their red Jory soils, which date back to lava flows occurring 15 million to 17 million years ago. This area has the highest concentration of vineyards (try 2,000 acres) in the Willamette Valley and most of that is dedicated to one grape — pinot noir. And because the vineyards reside between 200 and 1,000 feet above sea level, they don't have the frost problem that can occur at low elevations of the Willamette Valley. It's little wonder that the Dundee Hills are home to nationally and internationally renowned wineries, including the early pioneer winery De Ponte Cellars.

Owners Scott and Rae Baldwin have winemaking neighbors with excellent pedigrees, including Archery Summit and Domaine Drouhin. And like their neighbors, the Baldwins focus on Burgundy grape varieties such as pinot noir (of course), but they also make an unusual (for Oregon) Melon de Bourgogne white wine. De Ponte Cellars has developed a cult following of loyal fans who snap up cases of the Melon de Bourgogne. This is a wine crafted for Northwest seafood, particularly oysters, scallops, Dungeness crab, and sturgeon. However, it is the De Ponte Cellars pinot noir that shows exceptional finesse and will have you reaching for your wallet. The only downside to this wine is that it should be cellared for years to attain its peak taste. Tick-tock! Whereas great patience is in order for the pinot, the Melon de Bourgogne is ready to be drunk now. Luckily for me, I had the pleasure of meeting De Ponte Cellars' French-born, -educated, and -trained winemaker, Isabelle Dutartre. She often works the tasting room with other staff, pouring wine and introducing visitors to their wines. Through her thick French accent, her passion comes through loud and clear. A tasting fee of $10 includes a sampling of all four of De Ponte's current releases.

As the WineTrails guy, I brake for all tasting rooms. I must admit, however, that some wineries are more enjoyable than others. Much of this has to do with the overall demeanor of each winery, and I sense that attitude starts at the top and carries through to the staff. Despite the fact that De Ponte Cellars has all the trappings of pretension — glorious setting, great views and grand buildings — it succeeds in achieving a sense of country comfort, relaxation and, yes, fun. I'd be willing to bet that Scott Baldwin wouldn't want it any other way.

DE PONTE CELLARS
opened: 2001
winemaker(s): Isabelle Dutartre
location: 17545 Archery Summit Road,
Dayton, OR 97114
phone: 503-864-3698
web: www.depontecellars.com
e-mail: aaron@depontecellars.com
picnic area: Yes
tours: Yes
fee: $10 tasting fee refundable with purchase of 6
bottles or more
hours: Daily 11–5

BEST Views

DIRECTIONS: From Portland, follow I-5 south and take Hwy 99W exit toward McMinnville. Drive through Newberg and Dundee. Approximately 3 miles south of Dundee on Hwy 99W, turn right on McDougall Rd (just past the weigh station). Take the first right turn onto Breyman Orchards Rd (there's a blue sign that shows DePonte Cellars). Proceed about 1.5 miles and turn right onto Archery Summit Rd. De Ponte Cellars is the second driveway on the left — look for large sign and gated entrance.

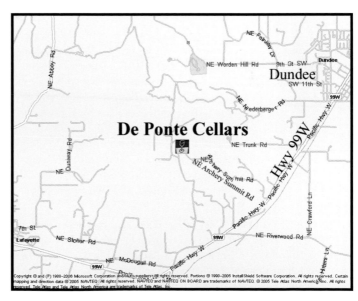

Domaine Drouhin Oregon 4

OK, I am breaking a self-imposed cardinal rule, but I must confess that Domaine Drouhin Oregon is one of my favorite wineries in the state. At the risk of not being welcomed at other wineries, let me explain why.

To begin with, note the name. It's not simply "Domaine Drouhin," it's "Domaine Drouhin Oregon." There is a subtle yet profound reason for this. Back in 1987, Robert Drouhin of Burgundy's Maison Joseph Drouhin purchased acreage in the Dundee Hills following a suggestion from David Adelsheim. Robert was well traveled and very familiar with Oregon and its potential for making great pinot noir. After all, back in 1980, his own winery, Beune-based Maison Joseph Drouhin, sponsored a blind tasting, and although its wine took first place, it was the second-place finisher from Oregon's Eyrie Vineyards that shook the established wine world. Robert Drouhin embraced Oregon and realized its potential.

At the time of the Oregon land acquisition (goodbye, Christmas trees — hello, pinot noir) Robert's daughter Véronique had just graduated from the enology program at the University of Dijon and sought to expand her winemaking résumé in the new world. Domaine Drouhin Oregon was born, but to no one's surprise, the early years were consumed with planting Burgundy vine clones on phylloxera-resistant root stalk, building the first gravity-fed winery in Oregon, and making early versions of pinot noir and chardonnay. It wasn't until 1992 that Domaine Drouhin Oregon Pinot Noir Laurène was released to critical acclaim. Named for Véronique's baby daughter, Laurène established Domaine Drouhin Oregon's reputation and ever since, the winery has received boatloads of accolades from such publications as *Wine Spectator* and *Wine Advocate*.

Now, here's a bit of a news flash: Rarely do I purchase a glass of wine at a winery, kick back, and relax. My time is usually very limited, and I typically have an agenda of six to eight wineries to visit in a day. Besides that, I need to keep my wits in order to scribble insightful thoughts (ahem) and operate my Nikon D200. However, on the July day that my partner, Kathleen, and I visited Domaine Drouhin Oregon, we broke the rules, purchased two glasses of the Pinot Noir Willamette Valley, and retreated to the outside patio. There, with spectacular views of the 90-acre vineyard and the rolling hills in the distance, we enjoyed the fruits of Véronique's labor. The silky taste of the pinot combined with the great views created a moment in time that we'll never forget.

DOMAINE DROUHIN OREGON
opened: 1988
winemaker(s): Véronique Drouhin
location: 6750 Breyman Orchards Road,
Dundee, OR 97115
phone: 503-864-2700
web: www.domainedrouhin.com
e-mail: info@domainedrouhin.com
picnic area: Yes
wheelchair access: Yes
fee: $10 refundable with $150 purchase
hours: Wednesday through Sunday 11–4

BEST Views

DIRECTIONS: **From Dundee** go southwest 2.3 miles on SR-99W [Pacific Hwy W]. Turn right (west) onto NE Archery Summit Rd and go 1.9 miles. Turn right (west) onto NE Breyman Orchards Rd and follow signs to the winery.

From McMinnville go south on 99W [Pacific Hwy W] about 8 miles. Turn left (west) onto NE McDougall Rd for .2 miles. Turn right (north) onto NE Breyman Orchards Rd and go 1.4 miles. Turn left to stay on NE Breyman Orchards Rd and go .4 miles to get to destination.

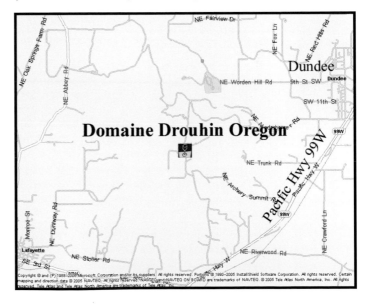

Wine Country Farm Cellars 5

Are you looking for a wine country experience that includes a great place to stay? Do you have a wedding in your future and need a romantic setting for it? Or maybe you just like going to wineries with spectacular views, gardens to explore, and an Arabian horse or two to view. If any of these criteria apply, Wine Country Farm Cellars is the place for you.

Owner Joan Davenport bought the 13-acre farm in 1990, and she's still living the dream. The property features the second-oldest vineyard in the Dundee Hills (planted in 1970), a bed-and-breakfast, and a barn built in 1870, in which Joan houses her Arabian

horses. This is a destination winery. You can arrive Friday, depart on Sunday, and never leave the property except perhaps to make a foray into Dundee or nearby McMinnville for a meal. While at Wine Country Farm, you can enjoy the hot tub, catch up on movies, ride a horse, retreat with coworkers, or get married. If you should opt to read a book, you might want to read *1,000 Places to See Before You Die* by Patricia Schultz — one of the destinations listed is Wine Country Farm. It is without doubt a most romantic setting.

The Wine Country Farm Bed & Breakfast features nine exquisite rooms, each uniquely decorated and appointed. Rooms, with nightly rates ranging from $150 to $225, have all the creature comforts, including Internet access (which is really convenient if you just happen to be writing a guidebook about wine touring in Oregon). Make an effort to visit the Arabian horses in the barn; they're a beautiful sight to behold with their distinctive small heads and large nostrils.

A separate room in the compound houses the winery's tasting room. For a refundable $5 tasting fee, visitors can sample a variety of wines created by Alberto Alcazar. Wines to be swirled and sipped include riesling, Müller-Thurgau (including a Müller-Thurgau dessert wine), chardonnay, and pinot noir.

WINE COUNTRY FARM CELLARS
opened: 1993
winemaker(s): Alberto Alcazar
location: 6855 NE Breyman Orchards Road,
Dayton, OR 97114
phone: 503-864-3446
web: www.winecountryfarm.com
e-mail: jld@winecountryfarm.com
picnic area: Yes
wheelchair access: Yes
weddings: Yes
fee: $5 tasting fee refundable with purchase
hours: Daily 11–5 during summer; Weekends 11–5
during winter

⭐ **BEST Lodging and views**

DIRECTIONS: South on 99W from Portland through Newberg and Dundee. 3 miles beyond Dundee just past truck weigh station, turn right on McDougal, go one block and turn right on NE Breyman Orchards Rd. Continue 2 miles to the end of road (the top of hill).

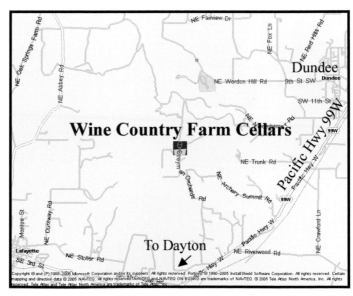

Domaine Serene 6

For shutterbugs, Domaine Serene is *the* place to be. A plethora of photo ops await visitors; you'll be thanking the techno gods for the invention of the digital camera, which allows you to snap, snap away. As you approach Domaine Serene, keep your eye out for panoramic views of this Tuscan-style winery in the distance, with its estate vineyards in the foreground. At the winery, potential shots include wrought-iron patio furniture in front of a Mediterranean-influenced wall, window shutters that exude elegance, and a

spacious tasting room that would impress Louis the XIV. Relative to other Oregon wineries, this place is truly over the top.

However, owners Ken and Grace Evanstad may beg to differ. After all, they feel their establishment should mirror the excellence of Oregon's pinot noirs; why take a back seat to wines from Burgundy, New Zealand, or California. Formerly of Minnesota, where Ken owned a pharmaceutical company, the Evanstads came west in late 1989 and purchased 42 acres in the Dundee Hills. That acreage would become Domaine Serene, named after their daughter. They might not have known much about growing grapes or making wine, but they brought with them considerable business expertise and a laser-sharp vision to make ultra-premium wines.

The Evanstads didn't let a little inexperience get in the way. Instead, they resolved to make superlative pinot noir, and given the number of awards and accolades they've accumulated over the years, they have succeeded.

Visitors to Domaine Serene are welcomed and asked to sign in at the tasting room entrance. A $15 tasting fee gains a visitor access to outstanding samples of pinot noir, chardonnay, and syrah made under the winery's Rockblock label. Visitors can sign up to become a member of one of three different Domaine Serene wine clubs, depending upon taste and budget, and purchase wine to take home. Make sure that wine is safely stowed for transit; at an average price of $75 per bottle for its pinot noirs, Domaine Serene will never be a leader in low prices. If it's not sold out, you can be the first on your block to purchase a $200 bottle of Domaine Serene's exclusive pinot noir cuvée called Monogram. Although many wine tourists and even connoisseurs might consider $200 a bottle to be pricey, it sends a message to the world that Oregon makes premier wines and should not be taken lightly.

DOMAINE SERENE
opened: 1990
winemaker(s): Eleni Papadakis
location: 6555 NE Hilltop Lane, Dayton, OR 97114
phone: 503-864-4600
web: www.domaineserene.com
e-mail: info@domaineserene.com
picnic area: Yes
fee: $15 tasting fee
hours: Wednesday through Monday 11–4

 **BEST Views**

DIRECTIONS: Heading southbound on I-5 from Portland, take exit 294 toward OR-99W/Tigard/ Newberg. Proceed about 16 miles to Dundee and turn right (west) onto NE Archery Summit Rd. Go 1.9 miles and turn right (west) onto NE Breyman Orchards Rd and go .4 miles. Turn left (west) onto NE Hilltop Lane, and look for winery on your right.

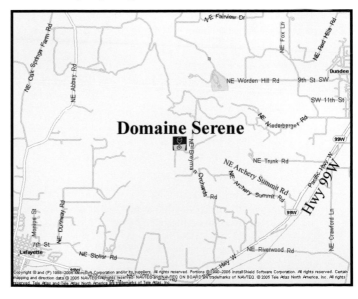

Vista Hills Vineyard & Winery 7

Dear John and Nancy McClintock and David and Cristy McDaniel,

I am writing to you, the owners of Vista Hills Vineyard & Winery, with a simple request. Please move out. I ask this favor so that I can live in the Treehouse, greet visitors, and tend the 42-acre vineyard.

I understand that this might be asking a lot, but please be assured that I will keep things in good shape. For example, I promise to maintain your beautifully built Northwest-style Treehouse: The exterior landscape and interior furnishings will not be neglected. Visitors will continue to marvel at the pond in front and gape when they enter as they look through the Treehouse windows toward the vineyards, the valley below, and the Coast Range in the distance. And you know that picnic table nestled in the fir and oak trees below? I promise to take good care of it and think of you often as I have a glass of Vista Hills pinot noir while marveling at the sunset.

I appreciate your commitment to giving back to the community. From what I understand about the Clint Foundation and its mission of providing student aid to working college students, I both applaud and promise to support it. That 10 percent of your profits that go to the Clint Foundation will continue under my stewardship.

Besides leaving me the keys to that gorgeous front door, I ask one more thing — that you leave the supply of pinot noir and pinot gris at the Treehouse. I'll need it, for the visitors who will continue to sample Vista Hills wines, the bike riders who will use the Treehouse as their base camp for group rides, and the weddings and other events that will continue to bring great joy to others. Oh, and I'll need some of it for myself. You see, everything about the taste and feel of your pinot noir reflects the *terroir* of this heaven-on-earth spot on top of the Dundee Hills. It's a homerun in my book.

The guest winemaker program that you have so artfully engineered will continue, featuring familiar names such as Montalieu, Mortimer, Sanders, Silva, Seufert, and Stevenson. All are master artisans, and their skills and talents will leave their marks on future vintages.

Thank you in advance for your consideration.

Steve Roberts, the WineTrails Guy

VISTA HILLS VINEYARD & WINERY
opened: 2007
winemaker(s): Guest winemakers
location: 6475 NE Hilltop Lane, Dayton, OR 97114
phone: 503-864-3200
web: www.vistahillsvineyard.com
e-mail: info@vistahillsvineyard.com
picnic area: Yes
wheelchair access: Yes
weddings: Yes
tours: Yes
fee: $10 tasting fee waived with purchase
hours: Daily 12–5 or by appointment

BEST Views

DIRECTIONS: From Portland and points north take I-5 south. Take exit 294 for 99W to Tigard / Newberg. Follow 99W through Tigard, Sherwood, Newberg, and Dundee. About 3 miles past the town of Dundee, turn right onto McDougall Road at the far end of the weigh station. Take first right onto Breyman Orchards Road and follow it up the hill for 2 mile. Near the top, turn left at Hilltop Lane, and follow the paved road until you see the Vista Hills Vineyard sign.

From points south, take 99W heading north. After going through the town of Lafayette, continue and pass the intersection with Hwy 18 (which will be on your right). Turn left onto McDougall just before the weigh station. Follow the directions above from McDougall Road to the winery.

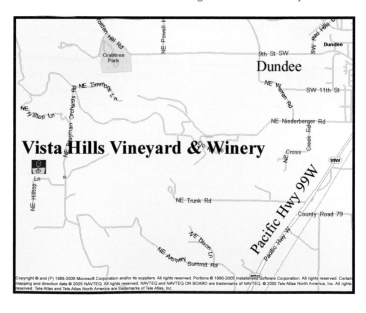

Winter's Hill Vineyard 🎱

First off, I love the name — Winter's Hill Vineyard. For me, it conjures up the image of a lone leafless tree perched on a snow-covered hill. The name, however, has more to do with Emily Gladhart's maiden name, Winter, than any romantic notions. In 1961, her parents purchased a fruit and grain farm in the Dundee Hills. Under the guidance of Emily, her

husband, Peter Gladhart, son Russell and his wife Delphine Gladhart, Winter's Hill Vineyard evolved.

Today the Winter's Hill Vineyard has a full 35 acres under production, mostly planted with pinot gris and pinot noir. The vineyard and the wines are certified as Salmon Safe and sustainable by LIVE of Oregon and the Pacific Rivers Council. The vineyard enjoys an ideal location facing west toward the Coast Range and experiences cool air from the ocean to mitigate hot summer days. The Jory soils, summer heat and cool nights all conspire to create superb grapes for the "pinotphiles" amongst us.

At the time of my visit, construction was under way for a new winery facility. You could see its footprint in the earth and equipment standing by. The target date for opening is 2009. The small tasting room where the family currently pours wine for eager fans and newbies will remain open. Within, there is plenty of space to sample wines, view quilts on exhibit, and shop for local merchandise from "local farmers, fishermen, and monks." If you haven't experienced the Brigittine Monks gourmet fudge, now is your chance. How about Trappist Abbey Fruitcake or Datenut Cake? My personal favorite, hazelnuts by Freddy Guys, are crunchy nuggets of pure joy.

Russell Gladhart's spouse, Delphine, who hails from Lyon, France, is the winemaker for Winter's Hill Vineyard. Armed with a degree in viticulture and enology, Delphine makes excellent wines for all seasons. Current production is around 5,000 cases. Winter is an excellent time to sip her pinot blanc and dessert wine. Spring and summer are perfect for her pinot gris and rosé. And autumn is the time to enjoy Winter's Hill pinot noir release.

If you can't find Winter's Hill Vineyard wines in your community, consider joining Winter's Hill Vineyard's Cellar Club. There's no charge for joining, and you benefit from significant discounts on your deliveries. What's more, Winter's Hill allows you to customize the wines you order. These wines are fantastic any time of the year.

WINTER'S HILL VINEYARD
opened: 1998
winemaker(s): Delphine Gladhart
location: 6451 Hilltop Lane, Dayton, OR 97114
phone: 503-864-4610
web: www.wintershillwine.com
e-mail: info@wintershillwine.com
picnic area: Yes
wheelchair access: Yes
fee: $5 tasting fee refundable with purchase
hours: Daily 12–5 May through October; Saturday
and Sunday 12–5 December through April,
and by appointment

BEST Views

DIRECTIONS: From Dundee take SR-99W [Pacific Hwy W] for 2.3 miles. Turn right (west) onto NE Archery Summit Rd and go 1.9 miles. Turn right (west) onto NE Breyman Orchards Rd and go .4 miles. Turn left (west) onto NE Hilltop Ln and go .3 miles. Arrive at 6451 NE Hilltop Lane.

From Dayton go east on SE Amity-Dayton Hwy [SE Ferry St.] for .1 of a mile. Turn left (northwest) onto SR-221 [SE 3rd St.] and go .3 miles. Take ramp (right) onto SR-18 [SR-233] for 1.3 miles to OR-18. Continue on SR -99W [Pacific Hwy W] for .5 miles. Turn left (west) onto NE McDougall Rd and go .2 miles. Turn right (north) onto NE Breyman Orchards Rd and go 1.4 miles. Turn left to stay on NE Breyman Orchards Rd and go .4 miles. Turn left (west) onto NE Hilltop Lane.

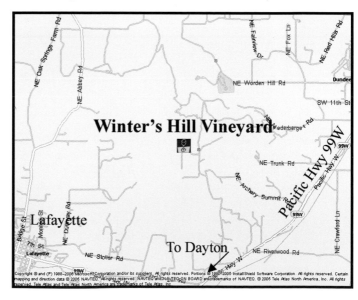

177

White Rose Wines 🤍 9

"Why is there a dragon on the label?" I asked upon entering White Rose Vineyard's low-ceilinged tasting room. Unfortunately, as soon as I got my question out, the tasting-room pourer needed to respond to an outstretched hand holding an empty wine glass.

Never mind, I thought, I would ask him later.

Soon I was part of the crowd holding out my wine glass for a taste. Sure enough, the pinot offered had that classic Dundee Hills *terroir*: cherry red, light, with flowery notes and a great finish, and devoid of big tannins — that's the Dundee Hills pinot noir's profile I have come to know. I looked around for owner/winemaker Greg Sanders to compliment him on this special pinot. Unfortunately, Greg wasn't in town that day, but had he been there I would have thanked him for this truly enjoyable pinot. I could have also queried him about that intriguing dragon on the label.

With a little bit of research I discovered that White Rose Vineyard's vines are 20- to 25-year-old Pommard clones from Dijon. Left untended, they might produce four to five tons of grapes per acre. However, through aggressive pruning, White Rose Vineyards produces only 1.25 tons per acre. The result is superconcentrated, intense flavors that other wineries such as Torii Mor, Panther Creek an St. Innocent have known about for years.

Greg makes about 1,500 to 2,000 cases of pinot noir annually, which fulfills his need to produce small-lot wines. He's not interested in running a 100,000-case production facility. Together with his vineyard and cellar teams, Greg is involved in each step of the winemaking cycle — from bud break to bottling. In essence, he gives birth to each vintage. So it stands to reason that his labels bear the names of his sons Mercotti and Quiotee, and daughter Nekaia.

Outside the big timbered tasting room and winery, visitors can soak in an amazing view of the vineyard with Willamette Valley in the distance. Grab a chair, kick back, relax, and try to remember to ask about the significance of that dragon!

WHITE ROSE WINES
winemaker(s): Greg Sanders
location: 6250 NE Hilltop Lane, Dayton, OR 97114
phone: 949-275-8021
web: www.whiterosewines.com
e-mail: angngreg@adelphia.net
picnic area: Yes
fee: $10 tasting fee
hours: Daily 11–5

BEST Views

DIRECTIONS: **From Portland** take I-5 South to exit 294 for 99W toward Tigard/Newberg. Follow SR-99W through Tigard, Sherwood, Newberg, and Dundee. About 3 miles past the town of Dundee, turn right onto McDougall Road, just at the far end of the weigh station. Take first right onto Breyman Orchards Road and follow up the hill for 1.75 miles. Near the top, turn left at Hilltop Lane and follow the paved road. Turn left and follow the gravel road until you see two houses. Just before the house entrance turn left, and you will see the winery just ahead.

If heading northbound on SR-99W past the town of Lafayette, continue and pass the intersection with Hwy 18 (on your right). Turn left onto McDougall Rd just before the weigh station. Take the first right onto Breyman Orchards Road. Follow Breyman Orchards Road up the hill for 1.75 miles. Near the top. Turn left at Hilltop Lane, and follow the paved road, turn left and follow the gravel road until you see two houses. Just before the house entrance turn left, and you will see the winery just ahead.

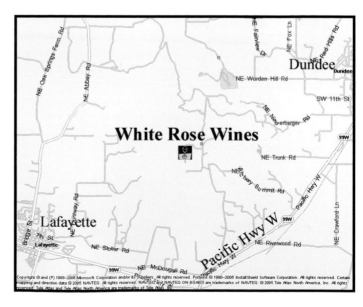

Stoller Vineyard and Winery 🔟

Do you think it's possible to be too green when it comes to environmentally conscious winemaking? Probably not, but Stoller Vineyard and Winery comes close.

At Stoller, you discover Willamette Valley's only solar power-driven, gravity-flow, and LEED (Leadership in Energy and Environmental Design) Gold-certified winery. Its nearby neighbor, Sokol Blosser, is LEED certified for its barrel room, whereas Stoller's

certification applies to its entire facility, hence the Gold level of certification. The winery integrates gravity flow, solar-powered electricity, and wastewater reclamation under one roof. In terms of sustainability, it sets the bar for other wineries.

Approaching Stoller Vineyard and Winery off McDougall Road, you see the prominent winery and the wide expanse of the 175-acre south-sloping vineyard. I found it hard to imagine that this used to be a turkey farm. When the turkey industry and the Stoller turkey business went south, Bill and Cathy Stoller saw the opportunity to turn the turkey farm into a premium vineyard. They understood that the south-facing slope, with its rocky soil and hardened Jory clay, is just the kind of terrain grape vines love. That was back in the mid-'90s, and today nearly half of the property is under production, primarily in pinot noir.

Pulling into the parking area, I saw the disc golf baskets nearby and regretted that I wouldn't have time to play a round. In Italy, you find bocce courts; in Oregon, you find disc golf courses. I looked around for the winery pugs, Pinot Noir and Chardonnay, but didn't see them. As I walked toward the tasting room, I recalled that in 2001, the Stollers began reserving part of the grape harvest for their own label. Other wineries — including Adelsheim, Argyle, and Domaine Drouhin — had purchased Stoller Vineyard fruit in the past, so the Stollers knew their grapes delivered.

In the tasting room, visitors experience an assortment of full-flavored pinot noirs and chardonnays, plus a delightful pinot noir rosé (perfect for pairing with turkey perhaps?). Winemaker Melissa Burr has crafted marvelous wines; *Wine Press Northwest* certainly thinks so. In its Spring 2008 issue, the wine magazine noted of the 2006 Stoller JV Pinot Noir, "It opens with inviting aromas of cherries, red peppercorns and blackberries, followed by richly structured flavors that reminded us of a freshly baked cherry pie." Cherry pie? I'm all over it!

STOLLER VINEYARD AND WINERY
opened: 2005
winemaker(s): Melissa Burr
location: 16161 NE McDougall Road,
Dayton, OR 97114
phone: 503-864-3404
web: www.stollervineyards.com
e-mail: info@stollervineyards.com
picnic area: Yes
wheelchair access: Yes
fee: $10 tasting fee refundable with 6
bottle purchase
hours: Daily 11–5

 BEST Views

DIRECTIONS: From Dundee take SR-99W [Pacific Hwy W] 4 miles heading southwest. Turn right (north) onto NE McDougall Rd and go .4 miles.

From Lafayette take SR-99W east for about 1 mile. Keep left onto NE McDougall Rd, go 1.1 miles, and arrive at 16161 NE McDougall Rd.

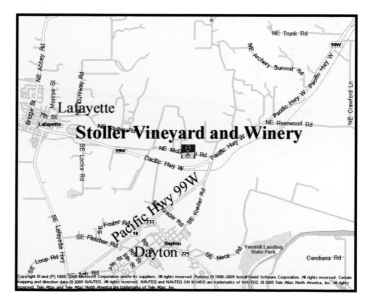

Anne Amie Vineyards 11

Anne Amie's owner is Dr. Robert Pamplin; its winemaker, Thomas Houseman; and its grape grower, Jason Tosch. The interplay between these three men is what distinguishes this winery. In 1999, Pamplin purchased Chateau Benoit with the goal of producing ultrapremium wines under a new label — Anne Amie Vineyards (named for his two daughters). Pamplin would require one lengthy entry in *Who's Who*. He's described as one of Oregon's most forward-thinking philanthropists and businessmen, which is evident by just glimpsing his résumé: businessman, philanthropist, farmer, minister and author of 13 books, including two Book-of-the-Month Club selections. He has earned degrees in

business, economics, accounting, education and theology. But that's just a gnat's eyebrow of his accomplishments; there's simply not enough space here to note the many businesses he runs.

Following a dancing career that led him to New York City, Thomas Houseman's interest turned to winemaking; his background includes stints at Husch Vineyards in California's Anderson Valley, followed by winemaking positions Down Under at a number of New Zealand wineries, which led to his role as assistant winemaker for Ponzi Vineyards in Oregon. When the Anne Amie Vineyards winemaking opportunity presented itself, he jumped at it, bringing his passion for pinot noir with him.

Jason Tosch, winegrower extraordinaire, got his degree in horticulture from Oregon State University and, like Houseman, worked at Ponzi Vineyards for two years prior to taking on the challenge of nurturing Anne Amie's many vineyards. Tosch's goals were to employ more sustainable practices in the vineyard. To that end, he's succeeded in obtaining both LIVE and Salmon Safe certifications for Anne Amie Vineyards.

I encourage all WineTrail enthusiasts, when visiting Anne Amie Vineyards, to take a just-purchased bottle or glass of Anne Amie wine and retreat to the outside deck. There, you can gaze over the magnificence of the vineyard below and the Coast Range to the west. Quite likely, your wine of choice will be the winery's flagship pinot noir. As you sip your pinot, just remember that it was the symbiosis, of owner, winemaker, and grape grower that brings you this pleasurable, memorable moment.

ANNE AMIE VINEYARDS
opened: 1999
winemaker(s): Thomas Houseman
location: 6580 NE Mineral Springs Road,
Carlton, OR 97111
phone: 503-864-2991
web: www.anneamie.com
e-mail: contactus@anneamie.com
picnic area: Yes
wheelchair access: Yes
fee: $5 for white flight and pinot noir; $10 for
extended flight refunded with purchase of $50
or more
hours: Daily 10–5 March through December; January
and February: Monday through Thursday by
appointment only, Friday through Sunday 10–5

DIRECTIONS: From Portland take I-5 south and exit at Hwy 99W. Follow 99W through Newberg, Dundee, and finally Lafayette. As you leave Lafayette, turn right at the blue highway sign for Anne Amie. Follow NE Mineral Springs Rd for approximately 1.5 miles until you see Anne Amie Vineyards sign. Take a right at the sign, and follow the lane a short distance to the winery.

From McMinnville, head north on SR-99W [NE Baker St.] for about 6 miles to the town of Lafeyette. Look for blue sign to Anne Amie Vineyards. Go left (northwest) onto NE Mineral Springs Rd and travel 2 miles to arrive at the winery.

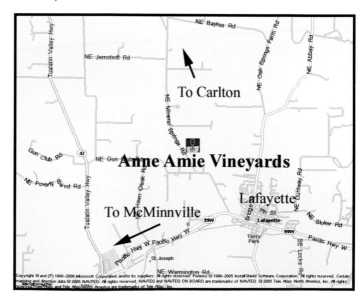

183

McMinnville
Wine Trail

Yamhill Valley Vineyards

The McMinnville Wine Trail can be summarized by the following: history, location and soil. When it comes to history, it was David Lett, an Oregon winemaking pioneer, who transformed a turkey processing plant into a winery in 1970. Now nearly 40 years later, The Eyrie Vineyards continues its reputation as an outstanding producer of fine wines. But they are not alone. Today over a dozen wineries have sprung up in close proximity to them, including Panther Creek Cellars, R. Stuart and Co., Anthony Dell Cellars, and Walnut City Wineworks.

Lying to the east of the Coast Range provides protection from the moist air of the Pacific and helps explain the relative dryness of the area. The soil itself is made of marine sedimentary loams and silts and provides for exceptional drainage characteristics. Industry specialists argue that grapes need to struggle to bring out the best in flavors. Hot summers, cool nights, relative dryness, loam and silt soils, all conspire to make McMinnville a unique agriculture area for growing noble grapes. It's little wonder that over 600 acres of grapes are under cultivation in the McMinnville sub-appellation of the Willamette American Viticulture Area. Get ready to see row upon row of wonderfully maintained vineyards in your visits to Evergreen Vineyards, Maysara Winery, and Yamhill Valley Vineyards.

McMinnville WineTrail
1 Stone Wolf Vineyards
2 Walnut City WineWorks
3 The Eyrie Vineyards
4 Anthony Dell Cellars
5 Panther Creek Cellars
6 R. Stuart & Co.
7 Evergreen Vineyards
8 Yamhill Valley Vineyards
9 Maysara Winery

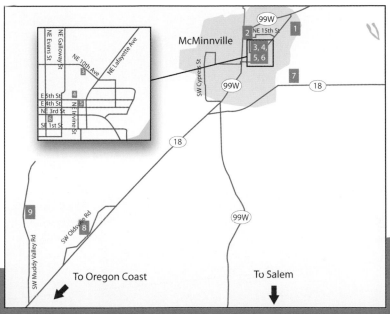

Region:	**North Willamette Valley Wine Country**
# of tasting rooms on tour:	**9**
# of satellite tasting rooms:	**1**
Estimate # of days for tour:	**2**
Getting around:	**Car and foot**
Key Events:	❑ **In March, McMinnville's Wine & Food Classic – call 503-472-4033 or visit www.macwfc.org for event schedule and ticketing.**
	❑ **Memorial Weekend in Wine Country – Willamette Valley – visit www.willamettewines.com.**
	❑ **In July, McMinnville's International Pinot Noir Celebration – call 800-775-4762 or visiting www.ipnc.org.**
	❑ **Wine Country Thanksgiving – Willamette Valley – call 503-646-2985 or visit www.willamettewines.com.**
Tips:	❑ **NW Wine Bar in McMinnville's historic district – fabulous. Call 503-435-1295 for hours.**
	❑ **Need a place to stay? Consider McMenamin's Oregon Hotel in downtown McMinnville. Call 888- 472-8427.**
	❑ **Budget a few hours for Evergreen Vineyards. It's out of this world!**

 Best: ❑ **Eats: R. Stuart & Co., Evergreen Vineyards.**
❑ **Gift shop: Evergreen Vineyards.**
❑ **Views: Yamhill Valley Vineyards, Maysara Winery.**

Stone Wolf Vineyards ▣

Located on the outskirts of McMinnville, right off Lafayette Avenue, Stone Wolf Vineyards is a convenient stop on the McMinnville WineTrail. It's a common occurrence on WineTrail treks to be greeted by a winery dog. Being that this is Stone Wolf Vineyards, wouldn't it be interesting to have a winery wolf to greet you? Second thought, that might not be good for business. Instead, Stone Wolf visitors are welcomed by a winery cat named Frank. He and Sinatra have something in common: the blue eyes. Hence, the feline's name.

Stone Wolf Vineyards produces its wine from one of two estate vineyards located in the Eola Hills of the Willamette Valley. At approximately 20 years of age, the vines are some of the oldest in the state. At Stone Wolf's relaxed tasting room, visitors can partake of a

number of its estate wines, including pinot noir, chardonnay, pinot gris, Müller-Thurgau, and its popular dessert wine called Idylle, made for people who have a sweet tooth — like me.

Linda Lindsay is the driving force and winemaker for Stone Wolf Vineyards. Linda's goal from the beginning was to make food-friendly wine. To this end, she makes judicious use of oak in order to lower the tannin effect. Consequently, these are wines you can purchase today and feel comfortable serving tonight with your roasted turkey or grilled chicken salad.

By the way, have you heard the legend of Stone Wolf? I had not, but according to the winery, "The stone wolf stands tall and proud as guardian of the vineyards. From his stone sanctuary, he silently protects the land, his watchful golden eyes wary of any threat. If you let the magic of the stone wolf fable grace you with its spirit and strength, we believe you will discover the magic of the crop he safeguards — as fruit on the vine, the wine in your hand, and finally in the gift of a memory we hope you will rekindle again and again." With this legend in mind, be sure to check out the winery's label — the wolf's staring eyes are mesmerizing.

However, the only animal I saw was Frank, and his blue eyes were anything but watchful. In between cat naps, he displayed a rather laissez-faire attitude toward any potential threat. He's a great representative for the winery: relaxed, happy-go-lucky, and approachable.

STONE WOLF VINEYARDS
opened: 1996
winemaker(s): Linda Lindsay
location: 2155 NE Lafayette Avenue,
McMinnville, OR 97128
phone: 503-434-9025
web: www.stonewolfvineyards.com
e-mail: stone@stonewolfvineyards.com
picnic area: Yes
fee: $3 tasting fee refundable with purchase
hours: Daily 12–5

DIRECTIONS: From McMinnville, go north onto SR-99W [NE Baker St.] and go 2.4 miles.
Turn right (south) onto NE Lafayette Ave. and proceed .5 miles. Look for the winery at 2155 NE
Lafayette Ave.

From Yamhill on SR-47 [S Maple St.] heading south 3.4 miles. Turn left (east) onto SR-47 [W Main
St.] and go .1 miles. Turn right (south) onto SR-47 [S Pine St.] 4.4 miles. Bear right (west) onto
SR-99W [Pacific Hwy W] and proceed .6 miles. Turn left (south) onto NE Lafayette Ave. for
.5 miles and arrive at the winery.

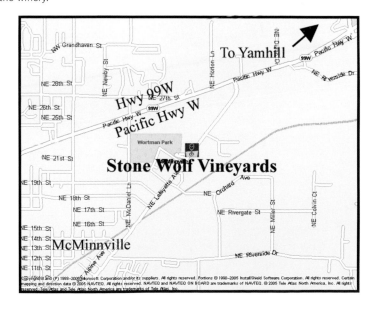

Walnut City WineWorks

It's not a stretch to say that McMinnville is the hub of Oregon wine touring; a couple of dozen wineries to experience, fine dining, great lodging, museums, and rich history all conspire to offer visitors a great getaway. The surrounding farmland is populated with vineyards galore, giving shutterbugs loads of photo opportunities.

However, I'll let you in on a secret: All that is McMinnville can be found under one roof at Walnut City WineWorks. Not that you can sleep there, mind you, but visitors will get

Jennifer Kadell, Courtney Trufant, Barrett Rostek, Miguel Lopez and Erin Baird (l to r).

to know a variety of wine labels and taste a host of varietals from a number of Willamette Valley's appellations — all in this one setting. The place is historical, too: The red building housing the wineworks was the home of a walnut-processing facility before morphing into the Walnut City WineWorks in 1999.

John Davidson and John Gilpin, the creators of Walnut City WineWorks, launched the winery to display their vineyard's fruit. With more than 200 acres of premium wine grapes — most of them pinot noir — John D. and John G. coined the motto "Growing great wines from the ground up." And speaking of great wines, it's not too often that you can visit a tasting room and experience a bounty of varieties under different labels. Among those represented are Walnut City WineWorks, Bernard-Machado, Robinson Reserve, and Z'IVO Wines. Make no mistake, pinot noir is front and center for these various brands, but there's room enough for chardonnay, viognier, cabernet sauvignon, and pinot gris for visitors to enjoy. All this production is under the watchful eye of chief winemaker Miguel Lopez and a bevy of assistant winemakers and cellar rats.

Walnut City WineWorks is not a custom crush facility. To gain entry, you must be a vineyard owner. Once admitted, participants can take advantage of equipment, space, and expertise in a collaborative environment.

In this unpretentious space, visitors can taste, savor, learn, and laugh.

WALNUT CITY WINEWORKS
winemaker(s): Miguel Lopez et al.
location: 475 NE 17th Street,
McMinnville, OR 97128
phone: 503-472-3215
web: www.walnutcitywineworks.com
e-mail: wine@walnutcitywineworks.com
fee: $5 tasting fee refundable with purchase
hours: Thursday through Sunday 11–4:30

DIRECTIONS: **From McMinnville** go east onto SE 1st St. and then an immediate left (north) onto SR-99W [NE Baker St.] for .9 miles. Turn right (east) onto NE 17th St. and proceed .2 miles to Walnut City WineWorks.

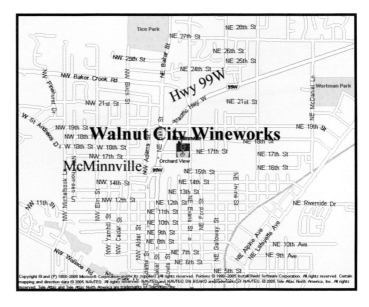

The Eyrie Vineyards 3

"[Eyrie] is the birthplace of quality wine in Oregon. The wines... are simply legendary."
— Larousse Encyclopedia of Wine

Launched in 1966 by David and Diana Lett (they planted pinot noir vines on their honeymoon), The Eyrie Vineyards has achieved many firsts, including growing and bottling the first pinot gris in America, and the first pinot noir and chardonnay in the Willamette Valley. David also evolved the single-vineyard concept by bottling pinot noir using vineyard-designated grapes. Eventually, through this labor of love, David, aka "Papa Pinot," put Oregon on the pinot map. He entered his wines in prestigious wine

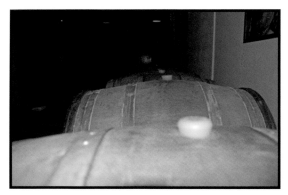

competitions in France in 1979 and 1980 and came away with top honors after competing against the traditional Burgundy biggies. Clearly, it must have sent the citizens of Beaune scurrying to their atlases to figure out where Oregon is located.

WineTrail note: Sadly David Lett passed away in October 2008 following a long illness. His original 13 acres of pinot noir plantings showed the world that Oregon produces great pinot noir. Today over 10,000 acres of pinot noir are planted throughout Oregon adding to his legacy as one of Oregon's wine growing pioneers.

David's winemaking style has influenced how wine is made in Oregon ever since. Throughout Oregon, you hear a common refrain about using a "hands off" approach to making wine as a way of preserving the flavor of the harvest. David employed this Burgundian method for producing pinot noir, which entails minimal racking, extended lees contact, complete and spontaneous malolactic fermentation, no fining, and minimal filtration. Although making pinot noir wine involves a minimalist approach, growing pinot noir (which has earned the nickname "heartbreak grape") requires major intervention in the vineyard: constant caring, pruning, and nurturing. This most vulnerable of noble grapes is susceptible to the vagaries of each year's wind, rain, and heat, and as a result, each vintage possesses its own flavor profile.

Visitors to The Eyrie Vineyards tasting room in McMinnville are surprised to enter a rather dated facility devoid of surrounding vineyards and an ultra-modern gravity-fed winery. However, David discovered early in his career that the refurbished poultry plant works just fine. Now under the direction and winemaking leadership of the Letts' son Jason, wine tourists come to experience the family's award-winning pinot noirs, pinot gris, chardonnay, and pinot blanc. Just as in France, the torch passes from one generation to another, and the family tradition continues.

THE EYRIE VINEYARDS
opened: 1966
winemaker(s): Jason Lett
location: 935 NE 10th Avenue,
McMinnville, OR 97128
phone: 503-472-6315
web: www.eyrievineyards.com
e-mail: info@eyrievineyards.com
fee: $5 tasting fee subject to change
hours: Wednesday through Sunday 12–5

DIRECTIONS: **From Portland and points north**, take I-5 south toward Salem/Tigard. Take the OR-99W exit (exit number 294) toward Tigard/Newberg. Merge onto OR-99W south and continue for about 20 miles. Turn left onto OR-18W (toward Ocean Beaches). Continue to follow OR-18W for about 6 miles. Take the McMinnville exit on the right and enter McMinnville. Turn right onto Lafayette Ave. (at the first stop light). Turn left onto 10th Ave. Eyrie is located on the northeast corner of 10th and Alpine.

From points south, take I-5 north toward Salem. Take OR-22 west toward Dallas and Ocean Beaches. Travel through Salem and continue on OR-22 for about 15 miles, until you reach Hwy 99W. Follow 99W north for about 20 miles into McMinnville. Turn right onto 3rd St. Follow 3rd until you reach Johnson St. (the streets are alphabetical). Johnson St. is also called Lafayette Ave. Turn left onto Johnson/Lafayette Ave. Turn left onto 10th Ave.

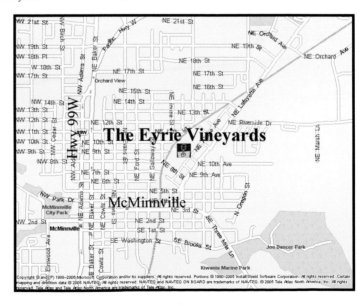

Anthony Dell Cellars

Truth is, I didn't actually make it to Anthony Dell Cellars. Not that I didn't try. I ventured to McMinnville's "Wine Quarter" on two occasions and, as luck would have it, the winery was closed. I took a couple of pictures and thought to myself to call ahead next time. However, with Panther Creek and The Eyrie Vineyards nearby, all was not lost.

Therefore, I leave it up to you, dear WineTrail trekker, to venture forth and discover for yourself Anthony Dell Cellars' story. Sure, I know a little about it from my research. Launched by Douglas Drawbond and Joy Means in 2002, the winery produces fewer than 1,000 cases of wine annually. You can expect to taste pinot noir and pinot gris that began in their Sunset Ridge Vineyards in the Eola Hills, and cabernet sauvignon, syrah and red table wine made from fruit sourced in the Rogue Valley, most of it from Del Rio Vineyards.

I love what they say on the Anthony Dell Cellars website. Check this out: "We're big into food. We believe wine is a food and should be enjoyed with other foods …. We believe that wine will get you through times of no money better than money will get you through times of no wine. Most of all, we believe in ourselves. Our wine is our art, our craft, our gift to the world." Now that's a healthy attitude, and I believe it gives an idea of what's in store for your visit. Odds are that Doug or Joy, or both, will be there pouring, the tasting room will be small, and you won't contend with busloads of wine tourists. To me, it's the perfect combination for a memorable experience!

If you do venture to Anthony Dell Cellars, please shoot me an email at info@winetrailsnw.com. Let me know what you discovered — what to look for, sample, and experience. I would be most appreciative. I promise, in the second edition of this book, to incorporate your feedback into a description of the winery and share with other WineTrail enthusiasts the nuances and unique character that define Anthony Dell Cellars.

ANTHONY DELL CELLARS
winemaker(s): Douglas Drawbond
location: 845 5th Street, Suite 300,
McMinnville, OR 97128
phone: 503-910-8874
web: www.anthonydellcellars.com
e-mail: info@anthonydellcellars.com
fee: Tasting fee may apply
hours: Friday through Sunday 12–5

DIRECTIONS: From Carlton go south on SR-47 [S Pine St.] for 4.4 miles. Bear right (west) onto SR-99W [Pacific Hwy W] and go 2.8 miles. Turn left (east) onto NE 5th St. and arrive at Anthony Dell Winery in .4 miles.

From Sheridan take SR-18 [Salmon River Hwy] north about 11 miles. Keep left onto Salmon River Spur and go .3 miles toward SR-99W/McMinnville. Bear right (northeast) onto SR-18 [Salmon River Spur] .3 miles. Keep straight onto SR-99W [SW Baker St.] and go 1.4 miles. Turn right (east) onto NE 5th St. and go .4 miles to Anthony Dell Winery.

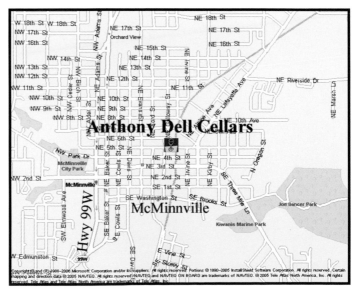

193

Panther Creek Cellars ⑤

The Lab's name is Zooey, and if there were a "mellowest wine dog" award, Zooey would be the recipient. Zooey is not a yappy dog; she doesn't feel the need to announce her presence nor does she seek your hand for petting. In this sense, Zooey symbolizes the

Panther Creek Cellars' confident manner, secure in the knowledge that it consistently produces some of Oregon's best pinot noirs.

Located in McMinnville's 1923 former power plant, Panther Creek Cellars excels in producing single-vineyard pinot noirs year after year. Winemaking falls under the watchful eye of Michael Stevenson, whose straightforward goal is to produce ultrapremium pinot noir that evokes the vineyard where the grapes are grown. Moderately priced, these wines are ready to take home and open the evening it's purchased, or conversely, cellared for many years.

Liz Chambers, the current owner of Panther Creek Cellars, purchased the winery from Ron and Linda Kaplan, who had purchased the winery from Ken Wright. If the name Linda Kaplan rings a bell, it's for good reason. She is the author of the critically acclaimed *My First Crush: Misadventures in Wine Country*. A fun and informative account of her experience on the front lines of Oregon winemaking, the book is sold at Panther Creek Cellars' tasting room (if still in stock). For folks with a modicum of interest in Northwest wines, this is the book for you. Linda's engaging writing style is chockfull of information about soil, climate, and vine trivia, but is also infused with humor and stories of real people doing real work.

Panther Creek's handsome red brick facility is both a tasting room and working winery. Here, WineTrail trekkers can swirl and taste the *terroir* associated with such notable vineyards as Temperance Hill, Freedom Hill, and Shea Vineyard. Can't make up your mind which vineyard-designated label you prefer? No worries, there's a pinot cuvée priced at around $30. And, lest you think that Panther Creek Cellars is all about pinot noir, it also offers pinot gris, chardonnay, and the rare melón from De Ponte Vineyard. Still, these whites account for only 10 percent of the 7,500 cases produced by Panther Creek Cellars annually.

WineTrail warning: As you depart the tasting room with your newly acquired bottles of wine, be careful not to trip over Zooey. She's likely to be sleeping or engaging in doggy yoga (the "downward-facing dog" pose, natch) and not notice you.

PANTHER CREEK CELLARS
opened: 1986
winemaker(s): Michael Stevenson
location: 455 NE Irvine Street,
McMinnville, OR 97128
phone: 503-472-8080
web: www.panthercreekcellars.com
e-mail: Info@panthercreekcellars.com
picnic area: Yes
fee: $5 refundable with purchase
hours: Daily 12–5

DIRECTIONS: **From McMinnville**, head south on SR-99W [SE Adams St.] a very short distance and turn left (east) onto SE 1st St. Proceed .5 miles. Turn left (north) onto NE Irvine St., go .2 miles and arrive at Panther Creek Cellars.

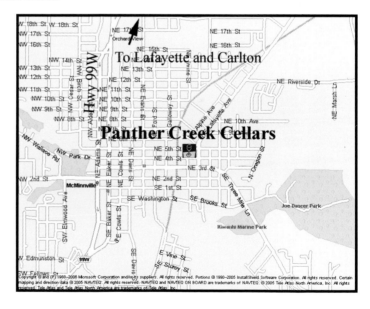

R. Stuart & Co. 6

The story behind R. Stuart & Co. is R. Stuart — or Rob Stuart to be exact — and the company he keeps. Rob's résumé features winemaking experience gained up and down the West Coast, with a special focus on pinot noir. Prior to starting R. Stuart & Co., Rob was

the winemaker for Erath Vineyards in nearby Dundee. However, it was only a matter of time before he created wine under his own label. The R. Stuart & Co. winery was born smack dab in the middle of McMinnville.

The "& Co." in the winery's name is the key to appreciating R. Stuart & Co., and I suspect the main company member

is Rob's wife, Maria — winery partner and the mother of their three children. She's the brains behind public relations, direct marketing, and special events for R. Stuart & Co. Needless to say, with a background that includes four years as the executive director of the International Pinot Noir Celebration (IPNC), she's well-qualified for the role.

Trish Ridgeway, the winery's sales director, is another Erath Vineyard veteran, who now makes her home in Ireland. On a regular basis, she takes a flight to the States to place R. Stuart & Co. wines in wine shops and select restaurants throughout America. This includes the company's second label, Big Fire wine, featuring literary poems on the label and liquid poetry in the bottle.

The low-key and relaxing R. Stuart & Co. Wine Bar is located in downtown McMinnville, on Third Street. At the wine bar, guests can sample R. Stuart & Co. wine flights, wine by the glass, or they can splurge for a bottle. Depending upon your taste buds' preferences, there's actually a lot to choose from, including pinot gris, a dry rosé, pinot noir (of course), a dessert wine, and a sparkling wine with the enchanting name Rosé d'Or. If quenching your thirst is a priority, there are also a couple of local beers on tap or in bottles to enjoy. What's more, there are plenty of nibblies to pair with the wines and beer. Choices abound, with such mouthwatering eats as *chèvre* in salsa rossa, savory Asiago cookies, Juniper Grove cheese tomme with Molly's Red Onion Marmalade, and an intriguing rustic Oregon country *pâté*.

Posted on one of the walls of the wine bar are the seven house rules. Space doesn't permit listing all seven here, but rule no. 7 speaks volumes about R. Stuart Co.'s *raison d'être*: "Good friends, good food, good wine. Period."

R. STUART & CO.
winemaker(s): Rob Stuart
location: 528 NE Third Street,
McMinnville, OR 97128
phone: 503-472-4477
web: www.rstuartandco.com
e-mail: winery@rstuartandco.com
fee: White/rose flight $6; Pinot noir flight $8
hours: Wednesday through Saturday 12–7;
Sunday 12–5

BEST Eats

DIRECTIONS: Heading southbound on I-5 from Portland, take exit 294 toward OR-99W/Tigard/
Newberg. Proceed about 22 miles toward McMinnville. Turn left (south) onto SR-18 [SR-233] and
go 6.4 miles. Turn right onto ramp toward Salmon River Spur. The road name changes to SE Three
Mile Ln. Bear right (northwest) onto NE 3rd St., go .4 miles, and arrive at 528 NE 3rd St.

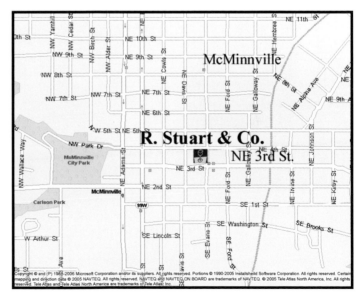

Evergreen Vineyards **7**

What are the chances of finding a tasting room situated in an air museum? You're probably thinking zero, zilch, nada. But one does exist. At McMinnville's Evergreen Aviation & Space Museum, visitors can sample wine, walk through the mammoth *Spruce*

Goose (Howard Hughes' famous HK-1 flying boat), and enjoy a movie at the IMAX Theatre. It's definitely family friendly here, and not many wineries can claim that. Here, the kids will drag their parents inside and be reluctant to leave.

With wine, it all starts in the vineyard, and Evergreen Vineyard is no exception. In possession of 160 acres of premium wine grapes — mostly pinot noir and pinot gris — Evergreen Vineyards began making wine in 2002 under the winemaking direction of Laurent Montalieu. Today visitors can sample Evergreen Vineyard wines at two different tasting rooms, both at the Evergreen Aviation & Space Museum, but in two separate buildings. WineTrail trekkers can taste a full line-up of pinot noirs, pinot gris, and rosé bearing the Spruce Goose label. For non-wine drinkers, a Spruce Goose pinot noir semi-sparkling non-alcoholic drink beckons.

On the way into the museum, take a moment to view the statue of Capt. Michael Smith, who died in car crash in 1995. It was Michael (and his father, Del Smith, president of Evergreen Aviation) who had the vision for the museum and the creative energy to successfully win the rights to move the *Spruce Goose* from Long Beach, Calif., to its new home in Yamhill County. I was told that the aircraft's former owner, the Disney Corp., paid $1 for the *Spruce Goose* but then spent more than $1,000,000 just to move the plane, which has a wingspan of nearly 320 feet. More than 200,000 visitors visit the Evergreen Aviation & Space Museum annually, and it's not all due to *Spruce Goose* fever. There's plenty of other aircraft to see, including a Lockheed SR-71A Blackbird — at 3.5 times the speed of sound, the fastest aircraft ever built — a model of a flying machine Leonardo da Vinci designed, and a replica of the Wright brothers' 1903 Flyer.

It's not necessary to purchase a ticket to the museum to experience the tasting room — it's free. However, a visit is incomplete without a tour of the museum, which opens at 9 a.m. daily. The cost to tour the museum is $13 for adults and $12 for AAA members.

EVERGREEN VINEYARDS
opened: 2002
winemaker(s): Laurent Montalieu
location: 500 NE Capt. Michael King Smith Way,
Evergreen Aviation Museum, McMinnville, OR 97128
phone: 866-434-4818
web: www.evergreenvineyards.com
e-mail: sales@evergreenvineyards.com
picnic area: Yes
wheelchair access: Yes
gift shop: Yes
fee: Complimentary wine tasting
hours: At Evergreen Aviation Museum (opens at 9);
tasting bars open daily 11–5

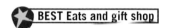 **BEST Eats and gift shop**

DIRECTIONS: When traveling south on I-5, take exit 294 for Tigard/McMinnville and follow the signs to McMinnville. Continue on Hwy 99W through Dundee until the Hwy 18 "Ocean Beaches" junction. Turn left on Hwy 18 and continue for approximately 4 miles. The Museum is on the right.

When traveling north on I-5, take exit 253 at Salem for Hwy 22/Mission St and follow the signs for Hwy 22/Mission St. through Salem. Stay to the left on Hwy 22 after crossing the Willamette River. Turn right (north) at the intersection with Hwy 99W. Continue northbound on Hwy 99W to the outskirts of McMinnville. Take the Hwy 18E exit and continue for approximately 4 miles. The Museum is on the left.

When traveling on Hwy 101, take Hwy 18 and continue until the "Y" just before entering the City of McMinnville. Stay to the right at the "Y" heading toward Portland and Dayton. Continue on Highway 18 for approximately five miles. The Museum is on the left.

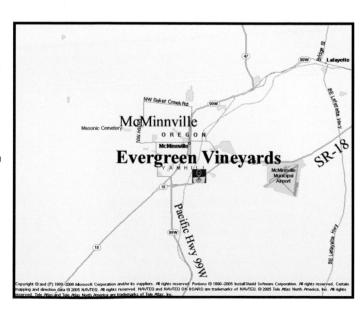

Yamhill Valley Vineyards 🎱

Noir, gris, and blanc: Since 1983, the pinot family has been alive and well at Yamhill Valley Vineyards. Situated on a 200-acre estate in the McMinnville America Viticultural Area (AVA), Yamhill Valley Vineyards focuses on estate-grown wines. Way back then,

Denis Burger and other investors recognized the unique quality of the soils and microclimate associated with this part of the Willamette Valley.

Over the years, legions of wine tourists have come to Yamhill Valley Vineyards (YVV) knowing that they will experience wines made from grapes grown right there. These are not blended grapes from various locations throughout the Willamette Valley. At YVV, you're tasting the unique flavors associated with this viticultural area. Well-known *Oregonian* wine critic Matt Kramer writes in his April 27, 2008, column, "[Yamhill Valley Vineyards pinot noir] is deeply colored, intensely flavored pinot noir of real character and depth allied to a just-right finesse and balance that keep it from being overly heavy or too fruit-intense." Kramer refers to this wine as a "someone wine," meaning that it comes from a small property and reflects an individualistic vision.

The individual at the center of YVV is winemaker Stephen Cary. Since 1991, when he joined the team at Yamhill Valley Vineyards, Stephen has shepherded each year's vintage. His focus is on day-to-day operations, but his experience provides him with a long-ranging view that stretches from one vintage to another. Stephen must be doing something right. The proof: YVV took home a gold medal at the 2008 Wine World Competitions in Chicago for its 2002 Tall Poppy Reserve Pinot Noir.

At the winery's light-filled tasting room, visitors can experience YVV's family of pinots, in addition to its estate riesling. Admittedly, the taste of the pinot gris was so good (imagine creamy lemon flavors) that my empty glass beckoned for a second helping — a rare occurrence for this WineTrails guy. With prices in the $25 range for its pinot noirs and low teens for its pinot gris, you might just want to pick up a bottle (or two) of these beauties and retreat to the outside picnic area. Definitely bring lunch or a light snack to enjoy on the outside deck. You're in the foothills of the Coast Range and in a rain shadow, so there's a good chance it won't be raining.

YAMHILL VALLEY VINEYARDS
opened: 1983
winemaker(s): Stephen Cary
location: 16250 SW Oldsville Road,
McMinnville, OR 97128
phone: 503-843-3100
web: www.yamhill.com
e-mail: info@yamhill.com
picnic area: Yes
fee: $5 tasting fee
hours: Daily 11–5 Memorial Weekend to December
23rd; closed January and February; March through
May open Thursday through Sunday

BEST Views

DIRECTIONS: From McMinnville go south on SR-99W [SE Adams St.] 1.2 miles. Keep straight onto SR-18 [SW Baker St.] and go 4 miles. Turn right (west) onto SW Oldsville Rd, go .4 miles, and arrive at Yamhill Valley Vineyards.

From Sheridan take S Bridge St south for .5 miles. Take ramp (right) onto SR-18 [Salmon River Hwy] for 5.6 miles. Bear left (north) onto SW Oldsville Rd and go 1.7 miles to Yamhill Valley Vineyards.

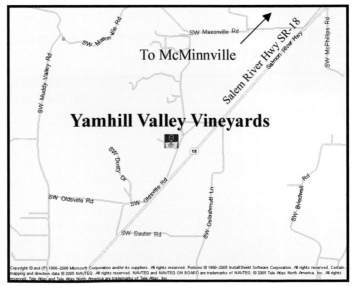

Maysara Winery 9

Turning into the entrance of this southern Yamhill County vineyard and winery, I stopped dead in my tracks. Reaching for my camera, I hopped out of my car to snap pictures of the sloping vineyard before me.

To appreciate Maysara Winery is to understand its 260-acre estate vineyard. Moe and Flora Momtazi have owned the property since 1997, and have been religious in applying

biodynamic practices, in the belief that healthy soil and healthy vines will produce superior grapes. If, as they say, 90 percent of producing good wine is a result of growing quality grapes, the Momtazis know where to focus their energies.

Biodynamic farming goes beyond not using pesticides and herbicides. Its main attributes are: 1) treating the whole vineyard as a living organism; 2) maintaining a healthy and diverse ecosystem embracing the rhythms of the earth as well as the cosmic influences; 3) employing soil husbandry and nutrient self-sufficiency (e.g., compost cocktails); and 4) never using genetically engineered plants and organisms. Bottom line: Consumers of Maysara wines can rest assured that they taste the pure fruit of Momtazi Vineyard.

Moe and Flora have backgrounds that read like a plot from a book. Following the fall of the shah of Iran in 1982, they both managed to immigrate to the United States. Moe leveraged his engineering background and gained admittance to Texas A&M. Eventually, the Momtazis made their way north and settled in McMinnville. Then, in 1997, they purchased the abandoned 532-acre wheat farm that would become Momtazi Vineyard. Today, with a 260-acre vineyard, they can proudly lay claim to the fact that they own the largest biodynamic vineyard in the Pacific Northwest.

Keeping the wine production in the family, the Momtazis have turned to their daughter, Tahmiene, a striking young woman whose youth belies her considerable education and winemaking experience acquired at other wineries both domestic and international. Inside the barrel-lined tasting room, visitors have the opportunity to sample pinot noir, pinot blanc, pinot gris, riesling, and rosé. I especially like the name of their rosé — Roseena Rosé. The word "roseena" is an ancient Persian term for a beautiful woman who naturally smells of roses. The Momtazis could readily apply it to their entire vineyard and winery.

MAYSARA WINERY
opened: 2001
winemaker(s): Tahmiene Momtazi
location: 15765 SW Muddy Valley,
McMinnville, OR 97128
phone: 503-843-1234
web: www.maysara.com
e-mail: Wine@maysara.com
picnic area: Yes
fee: $7 refundable with purchase
hours: Monday through Saturday 12–5

 BEST Views

DIRECTIONS: From McMinnville, head south on SR-99W [SE Adams St.] for 1.2 miles. Continue straight onto SR-18 [SW Baker St.] for 6.2 miles. Turn right (north) onto SW Oldsville Rd and go 1.6 miles. Turn right (north) onto SW Muddy Valley Rd and go .5 miles to the winery at .

From Amity, go west on 5th St [Bellevue-Hopewell Hwy] for .3 miles. The road name changes to Bellevue-Hopewell Hwy. Continue 5.9 miles. The road name changes to SW Muddy Valley Rd. Proceed 2.2 miles to the the winery at.

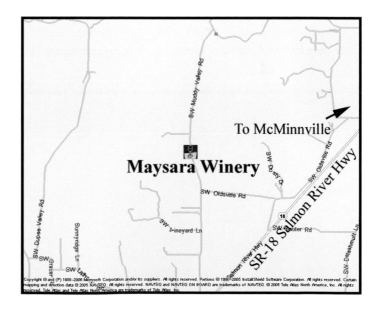

Eola - Amity
Hills North
p206

Mid Eola -
Amity Hills
p222

Eola - Amity
Hills South
p238

Salem -
Monmouth
p262

Salem

Mid Willamette Valley
WINE COUNTRY

Eola – Amity Hills North
Wine Trail

Outside Kristin Hill Winery's tasting room

Back in 1992 during the presidential election, Clinton's team coined the phrase, "It's the economy, stupid." Well, with apologies to Bill, the analogy to the Eola – Amity Hills Wine Trail North is "It's the agriculture, stupid." This is rich earth. This is farm country. This is a winegrowing region that requires a laid-back attitude to really appreciate. If you're type A and have a need to attack 10 wineries in one day, the Eola – Amity Hills Wine Trail North may not be your favorite.

You need to budget time for slow-moving farm trucks, stops at roadside fruit stands, and tasting room staff genuinely interested in how you are doing. Outside Amity (Latin for friendship) there's even a dedicated plot of land for tractor pulling contests! You'll need a car and plenty of carefree time to experience the products of Seufert Winery, Hauer of the Dauen, Methven Family Vineyards, Mystic Wines, Amity Vineyards, Kristin Hill Winery, and Coelho Winery of Amity. Pack your camera too — you're about to enter the scenic zone.

Eola – Amity Hills WineTrail North

1. Seufert Winery
2. Hauer of the Dauen
3. Methven Family Vineyards
4. Mystic Wines
5. Amity Vineyards
6. Kristin Hill Winery
7. Coelho Winery of Amity

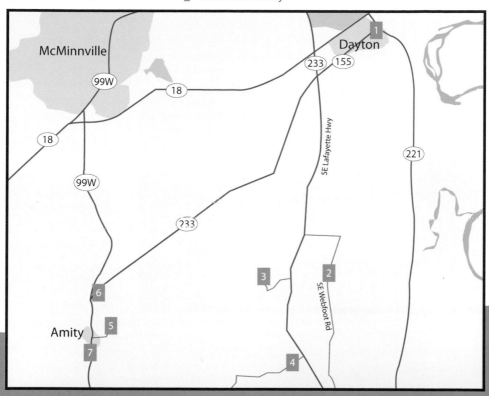

Region:	**Mid Willamette Valley Wine Country**
# of tasting rooms on tour:	**7**
Estimate # of days for tour:	**2**
Getting around:	**Car or bike**
Key Events:	❑ **In March, McMinnville's Wine & Food Classic –** **call 503-472-4033 or visit www.macwfc.org for event** **schedule and ticketing.**
	❑ **Memorial Weekend in Wine Country – Willamette Valley –** **visit www.willamettewines.com.**
	❑ **Wine Country Thanksgiving – Willamette Valley – call** **503-646-2985 or visit www.willamettewines.com.**
Tips:	❑ **Those well-kept rows of trees are hazelnut orchards.** **A mandatory stop to snap pictures.**
	❑ **See Appendix B – Wine Tour Planning, for planning** **your visit.**
Best:	❑ **Gift shop: Coelho Winery of Amity.**
	❑ **Views: Amity Vineyards, Methven Family Vineyards.**

Seufert Winery

For WineTrail enthusiasts, there's one thing to know about Seufert Winery: Look for the vineyard inside the bottle of wine. That is to say, owner/winemaker Jim Seufert (pronounced "sī-fert") is not tied to his own vineyard. He works with select vineyards in the Willamette Valley to make his wines, like a chef at a four-star Portland restaurant, free to buy from the best meat producers, vegetable and herb farmers, and seafood suppliers. Using minimalist winemaking practices, Jim focuses on the quality of the wine, on what he describes as "wine with soul."

He contracts for grapes from the best of the best in terms of organic vineyard practices. With Seufert's associations with names like Bishop Creek Vineyard, Momtazi Vineyard, Hawks View Vineyard, and Coleman Vineyard, consumers can sip with a clean conscience, knowing that sustainable methods went into the production of their wine. Visitors to Seufert Winery, in Dayton, can sample their way through the different areas of the Willamette AVA: Dundee, McMinnville, Carlton, Chehalem, and others. If you know someone who insists that all pinots of the Willamette Valley taste the same, take this person to Seufert Winery to experience the difference between darker, richer Yamhill-grown grapes and Dundee Hills' lighter, fruitier pinot noir. That'll cure *that* notion.

Here's a tip for getting the low-down on Seufert wines: Jim provides an easy-to-read taste profile on the back labels of all his wines. He characterizes each wine's flavor intensity, sweetness, acidity, oak influence, mouthfeel, and cellar life in a handy-dandy chart. In addition, the labels offer Jim's suggestions for which wines to pair with what foods, such as appetizers, light meals, pastas, hearty meals, and desserts. Life just got easier!

Please note that this worm-farm-cum-winery-and-tasting-room is cramped, but it's all part of the charm. Here you can engage Jim and get his winemaking philosophy, the various flavor profiles, and perhaps help on your golf swing (just kidding). Let him know what you're looking for, be it food pairings or simply a good hot-tub wine for later. He'll suggest a good match. (**WineTrail tip:** If you seek a wine to share with a friend or loved one, sans food, let me suggest Jim's Woven White blend of pinot gris, riesling, and chardonnay.) Delicious!

SEUFERT WINERY
opened: 2005
winemaker(s): Jim Seufert
location: 415 Ferry Street, Dayton, OR 97114
phone: 503-709-1255
web: www.seufertwinery.com
e-mail: jim@seufertwinery.com
fee: Complimentary wine tasting
hours: Weekends 12–5 June through November

DIRECTIONS: From Portland, follow Hwy 99 through Dundee. Go 4 miles past Dundee and turn left onto Hwy 18 towards the McMinnville bypass. Go 1 mile and take the Dayton exit – Hwy 221. Enter Dayton on 3rd St. and go to the four-way stop. Turn right onto Ferry St. and continue 1.5 blocks. Seufert Winery is on the right, across the street from City Hall.

From McMinnville, follow Hwy 18 east out of McMinnville. Two miles after the airport, turn right taking the Dayton exit – Hwy 221. Enter Dayton on 3rd St. at the four-way stop, turn right onto Ferry St. and up 1.5 blocks. Seufert Winery is on the right, across the street from City Hall.

From Salem go to West Salem and take Hwy 221 north. Follow Hwy 221 into Dayton where it becomes 3rd St. At the four way stop sign, turn left onto Ferry St. and go 1.5 blocks. Seufert Winery is on the right, across the street from City Hall.

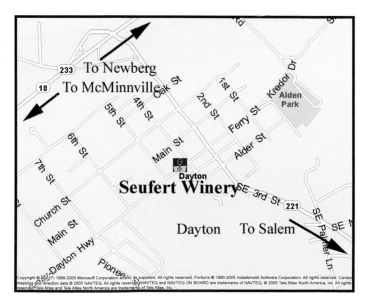

Hauer of the Dauen 2

Great name, don't you think? But what does it mean? Read on, dear WineTrail trekker.

The name Hauer of the Dauen is derived from the name of the winery's owners, Carl and Lores Dauenhauer. Armed with a big laugh and an equally sharp wit, Carl Dauenhauer notes that his name, from the High German language, translates to "the striking of the sun." High German is the language that Adolf Hitler forbade Germans to speak. I guess Adolf, unlike Carl, didn't have a sense of humor.

Carl Dauenhauer

Carl is a native Oregonian who spends most of his time tending his 110 acres of vineyards outside of Dayton. This is a certified biodynamic farm. His family's nursery-business background made it possible to plant a 40-acre vineyard in two and a half hours back in 1980. That's not a typo — it took two and a half hours for his family to plant 40 acres of vines! I thought he was kidding, but Carl assured me that he wasn't. Together, Carl and his large and well-organized family scored the earth and planted the vines like a well-oiled German machine.

Carl's current vineyard features seven different varietals: pinot noir, gamay noir, lemberger, pinot gris, gewürztraminer, riesling, and chardonnay. Although most of his fruit goes to such notable Oregon wineries as King Estate Winery, Eola Hills Wine Cellars, and A to Z Wineworks, he does set aside select grapes to produce 4,000 cases of Hauer of the Dauen's own. Most of the wine is sold directly from the winery, which sees a steady stream of fans.

This is an unpretentious winery, where Carl no doubt sets the relaxed atmosphere. At the entrance, there's a sign that reads, "Friends welcome. Relatives by appointment." It's definitely quirky, but it succeeds in making people feel welcomed. With the relatively low prices of its wines, Hauer of the Dauen is rewarded with a loyal fan base; this also helps explain why crowds line up to taste Hauer of Dauen wines at Oregon wine events and festivals. These are easy-drinking wines made for a singular purpose — enjoyment.

HAUER OF THE DAUEN
opened: 1999
winemaker(s): Carl Dauenhauer
location: 16425 SE Webfoot Road,
Dayton, OR 97114
phone: 503-868-7359
web: None
e-mail: hauerofdauen@aol.com
picnic area: Yes
wheelchair access: Yes
fee: $3 tasting fee
hours: Saturday and Sunday 12–5, or by appointment

DIRECTIONS: **Depart Dayton** on SE Amity-Dayton Hwy [SE Ferry St.] heading west for 1.3 miles. Road name changes to SR-233. Continue for .4 miles. Bear left (south) onto SE Lafayette Hwy and go 3.6 miles. Turn left (east) onto SE Alderman Rd and go .8 miles. Turn right (south) onto SE Webfoot Rd and proceed 1.4 miles. Arrive at 16425 SE Webfoot Rd.

From Salem take SR-221 [Salem-Dayton Hwy] 13.8 miles toward West Salem Business District. Turn left (west) onto SE Fairview Rd and go .6 miles. Turn left to stay on SE Fairview Rd and continue 1.2 miles. Turn right (north) onto SE Webfoot Rd and go .3 miles. Arrive to the winery.

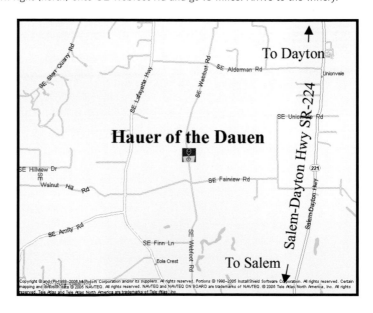

Methven Family Vineyards 🔢

It's not too often that I gloat about a wine club, but Methven Family Vineyards' club is an exception. Please understand that I'm biased. My partner, Kathleen, and I arrived

Jill and Allen Methven

on a Sunday only to find the winery closed because of a special wine club function. Undaunted, we walked in and introduced ourselves to Jill Methven, who was working the welcome desk. I explained that I was working on *Wine Trails of Oregon* and just needed to take a couple of pictures and then we would be on our way. However, despite my efforts to be unobtrusive, Jill welcomed us to the event, introduced us to her husband, Allen, and then placed us in the buffet line with plates in hand. Soon Kathleen and I made our way to the barrel room, where winemaker Chris Lubberstedt was pouring wines.

Now, here's the kicker. Chris was pouring wines, and club members then rated the four different out-of-the-barrels pinots being tasted. Using the feedback of wine club members, Chris then blended the wines into a special club reserve pinot cuvée for distribution exclusively to wine club members. With outstretched hand, Chris gave us generous pours, and we assumed the roles of Methven Family Vineyards Club members. Hey, when there's free wine at stake, I will pretend to be part of the catering crew if necessary!

In between munching on pulled pork, fresh fruit, and marinated olives, I managed to learn that the Methvens' 100-acre vineyard boasts 30 acres planted in pinot noir, pinot gris, riesling, and chardonnay. Using organic practices, the Methvens produce elegant wines representing the very best of Willamette Valley. Whereas other wineries have fancy names for their wine clubs, Methven Family Vineyards elected the generic name of Wine Club. But make no mistake; nothing else about this winery is common. Attention to detail is apparent from the greeting you receive to your impromptu membership into the club.

METHVEN FAMILY VINEYARDS
winemaker(s): Chris Lubberstedt
location: 11400 Westland Lane, Dayton, OR 97114
phone: 503-975-9153
web: www.methvenfamilyvineyards.com
e-mail: info@methvenfamilyvineyards.com
picnic area: Yes
fee: Tasting fee may apply
hours: Wednesday to Sunday 11–5, April through November. Friday to Sunday 11–5, December through March, or by appointment

Chris Lubberstedt pouring

 **BEST Views**

DIRECTIONS: **From McMinnville** take SR-18 south 3.5 miles. Turn right onto SR-233/Lafayette Hwy and go 5.1 miles. Turn right onto SE Westland Ln and arrive at Methven Family Vineyards.

From Salem take SR-22 west/Marion Street Bridge. Turn right on Wallace Rd/OR-221 toward Dayton. Bear right onto SR-221/Salem-Dayton Hwy/Wallace Rd NW for 11.5 miles. Turn left onto SE Lafayette Hwy and go 4.6 miles. Turn left onto SE Westland Ln and arrive at Methven Family Vineyards.

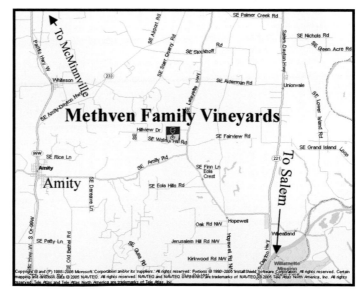

Mystic Wines

Don't you love visiting a tasting room housed in an old Craftsman-style farmhouse? For those of us who do, a trip to Mystic Wines in the rolling hills west of Salem provides that pleasant experience. With a glass of wine in hand, you can comfortably ensconce your weary bones in an oversized chair and relax. No doubt, the farmhouse's original owner had no clue in the 1920s that visitors to his home in the next century would be swirling and sipping in a winery tasting room!

Mystic Wines is a small, family-run Oregon winery established in 1992 by owner/winemaker Rick Mafit. His background includes a degree in enology from University of California–Davis and winemaking duties at various wineries. Then, in the early '90s, Rick came north from California to make big red wines using grapes primarily from The Dalles region in the Columbia Gorge. That said, if your goal is sampling pinot noir, Mystic Wines may not be the place for you. Rather, this is the place to experience Rick's merlot, cabernet sauvignon, zinfandel, syrah, and barbera. These wines are ready to drink upon release, yet will also benefit from additional cellaring.

With production at approximately 2,000 cases per year, each handcrafted batch is aged two years in the barrel. By the way, check out the beautiful monochromatic labels designed by Rick's son Dillon. Here's what Mystic Wines literature has to say about those labels, "Printed on actual 'cork' paper, the idea emulates reserve bottlings of many small wineries in Portugal. Each label varies with the patterns created by the natural cork and the way it absorbs the sepia ink, creating a uniquely attractive package."

Behind the tasting room is the new winery building, completed for the most part by Rick and friends. In a space this large, Mystic Wines can easily produce more than 2,000 cases annually. Fortunately for Rick, he's kept his day job as a sales representative for Scott Laboratories — one of the nation's largest producers of winemaking supplies. All Rick's fermentation, filtration, and packaging needs can readily be met. I suspect he gets a company discount.

Still, even with the opening of the new production facility, Rick notes, "The goal is to stay small, handle the wines and winery ourselves, and produce outstanding hand-crafted wines in limited quantities."

    www.winetrailsnw.com/wineries/mystic_wines

Richard Mafit

MYSTIC WINES
opened: 1992
winemaker(s): Richard Mafit
location: 11931 SE Hood View Road, Amity, OR 97101
phone: 503-581-2769
web: www.mysticwine.com
e-mail: tastingroom@mysticwine.com
picnic area: Yes
fee: Tasting fee may apply
hours: Saturday and Sunday 12–5

DIRECTIONS: **From McMinnville** take SR-99W southeast for 5.8 miles. Turn left (east) onto Bellevue-Hopewell Hwy [Nursery Ave.] and go .5 miles. Road name changes to SE Amity Rd. Continue for 4.2 miles. Turn right (south) onto SE Lafayette Hwy and go .8 miles. Turn right (west) onto SE Hood View Rd and arrive at the Mystic Wines tasting room in .3 miles.

From Salem take SR-221 [Salem-Dayton Hwy] north for about 12 miles. Turn left (west) onto SE Lafayette Hwy and go 2.6 miles. Turn left (west) onto SE Hood View Rd and continue .3 miles to the Mystic Wines tasting room at 11931 SE Hood View Rd.

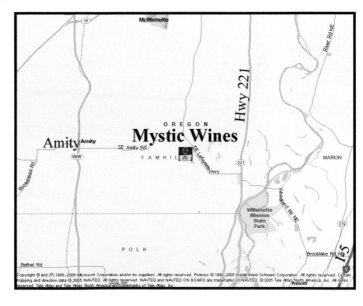

Amity Vineyards 5

To say that Myron Redford is legendary in the Oregon wine industry states the obvious. With the launch of his Amity Vineyards in 1974, Myron joined a handful of other pioneer wineries in Oregon, including Eyrie, Ponzi, Tualatin, and Erath vineyards. Now more than 30 years old, Amity Vineyards contends with more than 300 other Oregon wineries. With a full beard and blue eyes, Myron continues to reinvent his winemaking

craft and strive to create elegant pinot noirs with great finesse and structure.

Turning into Myron's vineyard, your car climbs a short distance to the weathered tasting room and winery. His estate vineyard surrounds you, and the view of the valley below in this northern part of the Willamette Valley is nothing short of spectacular. Once inside, visitors pay a small tasting fee for access to a variety of Amity Vineyards wines, including riesling, pinot blanc, gamay noir, Gewürztraminer, Maréchal Foch, and rosé, but the real star is Myron's pinot noir. Here you find reserve and single-vineyard wines, red wines, white wines, eco-friendly wines and sulfite-free wines. However, don't count on tasting Amity Vineyards 1983 Reserve Pinot Noir. It's not available. That's the one Robert Parker gushed over when he stated, "One of the best pinot noirs I have ever tasted." That review pretty much put Amity Vineyards on the map.

Beginning in 1990, Amity introduced ECO-WINE®, Oregon's first sulfite-free wine from organic grapes. Now its Eco-Pinot Noir is racking up medals like the Chinese Olympic gymnastic team, taking home the gold at the 2007 Northwest Wine Summit and the 2008 Oregon State Fair. It's a testimony to Myron's ability to evolve and meet the challenges that pinot (aka the "heartbreak grape") presents.

Although it's a challenge to continually make and refine your winemaking abilities, it's another thing to market your product. Even though he no longer contends with the notion of "you can't grow good wine in Oregon," Myron's current challenge is marketing to reduce inventory. Still, he and his staff manage to do this year after year, allowing WineTrail enthusiasts the opportunity to taste wine from a legend.

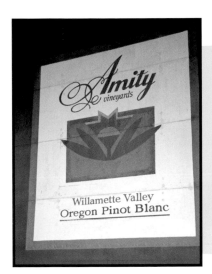

AMITY VINEYARDS
opened: 1976
winemaker(s): Myron Redford
location: 18150 Amity Vineyards Road,
Amity, OR 97101
phone: 503-835-2362
web: www.amityvineyards.com
e-mail: myron@amityvineyards.com
picnic area: Yes
fee: $5 tasting fee refundable with purchase
hours: Daily 11–5 June through October;
12–5 November through May; closed on
Thanksgiving, Christmas, and New Year's Day

 **BEST Views**

DIRECTIONS: From McMinnville take 99W south for 7 miles toward Amity. Turn left onto Rice Lane in Amity. Turn left onto Amity Vineyards Rd and follow signs to vineyard about .5 miles on the right.

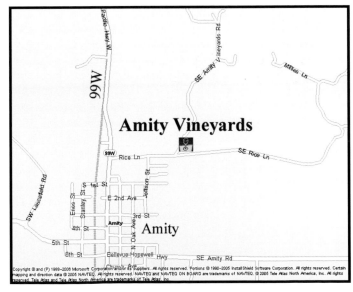

Kristin Hill Winery ⑥

The tree out front — the one that looks like it's upside down — is a Camperdown elm tree, and this little tidbit of trivia gives you a chance to impress friends and family when you visit Kristin Hill Winery. You could casually remark, "Isn't that a beautifully groomed Camperdown elm tree?" That's sure to raise an eyebrow.

Eric T. Aberg

As you approach the tasting room, which bears the name "Weinstube Aberg" stenciled on its side, you can further solidify your omniscient standing by asking, "Don't you just love wines made with the '*méthode champenoise*' technique?" That little term, "*méthode champenoise*," tells you that Kristin Hill Winery relies on traditional French methods for making champagne. However, it's an absolute no-no to refer to sparkling wine as "Champagne" — capital "C" — unless it's from the Champagne region of France."

For your further edification, "Weinstube" is German for "tasting room" and "Aberg" refers to the owner/winemaker Eric Aberg. The reference to "Weinstube Aberg" harks back to Eric's time in Europe serving in the U.S. Armed Forces. During his stay, Eric became intimately familiar with wines in Germany and France. That's where he got his know-how for producing estate pinot noir, pinot gris, chardonnay, Müller-Thurgau, gewürztraminer, rosé, and port. Following his stint in Europe, Eric took enology classes at the University of California–Davis while stationed at the Presidio in San Francisco. He then headed north to Oregon to make wine.

Once inside the tasting room, get ready for an enjoyable (and educational) session with Eric, who also tends the wine bar. Yes, he does pour a wide variety of Kristin Hill wines, but what WineTrail trekkers will remember is his production of sparkling wines and, in particular, Fizzy Lizzy. In this small family-owned and -operated winery, the cherry-infused Fizzy Lizzy sparkling wine is one of its most popular wines and it distinguishes Kristin Hill Winery from the pack. At the time of Kristin Hill Winery's first crush, there were only 22 wineries in Yamhill County. That was back in 1990. Today, with more than 100 wineries that call this viticultural region home, Kristin Hill Winery is a survivor.

By the way, the name Kristin Hill was coined from the name of one of Eric's four daughters — Kristin. Ironically, of all of his daughters, she is the only one who doesn't care for wine!

Camperdown elm tree.

KRISTIN HILL WINERY
opened: 1990
winemaker(s): Eric T. Aberg
location: 3330 SE Amity Dayton Highway,
Amity, OR 97101
phone: 503-835-0850
web: None
e-mail: kristinhill1@msn.com
picnic area: Yes
fee: Complimentary wine tasting
hours: Daily 12–5 March through December;
Saturday and Sunday 12–5 January and February

DIRECTIONS: **From McMinnville**, depart on SR-99W [SE Adams St.] heading south for 1.2 miles. Turn left (southeast) onto SR-99W [Pacific Hwy W] and continue 4.6 miles. Turn left (north) onto SE-233 [SE Amity-Dayton Hwy] and arrive at 3330 SE Amity-Dayton Hwy.

From Amity, head north on SR-99W [Pacific Hwy W] for 1.1 miles. Keep right onto SR-233 [SE Amity-Dayton Hwy] and arrive at 3330 SE Amity-Dayton Hwy.

Coelho Winery of Amity 7

Note the "W" across the top of the Coelho wine label. It stands for "wine," but if you look again, the "W" begins to look like rabbit ears. You're not imagining bunnies — the resemblance is intentional. You see, Coelho (pronounced co – EL – ho) means rabbit in the Portuguese language. It also happens to be the last name of owners Dave and Deolinda Coelho, who have Portuguese roots. It's little wonder then that the Coelho Winery of Amity wines have Portuguese names including: Paciência (patience), Renovação (renewal), Serenidade (serenity), Espontâneo (spontaneous), Divertimento (fun), and Fusäo (fusion). Consequently, visitors can come away with not only wine, but a language lesson to aid them on their next visit to Lisbon.

The generously sized tasting room at Coelho Winery offers respite for weary wine tourists. You may never want to come out. There is a cozy fireplace to gather around with glass in hand. Wine-related merchandise to purchase (someone has a great eye for gifts and gets our "Best Retail Shopping" award), local art and an ample wine bar also add to the pleasant experience. The building itself was built in the 1930s and still has its original post and beam timbers. However, like most of its visitors, you are here for the wine, and to that end, get ready to sample pinot noir, pinot gris, chardonnay, pinot noir rosé, petite sirah, red table wines and dessert wines. Most of these wines come from the Coelhos' 30-acre vineyard located a few miles away in the Eola Hills.

It's likely that your visit will include a lively conversation with the tasting-room staff and perhaps a "where are you from?" discussion with the folks next to you. There's a reason the name is Coelho Winery *of Amity* — amity means friendship and is derived from the Latin *amicus* meaning friend. The village of Amity prides itself on its friendliness.

Incidentally, the Portuguese word for friend is amigo. Saude!

COELHO WINERY OF AMITY
winemaker(s): Brian Marcy
location: 111 5th Street, Amity, OR 97101
phone: 503-835-9305
web: www.coelhowinery.com
e-mail: coelhowinery@onlinemac.com
picnic area: Yes
gift shop: Yes
tours: Yes
fee: $5 tasting fee
hours: Daily 11–5 May through mid-December; Friday,
Saturday and Sunday 11–5 January through April

 BEST Gift shop

DIRECTIONS: **From McMinnville** take SR-99W [Pacific Hwy W] approximately 9 miles and arrive at
111 5th St. in Amity. The winery is located on the right.

Mid Eola – Amity Hills
Wine Trail

Inside Cristom Vineyards tasting room

Can you say pinot noir, pinot gris, pinot blanc, chardonnay, viognier, and dolcetto? For the most part, these are cool climate grapes and representative of one of Oregon's newest viticultural areas — Eola Amity Hills AVA. In 2006 Eola – Amity Hills became a sub-appellation of Willamette Valley AVA.

If you are fortunate enough to visit in late summer/early fall, check out the pinot noir grapes. They have a distinctive dark pinecone look. Apropos to the pinot noir's name, pinot is French for "pine" and noir for "black." Cultivation-wise, this finicky grape provides low yields. A lot can go wrong: whether it's mildew or early fall rains, pinot noir is vulnerable to all sorts of attacks. All of this contributes to the mystique and charm of pinot noir and your quest to find the best pinot noir.

Mid Eola – Amity Hills WineTrail

1. Arcane Cellars at Wheatland Winery
2. Stangeland Vineyards & Winery
3. Witness Tree Vineyard
4. Cristom Vineyards
5. St. Innocent Winery
6. Bethel Heights Vineyard
7. Bryn Mawr Vineyards

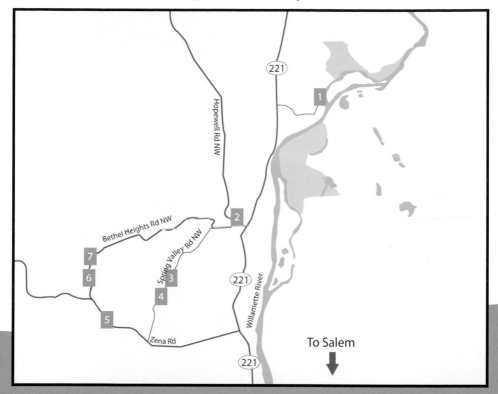

Region:	**Mid Willamette Valley Wine Country**
# of tasting rooms on tour:	**7**
Estimate # of days for tour:	**2**
Getting around:	**Car or bike**
Key Events:	❏ **In March, McMinnville's Wine & Food Classic – call 503-472-4033 or visit www.macwfc.org for event schedule and ticketing.**
	❏ **Memorial Weekend in Wine Country – Willamette Valley – visit www.willamettewines.com.**
	❏ **Wine Country Thanksgiving – Willamette Valley – call 503-646-2985 or visit www.willamettewines.com.**
Tips:	❏ **Need a place for an amazing wedding? Adjacent to St. Innocent Winery is the spectacular Event Center. Call 503-974-1658 for availability and pricing.**
	❏ **If you forgot your camera, splurge for a new one for this WineTrail!**
Best:	❏ **Views: Stangeland Vineyards & Winery, Cristom Vineyards, Bethel Heights Vineyard.**

Arcane Cellars at Wheatland Winery

Located along the Willamette River, Wheatland Winery requires visitors to swim across the swift current. Actually no, a short ferry ride awaits you if you are traveling east to west. Folks traveling on I-5 will take exit 263 and head west following signs to the Wheatland Ferry. Once you cross the Willamette River, it is a short hop to Arcane Cellars at Wheatland Winery. Approaching the winery through neighboring farms, you soak in wonderful views of the nearby Eola Hills.

Arcane Cellars at Wheatland Winery is a labor of love by a father-and-son team. Jeffrey Leal Silva manages the vineyard and facilities. His son, Jason Leal Silva, is responsible for making the wine. Thirty-something Jason also brings another talent to the business as a graphic artist and he's responsible for the winery's eye-popping signage and wine labels. Together, father and son (as well as a team of vineyard and winery assistants) produce a combination of estate wines and non-estate wines that rely on select vineyards in Oregon. In the cool of the tasting room, visitors have the difficult challenge of choosing among a host of wines to sample. In addition to Arcane's flagship pinot noir, WineTrail enthusiasts can taste its pinot gris, pinot blanc and viognier. For those who enjoy big reds, you'll want to taste the Wheatland Winery–labeled Bordeaux blends, and for fans of white wine, check out the unoaked chardonnay.

The name "Arcane Cellars at Wheatland Winery" might cause you to scratch your head, wondering who is arcane and what's with the wheatland reference. Essentially the wines made under the Arcane Cellars label are small-lot low-production wines. These are single-vineyard, estate-grown wines. Wines made under the Wheatland Winery brand are larger-production wines with fruit primarily sourced from the Columbia Valley and southern Oregon.

Pack a picnic or light snack and retreat with your bottle of wine to the outside patio. With views of the nearby field profuse with wildflowers, it's downright scenic. However, I must admit to a big regret as I headed to the ferry — I only bought one bottle of the Arcane Cellars pinot gris estate wine ($20). I should have bought a case. There's a reason the winery took home the gold medal from the 2008 prestigious San Francisco International Wine Competition for this wine.

ARCANE CELLARS AT WHEATLAND WINERY
winemaker(s): Jason Leal Silva
location: 22350 Magness Road NW,
Wheatland, OR 97304
phone: 503-868-7076
web: www.arcanecellars.com
e-mail: info@arcanecellars.com
picnic area: Yes
fee: $5 tasting fee
hours: Saturday and Sunday 12–4, or by appointment

DIRECTIONS: **From Dayton** head south on SR-221 [Salem-Dayton Hwy] for about 9 miles. Turn left (east) onto Wheatland Rd NW and go 1 mile. Bear left (northeast) onto Magness Rd NW and arrive at the winery in .6 miles.

From Salem take SR-221 [Salem-Dayton Hwy] 11.5 miles going north. Take a right (east) onto Wheatland Rd NW and continue 1 mile. Bear left (northeast) onto Magness Rd NW and arrive at the winery in .6 miles.

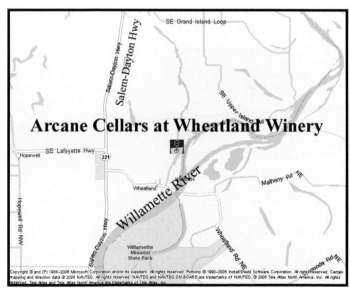

Stangeland Vineyards & Winery 2

Don't you love those oversized arched doors that grace the entrances of some wineries? I do. To me, they speak volumes about the artisan mindset, about attention to detail, and about making it clear that visitors are welcome. The extra-large tasting-room doors of Stangeland Vineyards & Winery do that for me. They're big — the hinges themselves must be 4 feet long. What's more, these are not assembly-line doors. It's as if the winery and tasting room were built around these doors.

Located northwest of Salem, on a south-facing slope, Stangeland Vineyards & Winery is the brainchild and *raison d'être* of husband-and-wife team Larry and Kinsey Miller. They planted the Stangeland Vineyard in 1978. Larry began making wine from their estate fruit in addition to grapes from other vineyards, and opened the winery in 1992. In many ways, the Millers are emblematic of many Oregon winery owners who are driven by craft and passion. With production at 1,500 cases per year, Larry keeps his day job and manages the winery and vineyard with Kinsey during his "spare time."

As Larry and Kinsey like to say, "There are no strangers at Stangeland," and they make good on that statement with a friendly staff and a variety of wines to experience, including pinot noir, pinot gris, chardonnay, and gewürztraminer. While there, you'll see T-shirts and wine labels bearing the distinctive red-and-white Norwegian flag. Turns out, Larry's grandmother came from Norway, and I suspect that the hilly farmland of the Eola Hills reminds many Norwegian transplants of the farmland outside of Oslo — sans snow.

By the way, Stangeland Vineyards & Winery offers a unique setting for special events, such as weddings, receptions, family reunions, birthdays, and business meetings. Stroll around the grounds of this hilltop winery and you'll understand how this winery can easily handle 150 guests for an event. But even if you don't have an upcoming event, the picnic tables can accommodate you and a glass of Stangeland's Estate Reserve Pinot Noir. It's a great way to experience the lush valley below while wondering how many people it took to hang those doors.

STANGELAND VINEYARDS & WINERY
opened: 1992
winemaker(s): Larry Miller
location: 8500 Hopewell Road NW, Salem, OR 97304
phone: 503-581-0355
web: www.stangelandwinery.com
e-mail: stangelandwinery@gotsky.com
picnic area: Yes
weddings: Yes
fee: Tasting fee may apply
hours: Saturday and Sunday 12–5 March through
December, or by appointment or chance 12–4

 **BEST Views**

DIRECTIONS: **From Salem,** cross the Willamette River exit north on SR-221 toward Dayton, go nine miles, turn left on Hopewell Road, .25 miles to driveway on route.

From Dayton, go south on SR-221 for 12 miles to Hopewell Road, turn right, go .25 miles to destination.

Witness Tree Vineyard

Witness Tree Vineyard, all 51.5 acres of it, lies in an ideal grape-growing spot in the Eola Hills. Imagine having a southeasterly exposure to take advantage of the morning light and the daytime heat. The vineyard's westerly ridge means that the evening temperatures get

lower than other parts of the valley, preserving those nice acids in the grapes. Essentially, you have the perfect conditions for growing exceptional grapes; owners Dennis and Carolyn Devine knew a good thing when they saw it.

A commanding oak tree living near the vineyard's ridgeline, the "Witness Tree" was present when the Oregon Trail pioneers settled in the valley. In 1854, the Witness Tree was designated a surveyor's landmark, a landmark with such a presence that the Devines decided to name their winery after it. Today, visitors to the winery can admire the tree from a distance, with camera in hand.

The Devines takes pride in the fact that 100 percent of their wines are estate produced. Every grape that goes into each bottle gets bud-to-bottle nurturing under the watchful eye of Steven Westby. Here, WineTrail trekkers can sample Witness Tree estate wines in the friendly confines of the intimate tasting room. They can anticipate tasting pinot blanc, viognier, chardonnay, pinot noir, dolcetto, and a dessert wine. Several of the wines bear the name of the Devines' grandchildren, including Witness Tree "Hanson" Pinot Noir, Witness Tree Dolcetto "Remari," and their dessert wine, Witness Tree "Sweet Signe."

Now here's a terrific marketing strategy: You can become a "futures" partner as part of the winery's "Witness Protection Program." During Memorial Day weekend, visitors to the winery can sample wines straight from the barrel. If you like a particular wine, you can buy it at a discount — when it is bottled. This ensures that you will receive a future allocation of the wine you like at bargain prices.

A brief walk around the property introduces you to a number of birdhouses residing among the vineyards. In this case, the inhabitants of these bird condos are part of the rodent-control program. You will also spy a number of ideal spots for picnicking, enjoying a glass of wine, or taking pictures. Ever present in the background is the Witness Tree, standing watch just as it did those many years ago, when the pioneers arrived.

WITNESS TREE VINEYARD
opened: 1987
winemaker(s): Steven Westby
location: 7111 Spring Valley Road NW,
Salem, OR 97304
phone: 503-585-7874
web: www.witnesstreevineyard.com
e-mail: info@witnesstreevineyard.com
picnic area: Yes
fee: $5 tasting fee
hours: Tuesday through Sunday 11–5 June through
August; Saturday and Sunday 11-5 September
through December and March through May;
January 15–17 and February 19–21, 11–5

DIRECTIONS: **From Dayton** take SE Amity-Dayton Hwy [SE Ferry St.] east .1 miles. Turn right (southeast) onto SR-221 [SE 3rd St.] and go 13.2 miles. Turn right (west) onto Oak Knoll Rd NW and go 1.7 miles. Turn left (south) onto Spring Valley Rd NW and travel .3 miles to destination.

From Salem go west onto SR-22 [SR-99E Bus] for .5 miles. Take ramp (right) onto SR-22 [Marion St. Bridge] and go .4 miles. Take ramp (right) onto SR-221 [Salem-Dayton Hwy] and go 7.3 miles toward West Salem Business District. Turn left (west) onto Oak Knoll Rd NW and go 1.7 miles. Turn left (south) onto Spring Valley Rd NW and go .3 miles to the winery.

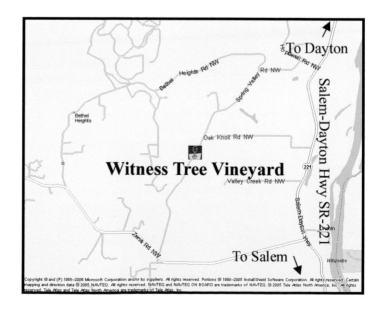

Cristom Vineyards 4

"Cristom's philosophy is about letting the land make the wines."
— Paul Gerrie, founder and owner

Paul and Eileen Gerrie came from Pittsburgh in the early 1990s, and they brought with them a burning desire to grow grapes and make wine. In collaboration with winemaker Steve Doerner, they succeeded, but in the process, they didn't forget their roots. When you're at Cristom Vineyards, make a point of examining their logo. It's a collage of images that includes coins, a duck decoy, a totem pole, rifle, pocket watch, Mount Hood, a hat, a boar's head and other meaningful memorabilia from the Gerries' past and their newfound home in Oregon. By the way, I think the boar's head is very cool.

Family is obviously important to Paul and Eileen. The winery's name is derived from the names of their two children, "Christine" and "Tom," and the half-dozen pinot vineyards you see from the tasting-room deck are named after family matriarchs Marjorie, Louise, Jessie, Eileen, Emilia, and Germaine. Even the antique rough-hewn mahogany doors at the entrance remind visitors that tradition lives on at Cristom Vineyards.

"The winemaker's job is to optimize what nature — the vineyard — provides."
— Steve Doerner, Cristom winemaker

Steve carefully crushes estate grapes, ferments with native yeasts and relies on nature to flow wines from fermenter to barrels by using gravity. He is a minimalist and uses a hands-off winemaker style, always striving to taste the vineyard's nuances. With a view of Mount Jefferson in the distance, visitors can sample wines described in their literature as "smooth, elegant, and subtle," including viognier, chardonnay, pinot gris, syrah, and pinot noir.

By the end of my visit, I had created a mental collage of Cristom Vineyards to help me remember this special place. My collage includes images of large wine glasses (I love it when tasting rooms use the big glasses), views of Mount Jefferson in the distance, the lovely Eola Hills, well-groomed vineyards, massive entrance doors, an antique phone on the wall, and beautiful flower beds populating the property.

CRISTOM VINEYARDS
opened: 1992 established
winemaker(s): Steve Doerner
location: 6905 Spring Valley Road NW,
Salem, OR 97304
phone: 503-375-3068
web: www.cristomwines.com
e-mail: winery@cristomwines.com
picnic area: Yes
gift shop: Yes
tours: Yes
fee: $5 tasting fee refundable with purchase
hours: Tuesday through Sunday 11–5 April
through Thanksgiving; December through March
by appointment only

BEST Views

DIRECTIONS: From McMinnville go south on SR-99W [Pacific Hwy W] for about 12 miles. Turn left (east) onto Bethel Rd and travel 1.2 miles. Keep straight onto Zena Rd for 3.8 miles. Turn left (north) onto Spring Valley Rd NW and go 1.4 miles. Arrive at 6905 Spring Valley Rd.

From Salem take SR-221 [Salem-Dayton Hwy] 6 miles toward West Salem Business District. Turn left (west) onto Zena Rd NW and go 2.2 miles. Turn right (north) onto Spring Valley Rd NW and look for the winery in 1.4 miles.

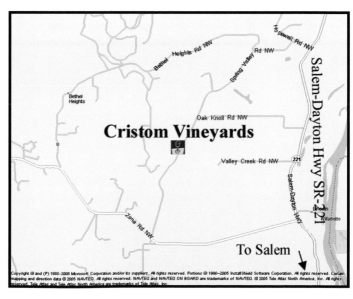

St. Innocent Winery 5

Approaching the new St. Innocent Winery, outside of Salem, you might think you are pulling into a Four Seasons Hotel. The only thing missing are matching black and white swans in the pond and a dude with white gloves to open your door.

Winemaker Mark Vlossak and other investors launched St. Innocent Winery in 1988. His dad's name was John Innocent Vlossak, and Mark chose the name St. Innocent as a tribute to his father, who taught him about wine as an accompaniment to life. St. Innocent's former residence was in an unattractive industrial area of Salem. To say that Mark was thrilled to close those digs and move to actual wine country is a great

understatement. However, this story is much more than a tale about moving into a new facility.

Don't let the beautiful grounds and new facilities turn your attention from the real star of the show — the land. This 133-acre estate in the Eola-Amity Hills was formerly the O'Connor Vineyard, which was, ironically, a major supplier of grapes to St. Innocent Winery. Based on a tip from Mark Vlossak, former Chicagoans Tim and Kari Ramey purchased the property from Pat O'Connor in 2002. After the purchase, the rechristened Zenith Vineyard benefited from the Rameys' philosophy of being "stewards of the land." Today they cultivate more than 80 acres of grapes, mostly of the pinot noir persuasion. Their sustainable farming methods are organic, and they have a LIVE certification to prove it. With wineries such as A to Z Wineworks, Seufert Winery, Adelsheim Vineyard, Biggio Hamina Cellars, St. Innocent Winery, and others as clients, the Rameys have a success on their hands. Not surprisingly, Mark is the winemaker for the Rameys' new wine label, Zenith Vineyard.

Adjacent to the winery is the luxurious Event Center managed by the Rameys perfect for corporate events and weddings. It is a separate business from St. Innocent Winery. Whereas most wedding centers pay singular attention to the bride's quarters, this event center makes sure that the guys weren't ignored. They've included a dedicated area for the men to relax, watch TV, and play video games.

Inside the light-filled tasting room, WineTrail enthusiasts can sample pinot noir, pinot gris, pinot blanc, chardonnay, and, of course, Mark's signature sparkling wines, made in the méthode champenoise style. His passion for making wine has not diminished since his first forays into making sparkling wine in the mid-'80s.

ST. INNOCENT WINERY
opened: 1988
winemaker(s): Mark Vlossak
location: 5657 Zena Road NW, Salem, OR 97304
phone: 503-378-1526
web: www.stinnocentwine.com
e-mail: markv@stinnocentwine.com
picnic area: Yes
wheelchair access: Yes
weddings: Yes – at adjacent Event Center
tours: Yes
fee: $5 tasting fee refundable with purchase
hours: Saturday and Sunday 11–4

DIRECTIONS: **From downtown Salem** take Liberty St. SE .4 miles. Turn left (west) onto SR-22 west and go .5 miles. Take SR-22 [Marion Street Bridge] and go .4 miles. Take ramp (right) onto SR-221 [Salem-Dayton Hwy] and travel 6 miles. Turn left (west) onto Zena Rd NW and continue 3.4 miles. Arrive at 5657 Zena Rd NW (on the right).

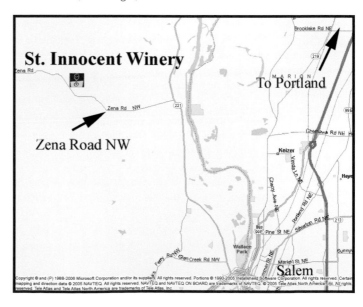

233

Bethel Heights Vineyard

I had previously tasted Bethel Heights Vineyard's pinot noir, but not by choice.
My partner, Kathleen, and I had been to one of our favorite restaurants, Nick's Italian
Café in McMinnville. We ordered a bottle of pinot noir to go with our dinner, and a
couple of minutes later, our server gave us the bad news that they were out of that wine.
No worries. I picked up the wine menu and ordered another Oregon pinot noir. A couple
of minutes later, the server reappeared, again with the same refrain — they were out of
that wine, too. However, she suggested an alternative wine that's "gorgeous and has a good
price point." We decided to give it a try.

She was right; It was gorgeous and didn't break the bank. The wine? A Bethel Heights Eola-Amity Hill Pinot Noir Cuvée.

Ironically, a week later we were in the Eola Hills to visit
Bethel Heights Vineyard. I was excited because I knew that I liked its wines and was
familiar with the fact that Bethel Heights Vineyards was one of the original vineyards in
the Eola Hills (planted in 1977). However, I didn't have a clue that the establishment had
a panoramic view of the valley below and Mount Jefferson in the distance. A beautiful
terrace wraps around the tasting room, giving visitors the opportunity to relax and enjoy
the view with the owners' Alaskan husky, Jack. I was in heaven.

Make no mistake, this is a family affair, with members of the Casteel family growing
the grapes, making the wine, running the tasting room, and managing the books. Twin
brothers Ted and Terry Casteel are at the center of the winemaking enterprise. Ted
manages the 51-acre vineyard surrounding the winery, and Terry makes the wine at a
clip of 10,000 cases annually. There are clear divisions of labor amongst the family —
except during crush. At that time, the roles dissipate and everyone rolls up the proverbial
sleeves to pitch in.

Visitors can taste other Bethel Heights Vineyard products, including chardonnay, pinot
blanc and pinot gris, but make no mistake: The focus here is on pinot noir, with most of
the vineyard planted with that most noble of Burgundian grapes.

BETHEL HEIGHTS VINEYARD
opened: 1977
winemaker(s): Terry Casteel
location: 6060 Bethel Heights Road NW,
Salem, OR 97304
phone: 503-581-2262
web: www.bethelheights.com
e-mail: info@bethelheights.com
picnic area: Yes
wheelchair access: Yes
fee: $5 tasting fee
hours: Tuesday through Sunday 11–5

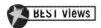

BEST views

DIRECTIONS: From Portland take I-5 south to Salem. Take Salem Parkway to center of town.
Follow signs that say "Ocean Beaches." Turn right onto Marion Street Bridge. Stay to the far right
when crossing the bridge. Exit right off of the bridge following signs to Dayton, McMinnville for
about 6 miles to the Lincoln Store. Turn left on Zena Rd. Stay on Zena for about 4 miles, turn right
onto Bethel Heights Rd. Drive .25 miles to winery.

From Amity, head south on SR-99W [Pacific Hwy W] for 5.1 miles. Turn left (east) onto Bethel
Rd and proceed 1.2 miles. Keep straight onto Zena Rd NW for 2.1 miles. Turn left (north) onto
Bethel Heights Rd NW and continue for .4 miles. Arrive at 6060 Bethel Heights Rd NW.

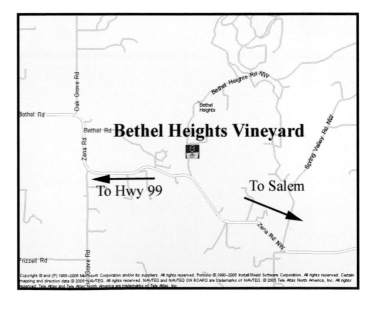

Bryn Mawr Vineyards ⑦

Bryn Mawr Vineyard is the consummate family-owned and -managed winery. It's small.
It's hands on. The owners do everything. They plant, prune, train the canes, remove
unwanted shoots, thin clusters and trim leaves. And that's just to get the vines to grow
grapes. Later, they have the task of turning fruit into wine, bottle by bottle, to produce

around 1,000 cases
annually. If you
look up "artisanal"
in the dictionary,
you may see a
picture of David
Lloyd-Jones and
Sharon Powers and
perhaps their two
girls and the family
dogs. This is a
working winery
with everyone
pitching in.

To appreciate the name Bryn Mawr Vineyards, you need to be there. The elevation is
higher than other parts of the Eola-Amity Hills AVA, and "bryn mawr" happens to mean
"high hill" in the ancient language of the Welsh people, to whom David and Sharon
can trace some of their family lineage. So the name rang true with the couple when
they arrived here from California in the late 1980s. The views of the valley below are
spectacular; it makes perfect sense that their slogan is "A Great Place to Grow Grapes
High on a Hill."

They succeeded in planting pinot noir and tempranillo vines for themselves and other
notable wineries. They emphasize organic methods for the vineyard. To this end, a flock of
Dorset sheep often munch their way through the vineyard while depositing their organic
contributions to fertilize the grounds.

By the way, this rather unassuming David Lloyd-Jones turns out to be quite the
renaissance man. First, visitors need to appreciate that the tasting room and house that
you experience were built by David — from the framing to the plumbing and electrical
work. That's on top of growing the grapes and making the wine. Also of note is that David
is a poet as demonstrated by this verse:

In every glass of wine, there's a view from a hill
Where a gentle wind complements the sun.
Where scent and touch of earth is warm,
And uplifts the spirit to soar
Like bird o'er valleys of grapes below.

David Lloyd-Jones

BRYN MAWR VINEYARDS
winemaker(s): David Lloyd-Jones
location: 5955 Bethel Heights Road NW,
Salem, OR 97304
phone: 503-581-4286
web: www.brynmawrvineyards.com
e-mail: davidlj@brynmawrvineyards.com
picnic area: Yes
tours: Yes
fee: Complimentary wine tasting
hours: Saturday and Sunday 11–5 from Memorial
Weekend to Thanksgiving Weekend

DIRECTIONS: **From downtown Salem**, turn left (north) onto Liberty St. SE and go .4 miles. Turn left (west) onto SR-22 [SR-99E Bus] and proceed .5 miles. Take ramp (right) onto SR-22 [Marion St. Bridge] and continue .4 miles. Take ramp (right) onto SR-221 [Salem-Dayton Hwy] and travel 6 miles. Turn left (west) onto Zena Rd NW and go 3.9 miles. Turn right (north) onto Bethel Heights Rd NW and arrive at the winery.

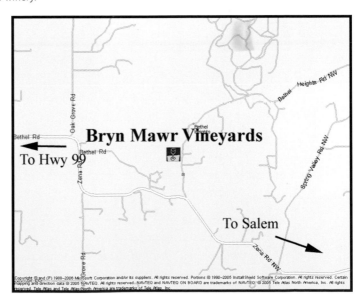

Eola – Amity Hills South
WineTrail

At Van Duzer Vineyards

For WineTrail enthusiasts who like to bike, this is the WineTrail for you. The Eola – Amity Hills WineTrail South offers scenic byways over rolling hills with wine stops along the way. Tom Huggins, founder of Eola Hills Wine Cellars, cooked up the idea of sponsoring a bike ride through wine country in the mid-90s. Though an avid bicyclist himself, he still might have been surprised by the large turnout of Oregon bike riders. Today the bike tour continues. During Sundays in August, Eola Hills Wine Cellars sponsors various rides to fit both beginner and advanced rider needs, ranging from 45 to 70 miles.

In addition to Eola Hills Wine Cellars, the Eola – Amity Hills WineTrail South will introduce you to amazing views, spectacular tasting rooms and most likely a one-on-one visit with a winemaker or two. From Redhawk Winery toward the east to Chateau Bianca Winery in the west, you would be wise to budget two or three days to savor this excursion.

Eola – Amity Hills WineTrail South

1. Redhawk Winery
2. Cubanisimo Vineyards
3. Kathken Vineyards
4. Orchard Heights Winery
5. Cherry Hill Winery
6. Firesteed Cellars
7. Left Coast Cellars
8. Van Duzer Vineyards
9. Namasté Vineyards
10. Chateau Bianca Winery
11. Eola Hills Wine Cellars

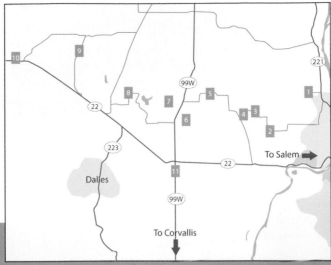

Region:	**Mid Willamette Valley Wine Country**
# of tasting rooms on tour:	**11**
Estimate # of days for tour:	**2 to 3**
Getting around:	**Car or bike**
Key Events:	❑ **Salem's Oregon Wine & Food Festival held at the Oregon State Fairgrounds. Call 503-580-2509 or go online to www.oregonstatefair.org.**
	❑ **Memorial Weekend in Wine Country – Willamette Valley – visit www.willamettewines.com.**
	❑ **Wine Country Thanksgiving – Willamette Valley – call 503-646-2985 or visit www.willamettewines.com.**
Tips:	❑ **During August weekends, Eola Hills Wine Cellars hosts bicycling in wine country complete with support van and evening barbeque. For details see www.eolahillswinery.com.**
	❑ **Kathken Vineyards hosts popular music concert series in summer. See www.kathkenvineyards.com for event information.**
	❑ **Sunday brunch anyone? Consider Orchard Heights Winery.**
	❑ **Chocolate to die for? Maybe. Check out gourmet chocolates at Cherry Hill Winery.**
	❑ **Cubanisimo Vineyards offers once a month salsa dance lessons. See www.cubanisimovineyards.com. Cha-cha-cha.**
Best:	❑ **Eats: Orchard Heights Winery.**
	❑ **Gift shop: Eola Hills Wine Cellars.**
	❑ **Lodging: Cherry Hill Winery, Chateau Bianca Winery.**
	❑ **Views: Cubanisimo Vineyards, Van Duzer Vineyards, Namasté Vineyards.**

239

Redhawk Winery

Talk about a leap of faith. Imagine never having grown grapes or made wine yet purchasing a winery with the intention of making a go of it. That's exactly what John and Betty Pataccoli did, leaving their Los Angeles confines in 2005 and buying a rundown winery north of Salem. But it wasn't just a spur-of-the-moment, impetuous lark that caused them to make such a bold move. Rather, they knew they were hooked on wine, having traveled to various wine regions of the world, including France. They had the wine

John and Betty Pataccoli (and Max)

bug all right. Moreover, they had a young son, and the rural splendor of this part of the Willamette Valley seemed a better fit to raise a child than their LA haunts. They chose wisely.

When they acquired Redhawk Winery, the Pataccolis had an inkling of what was in store: The vineyard needed rehabbing, the dark and dingy tasting room needed to be made more inviting, and the winemaking equipment required upgrades. Break out the checkbook. Fortunately, they live next to Russ Raney and the historic Evesham Wood Vineyard & Winery. Russ' assistance — especially during that first year — was invaluable, as John focused on the winemaking side of the business and Betty kept the books.

For visitors, the Pataccolis did a little something that brightens everyone's visit to Redhawk. They lightened up the tasting room by tearing down the dark, wood-paneled walls and re-oriented the tasting-room bar to allow visitors to view the picturesque valley below. Although this may seem like a no-brainer, it is surprising how many tasting-rooms views are squandered in favor of the staff and to the detriment of the visitor.

The Pataccolis also made a strategic decision to preserve the existing brand — Redhawk Winery. Over the years, a small army of loyal fans had developed, particularly for Redhawk's Grateful Red Pinot Noir. Only $14 a bottle, Grateful Red qualifies as a best buy that we are sure Jerry Garcia would have appreciated. Along with the Grateful Red Pinot Noir, Redhawk Winery also features other estate pinot noirs, dolcetto, pinot gris, and barrel-fermented chardonnay, in addition to cabernet sauvignon and red table wines made from grapes sourced from the Columbia Valley. All these wines have amazingly low prices that will likely have you reaching for your Visa or Master Card.

REDHAWK WINERY
opened: 1988
winemaker(s): John Pataccoli
location: 2995 Michigan City Road NW, Salem, OR 97304
phone: 503-362-1596
web: www.redhawkwine.com/index.php
e-mail: cellarmaster@redhawkwine.com
picnic area: Yes
fee: $5 tasting fee refundable with purchase
hours: Daily 11-5; Closed Thanksgiving Day, Christmas Day, New Year's Day, Easter and at kickoff on Super Bowl Sunday

DIRECTIONS: **From downtown Salem**, go west onto SR-22 [SR-99W Bus] .5 miles. Take ramp (right) onto SR-22 [Marion St. Bridge] and proceed .4 miles. Take ramp (right) onto SR-221 [Salem-Dayton Hwy] and continue 3.4 miles. Arrive at Michigan City Rd NW on left.

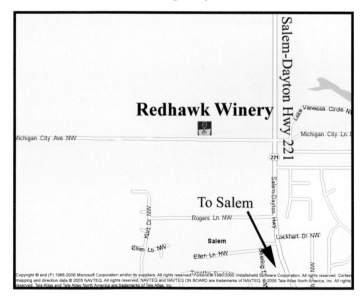

Cubanisimo Vineyards [2]

A chance encounter with a wadded-up piece of paper found on the streets of New Orleans brought Mauricio Collada to Oregon. It was an ad that sought physicians willing to relocate to Oregon and practice medicine. At the time, Havana-born Mauricio Collada Jr. had completed his medical studies in Florida and needed a place to begin his neurosurgery

practice. Mauricio also loved wine, thanks to a friendship he developed with a colleague from a winemaking family in Burgundy. This gave him an appreciation for pinot noir; he loved the elegance and complexity of this Burgundian grape and knew that Oregon's Willamette Valley was a hotbed of pinot activity. Mauricio landed in Salem and never looked back — except when it comes to his Cuban heritage.

The beach-like patio area, with its white-sand floor and inviting tables and chairs, has a distinctive Miami feel. All that's needed are some Cuban sandwiches, congas and a few sets of dominos and you have New Havana. It's "Cubanisimo Time!" The views here of the Willamette Valley looking south toward Salem are incredible. At 650 feet in elevation, this is one of the highest points of the Eola-Amity Hills AVA. This is a top 10 view.

You're here for a good time, for sure, but there's something deeper going on besides cigars and palm trees. It's also a love affair with pinot noir. Inside the cool tasting room, it is often Mauricio's daughter Christina who pours Cubanisimo Vineyard's wines. It's a manageable line-up of estate wines to sample — all delightful, including several pinot noirs, pinot gris and rosés of pinot noir. All the while, Cuban music is playing in the background, elevating the tropical mood and causing many a visitor to fantasize about leading a conga line with glass in hand under the light of a full moon.

The winemaker for Cubanisimo Vineyards is Rob Stuart. Beginning in the 1990s, Cubanisimo Vineyards supplied grapes to Erath Vineyards, where Rob Stuart worked as chief winemaker. Despite the fact that Rob launched his own label — R. Stuart & Co. — in nearby McMinnville their friendship and close working relationship continues strong as ever.

WineTrail tip: For WineTrail trekkers with a penchant for Latin swing, Cubanisimo offers salsa dance lessons once a month. In addition, enjoy salsa/jazz weekends during Memorial Day Weekend, Labor Day Weekend and Thanksgiving Day Weekend. Ricky Ricardo move over!

As the saying goes at Cubanisimo Vineyards, "Pride, passion, pinot. ¡Bienvenido!"

CUBANISIMO VINEYARDS
opened: 2003
winemaker(s): Rob Stuart
location: 1754 Best Road NW, Salem, OR 97304
phone: 503-588-1763
web: www.cubanisimovineyards.com
e-mail: vino@cubanisimovineyards.com
picnic area: Yes
wheelchair access: Yes
weddings: Yes
fee: $5 tasting fee
hours: Saturday and Sunday 12–5 April through
Thanksgiving, then by appointment

DIRECTIONS: **From Salem** go west on SR-22 [SR-99E Bus] .5 miles, take ramp (right) onto SR-22 [Marion St. Bridge] and proceed .4 miles. Take ramp (right) onto SR-221 [Salem-Dayton Hwy] and go .8 miles. Turn left (west) onto Orchard Heights Rd NW for 4.6 miles. Keep left onto Best Rd NW for .5 miles to arrive at the vineyard.

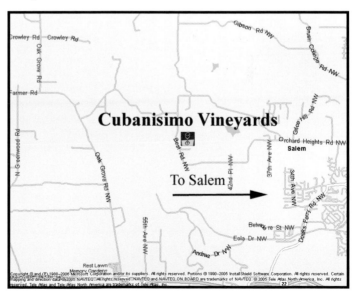

Kathken Vineyards 3

Lovers of music and wine can celebrate! Kathken Vineyards, located on the southern edge of the Eola-Amity Hills, is the place for you. Originators of an extraordinary summer music series, Ken and Kathy Slusser understand that nearly all people who enjoy music also enjoy wine. They get it. To that end, Kathken Vineyards sponsors a summer music series that features local and regional musicians, good food and lots of Kathken Vineyards

Ken and Kathy Slusser and granddaughter Jolie

wine. For just a small cover charge, WineTrail trekkers can experience major fun and excellent wine most Friday and Saturday nights in the summer. Blues and rock 'n' roll are served up with barbecue and pinot noir.

As the sun goes down during these events, the glow of the candled lanterns and bonfire light the way for WineTrail trekkers to make a beeline

to the beverage stand to purchase glasses of wine. There, they can buy a glass of pinot noir, pinot gris, a rosé of pinot noir, a late-harvest pinot gris, and a blend of reds composed primarily of Bordeaux grapes from southern Oregon with a dash of pinot noir from Kathken Vineyards.

Kathken Vineyards (the name is a melding of "Kathy" and "Ken") originated in the mid-'90s. At that time, the Slussers' youngest daughter was a student at the University of Oregon, and on one of their numerous trips to Eugene, the Slussers discovered Oregon wine. The seed was planted for having their own vineyard. That resulted in the purchase of 51 acres of prime vineyard land in the Eola Hills outside Salem. Today, 40 acres are under production — a full 32 are planted with pinot noir, and 8 acres are dedicated to pinot gris.

Don't forget to pack your camera for a visit to this winery. Although other nearby wineries can offer views of the valley floor, Kathken Vineyards doesn't. Rather, its view is looking upward from the tasting room/winery to the vineyard above. It's beautiful, but you find yourself thinking, as I did, about all the work associated with tending 40 acres of grapes. That's a lot of shoot removal, cane training and grape pruning. Whatever romantic notions you may have of purchasing a rural vineyard as the Slussers did and then cultivating year after year quickly evaporates once you gaze out over the vast acreage of grapes. Thank goodness we have folks like Kathy and Ken Slusser working the land to create music to our ears and wonderful wine.

KATHKEN VINEYARDS
opened: 2001
winemaker(s): Ken Slusser
location: 5739 Orchard Heights Road NW,
Salem, OR 97304
phone: 503-316-3911
web: www.kathkenvineyards.com
e-mail: kathkenvyd@aol.com
picnic area: Yes
wheelchair access: Yes
weddings: Yes
gift shop: Yes
fee: Complimentary wine tasting
hours: Saturday and Sunday 12–5 Memorial
Day to Labor Day

DIRECTIONS: **From McMinnville** drive south on SR-99W for 14 miles. Turn left (east) onto Frizzell Rd and go 1.2 miles. Turn right (south) onto Oak Grove Rd and travel 3.9 miles. Turn left (east) onto Orchard Heights Rd NW for .8 miles. Arrive at 5739 Orchard Heights Rd NW.

From Salem take Highway 22 west, turn right on Oak Grove Rd (look for Restlawn Cemetery and turn right just before the sign), follow Oak Grove approximately 2 miles to Orchard Heights Rd. Turn right on Orchard Heights Rd, travel past Orchard Heights Winery about .25 miles, and you will see the Kathken sign on the left-hand side.

Or Take Wallace Road to Orchard Heights Rd. Continue on Orchard Heights Road until you see the Bella Vista sign just before turning into the vineyard.

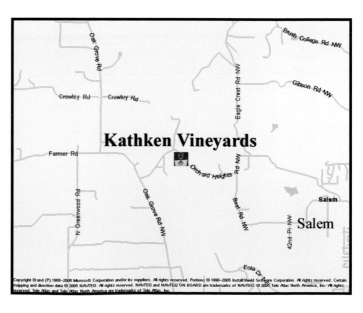

Orchard Heights Winery 4

Aloha!

Visitors find a touch of Hawaii and a whole lot more at Orchard Heights. This winery succeeds because it offers a unique experience. Yes, it has pinot noir and other Willamette Valley wines. However, what other wineries offer chocolate-covered macadamia nuts, caramel popcorn, and passionfruit wine? What other winery offers Sunday brunch?

What other tasting room has a gift shop with so much merchandise? Where else do you find terraced grounds and picnic areas that have the feel of a French chateau?

Orchard Heights Winery is a fusion of Hawaiian delights with Oregon wines and hospitality. Owner Gwen Purdy lives in Hawaii and is the sister of winemaker Carole Wyscaver. The connection with Hawaii explains the confections and macadamia-nut treats, as well as the "island tropical" wines, including passionfruit, tropical blend, mango, papaya, and pineapple. Forget the diet and try the Island Princess Macadamia Popcorn Crunch — it is simply delicious. For cork dorks in the crowd, there is plenty of traditional wine to be tasted, including muscat, gewürztraminer, pinot gris, pinot noir, and a red blend. The tropical wines are marketed under the label Island Princess.

Among the award-winning wines produced by Orchard Heights Winery are the '04 gewurztraminer, winner of a gold medal at the Oregon Wine and Food Festival; the '03 pinot gris, a bronze medal winner at the Oregon Wine and Food Festival; and the '04 Riesling, a silver medal winner at the Astoria Wine Festival.

Orchard Heights' scenic vineyard provides a wonderful setting for corporate events, weddings, and private parties. With plenty of wine to go around, there is no need to worry about such things. Your luaus are a guaranteed hit — Oregon style.

Mahalo!

ORCHARD HEIGHTS WINERY
winemaker(s): Carole Wyscaver
location: 6057 Orchard Heights Road NW,
Salem, OR 97304
phone: 503-769-4996
web: www.orchardheightswinery.com
e-mail: info@orchardhheightswinery.com
picnic area: Yes
weddings: Yes
gift shop: Yes
fee: $.50 per taste for white; $1 for reds. Fee waived
with purchase
hours: Daily 11–5

 BEST Eats

DIRECTIONS: **From Salem** take SR-22 [SR-99E Bus] west toward Marion St. Bridge. Take ramp (right) onto SR-221 [Salem-Dayton Hwy] for .8 miles. Turn left (west) onto Orchard Heights Rd NW and go 5.9 miles to the winery at 6057 Orchard Heights Rd NW.

Cherry Hill Winery 5

Approaching Cherry Hill Winery, you pass road signs informing you, "If you drink no noir, you pinot noir" and that you're in a "Cabernet-Free Zone"; there's also a speed limit sign asking you to keep it at 14 mph. You can spy the winery/tasting room in the distance past row upon row of pinot noir vines and a big pond set in a bowl in the landscape at the

base of the vineyard. There's a set of cabins and other buildings abutting the winery, with bicycles and kids' trikes scattered about. By the time I removed my car key, I knew these guys must be true "pinotphiles."

In 1998, Mike and Jan Sweeney purchased a piece of undeveloped property in the heart of the Eola-Amity Hills viticultural area west of Salem. With the property located on the same parallel as Burgundy, France, and with the south-facing slopes and mild climate, the Sweeneys must have been giddy with expectation. However, they were missing one key ingredient — vines. Along with a small army of vineyard workers, the couple set about planting the vines one at a time. Today, Cherry Hill Winery has planted more than 80,000 vines, accounting for 90 acres of pinot noir managed by Ken Cook and crew — all by hand.

Once I was inside the tasting room, my mouth watered at the prospect of sampling winemaker Chris Luby's productions: several vineyard-designated pinot noirs, including the winery's Papillon Estate Pinot Noir with the distinctive dog breed illustrated on its label. Visitors can also taste pinot gris and a dry pinot noir rosé. But make no mistake, Cherry Hill Winery is all about the pinot noir, with its Jory-soil-influenced dark cherry flavors and great finish. Chris uses neutral oak for aging, producing a tannin-tamed wine that delivers on flavor without being woody.

By the way, few wineries can boast that they offer a true wine country experience in one location. But Cherry Hill Winery can, with its dude ranch serving as a perfect spot for a romantic getaway or a corporate retreat. It's a viticultural retreat for those who want to know more about winemaking, ride a bike through wine country or relax with a book. The nearby Cook House caters breakfast in the morning and hors d'oeuvres in the evening. But here's the best part — the tasting room is a mere one-minute walk from your cabin.

CHERRY HILL WINERY
winemaker(s): Chris Luby
location: 7867 Crowley Road, Rickreall, OR 97371
phone: 503-623-7867
web: www.cherryhillwinery.com
e-mail: office@cherryhillwinery.com
picnic area: Yes
wheelchair access: Yes
tours: Yes
fee: $10 tasting fee refundable with purchase
hours: Monday through Friday 11–4 (call first); Saturday and Sunday 11–5, May 1 to October 1; Labor Day, Thanksgiving, and Memorial Day weekends

★ **BEST Lodging**

DIRECTIONS: **From Portland** take I-5 south to Salem and exit at Salem Parkway (exit 260). Follow signs for coast and the Marion St. Bridge. Take SR-22 across the Willamette River toward West Salem. Stay in the lanes marked "Oregon Coast & Beaches."

Continue approximately 5 miles west on SR-22 to Oak Grove Rd. Turn right onto Oak Grove Rd, and go 3 miles north to the first stop sign. Turn right, and travel approximately .7 miles to Crowley Rd. Turn left on Crowley Rd and continue .9 miles to 7867 Crowley Rd. Turn right, and continue approximately 1 mile to the winery. Cherry Hill Winery signs mark the way from SR-22.

From Eugene take I-5 north approximately 60 miles, and exit at the OR-22/OR-99E BUS exit towards Detroit Lake/Stayton (exit #253). Continue .2 miles then turn on SR-22/SR 99-E BUS. Follow signs for Marion St. Bridge and coast.

Take SR-22 across the Willamette River toward West Salem. Stay in lanes marked 'Oregon Coast & Beaches'. From there follow the same directions as above second paragraph.

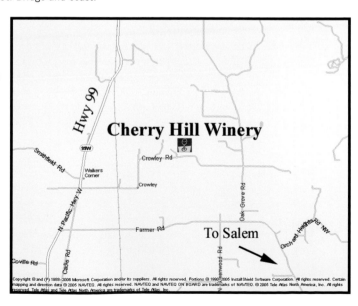

Firesteed Cellars ⁶

Do you enjoy a good rags-to-riches story that's downright American and inspiring? We've got one, and it belongs to Firesteed Cellars.

With its case production now at 80,000 cases per year, Firesteed Cellars ranks in the top five of Oregon wine producers. To understand how Firesteed accomplished this, you need to turn the clock back to the early 1990s, when the public's thirst for affordable red

wine hit a new high. Howard Rossbach, owner and founder of Firesteed Cellars, heard the plea and set about sharpening his pencil. He developed long-term contracts with Oregon pinot growers, identified a production facility with excess capacity, and found a winemaker consultant with time on his hand. The result? An everyday, quality pinot noir priced in the midteens and ready to be taken home and enjoyed the day it's purchased.

It didn't hurt that Howard came up with superior packaging. The label on the Firesteed Cellars is distinctive, looking like it belongs on a bottle of pinot three times the price.

So it was on a hot August day that we arrived at the Firesteed Cellars tasting room and winery 13 miles west of Salem on Hwy. 99W. Once inside the facility, you can't help but marvel at a massive wall of Firesteed Cellars wines stacked 15 cases high and 30 cases wide. That's a lot of pinot. Then you head to the cordoned "tasting room," where a talented interior designer somehow succeeded in making the area feel intimate. This is where you discover that Firesteed Cellars makes more than its everyday pinot noir, offering "more complex" pinot noirs, with higher price tags, such as a pinot gris, a pinot noir rosé, a Bordeaux-style red table wine, and its Italian-produced Barbera d'Asti. At only $12 a bottle for the red blend and barbera, visitors can find in these wines a respite from our economic woes.

And what foods pair well with these wines? I recommend checking out Martha Stewart's website (*www.marthastewart.com*) — OK, I confess that I've visited the site *on occasion* — to get her recipe for Spiced Butterflied Leg of Lamb, which features an anise-scented rub and fragrant olive oil. In pairing the lamb with a Firesteed Cellars Willamette Valley Pinot Noir, my only issue is having to wait until the lamb is ready before I enjoy a glass of this wine. Talk about a case of premature pairing!

FIRESTEED CELLARS
opened: 1992
winemaker(s): Bryan Croft
location: 2200 N Pacific Highway W,
Rickreall, OR 97371
phone: 503-623-8683
web: www.firesteed.com
e-mail: mbonner@firesteed.com
picnic area: Yes
gift shop: Yes
fee: $5 tasting fee refunded with purchase
hours: Daily 11–5; Closed Christmas and
New Year's Day

DIRECTIONS: **From Amity** take SR-99W [Pacific Hwy W] for 10.9 miles. Arrive at Firesteed Cellars at 2200 N Pacific Hwy W.

From Salem take SR-22 [Marion St. Bridge] 9.9 miles going west. Turn right (north) onto SR-99W and go 1.9 miles. Arrive at 2200 N. Pacific Hwy W.

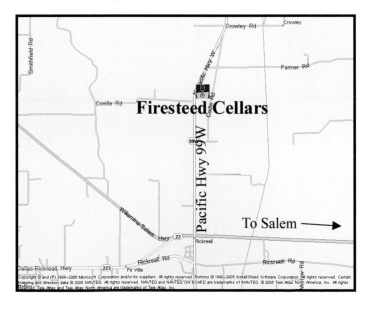

Left Coast Cellars 7

To visit Left Coast Cellars, you travel north from the town of Rickreall on Hwy. 99 until you arrive at the winery's gated entrance. From there, you execute no fewer than five left turns to get to the tasting room. Owners Bob and Suzanne Pfaff lived in Paris during the 1970s and no doubt visited that city's Left Bank on many occasions. There is, in fact, a streak of left-handedness running through the Pfaff family. The Pfaffs came fromColorado

to the "left coast" in 2003 when they acquired the 306-acre tract that would become… well, you guessed it: Left Coast Cellars.

Through some wise hiring choices, the Pfaffs developed an extended family of relatively young and talented vineyard, winemaking, tasting room and back-office personnel. These people, especially thirty-something vineyard manager and winemaker Luke McCollom, are the face of Left Coast Cellars. Luke was one of the first hires the Pfaffs made, and his background in the California wine industry was put to good use from the start. Today, on the primarily southern-sloping hills of the property, Luke and his team adhere to biodynamic and organic farming methods on nearly 100 acres of wine grapes. Bearing the names Field of Dreams, Latitude 45, Left Bank, Right Bank, The Bench, Truffle Hill, and The Orchards, the vineyards are the jewels of the estate. Each has a distinctive character suitable for various clones of pinot noir, pinot gris, and chardonnay. These vineyards are the key to the Left Coast Cellars success story.

However, from a visitor's perspective, the real story is the jaw-dropping beauty of the grounds. The 15-mph drive from the iron-gate entrance to the stylish tasting room allows your eye to drink in a spring-fed lake, undulating hills of meticulously groomed vineyards, artsy sculpture, stately white oaks, garden flowers, and Italian cypress trees. Framed by a natural bowl-like amphitheater, the Left Coast Cellars property is more of a private reserve on a Jurassic Park scale — minus the jungle foliage and Tyrannosaurus rex, of course.

As for the wines, Luke has succeeded in racking up a number of awards. For example, their 2004 Cali's Cuvée won a Critic's Gold at the prestigious 2007 Critics Challenge in San Diego. That's not a left-handed compliment; it's high praise for the wines he creates. Such recognition gives tasting-room staff a sense of pride when pouring Left Coast's offerings for eager visitors, including this left-handed WineTrail trekker.

LEFT COAST CELLARS
opened: 2007
winemaker(s): Luke McCollom
location: 4225 N Pacific Highway [99W],
Rickreall, OR 97371
phone: 888-831-4916
web: www.leftcoastcellars.com
e-mail: dm@leftcoastcellars.com
picnic area: Yes
fee: $5 tasting fee refundable with purchase
hours: Daily 12–5 February through December 23rd;
by appointment in January

DIRECTIONS: From McMinnville go southeast on SR-99W [Pacific Hwy W] 14.4 miles. Arrive at Left Coast Cellars at 4225 N Pacific Hwy W.

From Salem go north on Liberty St. SE for .4 miles. Turn left (west) onto SR-22 [SR-99E Bus] for .5 miles. Take ramp (right) onto SR-22 [Marion St. Bridge] for 9.9 miles. Turn right (north) onto SR-99W and go 4.1 miles to Left Coast Cellars.

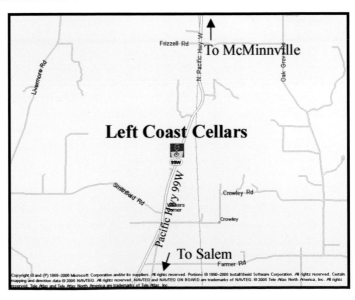

Van Duzer Vineyards 🎱

The westward views from the hilltop location of Van Duzer Vineyards stop you in your tracks. Beyond the vineyards lies the Coast Range and, specifically, a gap in the mountains called the Van Duzer Corridor. This passage through the Coast Range brings a cool breeze to the vineyards on summer afternoons. People and grapes love its cooling effect — winemakers swear by it. To celebrate this west wind, Van Duzer Vineyards drew upon Greek mythology and Zephyr, the god of the west wind, to adorn their labels. Their

version is more of a goddess, Zephyra, who, on a green background adorned with autumn grape leaves, holds a cluster of pinot noir grapes and looks you in the eye.

The proprietors of the 140-acre estate are Chicago-based Marilynn and Carl Thoma. As owners of the Stone's Throw Vineyards in California, they certainly knew what they were getting into when they purchased the property in 1998. However, with the Van Duzer Vineyards, they had the chance to add a new grape to their portfolio: pinot noir. To make this happen, they set about hiring a vineyard manager and a winemaker.

The vineyard management task fell on the shoulders of Norbert Fiebig, a German transplant. Charged with the task of making Van Duzer Vineyards a sustainable ecosystem, Norbert has achieved LIVE (low-impact viticulture and enology) and Salmon Safe certifications for the vineyards. He knows all 80 acres of cultivated ground, the many varieties of pinot clones, how the vines are trellised, and their orientation to the sun. And when it comes to the subject of good and bad bugs, Norbert becomes animated. With a clump of dirt in his hands, he can wax eloquently about the importance of lady beetles, green lacewings, and minute pirate bugs.

Since 1994, Jim Kakacek (pronounced "kuh-kay-sic") has made wine for Van Duzer Vineyards to the tune of 18,000 cases annually. Expect to taste several vineyard-designated and blended pinot noirs, pinot gris, and a pinot noir rosé. The tasting room itself looks as though it sprang from the pages of *Architectural Digest*, with plenty of glass to showcase the spectacular view to the west. Despite the surrounding splendor, I stood transfixed, gazing at the Van Duzer Vineyards' wine labels and the beauty of Zephyra and her cluster of ripe grapes. She seemed to be enticing me, saying, "Hey, WineTrail Guy, have you tried the Van Duzer Flagpole Block Pinot Noir?"

VAN DUZER VINEYARDS
opened: 1998
winemaker(s): Jim Kakacek
location: 11975 Smithfield Road, Dallas, OR 97338
phone: 800-884-1927
web: www.vanduzer.com
e-mail: info@vanduzer.com
picnic area: Yes
wheelchair access: Yes
gift shop: Yes
fee: Complimentary wine tasting
hours: Daily 11–5 March through December;
closed January and February

 BEST Views

DIRECTIONS: Accessed off of 99W, 8 miles south of Amity on Smithfield Rd, or off of Hwy 22 across from Hwy 223. Located on the northwest corner of Baskett Slough National Wildlife Refuge.

From downtown Salem head north onto Liberty St. SE for .4 miles. Turn left (west) onto SR-22 [SR-99E Bus] for .5 miles. Take ramp (right) onto SR-22 [Marion St. Bridge] and continue 13.2 miles. Bear right (north) onto Smithfield Rd and proceed .3 miles. Arrive at 11975 Smithfield Rd.

From Amity proceed south on SR-99W [Pacific Hwy W] 9.7 miles. Turn right (west) onto Smithfield Rd; go 3.2 miles and look for signs to the winery.

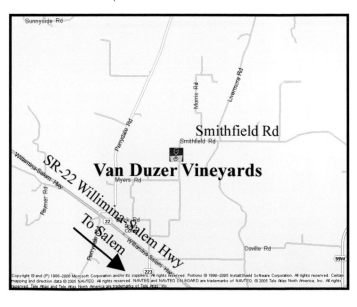

Namasté Vineyards 9

A journey of the heart brought Dave Masciorini and Chris and Sonia Miller to this rolling hilltop south of the Eola Hills. Call it a spiritual quest. All three possess a California background and had exposure to the wine industry. Indeed, owning a winery was a vision

they all shared; a place where they could live, play, and work in peace and harmony. So when the time came to name the newly acquired vineyard, it seemed only natural to call it Namasté Vineyards.

The Sanskrit word "namasté" means "I honor the Spirit in you, which is also in me" and is a common refrain heard in India and Nepal.

In keeping with the Eastern theme, a yin-yang-inspired sign greets visitors when they turn off dusty Van Well Road. From there it's a half-mile climb to the top of the hill. When you shut the car engine off, you notice the tranquility of the property. It's quiet. Life's pace slows down, and you can't help but notice the Adirondack chairs positioned to enjoy the view of the 200-acre vineyard. It provides the perfect setting for any special event, from a small intimate wedding to a large family reunion.

Looking at the tasting room from the outside, you would never know that the building is actually a Quonset hut bearing a façade with a set of French doors that hide the semi-circular roofline. Inside, the atmosphere is wonderfully uplifting, with a warm Mediterranean feeling given off by the golden-orange blown-in insulation on the ceiling, which contrasts sharply to the deep blue walls. On my visit, I had the honor of talking with co-owner Dave Masciorini, who was pouring samples of the winery's Willamette Valley wines, and as I tasted its array of whites (chardonnay, riesling, gewürztraminer, and a white blend called Peace) as well as couple of pinot noirs, Dave spoke about Namasté's entrepreneurial growth. Unlike many of the surrounding wineries that started with deep pockets, Namasté Vineyards' path has been incremental. Each year, it seems, the partners take on a new project, from insulating the tasting room to replacing the portable potty with a bathroom.

As owners of the vineyard and the wines brought forth from them, Dave, Chris, and Sonia must exercise due diligence in all aspects of Namasté Vineyards. Fortunately for them they have a neighboring winery with an excellent winemaker at their disposal — Chateau Bianca's Andreas Wetzel. They provide the yin and he brings the yang. The result is a convergence of joy, peace, and abundance at this winery. Namasté.

Dave Masciorini, Sonia Miller and Chris Miller (l to r).

NAMASTÉ VINEYARDS
opened: 2002
winemaker(s): Andreas Wetzel
location: 5600 Van Well Road, Dallas, OR 97338
phone: 503-623-4150
web: www.namastevineyards.com
e-mail: chris@namastevineyards.com
picnic area: Yes
weddings: Yes
fee: Complimentary wine tasting
hours: Saturday and Sunday 12–6 March through December, or by appointment

BEST Views

DIRECTIONS: From Salem go north on Liberty St. SE for .4 miles. Turn left (west) onto SR-22 [SR-99E Bus] and proceed .5 miles. Take ramp (right) onto SR-22 [Marion St. Bridge] and go 15.7 miles. Bear right (north) onto Van Well Rd and go 3.2 miles to Namaste Vineyards on right.

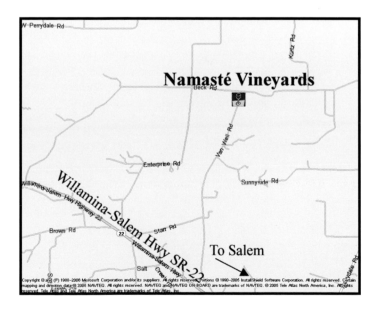

Chateau Bianca Winery 🔟

Opened seven days a week from 10 a.m. to 5 p.m., Chateau Bianca is a convenient stop for wine tourists and people taking Highway 22 to and from the Pacific coast. Situated near the Van Duzer corridor, the winery and vineyard benefit from the cooling effects of

the afternoon breeze. Simply turn into the winery's ample parking lot and enter its tasting room, where a large selection of wines and wine-related accessories await you.

Winemaking is in large part about tradition. Sure, you can gain such knowledge through courses at an enology program or by volunteering as a cellar rat. However, if you have four generations of winemakers in your family, you have a leg up on the competition. Such is the case with winemaker Andreas Wetzel. Being tall and having a broad smile helps Andreas to work with his crew, but it's the knowledge handed down from one generation to another that spells the difference — a difference with a German accent.

Andreas' parents, Helmut and Liselotte (aka Opa and Oma), are of German descent, and the couple began Chateau Bianca Winery in the 1970s with the planting of 12 different grape varieties on 50 acres near the Van Duzer Corridor of the Coast Range. They brought with them the German winemaking know-how of their ancestors, along with a family recipe for Glühwein, a mulled hot spiced wine perfect for the hot tub — just add cinnamon sticks.

Glühwein may be a signature offering at Chateau Bianca, but most of its production centers on pinot noir, pinot gris, and pinot blanc. Other wines include riesling, Gewürztraminer, Marechal Foch, chardonnay, port, and vin de glace (a dessert wine made from chardonnay). The wines are priced to go for an "irresistible value," ranging from the midteens to the high 20s for its estate pinot noir.

Interestingly, Opa and Oma are also proprietors and hosts of their estate bed and breakfast. Bearing the name Chateau Bianca Oregon Wine Country Bed & Breakfast, the establishment offers wine tourists a romantic getaway in the heart of wine country. Incredible views, a king-size bed, a private bath and a gourmet breakfast await visitors, all at an affordable rate. Can you name another place where you can brush up on your German language skills and sip a glass of Glühwein in the tub? Probably in the Rhine region of Germany, but nowhere else in Oregon!

CHATEAU BIANCA WINERY
opened: 1987
winemaker(s): Andreas Wetzel
location: 17485 Highway 22, Dallas, OR 97338
phone: 503-623-6181
web: www.chateaubianca.com
e-mail: customerservice@chateaubianca.com
picnic area: Yes
gift shop: Yes
tours: Yes
fee: Small tasting fee
hours: Daily 10–5; closed major holidays

Andreas Wetzel

BEST Lodging

DIRECTIONS: From McMinnville, head south 1.2 miles on SR-99W [SE Adams St.]. Keep straight onto SR-18 [SW Baker St.] for 16.3 miles. Turn left (east) onto Steel Bridge Rd and go 1.9 miles. Turn left (east) onto SR-22 [Willamina-Salem Hwy] for 4.8 miles. Arrive at Chateau Bianca Winery on right.

From downtown Salem, go north onto Liberty St. SE for .4 miles. Turn left (west) onto SR-22 [SR-99E Bus] for .5 miles. Take ramp (right) onto SR-22 [Marion St. Bridge] and continue 19.4 miles to the winery.

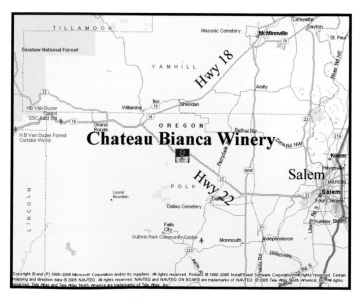

Eola Hills Wine Cellars 🔢

On my "1,000 Things to Do Before I Die" list is to cycle the Eola Hills Wine Cellars bike tour. It just seems to me that pinot noir and bike riding are a perfect pair — like peas and carrots. Rolling hills, vineyards, and an occasional stop at a roadside winery for a taste of pinot noir; what could be better than that?

Tom Huggins, the owner of Eola Hills Wine Cellars, had the idea for a Sunday ride in wine country back in the mid-'90s. A number of friends and family participated and had

a great time. Since then, every Sunday during the month of August, Eola Hills Wine Cellars sponsors bike touring through the Eola Hills wine country. With stops at a number of nearby wineries, you might wonder what to do with your purchases. It would be hard shifting gears while juggling a bottle of pinot noir. No worries, there is a SAG wagon in which to store your wine purchases along the way. As far as the pace and difficulty of the tour, Huggins and his team offer different routes for novice and hardcore cyclists. At the end of the day, you all meet back at Eola Hills Wine Cellars to enjoy a barbecue and wine.

A visit to Eola Hills Wine Cellars sans bicycle is also amazing. Just working your way through the gift shop is an exercise in restraint (or not!), because there are just so many goodies to purchase. The wine bar itself is like an oasis in a relatively large production room complete with aging barrels, bottling operations, and a full-size kitchen. At the oversized wine bar, visitors taste award-winning red and white wines including pinot noir, chardonnay, merlot, sangiovese, Maréchal Foch, zinfandel, syrah, pinot gris, sauvignon blanc, late-harvest Gewürztraminer, and port. With a case production of 60,000 annually, the winery must be doing something right, to say nothing of keeping winemaker Steve Anderson on his toes.

Be sure to take a glass of wine outside to enjoy on the picnic grounds. Stroll around and check out the artificial waterfall and koi pond. As you're snapping shots of this picturesque landscape, don't be surprised if you're overcome by an irresistible urge to reserve a spot on Huggins' next bike tour.

EOLA HILLS WINE CELLARS
opened: 1986
winemaker(s): Steve Anderson
location: 501 S Pacific Highway [99W],
Rickreall, OR 97371
phone: 503-623-2405
web: www.eolahillswinery.com
e-mail: ann-batson@eolahillswinery.com
picnic area: Yes
wheelchair access: Yes
weddings: Yes
gift shop: Yes
tours: Yes
fee: Complimentary wine tasting
hours: Daily 10–5; closed Thanksgiving and
Christmas days

BEST Gift shop

DIRECTIONS: **From McMinnville** head south on SR-99W [SE Adams St.] for 1.2 miles. Turn left (southeast) onto SR-99W [Pacific Hwy W] for 18.2 miles. Arrive at 501 S Pacific Hwy W on your right.

From Salem go west on SR-22 [SR-99E Bus] .5 miles. Take ramp (right) onto SR-22 [Marion St. Bridge] and continue 9.9 miles. Turn right (north) onto SR-99W, proceed .2 miles to cellars.

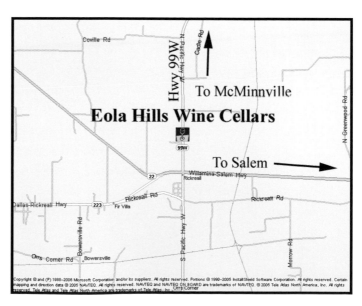

Salem – Monmouth
Wine Trail

Bird house at Ankeny Vineyard

One of the great joys of WineTrails of Oregon is the discovery of the old and the new. By that I mean the established winery bonded more than 30 years ago and the new winery that just opened its doors. In the case of the Salem – Monmouth WineTrail, wine tourists can check out the Honeywood Winery established in 1933 (that's not a typo) and the recently bonded Emerson Vineyards in Monmouth. Both have a story to tell. Both have their own signature wines that are totally different and appeal to different tastes. Aside from these wineries, visitors will enjoy the spectacular vistas that Willamette Valley Vineyards, Ankeny Vineyard, and Airlie Winery offer, as well as the down-home friendliness provided by Vitae Springs Vineyard.

If time permits, check out Salem for restaurants, artisan shops and a jaunt through the State Capitol grounds. This gives you a big dose of art and history and arms you well for the wine journey ahead.

1 Honeywood Winery
2 Willamette Valley Vineyards
3 Ankeny Vineyard
4 Vitae Springs Vineyard
5 Emerson Vineyards
6 Airlie Winery

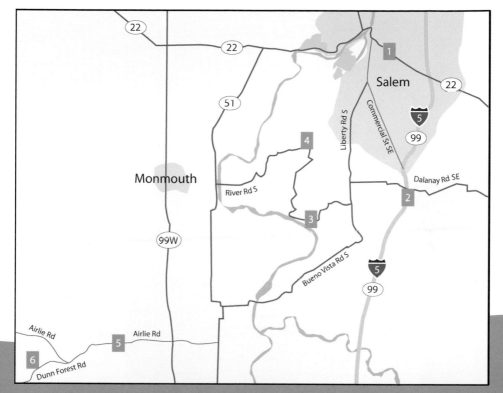

Region:	**Mid Willamette Valley Wine Country**
# of tasting rooms on tour:	**6**
Estimate # of days for tour:	**2**
Getting around:	**Car**
Key Events:	❑ **Salem's Oregon Wine & Food Festival held at the Oregon State Fairgrounds. Call 503-580-2509 or go online to www.oregonstatefair.org.**
	❑ **Memorial Weekend in Wine Country – Willamette Valley – visit www.willamettewines.com.**
	❑ **Wine Country Thanksgiving – Willamette Valley – call 503-646-2985 or visit www.willamettewines.com.**
Tips:	❑ **Consider hiring a limousine service such as Pro Limo 503-391-2900, 877-800-LIMO (5466).**
	❑ **See Appendix B – Wine Tour Planning, for planning your visit.**
Best:	❑ **Views: Willamette Valley Vineyards, Ankeny Vineyard, Airlie Winery.**

Honeywood Winery

Cork dorks need to check their attitude at the door. This winery may focus on fruit wines and other specialty wines, but it just so happens that Honeywood Winery is the grandfather of the Oregon wine industry. With the winery's roots reaching back to 1933, founders Ron Honeyman and John Wood did not want to call it "Honeywood." Still, the name came naturally, and it stuck.

Honeywood's list of fruit wines, specialty wines, and varietal wines is extensive. Nowhere else do you find such varieties of wine. Originally called Columbia Distilleries, the winery produced fruit brandies, cordials, and liqueurs. Eventually, Ron and John settled on making premium fruit wines and decided a name change was in order. That's when it became known as Honeywood Winery.

There's definitely a big community of fruit-wine lovers. Anything that has sugar in it is a candidate for becoming wine; those little yeast critters don't care if the sugar is from cherry or cabernet sauvignon, they'll convert it to alcohol. Think about pairing the following fruit wines with vanilla ice cream or pound cake: blackberry, boysenberry, black currant, red currant, cherry, loganberry, marionberry, pear, plum, raspberry, and rhubarb. These are in addition to such specialty wines as Golden Pineapple, Honeysuckle Supreme, and Tropical Sunset.

However, if you think Honeywood Winery is only about fruit and specialty wines, think again. It does offer a number of varietal grape wines, such as cabernet sauvignon, chardonnay, merlot, and pinot noir. These, together with its fruit and specialty wines, adds up to more than 40 different wines that Honeywood Winery produces for distribution throughout the United States.

The winery gift shop offers a multitude of wine-related items. From refrigerator magnets to wine stoppers, it's easy to shop for your favorite wine-loving relative. The bottom line: Honeywood Winery offers something for everyone.

HONEYWOOD WINERY
opened: 1933
winemaker(s): Paul Gallick
location: 1350 Hines Street SE, Salem, OR 97302
phone: 503-362-4111
web: www.honeywoodwinery.com
e-mail: info@honeywoodwinery.com
picnic area: Yes
gift shop: Yes
fee: Complimentary wine tasting up to 5 tastes
hours: Monday through Friday 9–5, Saturday 10–5, Sunday 1–5; closed Easter, Thanksgiving, Christmas and New Year's Day

DIRECTIONS: From I-5 take exit 253 and go west on Hwy 22 [Mission St.]. Turn left on 12th St. and then left on Hines St. SE. The winery is between 13th and 14th on your right.

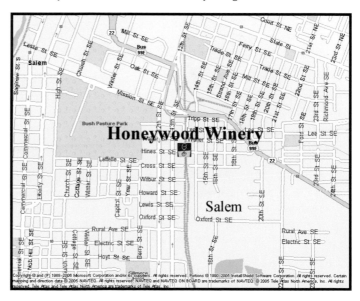

Willamette Valley Vineyards 2️⃣

The force behind Willamette Valley Vineyards is founder and principal owner Jim Bernau. Jim's over-the-top passion led to the acquisition of a plot of land south of Salem that was overgrown with blackberry bushes and Scotch broom. That was 1983, when Jim was a small-business lobbyist at the state Capitol, where he worked to create a budding Oregon wine industry. His neighbors surely thought this native Oregonian was a little wacky as they watched him clear the land with a tractor and run garden hoses to the young Vitis vinifera vines. His boots must have been permanently red from the property's Jory soil. Eventually, in 1989, Jim produced wine with the Willamette Valley Vineyards label and

demonstrated, along with other winemaking pioneers, that growing cool-climate varietals results in excellent wines of Burgundian heritage.

Jim understood that to make his dream a reality, he would need big bucks. But rather than find a few investors with deep pockets, he found thousands of investors with small pockets.

He drafted a public stock offering to create a cooperative of sorts to offer Oregonians a stake in a budding winery. It worked. Today, Willamette Valley Vineyards (WVV) is a community of more than 4,500 investors, and you can be sure that many of these investors happily participate in the wine club and the many events hosted at the winery throughout the year.

Each day, thousands of cars pass along the stretch of I-5 that runs parallel to the winery. The beauty of the vineyards and the towered building on the hilltop grabs the attention of many travelers. The lucky ones have time to take exit 248 off I-5 and negotiate a couple of turns to the winery's entrance. The tasting room offers a panoramic view from Illahee Hill toward other vineyard-covered hills to the west. The best part, however, is the complimentary wine tasting of vintage wines, and for $6, you can sample WVV reserve wines and take home a Riedel wine glass.

Chief winemaker Forrest Klaffke and his team use the fruit from four different WVV-owned vineyards (comprising more than 300 acres) to make pinot noir, pinot gris, and chardonnay. In typical Oregon fashion, Jim Bernau, his investors, and the staff of WVV focus intently on sustainable practices — all of these vineyards bear the LIVE certification and are Salmon Safe. There's something downright comforting about the purity of the wine you drink from Willamette Valley Vineyards.

WILLAMETTE VALLEY VINEYARDS
opened: 1989
winemaker(s): Forrest Klaffke
location: 8800 Enchanted Way SE, Turner, OR 97392
phone: 503-588-9463
web: www.willamettevalleyvineyards.com
e-mail: info@wvv.com
picnic area: Yes
wheelchair access: Yes
gift shop: Yes
tours: Yes
fee: Complimentary tasting & $6 reserve which, includes free Riedel wine glass
hours: Daily 11–6; closed major holidays

 BEST Views

DIRECTIONS: From Portland, take I-5 South to exit 248. Turn left, go under the freeway. Immediately turn right on Enchanted Way. Go 1 mile.

From Eugene, take I-5 North to exit 248. Turn right and immediately turn right onto Enchanted Way, go 1 mile.

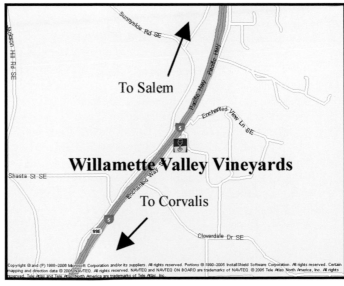

Ankeny Vineyard 3

The only thing friendlier than Hershey, the resident chocolate Lab at Ankeny Vineyard, is Joe Olexa, the vineyard's owner and resident dirt guy since 1982. With four college degrees under his belt — and none that had a thing to do with growing grapes — Joe caught the wine bug in the early '80s and never looked back. Today, he's the proud farmer of 35 acres of premium wine grapes.

The setting on this southern part of the Salem Hills affords visitors the chance to view the Ankeny National Bird Refuge from the property. If you like to swirl pinot while checking out ducks, geese, and swans, Ankeny Vineyard is the place to be. Joe, along with his tasting-room "wine duchess," Kathy Greysmith, usually are around to swap stories with visitors and explain the history of the property. Kathy is wonderfully welcoming as she leads visitors on a tasting tour of their estate white table wine, pinot gris, several pinot noirs, a pinot noir rosé, a Maréchal Foch and a red blend. My personal favorite was the Hershey's Red Pinot Noir, but I happen to be partial to wines with labels adorned with smiling dogs.

Be sure to take your glass to the outside patio, weather permitting, and enjoy. There's an outside chance that winemaker Andy Thomas will be around to provide tasting notes and winemaking secrets.

As the site of Cox Cemetery, Ankeny Vineyard is a historical property. A short hike up the hill will take you through Ankeny Vineyard wine grapes and past goats, emus, and llamas to arrive at the pioneer cemetery. The residents of Cox Cemetery include original settlers Tom and Martha Cox, who cultivated the current vineyard site in the mid-1800s, as well as about 100 other settlers buried in marked and unmarked graves. (**WineTrail note:** For further information about the Cox Cemetery, see www.oregonpioneers.com/marion/CoxCem.htm.) I was gazing at the view below and reflecting on those brave pioneers when my right hand felt a wet tongue. It was Hershey doing his friendly Lab thing and bringing me back to the here and now.

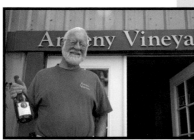

Joe Olexa

ANKENY VINEYARD
opened: 1980
winemaker(s): Andy Thomas
location: 2565 Riverside Road S,
Salem, OR 97211-5444
phone: 503-378-1498
web: www.ankenyvineyard.com
e-mail: ankenyvineyard@cs.com
picnic area: Yes
wheelchair access: Yes
fee: $5 tasting fee waived with purchase
hours: Daily 11–5

REST Views

DIRECTIONS: **From I-5**, take exit 243 west (Ankeny Hill) and follow the blue winery signs.

From Independence, at the flashing red light, go south on Route 51 for a quarter mile, turn left and cross the bridge over the Willamette River. Take the first right onto Riverside Rd S and follow the blue winery signs.

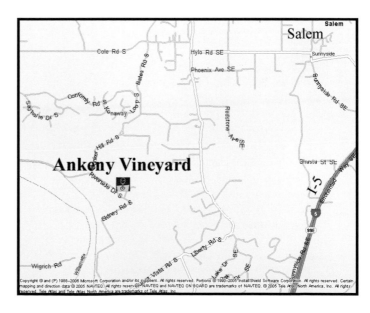

Vitae Springs Vineyard 4

During a U.S. Air Force stint in Europe in the early 1970s, Earl and Pam VanVolkinburg discovered German wines while residing in that country's Mosel Valley. With their newfound passion for growing grapes and making wine, the VanVolkinburgs returned to the states, where Earl began a private medical practice. However, one thing led to another, and they purchased a plot of land southwest of Salem that proved to be a great place for growing cool-weather grapes. That led to the planting of pinot noir, pinot gris, riesling, and a small amount of Grüner Veltliner.

The Grüner Veltliner grape has notable plantings in Austria along the Danube River. You rarely find it in the United States. In Oregon, fewer than 25 total acres are in production. This little factoid alone makes Vitae Springs Vineyard special. The charming, ready-to-drink white wine created with these grapes is packed full of citrus flavors and is easily drinkable by itself or served with seafood or such dishes as salad with grilled chicken or cheese-chicken tortellini.

When a family's two-car garage doubles as a tasting room, you know it's got to be a small operation. (In the case of Vitae Springs, there are fewer than 1,000 cases of wine produced each year.) In Vitae Springs' tasting room, you swirl and sip wine next to the family car and in the company of the VanVolkinburgs' white-coated West Highland terrier, who looks at you with big, teddy-bear eyes. Sydney, the dog, has an acute case of cuteness!

The VanVolkinburgs had come to the realization that the grapes they were cultivating on their 33 acres — 25 of which are planted with pinot noir — must be pretty wonderful, because wineries such as St. Innocent were signing long-term leases for their harvests. It seemed only natural that the family should start setting aside some of the grapes to make wine under the Vitae Springs Vineyard label. Fortunately for Earl and Pam, their son Joel and his wife, Michelle, have taken over many of the day-to-day grape-growing and winemaking chores. Joel's focus is the vineyard, which requires constant attention: pruning, managing weeds, training canes, trimming the canopy, and harvesting by hand. Equally important are the sales and market responsibilities assumed by Michelle. It's a family affair with each person having an assigned role, and it seems to work just fine.

Taste for yourself and you'll understand why it all works. Just remember to park your car outside the garage!

VITAE SPRINGS VINEYARD
opened: 1978
winemaker(s): Joe Dobbes, Jr.
location: 3675 Vitae Springs Road S,
Salem, OR 97306
phone: 503-588-0896
web: www.vitaesprings.com
e-mail: michelle@vitaesprings.com
fee: Tasting fee may apply
hours: Friday through Sunday 12–5,
or by appointment

Pam VanVolkinburg and winery mascot Sydney.

DIRECTIONS: **From downtown Salem**, head south on Commercial St. SE for about 1.5 miles. Keep right onto Liberty Rd S and go 1.8 miles toward Sprague High School/Rosedale. Turn right (west) onto Skyline Rd S for 1.9 miles. Keep right onto Vitae Springs Rd S and go 1 miles to arrive at the vineyard on the right.

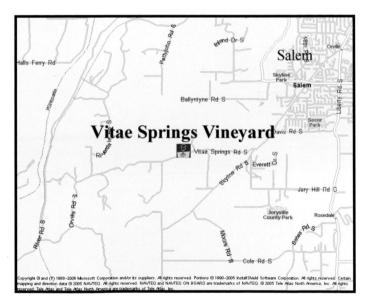

Emerson Vineyards 5

I know this may seem trivial, but it means a lot to this WineTrail trekker That the half-mile drive from the Airlie Road turnoff to this winery is paved. Somebody paid big bucks to give you a smooth drive without the dust. That someone is owner Tom Johns, a retired executive from a biotech firm in Boca Raton, Florida, who moved across the country to fulfill a dream — starting a winery in the Willamette Valley. However, this former executive is anything but retired. He's busy marketing the wine, managing the tasting room, and writing checks. Besides being really smart and savvy about business, Tom has another great asset that visitors discover: his infectious laugh.

The operation is a family affair with Tom's son Elliott Johns serving as its "wines and vines" person. A graduate of Oregon State University's fermentation science program, Elliott's résumé includes winemaking jobs at Elk Cove Vineyards and Chard Farm Winery in New Zealand. Elliott clocks long days at the winery managing 24 acres planted with vines (20 of which are various pinot noir clones) and producing 2,500 cases of wine per year. Other "experimental" grapes planted include viognier, Maréchal Foch, baco noir, Leon Millot and Oberlin noir. Ultimately, these grapes are destined for blending to soften, add texture or round out a wine.

Elliott's two dogs, Emmit and Birdy, are often at his heels. As Robert Parker Jr. wrote, "A dog is happiest when it is in the shadow of its owner." Incidentally, Emmit will likely need to get an agent soon. He's one of the dogs featured in the soon-to-be-published *Wine Dogs USA* book.

Tom came up with the attractive signage and packaging for the wine labels, borrowing from the Art Deco work of Charles Rennie Mackintosh, a contemporary of Frank Lloyd Wright. The intense blues, greens, and yellows found in the Emerson Vineyards logo carry through in the utilitarian doors of the tasting room and winery facilities. Even the name of the wine club reinforces the brand — The Waldo Society. However, beyond the packaging is that genuine smile and the caring attitude Tom shows visitors with each pour. Don't be surprised if he asks you a little about how your day is going. With his innate kindness and strong business acumen, he's a fine blend himself.

EMERSON VINEYARDS
winemaker(s): Elliott Johns
location: 11665 Airlie Road, Monmouth, OR 97361
phone: 503-838-0944
web: www.emersonvineyards.com
e-mail: info@emersonvineyards.com
picnic area: Yes
fee: $5 tasting fee
hours: Saturday and Sunday 12–5 between Memorial Day and Christmas, or by appointment

DIRECTIONS: **From Salem**, head west on SR-22 [SR-99 E Bus] for .5 miles. Take ramp (right) onto SR-22 [Marion St. Bridge] and go 9.9 miles. Turn left (south) onto SR-99W for 13.2 miles. Turn right (west) onto Airlie Rd and go 2.3 miles to 11665 Airlie Rd.

From Corvallis go north on SR-99W [NW 3rd St.] for about 13 miles. Turn left (west) onto Airlie Rd and proceed 2.3 miles to 11665 Airlie Rd.

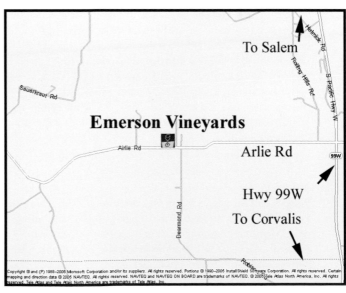

Airlie Winery 6

There are many great reasons to pack a picnic and head to Airlie Winery in rural Monmouth. Here's just one: Airlie Winery achieved the title of "Value Brand of the Year" from *Wine & Spirits* magazine in 2006. Its prices are in the low teens for most whites, and even its Vintner's Blend Pinot Noir sells for a reasonable $26.

Visitors to Airlie Winery would be wise to bring a cooler for all those bottles they'll be purchasing.

As they approach the winery, first-time visitors see the Airlie logo with its hot air balloon theme on the entrance sign. At this point you are forgiven for stopping to snap pictures. The setting itself is spectacular, with a small lake forming a bowl-like amphitheater for the vineyards and hilltop winery. There's a formal picnic area situated by the lake, where visitors can soak in the view and contemplate whether or not the lake has trout.

Owner Mary E. Olson is the creator of this idyllic space and manager of the Dunn Forest Vineyard estate. Her philosophy is to make affordable wines that are enjoyable when purchased. They don't need to lie in the cellar collecting dust for years; they're ready for grilled salmon or savory chicken that evening. With Elizabeth Clark as its winemaker, Airlie Winery produces as many as 8,000 cases of wine, which are sold throughout the United States. Its portfolio includes pinot noir, pinot gris, Gewürztraminer, Maréchal Foch, chardonnay, Müller-Thurgau and a white blend with the name "7." At only $12 a bottle, this blend of seven Willamette Valley white grape varieties flies out the door. Achieving a silver medal at the 2007 Oregon Wine Competition, Airlie's 7 wine is described by Airlie as being "like a gathering of great friends. Bring them together, let their best qualities shine and celebrate the mix." I love that.

As I left the friendly tasting room carting my newly purchased bottle of Dunn Forest Pinot Noir, I made sure to step over the resident Irish setters sleeping outside. I took in the fabulous view: People were drinking wine on the outside patio, exchanging the usual "where are you from?" pleasantries. The sky was blue and devoid of clouds. I spied Airlie's balloon logo and, wouldn't you know, the song "Up, Up and Away" by the 5th Dimension began to play in my head.

AIRLIE WINERY
opened: 1986
winemaker(s): Elizabeth Clark
location: 15305 Dunn Forest Road,
Monmouth, OR 97361
phone: 503-838-6013
web: www.airliewinery.com
e-mail: airlie@airliewinery.com
picnic area: Yes
weddings: Yes
fee: Complimentary wine tasting
hours: Saturday and Sunday 12–5

BEST Views

DIRECTIONS: **From downtown Salem**, head west on SR-22 [SR-99E Bus] for .5 miles. Take ramp (right) onto SR-22 [Marion St. Bridge] for 9.9 miles. Turn left (south) onto SR-99W for 13.2 miles. Turn right (west) onto Airlie Rd and proceed 4.3 miles. Turn left (south) onto Berry Creek Rd for .1 miles. Turn right (west) onto Dunn Forest Rd and continue 1.9 miles to arrive at winery.

If coming from Corvallis, take SR-99W [NW 3rd St.] for 12.8 miles. Turn left (west) onto Airlie Rd for 4.3 miles. Turn left (south) onto Berry Creek Rd for .1 miles. Turn right (west) on Dunn Forest Rd and drive 1.9 miles to arrive at Airlie Winery.

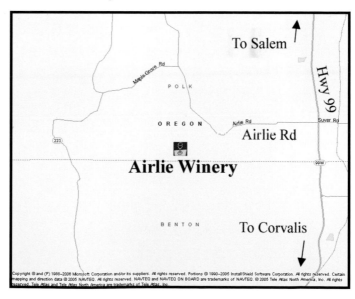

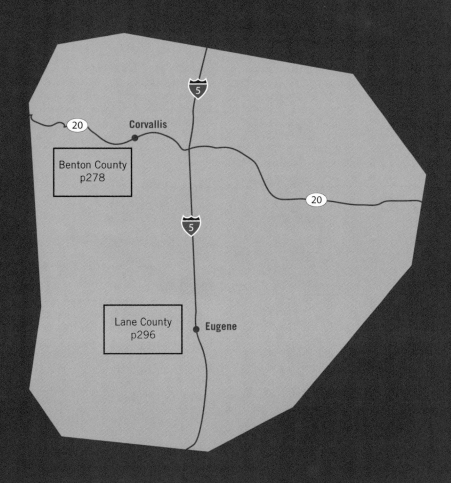

20

5

Corvallis

20

Benton County
p278

5

Lane County
p296

Eugene

South Willamette Valley

WINE COUNTRY

Benton County
WineTrail

Harris Bridge

Go Beavs! Corvallis is home to Oregon State University, as well as to a dozen wineries that enjoy critical acclaim and plenty of awards. The Benton County WineTrail focuses on eight wineries that have regular tasting room hours. Although some wineries in the northwest part of Benton County (namely Cardwell Hill Cellars, Harris Bridge Vineyard, Spindrift Cellars, and Pheasant Court Winery) can be tackled by bicycle, you will need a car for this WineTrail. From Springhill Cellars in the north to Benton-Lane Winery (which straddles the Benton and Lane County border) in the south a car is a must. Budget two days for this WineTrail and plenty of time to explore Corvallis for food and university culture. Being a college town, there are plenty of brew pubs and coffee shops to experience, not to mention a stroll through the campus. Just be sure to leave the Duck T-shirt at home.

Benton County WineTrail

1. Springhill Cellars
2. Pioneer Hopyard Vineyard
3. Pheasant Court Winery
4. Spindrift Cellars
5. Cardwell Hill Cellars
6. Harris Bridge Vineyard
7. Tyee Wine Cellars
8. Benton-Lane Winery

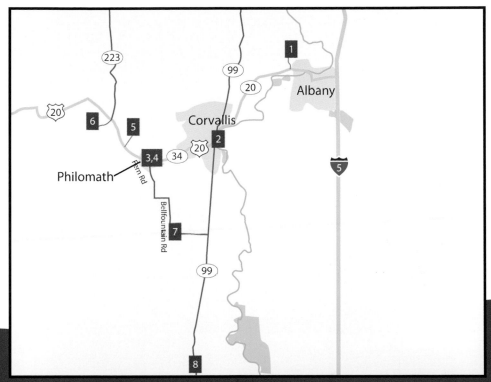

Region:	**South Willamette Valley Wine Country**
# of tasting rooms on tour:	**8**
Estimate # of days for tour:	**2**
Getting around:	**Car or bike**
Key Events:	❑ **Memorial Weekend in Wine Country – Willamette Valley – visit www.willamettewines.com.**
	❑ **In September, Corvallis' Rhapsody in the Vineyard – call 541-754-6624 or check out www.downtowncorvallis.org.**
	❑ **Wine Country Thanksgiving – Willamette Valley – call 503-646-2985 or visit www.willamettewines.com.**
Tips:	❑ **Much of this WineTrail is suitable for cycling. Be sure to pack a camera too!**
	❑ **Tyee Wine Cellars features outdoor music venue. See www.tyeewine.com for event information.**
Best:	❑ **Views: Cardwell Hill Cellars.**

Springhill Cellars ❶

Outside this winery's tasting room is a large bell, and beside the bell is a sign that states:

Springhill Hours:
Weekends 1 p.m. to 5 p.m.
Or by chance if you catch us ...
If you don't find anyone, ring the bell.
If we hear it, we'll run like heck.

With such a greeting, you know you are about to enter a relaxed and lighthearted tasting room. In this elongated, barrel-lined space, you're encouraged to step up to the bar, engage the pourer, and taste the wine. No question is too *naïve* to ask, and all opinions are welcomed.

In essence, this key stop along the Benton County WineTrail is a reflection of its owner and winemaker, Mike McLain. Mike is an easygoing person, despite the multitude of winemaking, vine-growing challenges he faces with each vintage — especially the very fickle pinot noir. As the owner of two vineyards — the Springhill Cellars vineyard that borders the winery and another, 12-acre site in the Eola-Amity Hills viticultural area — he has a deep sense of the fruit that goes into barrel. It's the challenge of showcasing each year's unique fruit that holds his interest and keeps him sharp as a winemaker.

It also doesn't hurt that Mike is the founder of the oldest real estate brokerage firm in the Willamette Valley specializing in winery and vineyard properties (McLain & Associates Vineyard Properties). For prospective buyers hoping to fulfill a dream of owning a winery/vineyard in the area, Mike is the person to know. His extensive knowledge of the Willamette Valley in general and its various viticultural areas in particular is an invaluable resource. If you want the details of Jory versus Willakenzie soils; temperature variations between hills and valleys; and what back roads to take to avoid farm trucks during harvest, Mike is the guy to see. No doubt, he could taste different pinot noirs blindfolded and tell you in what area of the valley the grapes grew.

Depending upon weather conditions, Springhill Cellars produces between 1,000 and 1,200 cases per year. Typically, the winery offers a couple of different estate pinot noirs, a pinot gris and a pinot noir rosé. Be sure you look at the artwork adorning the Springhill Cellars wine bottles. It is the work of artist neighbor Anna Tees, who specializes in paper collage art. When you enjoy a glass of Springhill Cellars pinot on one of the outside picnic tables, you can spot her house, which abuts the McLains' property.

Mike McLain

SPRINGHILL CELLARS
opened: 1998
winemaker(s): Mike McLain
location: 2920 NW Scenic Drive, Albany, OR 97321
phone: 503-928-1009
web: www.springhillcellars.com
e-mail: webmaster@springhillcellars.com
picnic area: Yes
fee: Complimentary wine tasting
hours: Saturday and Sunday 1–5 April through November

DIRECTIONS. From Albany go north on US-20 [Albany-Corvallis Hwy] for 2.2 miles. Turn right (north) onto NW Scenic Dr. and go 2.3 miles to arrive at the cellars.

From Corvallis go north onto US-20 [NW 2nd St.] 8.5 miles and go left (north) onto NW Scenic Dr. Travel 2.3 miles to 2920 NW Scenic Dr.

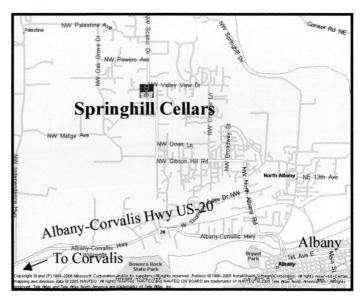

Pioneer Hopyard Vineyard 2

What's this, a tasting room within a jewelry store? Yep, and that store is Coleman Jewelers & Wine Shop in downtown Corvallis. For $1 per taste, visitors can sample wine and pick up a diamond ring. Whether it's pinot noir, pinot gris, or chardonnay, WineTrail trekkers can taste "the big three" wines from the Willamette Valley inside this historic store.

WineTrail note: As this establishment's name indicates, wine is also available for purchase. It offers a wide array of Northwest and California wines to choose from for those patrons rounding out their picnic or taking a bottle of wine home for dinner.

Store owner John Coleman is also the proprietor of the Pioneer Hopyard Vineyard, where these cool-climate grapes mentioned above grow. Named for the fact that the vineyard is on a former hop farm, the grapes are custom-crushed and bottled at the Eola Hills Wine Cellars by winemaker Steve Anderson. This is Steve's description of the Pioneer Hopyard Vineyard's 2003 chardonnay: "This chardonnay, produced from hand-selected grapes grown on that same soil give this varietal excellent character, complexity, and flavors. This delicate, fruity chardonnay boasts soft oak overtones with hints of citrus, honeydew, and pineapple. Non-chardonnay fans have remarked on the 'buttery, creamy texture.'" Anderson goes on to recommend an unusual movie-and-wine pairing, saying, "Due to its 'buttery, creamy texture,' [this chardonnay] is a great companion to a feel-good movie, replacing popcorn."

John Coleman lets the wine do the talking for him; he's rather introverted (or perhaps just focused on the jewelry side of the coin). However, his staff is eager to please and to answer questions while pouring Pioneer Hopyard Vineyard wines.

PIONEER HOPYARD VINEYARD
winemaker(s): Steve Anderson (Eola Hills Wine Cellar)
location: Coleman Jewelers & Wine Shop,
255 SW Madison Avenue,
Corvallis, OR 97333
phone: 541-753-3721
web: None
e-mail: jncjeweler@gmail.com
gift shop: Yes
fee: $1 per taste
hours: Friday 4–6; Saturday 1–4:30; Sunday through Thursday by appointment

DIRECTIONS: From Portland take I-5 south to exit 234A and go left (southwest) onto SR-99E [Pacific Blvd SE] for 1 mile. Bear right (west) onto US-20 [Albany-Corvallis Hwy] and travel 11 miles. Turn right (west) onto SW Madison Ave. to arrive at 255 SW Madison Ave.

Heading north on I-5 from Eugene take exit 228 toward OR-34/Lebanon/Corvallis. Go 10.1 miles on SR-34 [Corvallis-Lebanon Hwy] and turn left (south) onto US-20 [NW 2nd St.]. Turn right (west) onto SW Madison Ave. and arrive at Coleman Jewelers & Wine Shop.

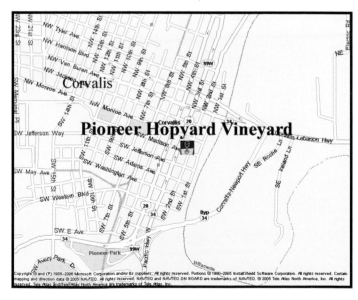

Pheasant Court Winery ❸

Charlie Gilson is the host with the most at The Wine Vault tasting room in downtown Philomath. Housed in the former Philomath Bank, the tasting room highlights the wines of Pheasant Court Winery and a variety of other local wines. In the center of the main room, Charlie pours samples to seated guests and provides a mixture of Wine 101 and tasting notes. He's friendly, informative, and approachable.

This old bank building has been around for nearly 100 years, and while visiting, you can still find telltale signs of the former financial institution. One example is the bank-vault door to the tasting room, which previously guarded personal valuables. The tasting room is located opposite the room bearing the sign "Da Boss"; this is where Charlie retreats to do the books and ponder his next vintage. He's clearly "chief janitor" and self-described one-man band of this operation.

Like a number of other select Oregon wineries, Pheasant Court Winery purchases its fruit from local vineyards. To this end, Charlie has established collaborative relationships with local growers to produce pinot noir, pinot gris, chardonnay, Maréchal Foch, and viognier. However, he does import his merlot grapes from the Rogue Valley.

Visitors will be tickled to know that besides experiencing great-tasting wine at Pheasant Court, they will also experience economic relief — there's no tasting fee!

PHEASANT COURT WINERY
opened: 2001
winemaker(s): Charlie Gilson
location: 1301 Main Street, Philomath, OR 97370
phone: 541-929-7715
web: www.pheasantcourtwinery.com
e-mail: info@pheasantcourtwinery.com
gift shop: Yes
fee: Complimentary wine tasting
hours: Saturday and Sunday 12–6

Charlie Gilson on the right

DIRECTIONS: From Corvallis go south onto US-20 [SR-34] for 5.9 miles toward Philomath. Arrive at 1301 Main St.

From Newport (Oregon Coast) head east on US-20 [Corvallis-Newport Hwy] 46 miles to Philomath. Arrive at 1301 Main St.

Spindrift Cellars 4

"Spindrift" usually refers to seaspray, particularly that blown from cresting waves during a gale. It also refers to a gem of a winery visitors can easily experience when heading from Corvallis to the Oregon coast, and vice versa. However, more than just a convenient stop in Philomath, Spindrift Cellars turns out to be a microcosm of outstanding southcentral Willamette Valley vineyards.

Owned by Matt and Tabitha Compton, Spindrift Cellars primarily relies on 250 acres of grapes from a number of vineyards that Matt manages through his company, West Vine Farms. He knows what he's buying, because his company nurtures each vine using

eco-friendly, sustainable practices. With pride, the Comptons note that their pinot gris, which comes from Deer Haven Vineyard, is "certified sustainable" and Salmon Safe. Matt views his duty as winemaker as preserving the essence of the varietal character through a combination of wild and cultured yeasts and the judicious use of oak. His goal is to produce food-friendly wine that's approachable and enjoyable, from first sip to last.

The Spindrift facility itself is bowling-alley big, with more than 8,500 square feet of space in which to make and sell wine. With this much capacity, it's no surprise that the Comptons lease space to other wineries, including Domaine Meriwether (which explains why visitors see bottles of Domaine Meriwether's sparkling wine in the tasting room). Another label visitors might see is the Comptons own second labels — Spinnaker. However, the wine with the distinctive wave crest on the label brings the focus back to Spindrift Cellars. For a nominal tasting fee, visitors can sip several Spindrift Cellars pinot noirs (its specialty), pinot blanc, pinot gris, and chardonnay.

At Spindrift Cellars, you are in a cork-free zone, so there's no need to fret about the cork shortage. Plus, the bottles are easy to open and can be stored upright. More and more Oregon wineries have embraced the twist-off cap trend. If you really must hear the sound of a popping cork, get someone to accompany the decanting ritual with the ol' finger-in-the-cheek sound effect. Sounds as good as the real thing.

SPINDRIFT CELLARS
opened: 2003
winemaker(s): Matt Compton
location: 810 Applegate Street, Philomath, OR 97370
phone: 541-929-6555
web: www.spindriftcellars.com
e-mail: info@SpindriftCellars.com
picnic area: Yes
tours: Yes
fee: $4 tasting fee
hours: Memorial Day Weekend through Thanksgiving Weekend, Tuesday through Friday 1–6; Saturday and Sunday 12–5. After Thanksgiving to end of May, Friday 12–6, Saturday and Sunday 12–5, or by appointment

DIRECTIONS: From Corvallis go south on US-20 [SR-34] 6.3 miles. Turn left (south) onto S 8th St. and arrive at Spindrift Cellars.

From Newport (Oregon Coast) go east on US-20 [Corvallis-Newport Hwy] 45.7 miles. Turn right (south) onto S 8th St. and arrive at the winery.

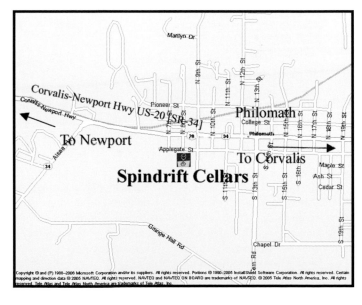

Cardwell Hill Cellars 5

Cardwell Hill Cellars is described by folks as having a "French country ambiance," and aside from the missing yellow mustard flowers, it definitely has that look and feel. The vineyard itself slopes down from Cardwell Hill (hence the name), with a chateau-like house set at the top of the slope. Outside the winery's light-filled tasting room, visitors can relax on the deck and picnic while enjoying a view of the vineyard and Mary's Peak in the distance. The scene epitomizes Oregon country elegance.

Dan and Nancy Chapel, who launched Cardwell Hill Cellars, are very much focused on the vineyard, where 36 acres of pinot noir and pinot gris are cultivated using earth-friendly sustainable practices; the vineyard bears both LIVE and Salmon Safe certifications. In terms of winemaking at their gravity-fed facility, Dan proudly remarks on the Cardwell Hill website, "Only the juice of the grape is removed from the vineyard — all of the rest is recycled back into the land." Now to this WineTrail trekker, that speaks to the purity of Cardwell Hill Cellars wines.

As you swirl and sip inside the beautifully appointed tasting room, note the sign stating, "Direct from the word of God, 1 Timothy 5:23, No longer drink only water, but use a little wine for the sake of your stomach and your frequent ailments." Trust me, though, no ailing stomach is needed to enjoy the taste of these elegant garnet-colored pinot noirs and the refreshing pinot gris. It's little wonder that the Chapels consistently take home awards from prestigious wine-tasting events, including the Dallas Morning News Wine Competition, Northwest Wine Summit, and Wine Press Northwest.

Located close to King Valley Highway (SR 223), Cardwell Hill Cellars is easy to find. Simply follow the blue signs to discover this touch of French country elegance ensconced in the graceful hillside.

CARDWELL HILL CELLARS
winemaker(s): Dan Chapel
location: 24241 Cardwell Hill Drive,
Philomath, OR 97370
phone: 541-929-9463
web: www.cardwellhillcellars.com
e-mail: chapel@cardwellhillwine.com
picnic area: Yes
wheelchair access: Yes
weddings: Yes
fee: $1 per taste
hours: Tuesday through Sunday 12–5:30

DIRECTIONS: From Corvallis take US-20 [SR-34] south for 11 miles. Turn right (northeast) onto SR-223 [King Valley Hwy] and go 1.1 miles. Turn right (east) onto NW Cardwell Hill Dr. and proceed .8 miles to the winery.

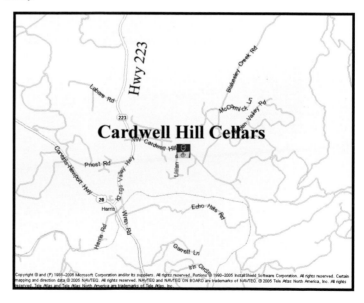

Harris Bridge Vineyard 6

I figured it was fitting to end my first day on the Benton County WineTrail at Harris Bridge Vineyard. It has a reputation for producing marvelous dessert wines from pinot noir and pinot gris, and I have a big sweet tooth. So going down the winding gravel road alongside Mary's River, I had to break out the drool cup in anticipation. However, I was to be disappointed in short order.

A sign on the door to the tasting room greeted me as I approached. It read, "Sorry we missed you. We're having a BABY!!! Hope to see you soon. Nathan, Amanda and ?????" [Baby ????? should have a name by now.]

It was a big reminder to call ahead to confirm that wineries are open. Sometimes wineries close shop because they've run out of wine; sometimes tasting rooms can't be staffed due to extenuating circumstances. In this case, the extenuating circumstance was the birth of a baby! It's a reminder to all wine tourists to be flexible and expect the unexpected while out in wine country. When you can, call ahead.

Nevertheless, I took the opportunity to stroll around the flower-populated grounds and view the 3 acres of grape vines, the old oak trees, the picnic grounds and a bocce court. But the key highlight for me was the historical covered bridge beside the property — the Harris Bridge, built in 1929 and the source of the winery's name. Inside the covered bridge, I could hear the gentle flow of Mary's River below as it made its way to join the Willamette River. It was easy to imagine old logging trucks making their way through this part of Harris Valley many years before.

As I walked through the covered bridge and caught sight of the nearby brick red-colored winery, I made a mental note to return here as soon as possible. Harris Bridge Vineyard has garnered major attention from local and regional lovers of dessert wines. Nathan's background in winemaking includes stints at Croft Vineyard, Argyle Winery and Eola Hills Wine Cellar, and these various experiences led to Nathan's unique focus on dessert wines.

Next time, I definitely will call ahead and then pack a picnic with peaches and cream to pair with Harris Bridge's dessert wines. In the meantime, I offer Nathan and Amanda my congratulations on the birth of their baby. I'm sure this is the best vintage yet!

HARRIS BRIDGE VINEYARD
opened: 1998
winemaker(s): Nathan Warren and Amanda Sever
location: 22937 Harris Road, Philomath, OR 97370
phone: 541-929-3053
web: www.harrisbridgevineyard.com
e-mail: harrisbridge@yahoo.com
picnic area: Yes
wheelchair access: Yes
fee: Small tasting fee
hours: Saturday and Sunday 12–6 June through
October; Memorial and Thanksgiving Day
weekends 12–6

DIRECTIONS: From I-5 follow Hwy 34 through Corvallis and Philomath. Continue on Hwy 20 past Philomath about 5 miles, then turn right onto Hwy 223. Take the next 3 immediate right turns and you will be on Harris Rd. The vineyard is 2.5 miles down Harris Rd, just before the covered bridge.

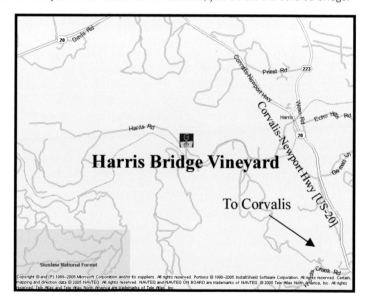

Tyee Wine Cellars 7

Oregon wine tourists might be used to estate wineries featuring local artists, summer concerts, plenty of picnic space, great views, and wedding facilities — the "full-meal deal," so to speak. But Tyee Wine Cellars takes it a step further (or should I say "steps further"?). Here you'll need your walking shoes for a mile-and-a-half nature walk that takes you through the historic Buchanan Family Farm, the location of Tyee Wine Cellars. Open weekends from April through November, the interpretive walking trail leads walkers past

oak groves, hazelnut orchards, a beaver pond, and the farm itself. Unfortunately, all visiting pooches will need to stay in the car — there's just too much wildlife to chase and bark at.

Borrowing a Native American word for "chief" (Tyee), this family-owned winery celebrates nearly a quarter-century of fine wine production.

Originally, the Buchanan family used a combination of estate and locally sourced grapes to produce their handcrafted wines. However, more recently they have come to rely exclusively on their own Beaver Creek Vineyards for grapes. Although their source of grapes has changed, their distinctive packaging, which features a Northwest Indian design on the label, has remained the same. At the winery's tasting room, WineTrail trekkers can taste current releases of gewürztraminer, pinot blanc, pinot gris, chardonnay, and pinot noir. Take a few moments, with wine in hand, to check out the art gallery located next to the tasting room. Local artists' works are featured each month, with an emphasis on nature genre.

The winemaker for Tyee Family Cellars literally grew up at the winery. Merrilee Buchanan Benson has worked closely with her family in the winery and vineyard most of her life, emerging as chief winemaker for the 2006 vintage. Now, from bud break to bottling, she shepherds the development of this delightful juice for the family's estate wines. All production processes use certified Salmon Safe viticultural practices to turn out about 2,000 cases of wine per year.

With a venue that lends itself to music concerts and winemaker dinners, it's a good idea to visit the Tyee Wine Cellar's website for event information when planning a visit. Given the wide variety of wines to sample, art to view, and music to listen to, you may just want to make a day of it. In addition to packing a picnic, be sure to include a good pair of walking shoes for that nature walk through the family's farm.

TYEE WINE CELLARS
opened: 1985
winemaker(s): Merrilee Buchanan Benson
location: 26335 Greenberry Road,
Corvallis, OR 97333
phone: 541-753-8754
web: www.tyeewine.com
e-mail: merrilee@storypages.com
picnic area: Yes
wheelchair access: Yes
weddings: Yes
fee: Complimentary wine tasting
hours: Saturday and Sunday 12–5 April through
December; Daily 12–5 June 15th through Labor Day

DIRECTIONS: From Corvallis take SR-99W [Pacific Hwy W] south for 7.1 miles. Turn right (west) onto Greenberry Rd and arrive at the winery in 2.5 miles.

From Eugene take Beltline Hwy west to exit 6. Head north on SR-99 9.7 miles. Turn left (northwest) onto SR-99W [Pacific Hwy W] for 17.6 miles. Turn left (west) onto Greenberry Rd for 2.5 miles and arrive at the winery.

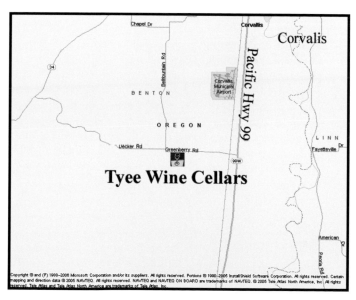

Benton-Lane Winery 🞐

Often, it's numbers that tell the story of a winery. In the case of Benton-Lane Winery, I uncovered those numbers. Twenty-thousand cases produced annually; 140 acres of vines under production; distribution to 46 states and several countries; and home of two of the Top 100 Wines in the World for 2006.

Not bad. But the numbers only tell part of the story. They don't elude to history, hard work, and love of the land. They don't speak about the characters who tend the vines and make the wines. Such is the case with Benton-Lane Winery.

California transplants Steve and Carol Girard came north to start a vineyard, founding Benton-Lane in 1988. They had successfully grown premium wine grapes in Napa Valley, but they wanted to grow pinot noir. After racking up considerable miles, they stumbled upon a perfect spot bearing the lovely name of "Sunnymount" in the southern reaches of Willamette Valley.

But they needed a name for their new vineyard, which just happens to straddle the Benton-Lane county line. Hence, Benton-Lane Winery got its name. However, the hard part came later when the Girards needed a label to showcase their pinot noir. For that, they turned to graphic artist Jim Moon of San Rafael, California, who, as it turns out, is a stamp collector. Jim drew his inspiration from the federal government's botched "Inverted Jenny" 24-cent stamp of 1918 on which a mail-carrier airplane was incorrectly printed upside down. A stamp border frames the wine label and for the center of the label, rather than using an upside-down vineyard, Jim chose undulating rows of vines with mountains in the background. The image was an immediate hit with Steve and Carol.

First-time visitors to Benton-Lane Winery will know they've arrived at the right place when they spot the large stamp-like sign out front. The distinctive tasting room and winery provide a wonderful venue for sampling various pinot noirs, pinot blanc, pinot gris, and rosé of pinot noir. Outside on the patio, visitors can relax in comfortable teak furniture and marvel at Mount Jefferson in the distance. If they feel like a stroll, they can explore Carol's herb and vegetable garden, which provides fresh produce for the many goodies served at winemaker dinners and other wine-pairing events.

There's no way to go postal in this idyllic setting. It certainly gets my stamp of approval.

BENTON-LANE WINERY
opened: 1991
winemaker(s): Chris Mazepink
location: 23924 Territorial Highway,
Monroe, OR 97456
phone: 541-847-5792
web: www.benton-lane.com
e-mail: info@benton-lane.com
picnic area: Yes
wheelchair access: Yes
fee: Complimentary wine tasting
hours: Monday through Friday 11–4:30, Saturday and
Sunday 11–5, April through November

DIRECTIONS: Heading southbound on I-5 about 15 miles south of Salem, take exit 234A forward Fair/
Expo/Knox Butte. Go left (southwest) onto SR-99E [Pacific Blvd SE] for 1 mile. Bear right (west)
onto US-20 [SR-99E] for .8 miles. Bear right (north) onto US-20 [SR-34] and stay on US-20 for
about 2 miles. Keep left onto SR-99W [Pacific Hwy W] for 17 miles. Turn right onto S 5th St.
[Territorial Hwy] and drive for 1.8 miles to the winery.

From Eugene take I-105 toward West Eugene and Delta Hwy. Turn right onto ramp toward Delta
Hwy/Beltline Hwy [Delta Hwy] for 1.8 miles. Take ramp (right) onto Beltline Hwy for 3.7 miles. At
exit 6, keep right onto ramp for .2 miles toward Eugene Airport/Junction City. Go left (north) onto
SR-99 for 9.7 miles. Turn left (northwest) onto SR-99W [Pacific Hwy W] drive 7.7 miles. Turn left
(south) onto S 5th St. [Territorial Hwy], go 1.8 miles to destination.

Lane County
Wine Trail

To this WineTrail trekker, the magical thing about Lane Country WineTrail is the mix of chateau-like settings and funky, break-out-the-tie-dyed-T-shirt-groovy wineries. This is the United Nations of WineTrails: diversity is the rule here, both in terms of the physical structure and the variety of wines to sample. And being open-minded is key to your enjoyment. You may surprise yourself and taste a Huxelrebe at High Pass Winery that will have you making reservations to the Rheinhessen region of Germany. Stranger things happen every day.

This is one of my favorite WineTrails to visit. I could return repeatedly without complaint. **WineTrail Tip:** Plan your day to end at King Estate Winery. With its fabulous views and first-class restaurant, your biggest challenge is deciding between their pinot gris and pinot noir. Tough duty!

Lane County WineTrail

1. Territorial Vineyards and Wine Co.
2. Pfeiffer Vineyards
3. High Pass Winery
4. LaVelle Vineyards
5. Secret House Winery
6. Noble Estate Vineyard & Winery
7. Sweet Cheeks Winery
8. Silvan Ridge-Hinman Vineyards
9. King Estate Winery
10. Chateau Lorane
11. Saginaw Vineyard

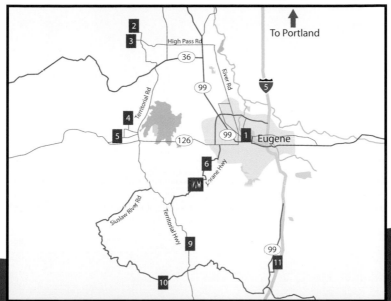

Region:	**South Willamette Valley Wine Country**
# of tasting rooms on tour:	**11**
# of satellite tasting rooms:	**1**
Estimate # of days for tour:	**3**
Getting around:	**Car or bike**
Key Events:	❑ **Memorial Weekend in Wine Country – Willamette Valley – visit www.willamettewines.com.**
	❑ **In June, Wineries of Lane County Summer Barrel Tour – call 800-992-8499 for more information and tickets.**
	❑ **In July, Eugene's Art and the Vineyard – call 541-485-2221 or go to www.artandthevineyard.org.**
	❑ **Lane County Wineries Thanksgiving – call 541-484-5307 or visit www.visitlanecounty.org.**
Tips:	❑ **Consider hiring a limousine service such as Sunshine Limo Service – call 541-344-LIMO (5466) or email info@sunshinelimoservice.com. For Off the Beaten Path Tours – call 541-998-2450 or email offthebeatenpathtransport@yahoo.com.**
	❑ **Need a place to get hitched? Consider the magnificence King Estate Winery.**

 Best: ❑ **Eats: Pfeiffer Vineyards, King Estate Winery.**
❑ **Picnic: Chateau Lorane.**
❑ **Views: Sweet Cheeks Winery, King Estate Winery.**

Territorial Vineyards and Wine Co.

The tasting room of Territorial Vineyards and Wine Co. is located in the heart of Eugene's funky Whiteaker neighborhood. During my visit, I chanced upon a summer block party, with streets closed to traffic, and plenty of tie-dye-garbed youth and portable potties. As I walked past the throngs of earth-friendly celebrants, I wondered what was in store for my visit. From a distance, I spied the Third Avenue tasting room, with its lacquered black paint job and pronounced block-letter "TERRITORIAL" across the top. It has that distinctive neighborhood bar feeling.

I entered a wine-tasting-room version of the hit TV show *Cheers*. The place rocked with folks having a decidedly good time. Instead of Ted Danson pouring, there were three women working behind the bar, exchanging friendly banter with patrons and fulfilling requests for pinot noir, pinot gris, riesling, chardonnay, and rosé. Folks welcomed me, and one of the smiling pourers asked if she could be of assistance.

Once I explained my mission, she made sure I had plenty of pinot to swirl and led me to the side door that opened to the 12,000-square-foot production space, which features an indoor crush pad and barrel room. I had the urge to shout to see if I could create an echo, but I figured that would have been a little weird. There was plenty of space for negotiating forklifts, hosting a big party, or tossing a Frisbee.

Founded by two wine-growing families, Alan and April Mitchell and Jeff and Victoria Wilson-Charles, Territorial Vineyards and Wine Co. is focused on estate wines. Located in the surrounding hills near Eugene, its vineyards bear the very cool names Equinox, Bellpine, and Toad Hall vineyards. All of its vineyards are certified LIVE (Low Input Viticulture & Enology) and Salmon Safe. Once the wines are barrel-aged in French oak, it's the task of winemaker John Jarboe to blend the vineyard-designated batches. An example is Territorial's Willamette Valley Pinot Noir, a blend of Pommard, Wädenswil, Jackson, and Dijon clones from the three Territorial vineyards. It's a symphony of sorts, with John conducting the orchestra.

Walking back to my car, past a jamming rock 'n' roll band and people dancing in the street, I realized that Territorial Vineyards and Wine Co. is true to the Eugene spirit. Their wines are pure expressions of the soil whence they came. It's authentically groovy.

TERRITORIAL VINEYARDS AND WINE CO.
winemaker(s): John Jarboe
location: 907 W Third Avenue, Eugene, OR 97402
phone: 541-684-9463
web: www.territorialvineyards.com
e-mail: wine@territorialvineyards.com
picnic area: Yes
wheelchair access: Yes
hours: Thursday 5–11, with live music; Friday and
Saturday 4–8, or by appointment

DIRECTIONS: Heading south or north on I-5 take exit 194B onto I-105 [SR-126] toward Eugene. Take SR-126 [SR-99] .4 miles toward SR-99/Florence. Turn right (north) onto Adams St. and go .2 miles. Arrive at 907 W 3rd Ave. — Territorial Vineyards and Wine Co.

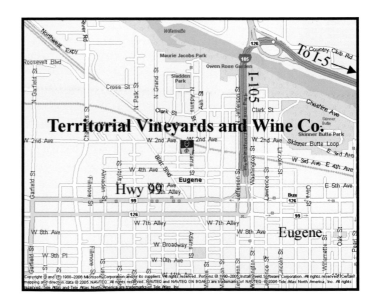

Pfeiffer Vineyards 2

Years ago, San Diego–based TV and radio personality Danuta Rylko placed this ad in the personals column of a local paper, "WF, 45, educated, attractive, author, conversationalist, skier, cyclist, likes Merlot, Mozart, rivers, cabin, books, seeking WM, 35-55, who knows how to spell." That ad fetched Robin Pfeiffer, a wine grower from Oregon who evidently submitted a correctly spelled response.

Robin succeeded in transplanting Danuta to the wine-growing world of the Willamette Valley west of Junction City. He had developed a vineyard on the family sheep farm

following a tip from some French visitors who were scouting the area for land to buy to grow grapes. Robin convinced his family to sell off the herd of sheep and replace the land with what would become a 70-acre vineyard. Not a baaaaad move.

The fact that Robin didn't know a lick about growing grapes (other than the fact that raisins came from them) didn't deter this former high school Spanish teacher from laying down undulating "S"-shaped rows of grapes and unevenly spaced vines. The result is outstanding fruit benefiting from strict organic practices. The sun not only nurtures the vines, but the winery as well with its installation of solar panels.

Produced in limited quantities, Pfeiffer Vineyards wines are sold only at the winery's Tuscan-villa-style tasting room or online via the winery's website. Inside the cavernous yet intimate tasting room, visitors experience premium wines: primarily pinot noir and pinot gris, along with select white wines and rosé. You will notice that the reserve pinot noir bears the name "Blue Dot," which is a reference to Robin's early winemaking years when he would mark bottles with a blue dot. These were the wines that his friends, with lip-smacking adoration, rated the highest. The winery's tasting fee covers wine samples, a delectable cheese torte, and a Riedel wine glass. It's all part of the "wow" factor you experience at Pfeiffer Vineyards.

The special relationship that Robin and Danuta share carries through to their "Villa Evenings" winemaker dinners. During Danuta's TV and radio career, she met a number of famous chefs and collected amazing recipes along the way. These recipes frame the menus for Villa Evenings dinners, which, of course, are complemented with Pfeiffer wines. As a bonus, Robin educates guests in the art of wine tasting, winning hearts and minds in the process. After all, he is a retired teacher who succeeded in winning the heart of Danuta many years ago.

Robin and Danuta Pfeiffer

PFEIFFER VINEYARDS
winemaker(s): Robin Pfeiffer
location: 25040 Jaeg Road, Junction City, OR 97448
phone: 541-998-2828
web: www.pfeiffervineyards.com
e-mail: via website
picnic area: Yes
wheelchair access: Yes
tours: Yes
fee: $5–$20 for tastes; keep the glass
hours: Saturday and Sunday 12–5

 BEST Eats

DIRECTIONS: From Corvalis head south on SR-99W [Pacific Hwy W] for 17 miles. Keep right onto S 5th St. [Territorial Hwy]. Road name changes to Territorial Hwy. Proceed 4.2 miles. Turn right (west) onto Ferguson Rd and go 2.9 miles. Turn left (south) onto Turnbow Ln, travel .6 miles. Turn right (west) onto Jaeg Rd for .9 miles and arrive 25040 Jaeg Rd.

From I-5 take exit 195 in Eugene onto Beltline Hwy and go 6.5 miles. At exit 6, right onto ramp and turn left (north) onto SR-99. Travel 8.6 miles. Turn left (west) onto W 1st Ave. and go .8 miles. Road name changes to High Pass Rd. Continue 6.6 miles. Turn right (north) onto Turnbow Ln and go .9 miles. Turn left (west) onto Jaeg Rd, travel .9 miles, and arrive at Pfeiffer Vineyards.

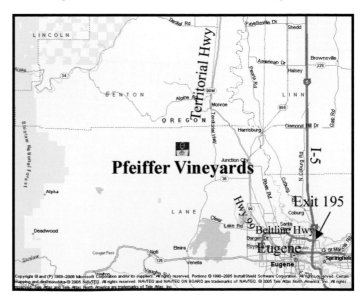

High Pass Winery ③

Can you say "Huxelrebe"?

The Huxelrebe is a white grape often used to make premium-quality sweet wines served as aperitifs or dessert wines. Huxelrebe is a delicious wine, but it's rarely found in Oregon unless one ventures to High Pass Winery. Located west of Junction City, High Pass Winery produces estate wines under the guidance of owner/winemaker Dieter Boehm at one of three vineyards: Walnut Ridge Vineyard, Priddy Ridge Vineyard, and High Pass Vineyard.

Rarely do we reprint a recipe, but with thanks to High Pass Winery, we offer this chocolate almond cake to pair with High Pass' Huxelrebe dessert wine:

7 ounces bittersweet chocolate, finely chopped
¾ cup unsalted butter
1 cup sugar (divided)
4 large eggs, separated, at room temperature
¼ teaspoon almond extract
¼ cup plus 1 tablespoon cake flour
¼ teaspoon salt
½ cup (3 ounces) almond meal (available at Trader Joe's)
Caramel sauce

Preheat the oven to 325 degrees. Butter and flour a Bundt pan. Combine the chocolate and butter and melt. Be very careful not to burn the mixture. Remove from the heat and whisk to combine. Whisk in ¾ cup of the sugar, the egg yolks, and the almond extract. Whisk in the almond meal and the flour. Beat the egg whites until they start to foam. Add the remaining ¼ cup sugar and beat until the whites form soft peaks. Using a rubber spatula, carefully fold one-third of the whites into the chocolate mixture, then fold in the remaining whites. Pour the batter into the prepared pan and smooth the top. Bake until the cake is puffed and a skewer inserted into the center comes out clean, 35–40 minutes.

Just before serving, using a fine-mesh sieve, dust the cake with confectioner's sugar and drizzle with caramel sauce. Serve with chilled High Pass Winery Huxelrebe and repeat after me: "Life is good, life is good, life is good.…"

High Pass Winery also produces silky-smooth pinot noirs, a pinot gris, a rosé of gamay noir, and another German white wine called Scheurebe — a wine with roots to the silvaner varietal grape. But whatever the wine, you can be sure that Dieter Boehm has personally "worked the vine to grow the wine." For a slice of heaven on earth, take time to bake the chocolate almond cake and bring it along to pair with the Huxelrebe dessert wine.

Conrad Pfeiffer entertaining at
High Pass Winery

HIGH PASS WINERY
opened: 1995
winemaker(s): Dieter Boehm
location: 24757 Lavell Road,
Junction City, OR 97448
phone: 541-998-1447
web: www.highpasswinery.com
e-mail: dieter@highpasswinery.com
picnic area: Yes
fee: Complimentary wine tasting
hours: Friday, Saturday and Sunday 12–5 during
summer, or by appointment

DIRECTIONS: From Junction City take W 6th Ave. (west) 1 mile. Turn left (south) onto Oaklea Rd and go .2 miles. Turn right (west) onto High Pass Rd and travel 7.9 miles. Turn right (north) onto Lavell Rd and look for signs leading to High Pass Winery.

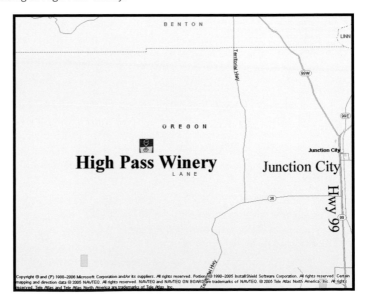

LaVelle Vineyards ④

Fifteen miles west of Eugene in the small town of Elmira is the LaVelle Vineyards property. Crossing the Hannavan Creek at LaVelle Vineyards, your journey takes you to a spacious parking lot. The winery's tasting room is visible on the hill, past terraced gardens and a patio that invites visitors to kick back and relax. However, at the tasting room's

doors is the name Forgeron Vineyards permanently carved on the door. I entered wondering if I had had a senior moment and arrived at the wrong winery, but was relieved to hear, "Welcome to LaVelle Vineyards, would you like to taste some wines?"

Turns out that prior to becoming LaVelle Vineyards, the winery's name was Forgeron Vineyards. That was back before 1994, when retired GTE executive Doug LaVelle fulfilled a dream by buying the defunct Forgeron Vineyards winery, with its 16 acres of neglected grapes. Thus ensued considerable effort to bring the winemaking equipment up to modern standards, redo the crush pad, renovate the tasting room, and rehab the vineyard. Eventually, Doug's son Matthew became part of the mix as director of operations. Today, LaVelle Vineyards "gently crushes" 300 tons of harvest fruit per year, including a combination of wines destined for the LaVelle Vineyards winery and custom-crushed wines.

Tasting-room visitors will give their arms a workout, with all the swirling to be done, what with so many wines to sample — riesling, pinot gris, chardonnay, viognier, gamay noir, merlot, pinot noir, rosé, and a sparkling wine made using the traditional *méthode champenoise* process. Using fruit from its estate vineyard, local grape growers and Washington's Columbia Valley, LaVelle Vineyards crafts a robust line-up of premium wines.

If, for some reason, you can't make it to LaVelle Vineyards winery in rural Elmira, I have good news. At Eugene's popular 5th Street Market, visitors can relax in the intimate confines of the LaVelle Wine Bar & Bistro. Open seven days a week, the wine bar offers WineTrails trekkers the same line-up of wines they would taste at the winery. And if you time your visit during weekend evenings, there's a good chance that your wine tasting will be accompanied by piano music inside the bar or a local band outside on the patio. The establishment is intimate and fun, and the perfect place to relax with friends and a glass of LaVelle Vineyards Vintage Select Gamay Noir, all the while wondering why this delightful wine isn't found throughout Oregon.

LAVELLE VINEYARDS
opened: 1972
winemaker(s): Matthew LaVelle
location: 89697 Sheffler Road, Elmira, OR 97437
phone: 541-935-9406
web: www.lavelle-vineyards.com
e-mail: info@lavelle-vineyards.com
picnic area: Yes
gift shop: Yes
fee: Complimentary wine tasting
hours: Daily 12–5

DIRECTIONS: From Eugene go west on SR-126 [W 11th Ave.] for 11.5 miles. Turn right (north) onto Territorial Hwy and go 1 mile. Turn left (west) onto Warthen Rd and travel 1.2 miles. Bear right (north) onto Sheffler Rd, drive 1.3 miles. Follow signs and turn right into the property.

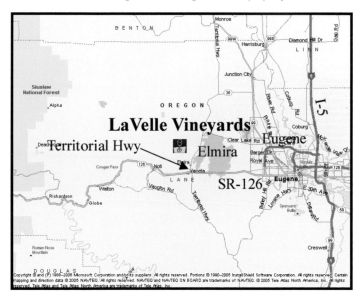

Secret House Winery 5

Fairy wings are optional here.

Secret House Winery, located on a 54-acre plot of land in Veneta, in the southern Willamette Valley, is the site of the annual Faerieworlds Festival. During July, fantasy lovers from all over gather here for a weekend of fun and celebration of life's magic. It's

all about art, music, and imagination. It's also a wonderful time to imbibe in the many wines of Secret House Winery.

Founded in 1991 by self-described former hippies Patti and Ron Chappel, Secret House Winery got its start because of a burglary. The Chappels had purchased the vineyard during the 1980s as an investment, but when their Oriental rug business was robbed, they opted to make a lifestyle change and move to Veneta to start Secret House Winery. Using grapes from different sources, including their own 27-acre estate vineyard, the couple set about creating high-quality wines at affordable prices. Their goal from the get-go has been to produce wines, such as pinot noir, that often sell for $40 and higher with a price tag in the low $20 range. In addition to pinot noir, Secret House also produces riesling, Müller-Thurgau, cabernet sauvignon, and sparkling wines affectionately known as sparklers. They also concoct a delicious red-blend wine called Vinotaboo — a blend of pinot noir and loganberry — that sells briskly.

The "Secret House" itself is a charming space in which to sample the Chappels' complimentary wines, view local artwork, and purchase wine-related accessories. You can spring for a bottle of wine and go outside to one of many picnic areas to take in your surroundings. Walk the grounds and see first-hand the many agreeable locations for weddings, corporate events, and that family get-together on your list of to-dos. You'll appreciate why Secret House Winery makes such a suitable outdoor music venue for Lane County.

Along the Lane County WineTrail, Secret House Winery is a must for the experience it offers. Feel free to don those fairy wings and celebrate art, music, and good wine.

SECRET HOUSE WINERY
opened: 1991
winemaker(s): Gary Carpenter
location: 88324 Vineyard Lane, Veneta, OR 97487
phone: 541-935-3774
web: www.secrethousewinery.com
e-mail: info@secrethousewinery.com
picnic area: Yes
weddings: Yes
fee: Complimentary wine tasting
hours: Daily 11 5; call for winter hours

DIRECTIONS: From Eugene head west on SR-126 [W 11th Ave.] for 14.5 miles. Turn right (north) onto Thomas Ln for .3 miles. Bear right (northeast) onto Suttle Rd and go .5 miles. Turn right (south) onto Vineyard Ln and arrive at the Secret House Winery.

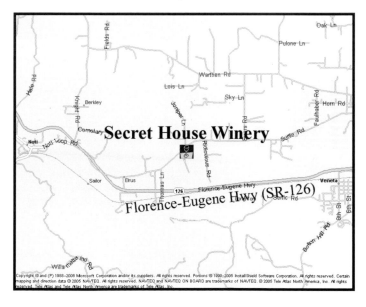

Noble Estate Vineyard & Winery 6

Pulling into the parking lot at Noble Estate Vineyard & Winery, my partner, Kathleen, and I popped out of the car and stopped short at the sight of a huge mastiff dog sitting on the porch. He stared at us, probably wondering if we were friend or foe. I assured him in my best "aren't you a cute dog" voice that we were friendly. As we walked down the garden path to the tasting room, it occurred to me that someone must be making regular Costco runs to buy food for this animal.

Situated on the outside of the quaint tasting room is a small pool, big enough for swimming short laps or executing a perfect cannonball on a smart-ass friend. Wrapped around the outside deck is a seating area with a beautiful view of the fir-treed grounds below. An outside cabana with deck furniture and a poolside barbecue grill beckoned us to relax. However, we were there for the wine tasting and made our way to the tasting room.

In 1999, Mark and Marie Jurasevich started Noble Estate Vineyard by planting pinot noir grapes. Exercising vine-by-vine hand crop management, they produce low tonnage crops ripe with intense flavors. As Marie notes in their literature, "It's all about capturing the sun." In addition to their own 6-acre vineyard, Mark has "acreage contracts" with select vineyards in the Willamette Valley and the Rogue River Valley. In total, Mark and his family produce about 1,200 cases of wine annually.

The charming tasting room offers wines to sample, comfortable furniture for relaxing, and plenty of wine-related accessories to purchase. For a small tasting fee, you can sample Mark's handmade beauties, including pinot noir, chardonnay, pinot gris from Willamette Valley grapes, and cabernet sauvignon and merlot from the warmer Rogue River Valley. All of the Jurasevichs' wines are graced by a distinctive noble fir tree label. Halfway through your tasting, you realize that these premium wines are crafted with singular attention and artfully presented. I couldn't help but purchase a bottle of the Pinot Noir Willamette.

On our way out, I showed my receipt to the giant mastiff to prove that I had purchased the Noble Estate wine I was holding. I wouldn't want that dog chasing me!

NOBLE ESTATE VINEYARD & WINERY
opened: 1999
winemaker(s): Mark Jurasevich
location: 29210 Gimpl Hill Road, Eugene, OR 97402
phone: 541-338-3007
web: www.nobleestatevineyard.com
e-mail: wines@nobleestatevineyard.com
picnic area: Yes
wheelchair access: Yes
gift shop: Yes
fee: $5 tasting fee
hours: Saturday and Sunday 12–5

DIRECTIONS: From downtown Eugene go west on W 11th Ave. for 1.2 miles. Keep straight onto SR-126 [W 11th Ave.] for 1.2 miles. Turn left (south) onto Bailey Hill Rd and go 2.1 miles. Turn right (west) onto Gimpl Rd, continue 1.7 miles, and arrive at Noble Estate Vineyard & Winery on the left.

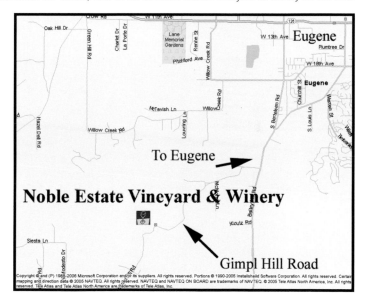

Sweet Cheeks Winery 🔟

Sweet Cheeks Winery is all about life's pleasures, including, of course, fine wine. Even the name itself is whimsical, with the word "cheeks," as you may have guessed, referring to the pair found on a person's backside. No kidding. Look closely at the crow-emblazoned logo and you'll notice sensually curving vineyards in the background. That's not by accident. Nor is the crow in the image, a nod to the nearby town of Crow, southwest of Eugene.

It's a vertical climb from the Briggs Hill Road entrance to the winery and tasting room. Even before entering the tasting room, you know the views are going to be spectacular. This fact explains the large patio with plenty of deck furniture for taking in the breathtaking scenery. Entering the spacious tasting room, with its warm colors, vaulted ceilings, large fireplace, and Old World stone floors, you realize that this winery is perfect for entertaining. It's little wonder that Sweet Cheeks Winery has a lively wine club, in which members can take part in events throughout the year. Get ready for winemaker dinners, harvest shindigs, release weekends, Thanksgiving bashes, and more.

Owner Daniel Smith served on the original board of Willamette Valley Vineyards. That experience must have been a great asset when he purchased what would become Sweet Cheeks' vineyard in 1989. Over the years, he has added to his holdings and now grows pinot noir, pinot gris, chardonnay, and riesling. Today, the estate vineyard accounts for 65 acres of the 140-acre south-sloping hillside.

To turn fruit into fine wine, Sweet Cheeks Winery employs thirty-something Aussie winemaker Mark Nicholl. Despite Mark's youth, his résumé includes considerable winemaking experience in Australia and France. His eclectic training has equipped him well for the "new world," although he was unfamiliar with Oregon wines when he arrived for the first crush in 2006. But no worries, mate. Now, a veteran winemaker, Mark takes on the unique challenges that each harvest presents, producing close to 10,000 cases annually.

Given all the great events and discounts on wine shipments that wine-club members enjoy, you may want to sign up to be a member before heading to your car. Membership has its challenges, however: You must determine which winemaker dinners to attend, what release parties to go to, and what to wear to the annual masquerade ball in October. Life is just full of difficult decisions!

SWEET CHEEKS WINERY
opened: 2005
winemaker(s): Mark Nicholl
location: 27007 Briggs Hill Road, Eugene, OR 97405
phone: 541-349-9463
web: www.sweetcheekswinery.com
e-mail: lorrie@sweetcheekswinery.com
picnic area: Yes
wheelchair access: Yes
weddings: Yes
tours: Yes
fee: Complimentary wine tasting
hours: Daily 12–6; Twilight Fridays 12–9

DIRECTIONS: From Eugene take W 11th or W 18th out to Bertelsen Rd. Turn left. Continue on Bertelsen to crossroads with Spencer Creek. Turn right on Spencer Creek Rd and continue for about 2 miles. Turn left on Briggs Hill Rd. The winery entrance will appear on the right in about 3.5 miles.

From Veneta/Beltline road take W 11th and Beltline to Veneta (about 10 miles). Turn left at the Veneta intersection. Go south about 9 miles to Briggs Hill Rd. Turn left on Briggs Hill Rd. Continue on Briggs Hill Rd for about 1 mile. The winery entrance is on the left.

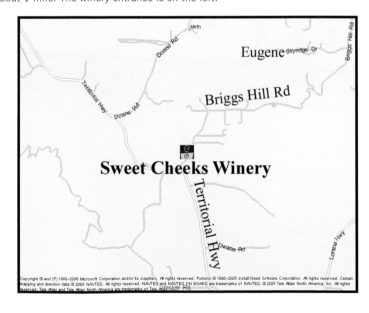

Silvan Ridge-Hinman Vineyards 🎱

The phrase "visitor's center" often doesn't apply to Oregon wineries. Rather, most wineries' tasting rooms serve as unofficial visitor's centers. However, in the case of Silvan Ridge-Hinman Winery, there truly is a visitor's center, which has been designed to accommodate major events, weddings, banquets, outdoor movies, and WineTrail trekkers like myself who are there to sample wine. A big dose of Old World charm and elegance informs the center's design throughout.

With origins dating back to 1979, when Doyle Hinman and David Smith opened Hinman Vineyards, Silvan Ridge-Hinman Vineyards is the oldest winery in Lane County. In 1993, Carolyn S. Chambers, a Eugene businesswoman and president of Chambers Communication Corp. (the local ABC affiliate), acquired the winery. (By the way, Carolyn's business accomplishments and lifetime achievements would fill a thick book. There's no doubt it would make a fascinating story.) Since 1995, Carolyn's daughter Elizabeth (Liz) Chambers has served as the general manager of the winery. Focusing on all aspects of the business, Liz has been instrumental in transforming the winery, with the label Silvan Ridge as its flagship. The name itself pays homage to her mother's maiden name, Silva.

If asked which winery to pack a picnic for, my answer would have to be Silvan Ridge — especially if you are lucky enough to visit the winery during one of its movie nights. During those evenings, you can uncork a bottle of wine on the lawn paired with a picnic. Then sit back and enjoy a classic movie with a dessert wine, such as Silvan Ridge Del Rio Portage, with its huge black-fruit flavor. On a clear night in this part of rural Lane County, the stars are out in full force.

Winemaker Jonathan Oberlander has the task of producing 25,000 cases annually; these are primarily filled with Rhone- and Bordeaux-style wines. When you are in Lane County, your varietal choices include both cool- and warm-weather grapes from the Willamette Valley and southern Oregon's Rogue River Valley viticultural areas respectively. It's a winemaker's playground and the enviable job of Jonathan to make a dozen different red and white wines.

Truly, Jonathan epitomizes the Silvan Ridge Winery. His youth speaks to the vitality and creativity of the Oregon wine scene. However, his training is grounded in tried-and-true, established winemaking techniques and processes. At Silvan Ridge, the elegant Old World charm of the winery meets New World boldness in a bottle. The result is delectable.

SILVAN RIDGE-HINMAN VINEYARDS
opened: 1979
winemaker(s): Jonathan Oberlander
location: 27012 Briggs Hill Road, Eugene, OR 97405
phone: 541-345-1945
web: www.silvanridge.com
e-mail: info@silvanridge.com
picnic area: Yes
wheelchair access: Yes
weddings: Yes
fee: Complimentary wine tasting
hours: Daily 12–5

DIRECTIONS: From Eugene, take W 11th to W 18th to Bertelson Rd and go left. Go to Spencer Creek Rd and turn right. Go 2 miles and turn left on Briggs Hill Rd. The winery entrance is 3.5 miles on the left.

From I-5 take exit 161 and head west onto Buck Creek Rd [County Rd 61] for .9 miles. Turn right (northeast) onto County Rd 212 [Curtin Rd] and go 2 miles. Bear left (north) onto County Rd 116 [Territorial Hwy] for 2.8 miles. Road name changes to Territorial Hwy. Proceed 13.3 miles. Turn right (north) onto Briggs Hill Rd and go .4 miles to 27012 Briggs Hill Rd.

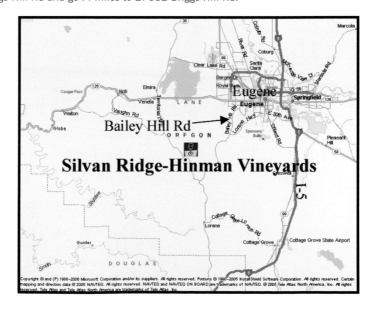

King Estate Winery ⑨

When you approach King Estate Winery from the Territorial Road entrance, one word comes to mind — majestic. It's usually a word reserved for French chateaus or Renaissance Tuscan villas. The drive through the 1,033-acre certified organic estate to the top of the hill, where the King Estate Winery sits, has a quietening effect on passengers, with the exception of their occasional "oohs" and "ahs." Once you've parked the car and taken a

gander, the panoramic view of the Lorane Valley below is nothing short of spectacular. Majestic *is* the word.

King Estate Winery is the dream of Ed King III and his father, Ed King Jr. Beginning in the early 1990s, Ed III began acquiring vineyards east of Eugene. However, the purchase of the Lorane Valley estate, where the present-day winery sits, is the crown jewel of the King Estate Winery properties. Over the years, a who's who of well-known industry pros have worked or consulted with the Kings to create one of Oregon's top wine producers.

Inside the lavish visitor's center, guests typically make a beeline to the wine bar, where King Estate Winery's pinot noir and pinot gris await. Before indulging your taste buds, however, you first will encounter the professionally trained staff. Indeed, they act more like concierges to your palate then simply wine-pouring zombies. Pourers walk you through the domaine-designated wines derived exclusively from the 465-acre King Estate vineyard, as well as the winery's Signature series, reflecting wines from top contracted vineyards in the Willamette Valley. You will understand why King Estate Winery has received top accolades and distinguished awards under the direction of its chief winemaker, John Albin.

However, wine always seeks pairing with wonderful food, and if the smells wafting from the winery's restaurant don't set your mouth awatering, the menu will. Open seven days a week (11 a.m. to 9 p.m.), the King Estate restaurant caters to both lunch- and dinner-time appetites. Get ready for such delights as BLT Pizzette or King Estate Seafood Sausage to satisfy lunchtime yearnings. For dinner, the menu will dazzle with such entrées as soy-glazed mahi mahi and (my favorite) Knee Deep Filet of Beef Tenderloin. Whatever meal you choose, many ingredients come right from the certified organic gardens and orchards of King Estate Winery. By the way, if you saved room for dessert, try the vanilla bean *crème brûlée*. You'll agree with me that it is truly majestic.

KING ESTATE WINERY
opened: 1991
winemaker(s): John Albin
location: 80854 Territorial Road, Eugene, OR 97405
phone: 541-942-9874
web: www.kingestate.com
e-mail: info@kingestate.com
picnic area: Yes
wheelchair access: Yes
weddings: Yes
tours: Yes
fee: Complimentary wine tasting of current releases
hours: Daily 11-8

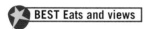 BEST Eats and views

DIRECTIONS: Heading southbound on I-5 past Eugene take exit 182 at Creswell. Go west on Oregon Ave. (becomes Camas Swale Rd and then Ham Rd) to Territorial Hwy. Left on Territorial to King Estate (about 2.5 miles).

Heading north on I-5, take exit 162 (toward Drain) to Curtin Rd. Go right on Curtin Rd to Territorial Hwy. Go left on Territorial (through Lorane) to King Estate (approximately 10.5 miles).

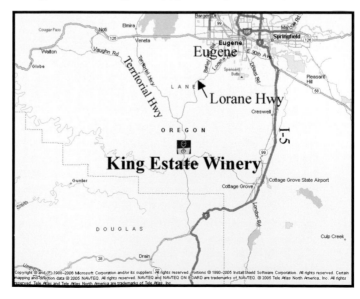

Chateau Lorane 🔟

Chateau Lorane's wine bar must be the longest in the state. It has to be in order to accommodate so many wines and so many fans. Groups of visitors form "tasting pods" sometimes two or three deep around friendly tasting-room staff. There's a steady level of loudness as people react to a wine or laugh at something the pourer has said. At Chateau

Lorane, WineTrail trekkers enter a fun zone of wine exploration.

Hands down, Chateau Lorane produces more wines — red, white, mead, fruit, and dessert — than any other winery in Oregon. Don't plan on a drive-by tasting experience at this winery. You might want to budget an afternoon, because you've entered the Bermuda Triangle of wine tasting. The owners of Chateau Lorane, Linde and Sharon Kester, are the reason behind the great variety of wines to taste. From the winery's beginning in 1992, their goal has been to produce wines to meet every taste. Consequently, whether you like dry, off dry or sweet, you are sure to find wines that you like. Whereas most wineries in this part of Oregon focus on pinot noir and pinot gris, at Chateau Lorane, the pinots get lost in an avalanche of choices, some of which will no doubt be new to many visitors. It's little wonder that the winery's slogan is "Come for the wine, stay for the view."

Here's a sampling of some of the rare varieties available to taste: Huxelrebe, cascade, chancellor, Leon Millot, Durif (aka petite sirah), pinot meunier, gamay noir, and baco noir. Many a WineTrail enthusiast comes here to experience these wines, because they simply don't have a month to drive around Oregon in search of these rare beauties.

But rest assured, Chateau Lorane pleases the taste buds of visitors with more traditional palates, too, offering Burgundy, Bordeaux, and other familiar European appellations. You can taste your way through such favorites as merlot, cabernet sauvignon, tempranillo, syrah, and pinot noir (many of them designated as "single vineyard") and not even realize that the winery offers unusual varieties, such as other fruit and dessert wines.

No matter what wine strikes your fancy, budget time to take a glass (or a bottle) to the outside deck, where you can sit amongst tall fir trees and enjoy a private lake below. Yep, a private lake, and it's all part of the charm and great variety that greet visitors to this extraordinary winery.

CHATEAU LORANE
opened: 1992
winemaker(s): David Hook
location: 27415 Siuslaw River Road, Lorane, OR 97541
phone: 541-942-8028
web: www.chateaulorane.com
e-mail: info@chateaulorane.com
picnic area: Yes
wheelchair access: Yes
weddings: Yes
fee: Complimentary wine tasting
hours: Daily 12–5 June through September; Saturday and Sunday 12–5 October through May

 BEST picnic

DIRECTIONS: From Eugene on E Broadway go west .5 miles. Turn left (south) onto Lawrence St. for .2 miles. Turn right (west) on W 11th Ave. [SR-126] for 1.2 miles. Turn left (south) onto Bailey Hill Rd for 4.6 miles. Keep straight onto Lorane Hwy for 8.3 miles. Turn left (south) onto Territorial Hwy for 5.8 miles. Turn right (west) onto Siuslaw River Rd and arrive at the winery in 1 mile.

Heading northbound on I-5 take exit 161 toward Anlauf/Lorane. Turn left (west) onto Buck Creek Rd [County Rd 61], go .9 miles. Turn right (northeast) onto County Rd 212 [Curtain Rd] for .4 miles. Turn left (northwest) onto County Rd 116 [Curtain Rd] go 2 miles. Bear left (north) onto County Rd 116 [Territorial Hwy] for 2.8 miles. Continue 4.1 miles. Turn left (west) onto Siuslaw River Rd and go 1 mile to the winery.

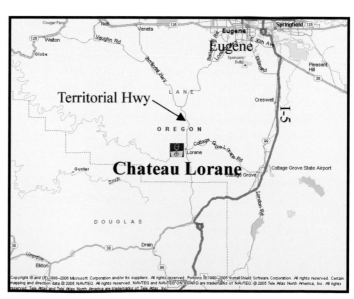

Saginaw Vineyard 🔢

Question: What do 30 ewes, 40 lambs, and one ram named Dude have in common? Answer: They all reside at Saginaw Vineyard, located near Cottage Grove. To varying degrees, they help with making wine, especially the lambs, who are just the right height for eating leaves and vines in the vineyard. That's Saginaw Vineyard's version of "canopy management."

Owners Scott and Cheryl Byler both grew up in the same town in Upstate New York, but their families didn't know each other. However, in one of life's ironies, both families moved across country to Phoenix, Arizona. Time marched on, and eventually Scott and

Cheryl met in high school and fell in love. For both, however, the heat and enormity of Phoenix became the incentives to head north to Oregon and eventually to purchase a rustic 100-year-old farmstead.

Since 1992, the Bylers have been growing 9 acres of premium wine grapes and 1 acre of blueberries. Tired of producing grapes for others, they launched their own winery in 2001 and christened their grape-wine labels "Saginaw Vineyard" and fruit-wine labels "Delight Valley Farms." In the 1905-built red barn, visitors can sample Saginaw Vineyard pinot noir, pinot gris, Maréchal Foch, chardonnay, and Müller-Thurgau. Also available for sampling are Delight Valley Farms blueberry and blackberry wines. We gladly purchased a bottle of the Delight Valley Farms blueberry wine after Cheryl suggested that we "imagine eating pound cake, cheesecake, or vanilla ice cream with this wine." Each 375-ml. bottle has a pound and a half of blueberries.

The Bylers are down-to-earth, hard-working people who have the perfect attitude for the demands of Saginaw Vineyard. I know it's cliché but what you see is what you get. From sunup to sundown, they are busy managing the farm with their loyal dogs, Petey and Buck, always at their side. During the summer, the Bylers host Friday Night Live evenings at the vineyard, which feature live music, plenty of good wine and beer, and an economical admission cost, as in free.

While in the tasting room, take time to explore the antiques and pictures on the wall. One of the pictures, dating from the early 1900s, is a photo of a large family outing at the farmstead. The rural splendor of a bygone era speaks for itself. Somehow, I think those folks would be very proud of what the Bylers have done.

Scott and Cheryl Byler with Buck

SAGINAW VINEYARD
opened: 2001
winemaker(s): Scott Byler
location: 80247 Delight Valley School Road,
Cottage Grove, OR 97424
phone: 541-942-1364
web: www.saginawvineyard.com
e-mail: Saginawvineyard@epud.net
picnic area: Yes
gift shop: Yes
fee: Complimentary wine tasting
hours: Daily 11–5; Closed Christmas, Thanksgiving,
New Year's Day, and Easter

DIRECTIONS: From I-5 take exit 176 toward Saginaw. Head north onto N Delight Valley School Rd for
.5 miles and arrive at Saginaw Vineyard.

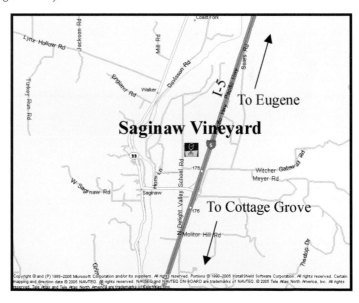

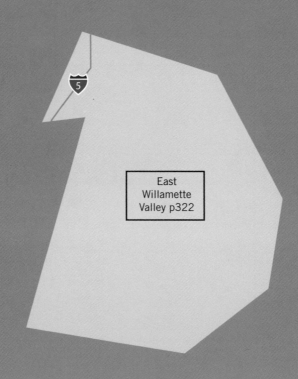

East
Willamette
Valley p322

East Willamette Valley
WINE COUNTRY

East Willamette Valley
WineTrail

Garden retreat at Piluso Vineyard & Winery

It's weird. You simply don't hear much said about the wineries in the Willamette Valley east of I-5. Given the short drive from Portland, you would think that the wineries of the East Willamette Valley WineTrail would be a popular destination for wine touring fans. I believe, however that this situation will change in the not-too-distant future, and throngs of wine tourists will discover the wineries of East Willamette.

This is rich farm country. It's picturesque, to be sure, with plenty of side trips to exercise your Visa. Definitely, no visit here is complete without a field trip to Silverton's Oregon Garden, featuring the only Frank Lloyd Wright–designed home in the Pacific Northwest. But it's the wines of East Willamette Valley WineTrails that keep us coming back for more.

East Willamette Valley WineTrail

1. St. Josef's Winery
2. Alexeli Vineyard & Winery
3. Vitis Ridge
4. Pudding River Wine Cellars
5. Silver Falls Vineyards
6. Piluso Vineyard & Winery

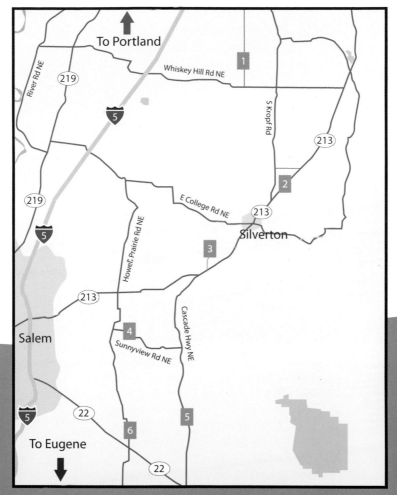

Region:	**East Willamette Valley Wine Country**
# of tasting rooms on tour:	**6**
Estimate # of days for tour:	**1 to 2**
Getting around:	**Car**
Key Events:	❑ **Memorial Weekend in Wine Country –** **Willamette Valley – visit www.willamettewines.com.**
	❑ **Wine Country Thanksgiving – Willamette Valley** **call 503-646-2985 or visit www.willamettewines.com.**
Tips:	❑ **Visit The Oregon Garden in Silverton –** **call 503-874-8100 for details.**
	❑ **See Appendix B – Wine Tour Planning, for planning** **your visit.**

St. Josef's Winery ❶

Josef Fleischmann, proprietor of St. Josef's Winery, has never forgotten his European roots. Josef, who grew up in a small Hungarian village near the German border, learned the art of winemaking from his relatives. That was some 60 years ago, before he arrived in the Willamette Valley and acquired farmland.

In 1978, Josef and his wife, Lilli, planted vinifera grapes, and to the delight of friends and family, the wine made from those grapes was delicious. Encouraged to start a winery,

they wondered what to call it. At the time, there were several wineries bearing the word "saint" in their names: Ste. Michelle, St. Innocent, St. Chapelle. Someone jokingly suggested the name St. Josef's Winery. It stuck.

Pulling into the parking lot, visitors see European touches galore, from the fountain courtyard area to the large double-door entrance. Guests feel as though they've been transported to a different time and place. In the distance, past the grape-stomping barrels, is a private spring-fed lake. Inside the winery, a grand foyer includes a staircase leading upstairs to rooms reserved for events. A side door brings you into a mural-adorned tasting room. It's all very Euro and enchanting, but that's not the best part.

Josef and Lilli also brought with them the Continental attitude that wine should be affordable. After all, in the small villages of Hungary, good wine at nominal prices is a part of life. Thus, WineTrail trekkers seeking a good buy for wine just entered heaven. All St. Josef's white wines are $9 per bottle. That's not a typo. All regular red wines (pinot noir, merlot, and cabernet sauvignon) are $15 each. Only St. Josef's reserve wines — the Kitara pinot noir and syrah wines and the KB Cabernet Sauvignon (short for Kirk's Best; Kirk is their son and vineyard manager) — cost a bit more, selling for around $20. Regulars at St. Josef's think that KB also stands for "Kick Butt," because the resulting cabernet kicks your you-know-what.

St. Josef's Winery maintains a regular schedule of events throughout the year. After all, there's much to celebrate. For example, during the summer, visitors can experience Cheeseburger in Paradise and Music at Jo-Lily Pond. In the fall, there's the Grape Stomping Festival and Neu Wein Celebration, followed by St. Josef's Day in the spring. When not conducting these events, the Fleischmann family welcomes weddings, family get-togethers, corporate events, and the like. The European charm never fails to delight at St. Josef's Winery!

ST. JOSEF'S WINERY
opened: 1982
winemaker(s): Joe Fleischmann
location: 28836 S Barlow Road,
Oregon City, OR 97013
phone: 503-651-3190
web: www.stjosefswinery.com
e-mail: info@stjosefswinery.com
picnic area: Yes
wheelchair access: Yes
weddings: Yes
gift shop: Yes
fee: $2.50 tasting fee
hours: Saturday and Sunday 11–5, or by appointment

DIRECTIONS: **From I-5 southbound** take the Canby/Hubbard exit 282A and continue to the second traffic light, Ehlen Rd. Take a left onto Ehlen Rd, heading east to Aurora. At the first traffic light in Aurora take a left, heading north on 99E toward Canby. Proceed .25 miles, crossing the Pudding River, to take a right onto Lone Elder Rd (steep hill). Drive approximately 3 miles to the light at Barlow Rd and take a right. St. Josef's Winery is located 3 miles south on, on the left (east) side of the road.

From I-5 northbound take Woodburn exit 271 and go right, heading east on Hwy 211. Drive 2 miles east to cross the 99E intersection (Safeway store). Continue E on Hwy 211 to Barlow Rd (5 miles). Take a left onto Barlow Rd (red blinking light) and drive 3 miles. The winery is on the right (east) side of the road.

From 205 southbound take Oregon City exit 9. Take a left at the light, heading to Canby on 99E. Continue along the Willamette River, driving through Canby, and crossing the Molalla River. After crossing the Molalla River, you will come to the Barlow intersection; take a left onto Barlow Rd. St. Josef's Winery is located 4 miles south on Barlow Rd, on the left (east) side of the road.

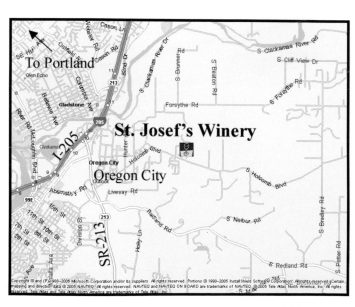

Alexeli Vineyard & Winery ②

Philip Kramer

Brothers Philip and Anthony Kramer know what they have gotten into. In 2007 they acquired Marquam Hill Vineyard & Winery from Joe Dobbes (the father of well-know winemaker son Joe Dobbes, Jr.) and understood the task ahead — rehabbing the vineyard, upgrading the gardens and picnic area and overhauling the tasting room. Fortunately, for the Kramer brothers they have considerable energy, youth and passion working in their favor. Philip's educational background, including a degree in mechanical engineering from Rensselaer Polytechnic Institute, is relied upon in redesigning the tasting room. By day, Anthony works at a social service organization in Portland and switches to his winemaking persona at night and on the weekends.

To put their signature on the winery, the Wisconsin-bred brothers changed the name of the winery. Formerly Marquam Hill the new winery's name is Alexeli Vineyard & Winery. If your GPS device says "Marquam Hill Vineyard & Winery", it's OK. You're at the right place. For the brothers it's a branding thing and a desire to distinguish them from the past.

With 20 acres of vineyards to rehab, Philip and Anthony have considerable "vine time" in store. However, the brothers are committed to a sustainable vineyard practices and their efforts focus on growing organic grapes and creating an eco-system for plants to thrive. Fruit quantity is secondary to fruit quality and the long hours ahead of them is the price to pay for creating a "green" vineyard.

At one end of the 60-acre property is a gazebo and private lake where visitors can take their bottle of wine and picnic on nice days. Take time to stroll through the vineyards and experience this splendid setting. It's a dream come true for two cheese heads from Wisconsin.

ALEXELI VINEYARD & WINERY
opened: 2008
winemaker(s): Joe Dobbes, Jr.
location: 35803 S Hwy 213, Molalla, OR 97038
phone: 503-829-6677
web: www.alexeli.com
e-mail: info@alexeli.com
picnic area: Yes
wheelchair access: Yes
weddings: Yes
tours: Yes
fee: Tasting fee may apply
hours: Friday, Saturday, and Sunday – call for hours

DIRECTIONS: **From Molalla**, take SR-211 [W Main St.] west 1.4 miles. Turn left (south) onto SR-213 [Cascade Hwy S] for 5. 3 miles. Arrive at Marquam Hill Vineyards.

From Silverton, take SR-213 [Cascade Hwy NE] east 8.3 miles and look for the winery sign.

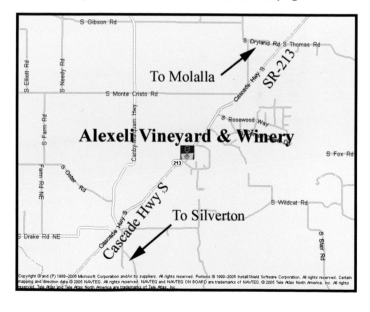

Vitis Ridge 3

Are you looking to escape the crowds and spend an enjoyable respite tasting wine? At Vitis Ridge, making visitors feel comfortable and open to tasting handcrafted wines is the owners' main goal; partners Chris and Sharon Deckelmann, Sally and Bruce Eich, and Glen Brunger make it their business. When you visit Vitis Ridge (which is open during the second weekend of each month), you can expect to have one of the partners pouring wine and making sure you're happy.

With plenty of wines to choose from (as many as 19!), chances are visitors will find a wine that they enjoy. Winemaker Glen Brunger produces about 2,800 cases annually. However, his portfolio of wines has a broad base; from big reds such as cabernet sauvignon, Maréchal Foch, syrah, and Malbec to fruit-forward smooth pinot noir and Beaujolais nouveau, there are plenty of reds to enjoy. Offerings of the white variety include pinot gris, riesling, and a white blend with the intriguing name d'Vine. Vitis Ridge's wines honestly express the varietal character and the region's appellations.

A transplant from the Midwest, Glen's love of pinot noir led him to a career of making wine. However, because focusing on pinot noir was too limited for him, he has began making more robust wines such as the aforementioned cabernet sauvignon and Maréchal Foch. Because of his ever-expanding repertoire, Glen has adopted the approach of producing a number of small batches of wines, rather than making one big batch of a single variety. It's a lot of work, but passion has a way of driving a person.

Honest. Uncrowded. Personal. Located just one mile north of the town of Silverton and the famous Oregon Garden, Vitis Ridge is a decidedly pleasing stop along the East Willamette Valley WineTrail.

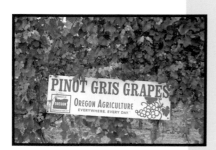

VITIS RIDGE
winemaker(s): Glen Brunger
location: 6685 Meridian Road NE,
Silverton, OR 97381
phone: 503-873-9800
web: www.vitisridge.com
e-mail: info@vitisridge.com
picnic area: Yes
wheelchair access: Yes
fee: Complimentary wine tasting
hours: Saturday and Sunday 12–5, 2nd weekend of
the month only except Memorial Day, Labor Day and
Thanksgiving weekends. Closed in January

DIRECTIONS: **Heading southbound on I-5** take exit 271 toward OR-214/Woodburn/Silverton. Go east on SR-214 [Newberg Hwy] for 2.5 miles. Turn right (south) onto SR-214 [SR-99E] and drive 1.2 miles. Turn left (east) onto SR-214 [Young St.] and travel 10 miles. Road name changes to Meridian Rd NE. Look for Vitis Ridge sign to the winery.

From Salem take SR-99E Bus [Salem Hwy] heading northeast for 2.7 miles. Turn right (east) onto Chemawa Rd NE. Proceed about 9 miles. Turn left (north) onto Mt Angel Hwy NE and go 1.1 miles. Turn right (east) onto Hobart Rd NE and go 2.5 miles. Road name changes to Meridian Rd NE. Arrive at 6685 Meridian Rd NE and look for Vitis Ridge sign.

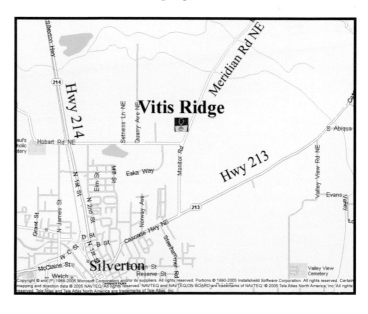

Pudding River Wine Cellars 4

The Pudding River wine label muses, "Life is good, the palate is pleased, and the rooster crows again!" For owner and winemaker Sean Driggers, that reference to the rooster crowing again has personal meaning. Prior to moving to rural East Willamette Valley in 2004, Sean and his wife, Stacey, lived a hectic life in Bellevue, Washington, pursuing mechanical-engineering careers. However, the adrenaline of the rat race began to wear thin and a longing for a less hectic life — where you can hear "the rooster crowing" — took over.

Located off Sunnyview Road in East Salem, the Pudding River Wine Cellars property was once a poultry farm. Sean's in-laws, John and Karen Bateman, recognized that the area produced premium wine grapes; why else would the well-established wineries in western Willamette Valley purchase grapes from this district they reasoned. Working the 4-acre vineyard resulted in the release of Pudding River Wine Cellar's first vintage (2006) of estate pinot noir to critical acclaim. In 2007, Pudding River wines gained acceptance into the Portland Indie Wine Festival. As the co-owner of a boutique winery, Sean took this opportunity to showcase the wines of an undiscovered Oregon wine region — East Willamette Valley.

Near the entrance to the winery is a two-story 1906 house that serves as the Driggers' home. This means that Sean's commute time to winery, vineyard, and tasting room is about one minute, 30 seconds — a far cry from rush-hour traffic in Bellevue. A separate red barn houses the tasting room for Pudding River Wine Cellars. Located upstairs, the whitewashed room is where you often find Karen Bateman, Sean's mother-in-law. With an engaging smile, she pours wine and entertains guests. It's a relaxed space in which to sample their rooster-labeled line-up of viognier, chardonnay, pinot noir, pinot gris, riesling, and pinot noir rosé. Sean must be doing something right: He's already garnered an 87 from *Wine Spectator* for his 2006 Willamette Valley Chardonnay. According to *Wine Spectator*, this chardonnay is "very good, a wine with special qualities." However, WineTrail trekkers should know that, given the small quantities of wine that Pudding River produces, certain wines are likely to be sold out.

The term "rising star" aptly describes Pudding River Wine Cellars, and its rise is a key reason we can say "adios" to the notion of East Willamette Valley as an undiscovered wine region. Clearly, life is good, the palate is pleased, and the rooster crows again!

PUDDING RIVER WINE CELLARS
winemaker(s): Sean Driggers
location: 9374 Sunnyview Road NE,
Salem, OR 97317
phone: 503-365-0391
web: www.puddingriver.com
e-mail: info@puddingriver.com
fee: Complimentary wine tasting
hours: Saturday and Sunday 11–5 May 31 through
September

DIRECTIONS: **On I-5** take exit 260B, toward Keizer. Head east onto Chemawa Rd NE and go 1.1 miles. Road name changes to Hazelgreen Rd NE. Go 5 miles. Turn right (south) onto Howell Prairie Rd NE and go 3.9 miles. Turn left (east) onto Sunnyview Rd NE and proceed .8 miles to winery on the right.

From downtown Salem go north on Liberty St. for .8 miles. Turn right (east) onto Center St. NE and go 3.9 miles. Turn left (north) onto Cordon Rd NE and continue 1.1 miles. Turn right (east) onto Sunnyview Rd NE and proceed 4.4 miles. Arrive at Pudding River Wine Cellars.

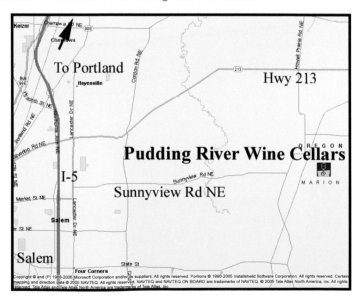

Silver Falls Vineyards 5

If you're looking for a place to get hitched, your search may be over. The place is called Silver Falls Vineyards, and the size of the property, the amenities, and the quick access to local attractions make it a convenient location for tying the knot. Imagine this: a 100-acre

majestic property located right off the Cascade Highway, plenty of parking, an estate vineyard, spacious grounds, and an inside banquet hall complete with piano and sound system. It's a wedding planner's dream.

When considering a place to exchange marriage vows, my concerns would be whether or not there's a mirror in which to check my bow tie, a kitchen to store my sister's Swedish meatballs, and ready access to the wine and other beverages. None of these worries pose a problem at Silver Falls Vineyards — especially the wine part.

Owned by Duane and Gail Defree, Silver Falls Vineyards is a family-owned and -operated winery. The 18-acre estate vineyard is truly "old vine" by Oregon standards, with most vines planted 30 years ago. The rich soil of East Willamette Valley provides an excellent home to four different varietals: pinot noir, pinot gris, riesling, and chardonnay. The harvested fruit is converted into wine at nearby Chateau Bianca winery by winemaker Andreas Wetzel. In addition to the varietal wines just mentioned, Andreas also makes a dessert wine called Sublime and a popular white blend named Silver Mist. As you would expect, Silver Falls also produces a sparkler with the perfect name of "Cheers" for those regularly occurring weddings. The Defrees distribute most of the wine directly from the tasting room at Silver Falls Vineyards for remarkably low prices. Most wines sell in the $15 range, to entice would-be visitors to venture east of I-5 to explore this uncrowded wine region.

The tasting room features a number of wine accessories to take home along with your wine purchase. Or, if you arrived for a wedding and forgot the gift, you can spring for one of those fancy wine openers or something artsy for the bedroom. Of course, with wines so reasonably priced, you may opt to get the bride and groom a case of the reserve pinot noir.

If the weather permits, take a glass of wine to the picnic area, located in a grove of old oak trees. There, you can contemplate the details of an upcoming wedding or wonder why viticulture scientists haven't come up with a seedless wine grape.

SILVER FALLS VINEYARDS
winemaker(s): Andreas Wetzel
location: 4972 Cascade Highway SE,
Sublimity, OR 97385
phone: 503-769-5056
web: www.silverfallsvineyards.com
e-mail: ddefrees@wvi.com
picnic area: Yes
wheelchair access: Yes
weddings: Yes
gift shop: Yes
fee: Complimentary wine tasting
hours: Friday through Sunday 11–6, March through
December, or by appointment

DIRECTIONS: From Silverton take SR-213 [Cascade Hwy NE] for 10 miles heading south toward Sublimity. Arrive at Silver Falls Vineyards.

From Salem head east on SR-22 [SR-99E Bus] for 13.7 miles. Turn right onto ramp toward Santiam/Sublimity. Turn left (north) onto Cascade Hwy SE for 3.8 miles and arrive at 4972 Cascade Hwy SE.

Piluso Vineyard & Winery 6

Pinky and Sandee Piluso came north from California in the late 1970s for a change in lifestyle. They succeeded in transforming their lives into those of wine-growing Oregonians. Pinky is the self-described "tractor driver," and Sandee is the winemaker, possessing degrees in both enology (i.e., making the wine) and viticulture (i.e., growing

the grapes) from Chemeketa Community College and University of California–Davis programs. It's unusual that a winemaker would have degrees in both fields, rarer still for a woman to have accomplished this in what is known to be a male-dominated industry.

Rather than spending big bucks on winemaking equipment, Sandee teamed up with Pudding River Wine Cellars to acquire advanced equipment and share winemaking space. This is collaboration on a grand scale, but around these parts, wineries helping each other is par for the course. By sharing resources with Pudding River, Sandee is able to focus on her own Piluso Vineyard & Winery label. (**WineTrail note:** The art that graces her wine labels is from critically acclaimed local artist Terry Peasley.) Perhaps this explains why she received a silver medal for Piluso's 2005 Estate Pinot Noir at the Northwest Wine Summit and an 88 rating from *Wine Spectator*. Expect Piluso Vineyard & Winery to receive a boatload of accolades and awards in the future.

Piluso Vineyard & Winery's motto is "Great wines begin with great grapes," and for that reason the battle is fought and won in the vineyard. From bud break through harvest, the Pilusos closely manage four clones of pinot noir (Pommard, 777, 828, and Wadensville) and a block of tempranillo. Their focus is on sustainable farming. Using a combination of estate and purchased grapes, Sandee plans future releases to include pinot noir, tempranillo, dolcetto, Maréchal Foch and an unusual gamay noir white wine.

Don't miss Sandee's special "vintner's garden" next to the winery's tasting room. Here amongst colorful flowers and indigenous plants, visitors can relax and truly enjoy Piluso Vineyard & Winery's award-winning pinot noir.

Sandee Piluso

PILUSO VINEYARD & WINERY
opened: 2003
winemaker(s): Sandee Piluso
location: 6654 Shaw Highway SE,
Aumsville, OR 97325
phone: 503-749-4125
web: www.pilusowines.com
e-mail: sandee@pilusowines.com
picnic area: Yes
wheelchair access: Yes
fee: Complimentary wine tasting
hours: Saturday and Sunday 12–5 June through September. Open October through December for holidays and special events. Closed January through March.

DIRECTIONS: **From I-5** take exit 253 toward OR-22/OR-99E Bus/Stayton/Detroit Lakes. Go east on SR-22 for 7.6 miles. Take exit 9 toward Shaw/Aumsville. Bear right (north) onto Shaw Hwy SE and go .5 miles. Arrive at destination.

From Salem take SR-22 east about 10 miles to exit 9. Bear right (north) onto Shaw Hwy SE and go .5 miles. Arrive at 6654 Shaw Hwy SE.

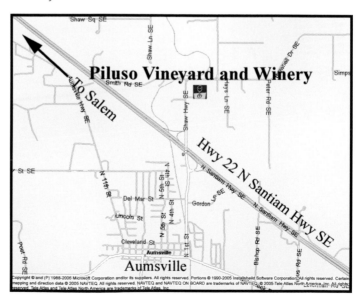

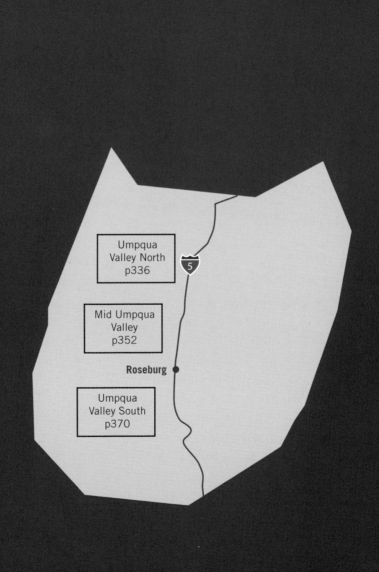

Umpqua
Valley North
p336

5

Mid Umpqua
Valley
p352

Roseburg

Umpqua
Valley South
p370

Umpqua Valley
WINE COUNTRY

Umpqua Valley North
WineTrail

Brandborg Winery

"America's last great undiscovered wine region," wrote nationally syndicated columnist Dan Berger in reference to the Umpqua Valley wine region. Well, maybe so, but this is one WineTrail trekker on a mission to change that… especially when it comes to the wineries of Umpqua Valley WineTrail North.

The Umpqua Valley AVA is nothing short of spectacular. With the moniker of "the land of a hundred valleys," the Umpqua Valley is characterized by one word: diversity. Diversity of soils, temperature, and moisture creates a diversity of wine-growing grapes. To the north, in and around the town of Elkton reside wineries that rely on cool-weather grapes not unlike the Willamette Valley's. Being only forty miles from the coast, Elkton gets an annual dose of 50 inches of precipitation and plenty of cool nights. The result is an abundance of riesling, pinot noir, pinot gris, pinot blanc, and gewürztraminer to go around.

Umpqua Valley WineTrail North

1 River's Edge Winery   **3** Brandborg Winery   **5** Sienna Ridge Estate
2 Anindor Vineyards   **4** Bradley Vineyards   **6** MarshAnne Landing

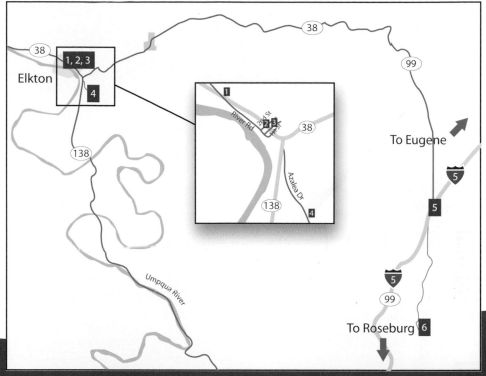

Region:	**Umpqua Valley Wine Country**
# of tasting rooms on tour:	**6**
Estimate # of days for tour:	**1 to 2**
Getting around:	**Car**
Key Events:	❑ **In March, Canyonville's Annual Greatest of the Grape – call 541-673-7575 or go to www.umpquavalleywineries.org to order tickets.**
	❑ **In April, Roseburg's Umpqua Valley Barrel Tasting Bus Tour – call 800-444-9584 or see www.umpquavalleywlneries.org.**
	❑ **In May, Umpqua Winery Association's Memorial Day Open House – call 541-679-6642.**
Tips:	❑ **Great food at Sienna Ridge Estate – wonderful spreads and dips.**
	❑ **Pack your fishing pole and stay at Steamboat Inn on North Umpqua River. Historic charm.**
	❑ **Consider hiring a limousine services such as Oregon Wine Country Tours – 800-704-2943 or see www.oregonwinecountrytours.com.**
Best:	❑ **Gift shop: MarshAnne Landing.**
	❑ **Views: Bradley Vineyards, MarshAnne Landing.**

River's Edge Winery ▣

Overlooking the Umpqua River in the tiny town of Elkton (pop. 170) is the friendly River's Edge Winery. The view of the river from the tasting room is break-out-the-fishing-pole spectacular. Within a day, the white-capped river water will reach the Pacific Ocean, which is only 36 miles from Elkton as the crow flies. Given the area's proximity to the ocean, the climate here is much like the Willamette Valley, rather than the hotter environs

of the southern Umpqua Valley. Summertime temperatures often climb above 90 degrees during the day and drop at night to the mid-50s, influenced by the nighttime breeze from the Pacific. The grapes love it.

The proprietors of River's Edge Winery, Michael and Vonnie Landt, are the proud owners of two of the state's oldest vineyards. Located outside of Elkton, their estate vineyards — Elkton Vineyard and Black Oak Vineyard — produce primarily pinot noir with a dash of gewürztraminer. Totaling 11 acres, both vineyards were planted in 1972. If good wine comes from older vines, this winery has an edge on the others. To supplement their grape production, the Landts acquire more grapes from Bradley Vineyard (their neighbor) and Grace Hill Vineyard, located north in the Willamette Valley.

From the start, Michael and Vonnie's focus has been on "handcrafted" wines. This starts in the vineyard, where each vine is meticulously treated, and grapes are harvested by hand. At the winery, the clusters are sorted by hand, and each batch is aged in separate barrels to create single vineyard reserve wines or blended as a cuvée. The resulting artisan wines include a number of pinot noirs (including a relatively sweet, lip-smacking Dulcet Cuvée with 16.4 percent alcohol). The white wine line-up includes a dry and semisweet gewürztraminer, and a pinot gris.

Although the River's Edge portfolio of wines reflects what you would expect to find in the Willamette Valley, the similarity ends there. The reason? The unique microclimate and soil conditions found at River's Edge's vineyards give an entirely different expression to these wines. What's more, Michael and Vonnie rely on a combination of different new and not-so-new French, American, and Hungarian oak to impart unique flavor profiles.

While in the tasting room, take your eyes off the spectacular river below to sneak a peek at the barrel room behind the wine bar. Nestled there since the winery's launch in 1998 are the fruits of Michael and Vonnie Landt's artisan labors.

RIVER'S EDGE WINERY
opened: 1998
winemaker(s): Michael Landt
location: 1395 River Drive, Elkton, OR 97436
phone: 541-584-2357
web: www.riversedgewinery.com
e-mail: wines@riversedgewinery.com
picnic area: Yes
wheelchair access: Yes
hours: Daily 11–5 during summer; Wednesday through Sunday until end of November; closed in winter and spring except by appointment with 24 hours advance notice

DIRECTIONS: **Heading southbound on I-5 past Eugene** take exit 162 toward OR-38/Drain/Elkton. Continue on OR-38 about 21 miles to Elkton. Turn left (south) onto River Dr. and arrive at River's Edge Winery.

Heading northbound on I-5 from Medford take exit 136 toward OR-138/Sutherlin/Elkton. Turn left (west) onto SR-138 and proceed 24.2 miles. Turn left (west) onto SR-38 [W Central Ave.] and go .8 miles. Turn left (south) onto River Dr. and arrive at winery.

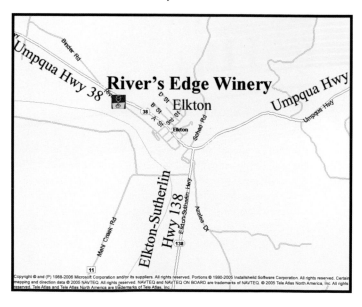

Anindor Vineyards ②

Entrepreneurs Rod and Nina Pace lead an amazing life. The couple is always on the go; his mining background takes them to other western states, including Arizona, where they have a second residence. However, the Paces' winemaking passion keeps them coming back to their vineyard home just outside the town of Elkton. Rod's background in agriculture (he took grape-growing classes in college) brought them to this northern part of the Umpqua region, where he could grow premium pinot noir, pinot gris, gewürztraminer, pinot blanc, and riesling. It's a farmer's dream. In fact, Rod and Nina refer to themselves as "grape ranchers"!

The name "Anindor" comes from Nina's and Rod's names spelled backwards and combined, and the moniker applies to both their vineyard and wine label. At Anindor Vineyards, sharp-shinned hawks do a great job of scaring away grape-eating birds, such as robins. It's little wonder then that an image of this hawk graces the label on their wine bottles as well as other Anindor branding. The eco-friendly vineyard is certified sustainable by LIVE (Low Input Viticulture & Enology). However, with their desire to distribute their wines themselves to friends, family, and loyal fans, the Paces needed one more thing — a tasting room.

Located in a former hot-dog stand and bike shop on Second Street, the Anindor Vineyards tasting room provides an intimate space in which to experience its wines. For WineTrail trekkers who enjoy a manageable line-up of wines to sample, Anindor Vineyards offers the perfect wine-tasting oasis. For white wines, you can experience gewürztraminer, pinot gris, and riesling. For reds, your choice is pinot noir. All of them are estate grown. All are small-batch productions. And all are certifiably delicious, as approved by this tasting-room crawler.

The tasting room's porch sits alongside Elkton's main street and provides a shaded space to sit under and watch the world go by. I understand that food pairs nicely with pinot noir, but I discovered that a glass of Anindor Vineyards Pinot Noir on its own is great for sipping as you watch the traffic flow.

Cheers!

ANINDOR VINEYARDS
winemaker(s): Rod Pace
location: 325 2nd Street, Elkton, OR 97436
phone: 541-584-2637
web: www.anindor.com
e-mail: nina@anindor.com
picnic area: Yes
fee: Complimentary wine tasting
hours: Wednesday through Sunday 11 – 5, May
through December; closed January through April

DIRECTIONS: Heading southbound on I-5 take exit 162 toward OR-38/Drain/Elkton. Continue on OR-38 about 21 miles to Elkton. Look for Anindor Vineyard's tasting room on the right in Elkton's town center.

Heading northbound on I-5 from Medford take exit 136 toward OR-138/Sutherlin/Elkton. Turn left (west) onto SR-138 and proceed 24.2 miles. Turn left (west) onto SR-38 [W Central Ave.] and go .8 miles. Look for Anindor Vineyard's tasting room on the right in Elkton's town center.

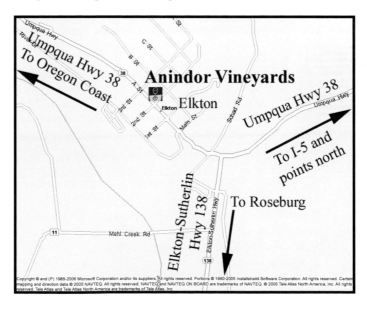

Brandborg Winery 3

In 2008, *Wine Press Northwest* named Brandborg Winery the Oregon winery to watch. That's high praise for a winery in the little ol' town of Elkton, population 170.

Terry and Sue Brandborg relocated from the Bay Area in pursuit of making pinot noir at the start of 2002. The winemaking wasn't the challenge for Terry. After all, he had

been making wine for a number of years prior the move and knew all about converting grapes into wine. Rather, it was relocating to a small town that posed the biggest problem. Goodbye, gourmet restaurants — hello, corner café.

A half-dozen years later, Terry and Sue readily agree that the move worked out fine. Residing on a 145-acre plot of land with a great view of the surrounding valley and growing pinot noir translates into a little heaven on earth. Although their Ferris Wheel Estate Vineyard accounts for only five acres now, expect to see the vineyard acreage increase. In the meantime, they source grapes from other local growers to make pinot gris, pinot blanc, pinot noir rosé, gewürztraminer, and several different pinot noirs. By the way, if you find yourself a little peckish during your visit, as I did, try not to think of rotisserie chicken and grilled asparagus when tasting the pinot. It leads to excessive drooling.

The Brandborg Winery tasting room is located directly on the highway that runs through Elkton. The spacious room features vaulted ceilings and an upstairs seating area with a bird's eye view of the tasting area and generous gift shop below. Outside is an inviting patio where visitors can linger and contemplate making a move to Elkton as the Brandborgs did. If you need nibbles to nosh on with your wine, check out the deli case. Back inside, you might note that there's more than enough room for bands to perform. If so, the Brandborgs already thought of that and host regular appearances by local artists all year around.

To some, Brandborg Winery might be up and coming. However, to this WineTrail trekker and a host of loyal fans, it has already arrived. There's a reason why the Brandborgs make nearly 9,000 cases of wine per year. People buy it. That in itself is proof positive that Brandborg Winery is here to stay.

BRANDBORG WINERY
opened: 2002
winemaker(s): Terry Brandborg
location: 345 First Street, Elkton, OR 97436
phone: 541-584-2870
web: www.brandborgwine.com
e-mail: terry@brandborgwine.com
picnic area: Yes
wheelchair access: Yes
gift shop: Yes
tours: Yes
fee: $5 tasting fee refundable with purchase of 6 or more bottles
hours: Daily 11–5; Closed major holidays

DIRECTIONS: From I-5 southbound about 30 miles past Eugene take exit 162 onto SR-38 [SR-99] toward Elkton. Proceed 6.6 miles. Turn right to stay on SR-38 [SR-99] for 14.1 more miles. Look right for Brandborg Winery's tasting room in Elkton's town center.

Heading north on I-5 about 12 miles past Roseburg take exit 136 toward Elkton. Turn left (west) onto SR-138 and proceed 24.2 miles. Turn left (west) onto SR-38 [Umpqua Hwy] and go .2 miles. Look for Brandborg Winery's tasting room in Elkton's town center.

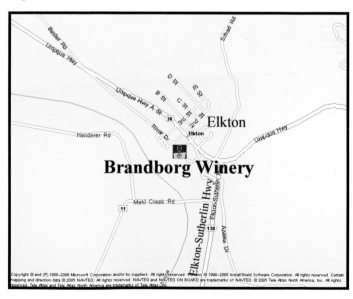

Bradley Vineyards 4

Bradley Vineyards offers something different from other Elkton-based wineries — its tasting room is at the vineyard. Just one mile south of Elkton's town center, visitors will find Bradley Vineyards' 25 vine acres, winery and tasting room. Still, guests might be hesitant to make the trek outside of town and turn off the highway onto the unpaved road leading to the winery.

This explains the Burma Shave–inspired signs telling visitors:

"Row after row
Drive to the top
To taste what they grow"

Since 1983, John and Bonnie Bradley have been growing grapes in this remarkable area. The vineyard includes wine varieties you come to expect in this marine-cooled climate: pinot noir, gewürztraminer, and riesling. In addition to these wines, the Bradleys also produce a wine unique to Umpqua — Baco noir. However, these grapes are grown much farther south in the Umpqua region.

If you are working your way north to south in the Umpqua, this will probably be your first exposure to Baco. A turn-of-the-century cross between folle blanche and *Vitis riparia* by the famous French hybridizer François Baco, this grape is grown principally at the Melrose, Girardet and Reustle-Prayer Rock vineyards to the south. The elegant taste of Baco noir will likely have you scratching your head wondering why we don't see this wine throughout the Northwest.

The views from the tasting-room deck include the vineyards in the foreground and the stunning Coast Range in the distance. On summer evenings, the golden light is spectacular and gets even better with each sip of Bradley Vineyards pinot noir. Beside the tasting room is a venue for weddings. It's easy to imagine friends and family gathered for a perfect wedding at Bradley Vineyards. During those events, perhaps the Bradleys should change their roadside signs to read:

Row after row
Drive to the top
And bring your sweetie in tow.

www.winetrailsnw.com/wineries/bradley_vineyards

Row after row

BRADLEY VINEYARDS
opened: 2001
winemaker(s): John Bradley
location: 1000 Azalea Drive, Elkton, OR 97436
phone: 541-584-2888
web: www.bradleyvineyards.com
e-mail: bbradley@cascadeaccess.com
picnic area: Yes
weddings: Yes
fee: Complimentary wine tasting
hours: Wednesday through Sunday 11–5 June through November

 BEST Views

DIRECTIONS: **From I-5 southbound about 30 miles past Eugene** take exit 162 onto SR-38 [SR-99] toward Elkton. Continue 6.6 miles. Turn right to stay on SR-38 [SR-99] for 13.9 miles. Turn left (south) onto SR-138 [Elkton-Sutherlin Hwy], then turn left (east) immediately onto Azalea Dr. and proceed .9 miles to Bradley Vineyards.

Heading north on I-5 about 12 miles past Roseburg take exit 136 toward Elkton. Turn left (west) onto SR-138 and proceed 22.6 miles. Turn right (east) onto Wells Rd and go .3 miles. Bear left (east) onto Azalea Dr. for 1 mile to arrive at 1000 Azalea Dr.

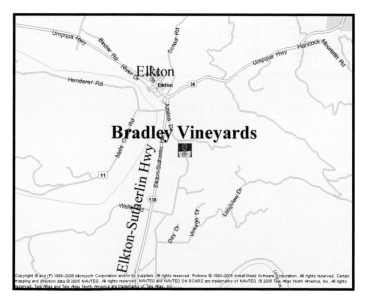

Sienna Ridge Estate 5

The typical tasting-room experience usually involves visitors nibbling on tiny crackers between sips. That's not the case at Sienna Ridge Estate winery. Here, visitors enjoy *hors d'oeuvres* as part of their tasting journey. However, I am not suggesting that you visit Sienna Ridge for the food. Rather, go with the wine in mind, but if your tummy starts making demands, partake in the snacks.

Sienna Ridge Estate's tasting room has some history. Located on John Long Road right off I-5 near Oakland, the structure housing the tasting room was built by John Long's son Robert in 1906. John Long himself had obtained a land grant in the Oregon Territory in 1847, which established the farm. Featuring plenty of windows to create a light-filled atmosphere, hardwood floors, large porch, and an expansive deck big enough to host music concerts (which it does), Sienna Ridge Estate's tasting room is more like a field trip than a simple tasting foray.

The owner of Sienna Ridge Estate winery is Anchorage resident Wayne Hitchings. Despite the distance, he is anything but a remote landlord. Although his successful architectural supply business keeps him in Alaska for much of the year, he often commutes south to attend to the myriad details of running a winery. Not only is there the winery business to manage, but there's also his 267-acre vineyard, one of only three individual vineyards designated as American Viticultural Areas (AVAs) in the United States. That's right, his vineyard is its own viticultural area, featuring red Jory soil (hence the winery name's reference to sienna). But it's the taste that matters, and according to Sienna Ridge literature, the microclimate and soil work together to create "small, tight clusters of grapes bursting with flavor." The name of this single-vineyard AVA is Red Hill Vineyard, and visitors can view the vineyard, across the road from the winery, by climbing up the hillside.

Sienna Ridge offers a number of varietals: pinot noir, pinot gris, pinot blanc, chardonnay, merlot, cabernet sauvignon, riesling, gewürztraminer, along with a late-harvest riesling and late-harvest gewürztraminer. For a nominal tasting fee, visitors can opt for a white wine flight or a red wine flight. But if you are like this WineTrail trekker, you can double the tasting fee and enjoy both flights. Fortunately, there's more than Ritz crackers to nibble between swirls and sips. At Sienna Ridge Estate, your biggest challenge may be discovering which wine pairs best with which appetizer. It's a delicious adventure!

SIENNA RIDGE ESTATE
winemaker(s): Terry Brandborg
location: 1876 John Long Road, Oakland, OR 97462
phone: 541-849-3300
web: www.siennaridgeestate.com/
e-mail: siennaridge@centurytel.net
picnic area: Yes
fee: $5 for whites; $5 for reds; $10 for full flight
hours: Daily 12–6

DIRECTIONS: Heading southbound on I-5 (about 40 miles south of Eugene) take exit 150. Turn left (south) onto SR-99 [CR-389] and go .3 miles. Turn left (southeast) onto John Long Rd and proceed .9 miles to the winery.

Heading northbound on I-5 (about 24 miles north of Roseburg) take exit 148. Turn left (northeast) onto County Road 126A [Goodrich Hwy] and go .1 miles. Keep straight onto John Long Rd and continue .7 miles to Sienna Ridge Estate.

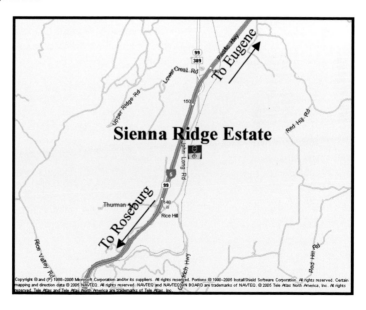

MarshAnne Landing 6

At first, I wondered what this winery's UFO logo had to do with syrah. However, when I walked into the tasting room and got a "Welcome to MarshAnne Landing," it began to dawn on me. Co-owner Frances Cramer pronounced "MarshAnne" like something having to do with the fourth planet from the sun — "Martian."

In the mid-'90s, Greg *Marsh* and Frances *Anne* Cramer moved to Oregon from Maryland in search of a new life and to make wine. As far as I know, they were transported via a regular airplane rather than hopping a space shuttle. Greg, who has a doctorate in chemistry, had developed a penchant for making wine in the basement. Frances' background is in computer science. Both loved Rhône-style wines — syrah, marsanne, viognier, and grenache — and believed that the warmer Umpqua region would prove best for these warm-weather grapes. The couple ultimately settled on a 109-acre "landing" site located four miles north of Oakland.

Inside the newly constructed (2006) tasting room, visitors encounter an elegant, light-filled space complete with an inviting fireplace and a set of French doors that open onto the outside deck. From there, you can ogle the Cramers' 20-acre estate vineyard. Back inside the high-ceilinged tasting room, there is plenty of art to keep visitors occupied. At the time of my visit, 17 different local artists were exhibiting their work, which included quilts, paintings, and woven art. Opera music was playing in the background.

With the goal of making "out of this world" wines, the Cramers create approachable, food-friendly wines. In keeping with their love of Rhône-style wines, they offer syrah and grenache red wines, including a red blend called Cote de Umpqua, which, unfortunately, has a way of selling out. They also feature Bordeaux varietals, including a merlot-cabernet blend they call Red Planet. White "landing fluids" included a crisp viognier that went great with the 90-degree temps outside.

While partaking of their wines and listening to Frances talk about her affection for the Umpqua, it dawned on me that there was another reason for the flying saucer on the logo. It conveys a sense of humor and an approachability that lets the drinker know that these wines are not snooty. At MarshAnne Landing, you can feel right at home, imagining yourself rubbing elbows with astronauts while admiring a wine label bearing the image of the Southern Cross.

MARSHANNE LANDING
opened: 2002
winemaker(s): Greg Cramer
location: 175 Hogan Road, Oakland, OR 97462
phone: 541-459-7998
web: www.marshannelanding.com
e-mail: gregnfran@hughes.net
picnic area: Yes
wheelchair access: Yes
gift shop: Yes
fee: $5 tasting fee
hours: Wednesday through Sunday 11–5

BEST Views and gift shop

DIRECTIONS: Heading south on I-5 take exit 150, Yoncalla, turn left over the freeway and proceed south on John Long Rd for about 1 mile to Goodrich Hwy (opposite Pilot Gas station). Turn left and drive 3 miles to Hogan Rd. A blue winery tour sign just before Hogan Rd advises travelers to turn left to winery.

Heading north on I-5 take exit 148, Rice Hill and proceed under freeway to John Long Rd. Turn right after blue winery tour sign on Goodrich Hwy. Proceed about 3 miles to another blue winery tour sign and turn left on Hogan Rd to arrive to destination.

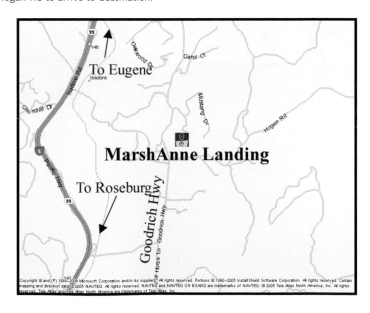

Mid Umpqua Valley
WineTrail

Umpqua River

You could argue that this is the only Oregon WineTrail you need to visit. Why? Because of the tremendous variety of wines you can experience! Everything from cool climate pinots to hot weather merlot is for tasting in the Mid Umpqua Valley WineTrail. Plus, here's your chance to swirl and sip unusual wine varieties. For example, check out Melrose's baco noir or Reustle-Prayer Rock's grüner veltliner. If awards were given out for red and white blend names, this WineTrail would take home the medals. How about these red blend names: Palotai's Bull's Blood, or Misty Oaks' Gobbler's Knob? There are also plenty of dessert-style ice wines to experience. In total, this WineTrail features two dozen wine varieties.

Need a place to stay or eat? Nearby Roseburg offers a variety of motels and quaint inns to meet various budgets and tastes. Plus, pack your walking shoes. Roseburg's Stewart Park offers well maintained walking trails to get the heart pounding while you enjoy the beauty of the South Umpqua River.

Mid Umpqua Valley WineTrail

1 Misty Oaks Vineyard
2 Henry Estate Winery
3 Reustle-Prayer Rock Vineyards
4 Becker Vineyard
5 Julianna Vineyards
6 Palotai Vineyard and Winery
7 Melrose Vineyard
8 HillCrest Vineyard

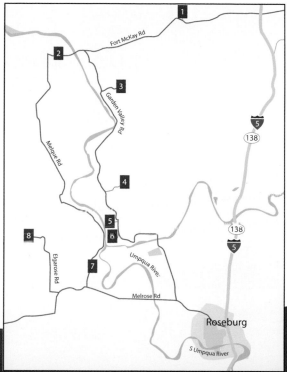

Region:	**Umpqua Valley Wine Country**
# of tasting rooms on tour:	**8**
Estimate # of days for tour:	**2**
Getting around:	**Car**
Key Events:	❑ **In March, Canyonville's Annual Greatest of the Grape – call 541-673-7575 or go online to www.umpquavalleywineries.org to order tickets.**
	❑ **In April, Roseburg's Umpqua Valley Barrel Tasting Bus Tour – call 800-444-9584 or see www.umpquavalleywineries.**
	❑ **In May, Umpqua Winery Association's Memorial Day Open House call 541-679-6642.**
Tips:	❑ **Pack your fishing pole and stay at Steamboat Inn on North Umpqua River. Historic charm.**
	❑ **Consider hiring a limousine services such as Oregon Wine Country Tours 800-704-2943 or see www.oregonwinecountrytours.com.**
Best:	❑ **Eats and views: Reustle-Prayer Rock Vineyards.**
	❑ **Gift shop and Views: Melrose Vineyard.**

Misty Oaks Vineyard ❶

Misty Oaks Vineyard is the first stop along the Mid-Umpqua Valley WineTrail. In many ways, it is typical of other nearby wineries, yet it has some unique touches.

Like many winemakers in the Umpqua, Steve and Christy Simmons came to Oregon to grow grapes and make wine. In their case, they began their new life in 2000, after

spending 30 years in Alaska, the "Land of the Midnight Sun." The Simmons purchased vineyard property in the so-called Tyee foothills of Umpqua. No doubt they were giddy with excitement and just a little stunned, as in "Oh my God, what have we done?" As they note on their website, starting their winery was an opportunity to get "dirt under the fingernails" and experience "skunks on the porch."

This adventurous move also led to making good friends and experiencing winemaking collaboration Oregon style. After all, a helping hand and sage advice make the difference when it comes to planting grapes and making wine.

There is something magical about the sight of a stately oak standing tall among vineyard rows. It's a common scene throughout the Umpqua region, yet it never fails to delight. Add a veil of mist for atmosphere and the image would be postcard perfect. But during my hot August visit to Misty Oaks Vineyard, there was no mist in sight. No matter. At an elevation that approaches 1,000 feet, the winery does offer breathtaking views to the valley below.

For me, the best feature of Misty Oaks Vineyard are the names of its wines, which have been labelled after some of the Simmons' experiences in the vineyard. Their red blend goes by "Gobblers Knob," a nod to the wild turkeys that trot about the property. How about Stuckagain Heights Pinot Noir? There *has* to be a story there. Friendswood Gewurztraminer had me Googling its name, but all I discovered was the location of Friendswood, Texas. My favorite Misty Oaks wine name is Constitution Ridge Pinot Blanc, that for me implies a sense of strength.

It's clear that Alaska is a chilly memory for Steve and Christy. Their lives are about the vines and the wines. They live in the present — pruning vines, destemming grapes, and blending reds. The demands of their vineyard likely have them jumping out of bed a little earlier in the morning, ready for another day of making wine — and memories fit to earn a name on one of their bottles.

MISTY OAKS VINEYARD
opened: 2004
winemaker(s): Steve and Christy Simmons
location: 1310 Misty Oaks Lane, Oakland, OR 97462
phone: 541-459-3558
web: www.mistyoaksvineyard.com
e-mail: info@mistyoaksvineyard.com
picnic area: Yes
wheelchair access: Yes
fee: Complimentary wine tasting
hours: Friday through Sunday 11–5 Memorial Day weekend through Thanksgiving weekend, and by appointment

DIRECTIONS: Heading south on I-5 take exit 136 onto SR-138 toward Sutherlin/Elkton. Turn left (west) onto SR-138 [W Central Ave.] and go 3.9 miles. Turn left (west) onto Stump Ranch Ln and proceed 1.7 miles. Turn right (west) onto Cole Rd and then right onto Misty Oaks Lane.

Heading north on I-5 about 12 miles north of Roseburg take exit 136 toward Sutherlin/Elkton. Turn left (west) onto SR-138 [W Central Ave.] and go 4 miles. Turn left (west) onto Stump Ranch Ln and proceed 1.7 miles. Turn right (west) onto Cole Rd and travel a short distance to Misty Oak Lane. Turn right and look for the winery.

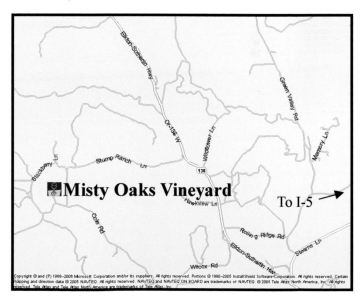

Henry Estate Winery 2

I was the accidental wine tourist who stumbled onto the Henry Goes Wine festival at the Henry Estate Winery. For more than 20 years, the Henry family has hosted the daylong bash as a way of saying "thanks" to its many fans. The shindig is held the third Saturday of each August; come early and bring an empty belly for succulent barbecue and flavor-packed wines. This is your opportunity to watch horseshoes being tossed, hop on a wagon ride, and listen to local bands.

The winery's slogan is "A Family Tradition," and for good reason. Scott Henry III founded the vineyard in 1972 with the planting of 12 acres of premium wine grapes. Since then, he has expanded to 40 acres, begun a winery and immersed his offspring in the business. His son, Calvin Scott Henry IV (Scotty), is the chief winemaker and responsible for producing 16,000 cases annually, making Henry Estate Winery the largest winery in the region. Daughter Syndi (married to another Scott) manages the tasting room and coordinates events, including the aforementioned Henry Goes Wine celebration. Her kids help, too, with mass mailings and other elf-type duties. All this makes you wonder if there is a Henry VIII waiting in the wings.

Located alongside the beautiful Umpqua River, the vineyard's rich soil provides the perfect ground for growing pinot noir, pinot gris, chardonnay, gewürztraminer, Müller-Thurgau, riesling, and merlot. However, the emergence of the vineyard took time to develop and considerable ingenuity. Soil and weather factors necessitated the engineering prowess of Scott Henry III to develop a unique trellis system for growing grapes. A number of vineyards have since embraced the Scott Henry Trellis System.

Rarely do you find a winery that is kid friendly, embraces dogs, and provides a parking lot in which you can easily maneuver the family Winnebago. That's the case at Henry Estate Winery, where children, dogs, and RVs are welcome. Inside the tasting room, take time to explore the retail area, where wine-related merchandise awaits. The tasting bar gives visitors the chance to taste numerous "best buy" wines. Here, pinot gris will set you back $15 a bottle. And it's little wonder that many visitors cart away a case of Henry's Oregon Pinot Noir, which goes for about $180.

Take time to walk through the splendid memory garden outside the winery. Scott dedicated the winery to his mom and dad, adding to the "family tradition" of this renowned establishment.

HENRY ESTATE WINERY
opened: 1978
winemaker(s): Calvin Scott Henry IV
location: 687 Hubbard Creek Road,
Umpqua, OR 97486
phone: 541-459-5120
web: www.henryestate.com
e-mail: winery@henryestate.com
picnic area: Yes
gift shop: Yes
tours: Yes
fee: Complimentary wine tasting
hours: Daily 11–5

DIRECTIONS: From Roseburg heading south on I-5 take exit 136. Keep left to stay on ramp. Turn left (west) onto SR-138 [W Central Ave.] for .3 miles. Bear left (west) onto County Rd 9 [Fort McKay Rd] for 6.3 miles. Bear right (west) onto County Rd 6B [Hubbard Creek Rd] for .6 miles. Arrive at Henry Estate Winery.

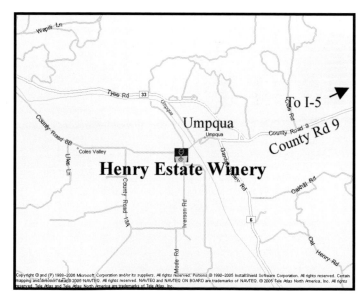

Reustle-Prayer Rock Vineyards ❸

"Enter as strangers — leave as friends" is the motto visitors experience at Reustle–Prayer Rock Vineyards. Transplants from the New York City area since 2001, Stephen and Gloria Reustle found an ideal location in the Umpqua region to lay down a vineyard. Stephen

Reustle-Prayer Rock

had enjoyed a very successful business career in New York, which he parlayed into the creation of an extraordinary winery. However, he and Gloria also leveraged another asset — a strong Christian foundation. The fact that Jesus' first miracle was turning water into wine was a nice endorsement from on high.

In 2004, they began making wine, producing fewer than 500 cases. Unfortunately, a Washington bureaucrat didn't appreciate what the Reustles had etched on their corks. Failing to get approval from the Department of the Treasury's Alcohol and Tobacco Tax and Trade Bureau, the Reustles received the following statement from a federal reviewer: "Delete 'Drink your wine with a happy heart God approves of this' reference." Evidently, alluding to wine as a heart-happy food is a no-no.

The top of Prayer Rock Vineyards affords a bird's eye view of the property. Here, you can look down into the bowl of rolling vineyards, winery buildings, and the Reustles' home. It's also the site of the rock where Stephen visited and prayed for God's blessing when they arrived. They live lives of abundance. But they don't keep it to themselves — they pass it along.

At their new tasting room, which features the only cave-like barrel-room setting in southern Oregon, visitors receive a healthy dose of wine education, wonderful appetizers, and generous tastes of award-winning wines. I love the distinctive orange and black packaging that envelopes each bottle of pinot noir, tempranillo, viognier, riesling, syrah, merlot, rousanne, semillon, grüner veltliner, grenache, pinot gris, and sauvignon blanc. (**WineTrail note:** Notice the wide range of warm- and cool-weather varietals — a sure sign you're in the Umpqua!) By the way, the grüner veltliner is a rarity of sorts not only in Oregon, but also in the United States. This surprisingly flavorful white wine from Austria pairs wonderfully with grilled chicken, fish, and summer salads.

Is Reustle–Prayer Rock Vineyards a spiritual experience? I think so. Can you call this plot of land a piece of "heaven on earth"? Yes, I believe you can. Will your visit transform you? Yes, it will. Enter as strangers — leave as believers.

Gloria and Stephen Reustle

REUSTLE-PRAYER ROCK VINEYARDS
winemaker(s): Stephen Reustle
location: 960 Cal Henry Road, Roseburg, OR 97470
phone: 541-459-6060
web: www.reustlevineyards.com
e-mail: wine@reustlevineyards.com
picnic area: Yes
wheelchair access: Yes
tours: Yes
fee: $10 tasting fee
hours: Monday through Saturday 10–5

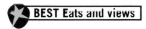 **BEST Eats and views**

DIRECTIONS: Heading south on I-5 take I-5 exit 136. Bear right and proceed to intersection. At stop sign turn left (west) toward Dairy Queen/Taco Bell. Go left at Ft. McKay Rd. Proceed 2 miles and go left at Gross Ln. At the end of Gross Ln (about 1 mile) go right at Oak Hill Rd and continue for about 2 miles. When Oak Hill Rd turns into a one lane road, slow down and turn left at 7612 Oak Hill Rd. Stay straight, pass through iron gate, and go 0.7 miles to the tasting room.

Heading north on I-5 take exit 125. At traffic light turn left at Garden Valley Rd. Proceed on Garden Valley Rd for 12 miles. After mile marker 12, slow down and turn right at Cal Henry Road. Proceed to first driveway on the left. Go left through the iron gate and to the tasting room.

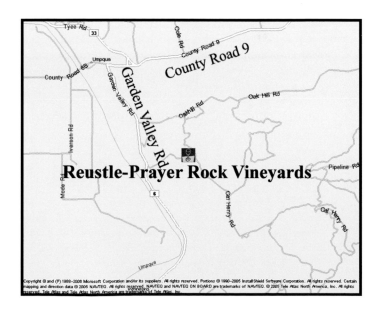

Becker Vineyard 4

OK, I understand that this page is for waxing somewhat eloquently about a winery's fantastic wines, its great tasting room, its eco-friendly vineyard practices, its summer concert series, and the stunning views. However, when it comes to Becker Vineyard, the storyline begins and ends with the proprietors of this marvelous winery — Charles (Charlie) and Peggy Becker. Sure, they offer a lovely line-up of wines in a gorgeous setting, but the chemistry of these two makes the difference. They are a such a cute couple, with loads of energy.

Peggy and Charles Becker

This is the story of two very hard-working people who met in midlife at a nature preserve and fell in love. They are still in love, despite the fact that launching and maintaining the winery/vineyard is all consuming. That's in addition to keeping their day jobs, no less. During the week, Peggy works at a local healthcare clinic, and Charlie is a house painter. He's also an accomplished builder and personally constructed their new tasting room. I suspect he also painted it. In addition, Peggy is a master gardener of sorts, and a quick inspection of the nearby gardens, which includes a rare big leaf magnolia tree, is a testament to her green thumb.

Together with their chocolate Lab, Moka, the couple produces small batches of premium wines, most of which are sold at the tasting room. Visitors will experience a yummy portfolio of wines, including pinot gris, pinot noir rosé, pinot noir, cabernet sauvignon, and syrah. That is, if they aren't sold out. When done with the tasting, there's a nature walk around the Beckers' property that's excellent for getting to know the flora of this great region.

Balancing camera and notebook in one hand, I shook their hands and said my goodbyes. Little did they know that I felt like hugging them, but given the fact that we had met just 45 minutes earlier, that might have been a little awkward.

www.winetrailsnw.com/wineries/becker_vineyard

BECKER VINEYARD
opened: 2008
winemaker(s): Charles Becker
location: 360 Klahowya Lane, Roseburg, OR 97470
phone: 541-677-0288
web: www.beckerwine.com
e-mail: winemaker@beckerwine.com
picnic area: Yes
wheelchair access: Yes
fee: Complimentary wine tasting
hours: Weekends and holidays 11–5

DIRECTIONS: Heading southbound on I-5 past Eugene take exit 129 toward OR-99/Winchester/N Roseburg. Bear right (west) onto County Rd 115 [Del Rio Rd]. Proceed 2.9 miles. Turn left (west) onto local road and continue .6 miles. Keep left onto Klahowya Ln and travel 1.3 miles. Arrive at Becker Vineyard and follow signs to winery.

Heading northbound on I-5 north of Roseburg take exit 125 toward Garden Valley Blvd/Roseburg. Turn left (west) onto NW Garden Valley Blvd and go 1.6 miles. Road name changes to County Rd 6 [NW Garden Valley Blvd]. Proceed .6 miles. Bear right (north) onto County Rd 31A. Continue .6 miles. Road name changes to County Rd 31D [Garden Valley Rd]. Proceed 1.4 miles. Road name changes to CR-6 [Garden Valley Rd]. Continue 1.2 miles. Turn right (east) onto Upper Cleveland Rapids Rd and go .9 miles. Bear right (east) onto Klahowya Ln, go .2 miles, and arrive at 360 Klayhowya Ln.

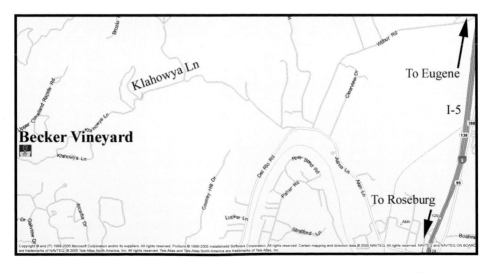

Julianna Vineyards 5

You know you are fairly far south in Oregon when you stumble onto a "pinot-free zone." That would describe 22-acre Julianna Vineyards. Don't come here expecting to taste pinot noir. Rather, warm-weather grapes are the varietals of choice for proprietors Henry and Debbie Russel. At Julianna Vineyards, classic Bordeaux varietals dominate alongside the Umpqua River, with the Callahan Mountains in the backdrop.

Midwesterners Henry and Debbie know a lot about European grapes. After all, their military service in the U.S. Air Force had them stationed there for many years. This afforded numerous opportunities to hop in the family car and make forays to Bordeaux, the Rhine, the Rhône and other grape-growing regions. Later they had a stint in California, where again they could exercise their wine-loving passion. Not surprising, when the opportunity arose to purchase a vineyard next to the Umpqua River 10 minutes from downtown Roseburg, they pounced on it.

When asked about the name, Henry responded that they named the winery Julianna after his "greatest generation" mother. Relying on environmentally safe practices and dry farming (i.e., no irrigation), the Russels grafted 20-plus-year vines on original rootstalk. Varieties planted include cabernet sauvignon, cabernet franc, Maréchal Foch, merlot, sauvignon blanc, semillon, chenin blanc, and riesling. Few vineyards in Oregon grow both semillon and chenin blanc. A chinook salmon is the central image for the Julianna logo and label. Given the winery's sustainable practices and proximity to the Umpqua River, a wild salmon makes sense.

In 2008, the Russels opened an all-stone winery and tasting room next to the vineyard. Inside this intimate space, Henry pours and sells wines to admiring visitors. Harking back to his time in Europe, Henry notes, "Great wines should be affordable," and to this end, many of their wines retail in the teens, and even the red Bordeaux varietals are in the low 20s. By the way, if you do find a wine you like, now would be the time to reach for your wallet. Don't go looking for Julianna Vineyards wines at Fred Meyer — Henry distributes his creations only at the winery.

Along the banks of the Umpqua River at this winery featuring warm-weather grapes, visitors have an opportunity to experience what Henry describes as "heaven on earth." Estate wines take center stage, and all is good.

JULIANNA VINEYARDS
winemaker(s): Henry Russel
location: 707 Hess Lane, Roseburg, OR 97470
phone: 541-677-9251
web: www.juliannavineyards.com
e-mail: info@juliannavineyards.com
wheelchair access: Yes
fee: $2 tasting fee
hours: Weekends 11–5 and holidays; call for private tasting or appointments at other times

Henry Russel

DIRECTIONS: Heading north or south on I-5 take exit 125 toward Garden Valley Blvd/Roseburg. Take NW Garden Valley Blvd and proceed 1.6 miles (west). Road name changes to County Rd 6 [NW Garden Valley Blvd]. Continue .6 miles. Bear right (north) onto County Rd 6 [Garden Valley Rd] and go 2.5 miles. Turn left (south) onto Old Garden Valley Rd followed by a right (west) onto W Hess Ln and arrive at winery.

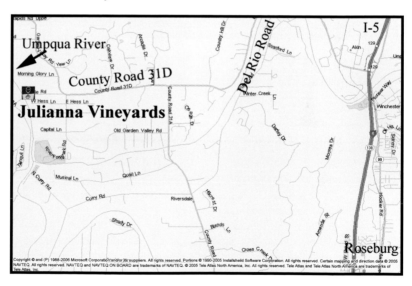

Palotai Vineyard and Winery 6

I have *National Geographic* to blame. I came to Palotai Vineyard and Winery to taste Gabor Palotai's Bull's Blood, but as luck would have it, it was out of stock. Gabor noted that a one-sentence line in a 2008 issue of *National Geographic* wiped out his remaining stock of Bull's Blood. I've heard of *Wine Spectator* influencing wine sales, but *National Geographic*?

Still, all was not lost. There was much to sample, including Gabor's award-winning syrah. In 2007, his estate syrah received the "Greatest of the Grape" award from those attending Douglas County's showcase wine-tasting event. That's high praise. But Palotai offers a host

Gabor Palotai

of other wines to dip into, including a delicious white blend called Bella Bianca, a red blend with the name of Indigo, as well as tempranillo, Baco noir, Maréchal Foch, zinfandel, and others.

Gabor's wines are fabulous, but the real surprise for me is the man himself. He was in his full Hungarian glory and dished out one-liners to visitors, who were clearly entertained. He noted that behind a speaker's podium, he would be stiff and speak in a monotone, but behind his wine bar, he can be his relaxed, good-natured self. He was funny, engaging, and, with his rakish hat, positively charming.

In 1983, Gabor got a student visa to study in the United States, away from then Communist-controlled Hungary. When it came time to return, the plane that arrived in Budapest was missing a passenger. Gabor had defected to America. Initially living in Sacramento, where he trained horses, Gabor never forgot his Hungarian roots — especially what he had learned about making wine at a young age from his grandfather. Small-lot wines made by hand, barrel-aged, and drinkable right after bottling. Not surprisingly, you won't find his wine touching French oak. Here, Hungarian oak is the wood of choice. At $650 to $700 a barrel, he saves, compared to the high-priced French barrels, and the relatively tight wood grain and toast of the Hungarian oak imparts a distinct flavor Gabor seeks.

In 2003, Gabor launched Palotai Vineyard and Winery alongside the Umpqua River. At four acres, his vineyard is small but manageable. Gabor works the land vine by vine, knowing what clusters to drop, when to pick, and how best to bring out the flavor of the *terroir*. At Palotai Vineyard and Winery, visitors experience "Old World craftsmanship" even when the Bull's Blood is sold out.

PALOTAI VINEYARD AND WINERY
opened: 2001
winemaker(s): Gabor Palotai
location: 272 Capital Lane, Roseburg, OR 97470
phone: 541-464-0032
web: www.palotaiwines.com
e-mail: gabor@mbol.us
picnic area: Yes
fee: $2 tasting fee
hours: Daily 11–5

DIRECTIONS: Heading north or south on I-5 take exit 125 toward Garden Valley Blvd/Roseburg. Take NW Garden Valley Blvd and go 1.6 miles (west). Road name changes to County Rd 6 [NW Garden Valley Blvd]. Continue .6 miles. Bear right (north) onto County Rd 6 [Garden Valley Rd] and go 2.5 miles. Turn left (west) onto Old Garden Valley Rd and travel 1.7 miles. Turn left (west) onto Capital Ln and arrive at the winery in .2 miles.

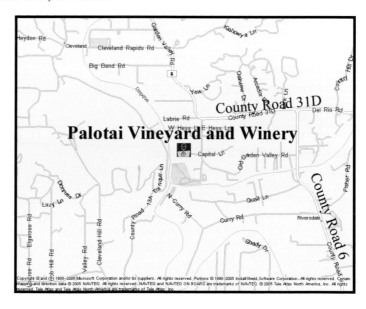

Melrose Vineyard 7

Located aong the banks of the South Umpqua River, Melrose Vineyard occupies a former French settlement. Today it's the site of 150 acres of premium grapes, a place where people get married, and wine and gifts are sold. Just walking into the lovingly restored 100-year-old barn and seeing the gift shop's quality merchandise is impressive. However, when you step out on the deck and view the property below, your jaw drops. It's little wonder that

Melrose Vineyard ranks in our top 10 for gift shops and wedding venues.

Ironically, Melrose Vineyard is a winery without being a winery. Yes, proprietors Wayne and Deedy Parker grow grapes — lots of them, with more acreage to be added downstream — but they don't actually make the wine. For that, they turn to local wineries/winemakers to custom-crush their grapes and apply the Melrose Vineyard wine label. However, don't assume that the relationship between grape grower and winemaker is superficial. In fact, there's a whole lot of collaboration going on between them.

Arriving from Fresno in the mid-'90s with 20 years of grape-growing experience under their belts, the Parkers knew the work required with vineyards. Perhaps they weren't certain if the land would deliver such quality grapes, but the feedback from wineries using their grapes proved positive, and long-term contracts to supply grapes were drawn up. Wayne employs the Scott Henry Trellis system, developed by his nearby neighbor, to grow 10 different grape varietals: pinot noir, pinot gris, viognier, riesling, syrah, tempranillo, Baco noir, merlot, dolcetto, and pinotage. The Baco noir and the pinotage varietals place Melrose Vineyard in a rarefied realm; it's hard to find these varietals growing in Oregon — especially the South African–grown pinotage grape.

Hospitality takes center stage at Melrose Vineyard, where even the dogs — Missy, Rosie, and Bacus — greet you with wagging tails. Once inside, it is apparent that someone has a good eye for merchandise. (If I were sent to fetch stuff to sell, I would likely come back with the "Stop Your Whining" cocktail napkins.) Tasting-room manager Deb Wandrus does an exceptional job of making visitors feel at ease while educating folks about Melrose Vineyards' remarkable story. Once she explained how the different tasting-room fees worked, it was a no-brainer to choose the $7-for-eight-tastes option, which includes a logo-adorned stemware glass. Now, that's a deal!

MELROSE VINEYARD
opened: 1996
winemaker(s): Various winemakers
location: 885 Melqua Road,
Roseburg, OR 97470
phone: 541-672-6080
web: www.melrosevineyards.com
e-mail: info@melrosevineyards.com
picnic area: Yes
wheelchair access: Yes
weddings: Yes
gift shop: Yes
tours: Yes
fee: Complimentary wine tasting for up to 3 tastes;
$5 for 8 tastes and $7 for 8 tastes and a logo glass
hours: Daily 1–5 or by appointment; closed Christmas
and New Year's Day

BEST Views and gift shop

DIRECTIONS: Heading north or south on I-5, take exit 125 and travel west on Garden Valley Blvd to Melrose Road. Turn left on Melrose Rd and right on to Melqua Rd, by the Melrose store. Go .5 miles and look for restored old barn, which serves as the tasting room and gift boutique.

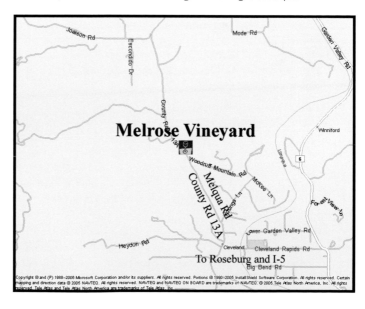

HillCrest Vineyard 🎱

HillCrest Vineyard is ground zero for Oregon's modern-day wine history, and the reason is simple. It is the oldest continuously running winery in Oregon that produces *vinifera* premium wines. Native Californian Richard Sommers began HillCrest Vineyards in 1961 with the intent of growing riesling. It's little wonder that Richard is sometimes referred

to as the father of today's Oregon winemaking world. When visiting, you might catch the "BW 44" notation here and there — it's a reference to the fact that HillCrest Vineyard was the 44th bonded "alcohol producer" in Oregon and the first winery bonded after Prohibition. That's old.

Dyson DeMara

In 2003, Dyson and Susan DeMara purchased HillCrest Vineyard. It has been a sprint since then to uproot old rootstalk, replant, and produce wine meeting their high standards. Most days, Dyson is working the tasting room pouring and educating. Many visitors know of the HillCrest legacy and come from afar to visit. I suspect, they are pleased, as I was, to see the building's weathered wood outershell and rustic tasting room. However, at the tasting bar, the old ends and the new begins with the renewed energy and passion that Dyson brings.

Using locally sourced grapes while his vineyard comes into full production, Dyson produces around 1,400 cases of wine annually. It's an impressive array of wines: cabernet sauvignon, chardonnay, grenache, Malbec, merlot, pinot noir, riesling, sauvignon blanc, viognier, and zinfandel. My personal favorite was a full-bodied red blend having a great mouthfeel and lasting finish called HillCrest Vineyard Massimo. It seemed to say, "Pair me with hearty food," so I went in search of a steak to dine on, but failed to find one.

As I drove away, I had the thought that change is good. During my travels around Oregon, I have come upon a few wineries with new owners who have brought exciting changes and new vigor. Redhawk Winery and Alexeli Vineyard & Winery (formerly Marquam Hill Vineyard) in the Willamette Valley come to mind. That's my sense about HillCrest Vineyard — I am thrilled for Dyson and Susan. Later that night in Roseburg, I saw a sign outside a downtown restaurant that proclaimed, "Under new management." I decided to give it a shot. You can bet that, like the DeMaras, it is eager to please.

HILLCREST VINEYARD
opened: 1961
winemaker(s): Dyson DeMara
location: 240 Vineyard Lane, Roseburg, OR 97470
phone: 541-673-3709
web: www.hillcrestvineyard.com
e-mail: info@hillcrestvineyard.com
picnic area: Yes
wheelchair access: Yes
tours: Yes
fee: Tasting fee may apply
hours: Daily 11–5

Bonded Winery 44

DIRECTIONS: From Roseburg, take exit 125 on I-5 and proceed west. Turn left (west) onto NW Garden Valley Blvd and go 1.6 miles. Road name changes to County Rd 6 [NW Garden Valley Blvd]. Go .6 miles. Turn left (west) onto CR-167 [Melrose Rd] and continue 1.3 miles. Road name changes to CR-13 [Melrose Rd]. Proceed 2 miles. Road name changes to County Rd 51B [Melrose Rd]. Proceed 1.1 miles. Turn right (west) onto County Rd 90 [Doerner Rd] and go .4 miles. Turn right (north) onto Elgarose Rd and travel 2.6 miles. Turn left (south) onto Vineyard Ln and arrive at Hillcrest Vineyard.

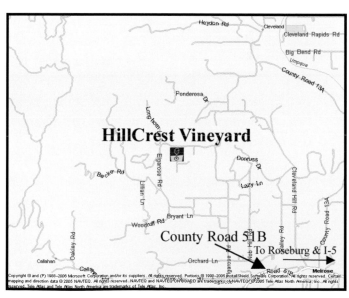

Umpqua Valley South
WineTrail

Girardet Wine Cellars

For wine tourists, a trip to the Umpqua Valley is a balancing act. Beyond amazing wineries to visit are the region's natural wonders and other treasures to check out. Crater Lake National Park and the Diamond Lake recreation area are easy day trips from Umpqua's major city, Roseburg. Fly fishing on the Umpqua River is a pastime enjoyed by many visitors and can be easily budgeted with wine tasting. If not fishing the river, consider floating on it via a white-water rafting excursion. This is an area rich in hiking and biking opportunities as well.

In between hiking, fishing, biking, and serious picture taking, WineTrail trekkers can visit some gorgeous wineries. Working your way east to west, Spangler Vineyards is an oasis right off I-5. Further east are Abacela Vineyards & Winery, Wild Rose Vineyard, and Girardet Wine Cellars featuring great views, unusual wines, and wonderful picnic opportunities. If time permits, drive west on Hwy 42 to Remote, Oregon and sample the wines of Old Bridge Winery. From there it is a short hop to the Pacific Ocean, where you can enjoy seafood with that bottle of wine you purchased from the Umpqua.

Umpqua Valley WineTrail South

1 Spangler Vineyards   **3** Wild Rose Vineyard   **5** Old Bridge Winery
2 Abacela Vineyards & Winery   **4** Girardet Wine Cellars

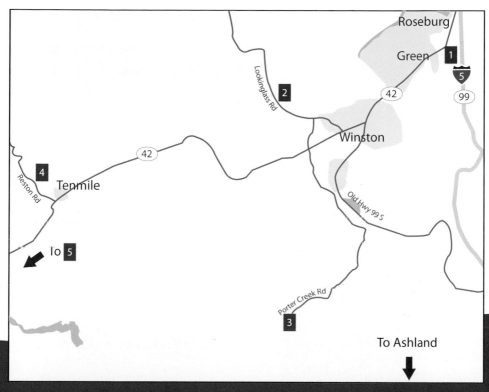

Region:	**Umpqua Valley Wine Country**
# of tasting rooms on tour:	**5**
Estimate # of days for tour:	**1 to 2**
Getting around:	**Car**
Key Events:	❑ **In March, Canyonville's Annual Greatest of the Grape – call 541-673-7575 or go online to www.umpquavalleywineries.org to order tickets.**
	❑ **In April, Roseburg's Umpqua Valley Barrel Tasting Bus Tour – call 800-444-9584 or see www.umpquavalleywineries.**
	❑ **In May, Umpqua Winery Association's Memorial Day Open House – call 541-679-6642.**
Tips:	❑ **Pack your fishing pole and stay at Steamboat Inn on North Umpqua River. Historic charm.**
	❑ **Consider hiring a limousine services such as Oregon Wine Country Tours, 800-704-2943. See www.oregonwinecountrytours.com.**
Best:	❑ **Gift shop: Spangler Vineyards.**
	❑ **Views: Abacela Vineyards & Winery.**

Spangler Vineyards ❶

In 2004, Pat and Loree Spangler purchased Spangler Vineyards. Fortunately they didn't need to start from scratch. They bought an existing winery and vineyard on the outskirts of Roseburg, after being put off by Napa's high prices. Another selling point: Southern Oregon offered the perfect place to grow Bordeaux grapes. Sure, Oregon's reputation is wrapped up in pinot noir, but in the Land of 100 Valleys, the Spanglers could show the world that Umpqua produces other fine wines. They knew they could successfully grow warm-weather grapes, such as cabernet franc and tempranillo, that were every bit as good

Pat Spangler

as those cultivated in other wine-growing regions of the world. After all, as celebrated Californian wine writer Dan Berger put it, Umpqua is "the last great undiscovered wine region."

Pat and Loree met in Chicago at a wine-tasting party. Their love for wine and Pat's winemaking hobby led to a well-stocked wine cellar and numerous trips to Napa, where the couple discovered the region's exceptional wines. And oddly enough, Pat's place in suburban Chicago actually had vinifera wine grapes growing in the backyard — an omen of things to come, perhaps?

The move to Roseburg meant more than finding a good place to make wine. It also gave the Spanglers a great place to raise their young daughter, Sydney; the area has good schools, great outdoors, and plenty of parks. In addition to the three human Spanglers, other family members include an Akita (Jasmine) and a German shepherd (Sage). Both dogs are semi-permanent fixtures at the winery and members of the winery's welcoming committee.

Spangler Vineyards' tasting room provides an inviting space for sampling the winery's many award-winning wines. You can also finish your holiday shopping or score on a great gift for a loved one (or for yourself). Loree has a great eye for unique and high-quality merchandise that happens to pair perfectly with their best-in-show wines. Thanks to Spangler Vineyards, Oregon's pinot-centric reputation will need to make room for a new kid on the block.

Pat and Loree Spangler

SPANGLER VINEYARDS
opened: 2004
winemaker(s): Pat Spangler
location: 491 Winery Lane, Roseburg, OR 97471
phone: 541-679-9654
web: www.spanglervineyards.com
e-mail: info@spanglervineyards.com
picnic area: Yes
wheelchair access: Yes
gift shop: Yes
tours: Yes
fee: Tasting fee may apply
hours: Daily 11–5

BEST Gift shop

DIRECTIONS: On I-5 heading north or south about 4 miles South of Roseburg, take exit 119. Go west onto Coos Bay–Roseburg Hwy for .2 miles. Keep straight onto SR-42 [SR-99] for .1 mile. Turn left (south) onto Winery Ln and go .4 miles to Spangler Vineyards.

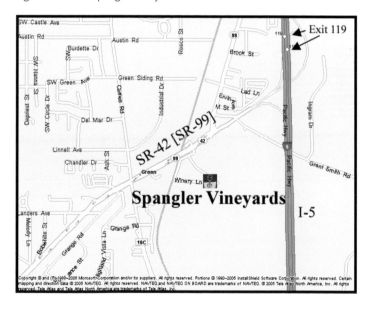

Abacela Vineyards & Winery 🄲

Prior to my visit to Abacela Vineyards & Winery, I needed to beef up my knowledge of tempranillo. Here's what Wikipedia.com had to say: "Tempranillo is a variety of black grape widely grown to make full-bodied red wines in its native Spain. It is the main grape used in Rioja, and is often referred to as Spain's 'noble grape.'"

Proprietors Earl and Hilda Jones fell in love with tempranillo in the early 1990s, discovering that it matched wonderfully with their favorite fingerfood, tapas. Consequently, they set about finding the perfect spot to grow this grape, examining reams of weather data rather than focusing on the soil. After all, this grape thrives in temperate climates: warm days followed by cool nights with a fair amount of precipitation. Their unusual analysis landed them outside of Roseburg in southern Oregon at a vineyard with the unsteady name of Fault Line Vineyards. Not surprisingly, the Joneses' vineyard is at the same latitude as Spain's Rioja and Ribera del Duero regions. The sensitive tempranillo grapes love it. The Joneses called their winery Abacela, borrowing the Spanish word meaning "to plant a young vine."

In 2001 at the prestigious San Francisco International Wine Competition, Abacela was awarded a double gold for its 1998 tempranillo. The fact that it bested 19 Spanish tempranillo entries put Abacela Vineyards & Winery on the proverbial map.

Abacela's flagship wine may be tempranillo, but visitors can still sample a number of other wines at this spectacular winery, which features a Mediterranean-style tasting room and winery. In addition to a variety of traditional wines (e.g., merlot, petit verdot, and syrah), visitors can try Abacela's albariño and dare each other not to think about seafood when they are tasting this delightfully crisp white wine. Abacela Vineyards & Winery also produces port-style wines from Portuguese grapes such as tinta cão. All this is under the direction of 30-something Andrew Wenzl, who happens to be one of the nicest winemakers you will ever meet.

I took home a bottle of Tempranillo Umpqua Cuvée and paired it with a tapas-like dish of prawn and bacon brochettes. I realized then what Earl and Hilda Jones understood many years ago — that tempranillo goes great with the good things in life. Down the road, if I decide to open a tapas bar, I'll establish a direct pipeline to Abacela Vineyards & Winery. I think I would call the establishment Tapas Tempranillo, in honor of Earl and Hilda.

Andrew Wenzl

ABACELA VINEYARDS & WINERY
opened: 1997
winemaker(s): Andrew Wenzl
location: 12500 Lookingglass Road,
Roseburg, OR 97471
phone: 541-679-6642
web: www.abacela.com
e-mail: wine@abacela.com
picnic area: Yes
wheelchair access: Yes
fee: $5 tasting fee refundable with purchase
hours: Daily 11–5

 **BEST Views**

DIRECTIONS: Leave I-5 at exit 119 onto US-42 west/US-99 south. Head west 2.8 miles to Winston's only traffic light, turn right and follow US-42 west 1.6 miles to the caution light at Brockway Store, and turn right (north) onto Brockway Road. At stop sign, turn left onto Lookingglass Road. Turn right just past the grapevines into a gated driveway.

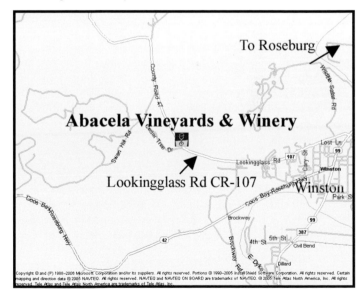

Wild Rose Vineyard ❸

At the end of a gravel road in the small village of Winston lies the nine-acre Wild Rose Vineyard. As I drove up, a lone man and his dog stood outside the tasting room as if waiting for me. It was winegrower Carlos Figueroa and his dog, Kinsey. I quickly learned that Carlos had an engaging smile, matched by a friendly disposition. We walked into the shaded garage-style tasting room, where a wine bar stood at one end and various art pieces

executed by Carlos' daughter, including a green frog sculpture and paintings, occupied the sides of the room. Kinsey found a spot on the cool concrete.

Carlos is a retired engineering instructor from Umpqua Community College who clearly is not one to sit back and watch the grass grow. He's a man of many projects, from planting an eight-acre vineyard and launching a winery to growing an herb garden, to name just a few. His non-irrigated vineyard produces one ton of grapes per year. Carlos' spouse, Denise, is an active partner in the endeavor. Together they have cleared the land (leaving a number of the wild-rose plants intact) and worked to obtain LIVE (Low Input Viticulture and Enology) certification. They wish their vineyard to be free of pesticides, to assure wine buyers that Wild Rose Vineyard wines are organic.

The family-owned and -operated winery produces small lots of estate wines (about 500 cases annually) adorned with brightly colored wine labels — they definitely "pop" in the display case. Visitors can anticipate complimentary wine tastings, which include samples of pinot gris, pinot noir, cabernet sauvignon, merlot, late-harvest pinot gris, and a port-like pinot gris with a name that captured my attention — "Tears of the Rose."

In the cool of the tasting room, Carlos ticked off a number of projects he has lined up for the future. From expanding the winemaking facility to moving the tasting room upstairs, his calendar is filled for the next 10 years. So much for retirement. Behind the winning smile, this former chemical engineer has miles to go and dreams to realize.

WILD ROSE VINEYARD
opened: 2002
winemaker(s): Carlos Figueroa
location: 375 Porter Creek Road, Winston, OR 97496
phone: 541-679-1433
web: www.wildrosevineyard.com
e-mail: cfigueroa@hughes.net
picnic area: Yes
fee: Complimentary wine tasting
hours: Daily 11–5

DIRECTIONS: From Roseburg take I-5 south about 4.5 miles to exit 119. Bear right (west) onto Coos Bay–Roseburg Hwy. Keep straight onto SR-42 [SR-99] and go 2.9 miles. Keep straight onto SR-99 [CR-387] and go 3.1 miles. Turn right (south) onto Rice Creek Rd and go 2.3 miles. Turn right (west) onto Porter Creek and travel .6 miles to Wild Rose Vineyard.

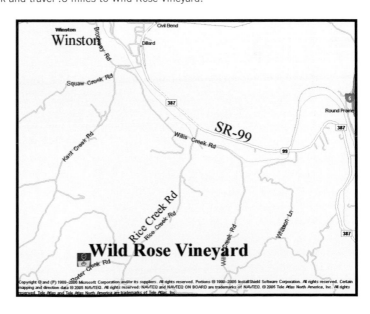

Girardet Wine Cellars ❹

Sure, you've heard of pinot noir, but what about Baco noir? Unless you are a devoted fan of Umpqua wines or claim to be a distant relative of its inventor, Francois Baco, chances are you likely have not heard of this grape. That will change, however, when you visit Girardet Wine Cellars in rural Tenmile, outside of Roseburg. Goodbye, pinot — hello, Baco.

I must confess that I am a recent Baco convert. Truth is, I had not heard of it before my sojourn in the Umpqua area. Now I wonder why we don't find Baco noir in everyone's cellar. The tasting notes on the Girardet Wine Cellars website states this about its Baco

noir, "Displays a deep crimson color with great legs. Sweet, vibrant aromas of sun-ripened fruits with a little toasted vanilla. Silky fruit flavors build slowly and then linger on with toasty, spicy flavors in the finish. Incredibly drinkable with a luscious mouthfeel." I love that word "silky."

Girardet Wine Cellars is the product of Swiss-born Philippe Girardet and his wife, Bonnie. They met in the 1960s in California, but a trip to southern Oregon convinced them this would be an ideal location for growing premium wine grapes. Perhaps the location reminded Philippe of his native Switzerland, with its sloping hillsides in close proximity to the Rhône River. By the early 1970s, the couple had planted their vineyard, and today they grow more than 30 varietals of non-irrigated premium grapes.

Keeping it in the family, son Marc is now the vintner for Girardet Wine Cellars. In addition to Baco noir, Marc hand-crafts other varietals, including pinot noir, cabernet sauvignon, and their hugely popular Grand Rogue blend, which consists of 14 different grape varietals and is priced to sell at $14 a bottle. At that price, you might want to pick up a couple of cases! Also, if you are a fan of non-oaky chardonnay that still has a buttery flavor, check out Girardet Wine Cellars Chardonnay — a blend that uses 30 percent new oak.

At 12,000 cases a year, Girardet Wine Cellars is one of the largest producers of fine wine in the Umpqua region. A steady stream of visitors finds its way to the winery, where Girardet sells most of its wines. Family owned and operated, Girardet Wine Cellars is a big reason why Umpqua is no longer the last great undiscovered wine region.

GIRARDET WINE CELLARS
opened: 1983
winemaker(s): Marc Girardet
location: 895 Reston Road, Roseburg, OR 97470
phone: 541-679-7252
web: www.girardetwine.com
e-mail: genuine@girardetwine.com
picnic area: Yes
wheelchair access: Yes
gift shop: Yes
tours: Yes
fee: Complimentary wine tasting
hours: Daily 11–5

DIRECTIONS: From Roseburg heading south on I-5 take exit 119 turning right onto ramp. Bear right (west) onto Coos Bay–Roseburg Hwy for .2 miles. Keep straight onto SR-42 [SR-99] for 12 miles. Turn right (west) onto County Rd 5C [Reston Rd] and go .8 miles. Arrive at 895 Reston Rd. (Note: look for the signs 9 miles after Winston.)

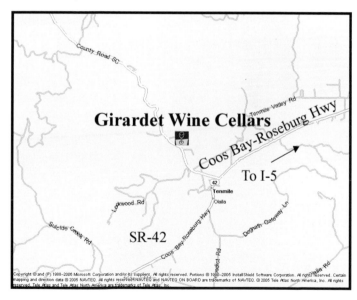

Old Bridge Winery 5

Metamorphosis is derived from the Greek language and means "change of form."

George and Angie Clarno know all about metamorphosis. After nearly 60 years of marriage, they have lived many lives. Along the way, they owned a logging company, a hunting-guide service, a taxidermy business, and a saw shop. You name it, they've done it. So when it came to opening a winery, it was no big deal for George and Angie to launch Old Bridge Winery.

Located in the small town of Remote, Oregon, off Highway 42, Old Bridge Winery is across the road from Sandy Creek Bridge. Until the 1950s, this covered bridge was part of the main road that led to and from the Pacific Ocean from Roseburg. Now, it is a historic landmark and serves as a backdrop for picture-taking families on their way to the coast.

Inside the manufactured home that serves as the tasting room and annex for the winery, Angie welcomes visitors and introduces them to Old Bridge wines. She explains that George has been making wine for more than 50 years, in between running his logging business, leading hunting expeditions in British Columbia, and bagging elephants in Africa (note the elephant tusk in the tasting room). As it turns out, George still has a commercial pilot's license, allowing the couple to make day trips to a variety of places around the Pacific Northwest. Among all these adventures, however, one avocation remained front and center: making wine. You could say George's hobby was out of control.

Pouring from bottles and jugs, Angie takes visitors through a smorgasbord of traditional European wines, fruit wines, and an enchanting sparkling wine called Spirit of Cranberry. It just might be the only sparkling cranberry wine in Oregon. She explains that her biggest joy occurs when people exclaim that they like the wine. At prices between $10 and $20 per bottle, visitors have reason to celebrate. However, everyone gets to celebrate in the fall when the Clarnos host a daylong barbecue and bring in a chef from Portland to prepare the fixin's.

After taking some photos and gathering my notebook to leave, I asked Angie about their next adventure. She replied that she's afraid to ask George that question. She's happy with their current lives and not quite ready for another career change. I guess she figures it's time to settle down.

OLD BRIDGE WINERY
opened: 2001
winemaker(s): George Clarno
location: 50706 Sandy Creek Road,
Remote, OR 97458
phone: 541-572-0272
web: None
e-mail: None
picnic area: Yes
fee: Complimentary wine tasting
hours: Tuesday through Sunday 11–5, May
through December

DIRECTIONS: From Roseburg heading south on I-5 take exit 119 toward OR-99/Winston and Coos Bay. Bear right (west) onto Coos Bay–Roseburg Hwy [SR-42] and keep straight onto SR-42. Go 35.9 miles just past the tiny community of Bridge. The winery is located at the covered bridge at Sandy Creek Rd. on the right.

From Coos Bay take US-101 south for 6 miles. Keep left onto SR-42 [Coos Bay–Roseburg Hwy] for 9.9 miles. Bear right (east) onto Coquille-Bandon Hwy for .9 miles. Keep straight onto SR-425 [Coquille-Bandon Hwy] for .4 miles. Bear right (east) onto SR-42 [Coos Bay–Roseburg Hwy] for 25.3 miles. Arrive at Sandy Creek Rd.

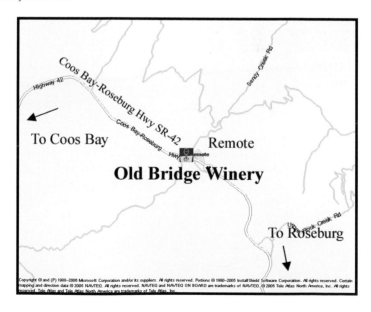

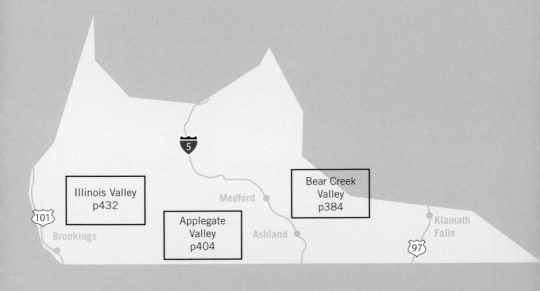

Illinois Valley
p432

Bear Creek
Valley
p384

Medford

Applegate
Valley
p404

Ashland

Klamath
Falls

Brookings

101

97

Rogue Valley
WINE COUNTRY

Bear Creek Valley
Wine Trail

Del Rio Vineyards and Winery

O thou invisible spirit of wine! If thou hast no name to be known by,
let us call thee devil! — William Shakespeare 1564–1616
Othello [1604–1605], act II, sc. iii, l. 285

If you're planning a trip to the Rogue Valley for wine touring I am immensely jealous. The fact is, I love this wine country region and can return again and again to sample the wines, take in a Shakespeare play, enjoy a splendid meal at one of the region's many fine restaurants, bike the Bear Creek Greenway Trail, and more.

The Bear Creek Valley Wine Trail runs north and south through the Rogue Valley. I-5 runs parallel for many miles. From the Del Rio Vineyards and Winery in the north to Weisinger's of Ashland in the south, the Bear Creek Valley Wine Trail includes nine wineries featuring grape varietals from this region. The Rogue Valley got its federal designation in 2001 as an American Viticultural Area and distinguishes itself from other Oregon regions as the warm-weather grape area. Prepare your palate for merlot, cabernet sauvignon, pinot noir, syrah, chardonnay, pinot gris, riesling, cabernet franc, viognier, and tempranillo.

Region:	**Rogue Valley Wine Country**
# of tasting rooms on tour:	**9**
Estimate # of days for tour:	**2**
Getting around:	**Car**
Key Events:	❑ **Running from late February until early November, Ashland's Oregon Shakespeare Festival – see www.osfashland.org or contact 541-482-4331.**
	❑ **In May, Medford's Art in Bloom Festival – call 541-608-8524 or visit www.visitmedford.org.**
	❑ **From June to September – Jacksonville's Britt Festival – call 541-779-0847 or visit www.brittfest.org.**
Tips:	❑ **Consider hiring a limousine service such as Ashland Wine Tours, 541-552-WINE (9463) or Jules of the Valley Wine Tours 541-973-9699.**
	❑ **Many excellent restaurants to choose from – Monet, Chateaulin, Amuse, New Sammy's Cowboy Bistro (Talent) or Lela's Cafe to name some.**
	❑ **Excellent overnight accommodations including Ashland Springs Hotel, Ashland's Inn and Garden Springs at Lithia Springs and the TouVelle House Bed and Breakfast in Jacksonville.**
Best:	❑ **Eats and Gift shop: RoxyAnn Winery.**
	❑ **Lodging: Weisinger's of Ashland.**
	❑ **Views: Del Rio Vineyards and Winery, RoxyAnn Winery, Trium, Weisinger's of Ashland.**

el Rio Vineyards and Winery

Located near Gold Hill in the Rogue River Valley, Del Rio Vineyards and Winery is the largest vineyard in the region, with more than 200,000 vines. Yes, it does have pinot noir and pinot gris, but more importantly (at least to a couple of dozen wineries to the north), it produces a number of warm-weather grapes, including syrah, merlot, cabernet sauvignon, cabernet franc, and Malbec. The reason? The vineyards' southern slope exposure at the 42nd parallel and a relatively low elevation all conspire to generate the significant "heat units" that warm-weather grapes so adore.

Winery tourists visiting the Willamette Valley are often surprised to discover classic Bordeaux- and Rhône-style wines here. When asked where they source their grapes from, tasting-room personnel at area wineries such as Cana's Feast Winery, Tyrus Evan, Sylvan Ridge, Penner-Ash Wine Cellars, and Soléna Cellars routinely answer with a common refrain "Del Rio Vineyards." When it comes to producing warm-weather varietals, Del Rio Vineyards shines, proving that southern Oregon is not just for attending Shakespeare plays and rafting whitewater.

With prestigious wineries throughout Oregon relying on their fruit, it's little wonder that Del Rio owners Lee Traynham and Rob Wallace decided to make wine under their own label. They understand that it all starts in the vineyard. It was their vision (and gamble) in the 1990s that laid the framework for Del Rio Vineyards. The creation of the winery and visitors center is an extension of that original concept.

Del Rio Vineyards and Winery offers more than an opportunity to experience great wine. Located in an old hotel built during the Civil War era, the well-appointed tasting room can turn out to be a field trip as well — especially for history buffs. It also provides a relaxing space in which to sample wine. Outside, there is plenty of open area devoted to picnicking. The view of the nearby vineyard occupying the hillside is nothing short of spectacular. It's hard to imagine that prior to the rows of vineyards, there were hundreds of acres of prime orchard property planted with pears, apples, cherries, peaches, apricots, walnuts, and filberts. Today, economic realities have farmers pulling fruit trees out and replacing them with cabernet sauvignon.

With the slogan "Great grapes, great wines, great times," diversity rules at Del Rio Vineyards and Winery — diversity of the grape, that is.

DEL RIO VINEYARDS AND WINERY
opened: 1997
winemaker(s): Jean-Michel Jussiaume
location: 52 N River Road, Gold Hill, OR 97525
phone: 541-855-2062
web: www.delriovineyards.com
e-mail: taste@delriovineyards.com
picnic area: Yes
wheelchair access: Yes
weddings: Yes
gift shop: Yes
fee: $5 tasting fee
hours: Daily 11–5 September through May; 11–6 June through August

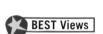

BEST Views

DIRECTIONS: **From the south** take I-5 north to exit 43. Turn right off freeway ramp and then right onto Hwy 99. Continue across bridge over Rogue River. Turn left on North River Rd. Take the first right into Del Rio Vineyards.

From the north take I-5 south to exit 43. Turn left off freeway ramp and then right onto Hwy 99. Continue across bridge over Rogue River. Turn left on North River Rd. Take the first right into Del Rio Vineyards.

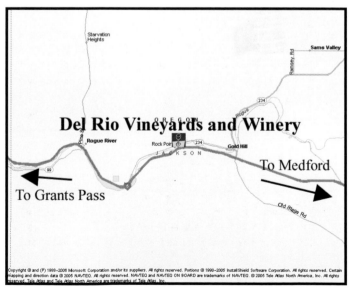

Crater Lake Cellars [2]

A gazillion tourists drive by Crater Lake Cellars on their way to Crater Lake National Park and don't realize they have passed a gem of winery in the sleepy town of Shady Cove. Tucked between the Union 76 gas station and Bel Di's Restaurant along Highway 62 is the diminutive winery and tasting room of Crater Lake Cellars. It's intimate, friendly, and a great place to discover this area's enchanting history.

Owners Steve and Mary Gardner are a match made in winemaking heaven. Steve, who has a background in chemistry, becomes animated discussing fermentation science. Mary's background includes a solid dose of marketing with a degree in that field from the University of Oregon. Together they make a full slate of wines: pinot gris, chardonnay, pinot blanc, gewürztraminer, muscat, syrah, pinot noir, merlot, cabernet sauvignon, cabernet franc, dessert red and white wines, and a red blend. There's even an unusual "white grenache" wine to baffle experienced wine tourists who think they have tasted it all.

Gracing the Gardners' Wood House White Wine is a photo of the area's historic Wood House, off Highway 62 at Eagle Point. The community faces the loss of this historic landmark. However, thanks in large part to Steve and Mary, it may be possible to preserve the building for future generations, because a portion of the proceeds from sales of their wine go toward its preservation.

The Fire House #4 Red Wine's label, with its image of an original 1956 firefighter's helmet, commemorates those who protect the community. No doubt, those earlier firefighters would be stunned to see that their former district fire hall is now occupied by a winery. In keeping with tradition, Mary took a picture of her dad's 1949 Packard in front of the covered bridge at Eagle Point. That charming photo now adorns bottles of their pinot noir.

Inside the intimate tasting room, the blue cedar interior creates a relaxing atmosphere in which to sample their wines. The custom-made door has a speakeasy to permit visitors to keep an eye on a sleeping kid or a dog in the car. Tasting these delightful wines is one thing, but budget plenty of time for Mary to share the many stories found on the bottles.

CRATER LAKE CELLARS
opened: 2004
winemaker(s): Steve Gardner
location: 21882 Highway 62, Shady Cove, OR 97539
phone: 541-878-4200
web: www.craterlakecellars.com
e-mail: info7@craterlakecellars.com
picnic area: Yes
wheelchair access: Yes
hours: Daily 11-5:30; Closed Thanksgiving, Christmas, and New Year's Day

DIRECTIONS: **From Medford** take Jacksonville Hwy heading west. Turn right (north) onto W McAndrews Rd and go .2 miles. Turn left (northwest) onto Sage Rd. Travel .5 miles. Turn right (northeast) onto SR-238 [Jacksonville Hwy] and go .7 miles. Bear right (east) onto SR-62 [Crater Lake Hwy] and go 20.1 miles. Arrive at 21882 Highway 62 in Shady Cove – located on the right-hand side between the 76 gas station and Bel Di's Restaurant.

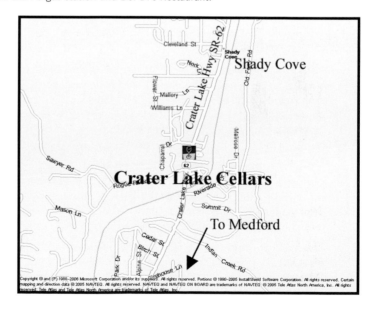

Agate Ridge Vineyard & Winery 3

Happiness for Kim Kinderman was watching Alabama recede in her rearview mirror. Needing a life change, Kim packed up her car (including her dog, Winnie) and came west.

She managed to find a 126-acre farm off Highway 62 in Eagle Point, complete with a 100-year-old farmhouse, stunning views and plenty of land for a vineyard. Fortunately for Kim, her father and brother, Don and Greg Kinderman, joined her as resident handymen,

vine pruners and builders of their new winery and barrel room. However, planting 30 acres of grapes — and 100 acres of deer fence — wasn't something the guys had anticipated. Yet they wouldn't have it any other way.

Today, they produce a full slate of red and white wines, which are sold at the winery as well as other notable locations such as nearby Harry & David and the Rogue Creamery. Visitors to the winery can sample a red line-up of syrah, cabernet sauvignon, petite sirah, zinfandel, pinot noir, and red blends. For whites, the Kindermans offer viognier, pinot gris, sauvignon blanc and a roussanne/Marsanne white blend. Their goal is to steadily ramp up production to no more than 6,000 cases annually.

A visit inside the old-farmhouse tasting room is well worth the trip, but if weather permits, get a glass of Agate Ridge wine and retreat to the outside picnic area. There you will discover wonderful vistas of the surrounding vineyard, Lower and Upper Table Rock, and Mount McLaughlin in the distance.

This family possesses a can-do attitude. When told the weather was too warm for pinot noir, they planted 2 acres of pinot in the vineyard. Now, their pinot noir sells in Portland-area wine shops. When I asked Kim why the vineyard rows are 9 feet apart, she responded that was the size needed for the tractor to get through. When they needed outdoor furniture, Don built the picnic tables. The family has also gone "green" — part of their electricity comes from their wind machine. Given the Kindermans' willingness to take on life's challenges, I am sure that if the wind died and the tractor failed to start, they'd still produce and enter their pinot noir in some prestigious wine-tasting competition. And win.

AGATE RIDGE VINEYARD & WINERY
opened: 2006
winemaker(s): B. Kiley Evans
location: 1098 Nick Young Road,
Eagle Point, OR 97524
phone: 541-830-3050
web: www.agateridgevineyard.com
e-mail: info@agateridgevineyard.com
picnic area: Yes
fee: $5 tasting fee
hours: Tuesday through Sunday 11–5

Kim Kinderman

DIRECTIONS: Agate Ridge Vineyard is located along the "Gateway to the Lakes" corridor in Eagle Point, Oregon, 10 miles from I-5. **Travel on I-5 towards Medford** until you reach Oregon Hwy 62, also known as Crater Lake Hwy, at I-5 exit 30. Travel north on Hwy 62 for 10 miles to Eagle Point. Watch for signs for Nick Young Rd, directly across from the Harnish Wayside Welcome Center. Turn left and travel 1 mile to destination.

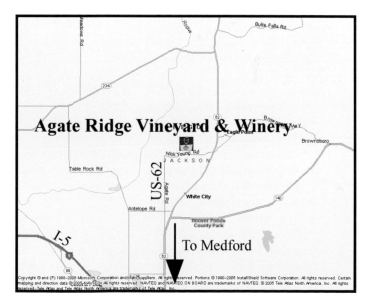

391

RoxyAnn Winery 4

My sister who lives in California was planning a visit to the Rogue Valley to take in a Shakespeare play or two, explore Ashland, and dine at a few restaurants. She noted that she and her husband only had Saturday afternoon to spend tasting wine and she wanted my advice about where to go. I suggested RoxyAnn Winery in Medford.

I'm sure she was surprised that I didn't tick off three or four wineries, but I felt confident in my recommendation. I told her that at RoxyAnn Winery, she'd experience locally produced wines and fruit orchards in an historic setting. She seemed hesitant, but I reassured her, "Don't worry, you'll love it."

I visited RoxyAnn on an earlier occasion and had been delighted to find a tasting room located inside a restored white and green-trimmed barn, a structure that is listed on the National Register of Historic Places. Its interior is light, colorful, spacious, and populated by friendly, well-trained staff. RoxyAnn wines are available for purchase here, along with a number of other Oregon wines that are custom-crushed at the RoxyAnn winemaking facility.

Gus Janeway is the chief winemaker for RoxyAnn Winery, as well as for a half-dozen other Oregon wineries that use RoxyAnn's winemaking facility. In between pressing and bottling, Gus serves as the president of the Rogue Valley Chapter of the Oregon Winegrowers Association. He also finds time to produce wine under his own label, Velocity (sold inside the RoxyAnn tasting room). When it comes to RoxyAnn wines, the list of varietals is extensive — pinot gris, viognier, merlot, syrah, and tempranillo — and it also produces dessert wines and red blends. My sample of RoxyAnn's claret (a Bordeaux blend of merlot, cabernet sauvignon, and cabernet franc) had me fishing for my wallet to buy a bottle to take home.

Throughout the summer, RoxyAnn is an active participant in the Community Supported Agriculture program, a program that supports local growers of fruits, herbs, flowers, and vegetables. Program members pick up their boxes of fresh produce at the winery.

My sister's trip? My sister Carole and her husband Bob had a fabulous time and noted that they had no problem finishing off a bottle of RoxyAnn's Parsons Reserve while enjoying the outdoor gardens. I knew they would. Perhaps James Joyce said it best, as quoted in RoxyAnn's literature, "What is better than to sit at the end of the day and drink wine with friends?"

ROXYANN WINERY
opened: 2002
winemaker(s): Gus Janeway
location: 3285 Hillcrest Road, Medford, OR 97504
phone: 541-776-2315
web: www.roxyann.com
e-mail: via website
picnic area: Yes
wheelchair access: Yes
weddings: Yes
gift shop: Yes
tours: Yes
fee: $3 tasting fee refundable with purchase
hours: Daily 11–6

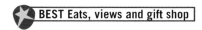

BEST Eats, views and gift shop

DIRECTIONS: **From south of Grants Pass** about 25 miles take exit 30 off I-5 heading toward OR-62 / Medford/Crater Lake. Turn left (northeast) onto SR-62 [Crater Lake Hwy] and go .1 mile. Turn right onto ramp, then left (south) onto Biddle Rd and proceed .6 miles. Turn left (east) onto E McAndrews Rd and travel 2.4 miles. Keep right onto ramp and turn right (south) onto N Foothill Rd for .7 miles. Turn left (east) onto Hillcrest Rd and proceed .3 miles. Look for signs to the winery.

From Medford go east on 8th St. [Jacksonville Hwy] for .1 mile. Bear right (east) onto E Main St., go 1.2 miles. Bear left (northeast) onto Valley View Dr. for .2 miles. Turn right (east) onto Hillcrest Rd, 1.3 miles later and arrive at winery.

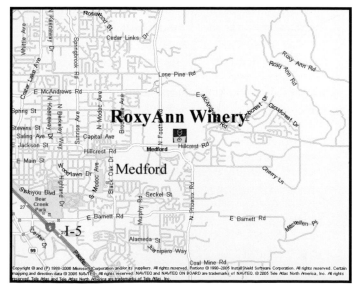

Paschal Winery 5

At the entrance to Paschal Winery, visitors get a glimpse of what's in store. As you look toward the hilltop, the Italian-style tasting room, with its warm golden colors and red slate roof, may have you thinking of Tuscan blends and pinot grigio. Your drive up takes you past the Paschal vineyards to the generous parking area, where you'll see an expansive lawn leading down to a pond. You're in the heart of Bear Creek Valley, and the surrounding Siskiyou Mountains provide a spectacular backdrop.

Inside Paschal's tasting room, the Mediterranean ambiance continues with a warm color scheme and a set of French doors leading out to a comfortably furnished deck. Cypress trees and sculptures down near the pond complete this picture of *la vita dolce*. Tucker

might be around — he's the easygoing black Lab that won the canine lottery when he became a member of this family.

Paschal Winery is the heart and soul of owners Roy and Jill Paschal. They began growing grapes on the property in the mid-'90s. However, when they tasted the fruit of their labors — literally — they realized that they needed to make their own wine from the fruit. Noted Oregon winemaker Joe Dobbes, Jr. has been doing so for Paschal Winery since 2002. He produces a variety of wines, which includes a healthy dose of Italian-style wines such as pinot gris and a red blend of sangiovese and dolcetto with the decidedly Italian name of Civita Di Bagnoregio.

In addition to sampling the wines mentioned above, it would be a crime for visitors not to take advantage of the warm-weather varietals produced by the Rogue Valley AVA. WineTrail trekkers can sip tempranillo, syrah, Bordeaux-style red blends and a delicious white blend named in honor of the winemaker's daughter, Maya's New White Wine.

It so happens that Paschal Winery is event central for the Rogue Valley. It hosts regular wine and music events the third Friday of each month, which have become popular with the locals. These events highlight regional musical acts and art shows throughout the year. For those in search of a place to wed or a site for that next corporate shindig, Paschal could fill the bill very nicely. With ample parking, excellent caterers, a huge lawn, tremendous views, rotating art exhibits, lots of wine, and a professional staff that give guests the royal treatment, Paschal Winery is perfect place for pairing wine with life's celebrations.

PASCHAL WINERY
opened: 1998
winemaker(s): Joe Dobbes, Jr.
location: 1122 Suncrest Road, Talent, OR 97540
phone: 541-535-7975
web: www.paschalwinery.com
e-mail: web@paschalwinery.com
picnic area: Yes
weddings: Yes
fee: 2 complimentary tastings; $5 tasting fee for 3 whites and 5 reds; $10 supreme tasting fee for additional premium wines
hours: Daily 11–6 during summer; Tuesday through Sunday 11–5 during winter

DIRECTIONS: **From Medford** take 8th St. [Jacksonville Hwy] 1 mile heading east. Turn right (southeast) onto SR-99 [S. Central Ave.] for .8 miles. Bear right (south) onto SR-99 [S Riverside Ave.] and go .3 miles. Bear left (southeast) onto SR-99 [S Pacific Hwy] and go 5.8 miles, [S Pacific Hwy changes name to Main St. for a while]. Bear left (east) onto Suncest Rd for .9 miles. Turn right to stay on Suncrest Rd and arrive at Paschal Winery in .2 miles.

From Ashland head northwest on SR-99 [N. Main St.] for 1.5 miles. Keep straight on SR-99 for about 4 miles. Turn right (east) onto Suncrest Rd and go .9 miles. Turn right to stay on Suncrest Rd for .2 miles and arrive at destination.

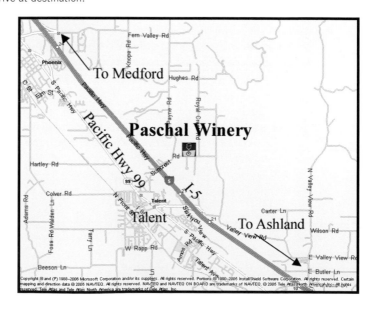

EdenVale Winery ⑥

A visit to EdenVale Winery is both a wine-tasting excursion and a field trip in history. However, before we dive into the juicy details, I need to clarify that the EdenVale tasting room is known as the Rogue Valley Wine Center, and it's part of the Eden Valley Orchards–Voorhies Mansion. Whatever the name, a visit to the winery takes you to the birthplace of Oregon's commercial pear industry — the Eden Valley Orchards, launched by Joseph H. Stewart in 1885.

The woman working in the tasting room during my visit couldn't say enough good things about the owners of the winery — the Root family. It seemed her feelings were genuine.

When asked about the history of the property, she responded, "I wish Anne [Root] was here. She could tell you a lot about the history of the property. The Roots view themselves as stewards of the land and the valley's traditions."

Interesting to know, I thought. But I was more curious about the fact that, in addition to EdenVale wines, the Roots sell other boutique wines in their tasting room. "What's up with that?" I asked. Again, the pourer stated, "Anne could give you a better answer, but I know that their concern is for the welfare of the Rogue Valley's wine industry. If we can promote small-time wineries, it helps everyone's cause." However, it was EdenVale's Pear House Collection of syrah, tempranillo, cabernet franc, cabernet sauvignon, and claret that held my attention.

I looked out through the window and noticed that winery employees were setting up for a wedding. Someone was aligning the white chairs, and a photographer was snapping pictures of the bride and groom before the crowd arrived. I turned to the pourer to ask a question about EdenVale events, but before I could frame my question, she noted, "The Roots are big into hosting events and celebrations. They sponsor a jazz night every Thursday night during the summer. We're always busy!"

By then, I had gotten the point. As the fourth generation of the Roots family in this valley, its current members continue to carry on the familial passion for this special place and its rich agriculture. Their pride spills over, and visitors experience it in the tasting room. After my visit, I didn't see the need to interview any of the Roots themselves. Unbeknownst to them, their ambassador working the tasting room that day had succeeded in telling their story with great eloquence.

EDENVALE WINERY
winemaker(s): Patrick Fallon
location: 2310 Voorhies Road, Medford, OR 97501
phone: 541-512-2955
web: www.edenvalewines.com
e-mail: wine@edenvalleyorchards.com
picnic area: Yes
wheelchair access: Yes
weddings: Yes
tours: Yes
fee: Complimentary wine tasting; $5 tasting fee for 3 reserves; $10 for all
hours: Tuesday through Saturday 10–6, Sunday 12–4, March through November; Tuesday through Saturday 10–5, Sunday 1–4, December through February

DIRECTIONS: **From Medford** take 8th St. [Jacksonville Hwy] 1 mile going east. Turn right (southeast) onto SR-99 [S Central Ave.] and go .8 miles. Bear right (south) onto SR-99 [S Riverside Ave.] for .3 miles. Bear left (southeast) onto SR-99 [S Pacific Hwy] for .7 miles. Turn right (west) onto Stage Rd S and go .2 miles. Turn left (south) onto Voorhies Rd and proceed .2 miles to EdenVale Estate Winery.

From Ashland take SR-99 (northwest) for about 10 miles. The road name changes from S Pacific Hwy to N Pacific Hwy, to Bear Creek Dr., to N Manin St. Regardless, keep straight on SR-99. Turn left (west) onto Stage Rd S. and go .2 miles. Turn left (south) onto Voorhies Rd for .2 miles to 2310 Voorhies Rd.

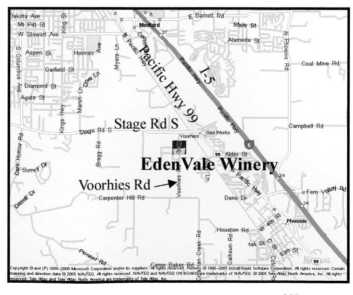

Trium

Part of the magic of visiting wineries for the first time is that you never know what you'll find. I've been to hundreds of tasting rooms throughout the Pacific Northwest and I have learned one thing: Expect the unexpected. Such was the case with my visit to Trium.

The woman behind the tasting-room bar greeted us with "Welcome to Trium winery." but that's where the small talk stopped. Turns out, the woman was not some neighbor tending the tasting room while the owners are in the cellar blending wines. Rather, our guide to Trium was Laura Lotspeich, one of its co-owners and the manager of Pheasant Hill Vineyard, along with her husband, Kurt Lotspeich.

Laura talked about their vineyard and their guiding philosophy: "Wine is made in the vineyard." In this case, wine is made in Pheasant Hill Vineyard, as well as two other vineyards — Gold Vineyard (owned by Rebecca and Randy Gold) and Evans Creek Vineyard (owned by Nancy Tappan and Vernon Hixson). The name Trium is Latin for "of the three," and all three vineyards are certified as LIVE (Low Input Viticulture & Enology) and Salmon Safe.

Starting with white wine, Laura introduced us to Trium's luscious pinot gris, followed by a silky viognier. She then moved on to a full-bodied cabernet sauvignon and finally to their signature Trium Growers' Cuvée (which I happily sprung for). All the wines' labels feature a distinctive woodblock image of a 16th-century vineyard worker. While pouring, Laura noted that they use one-third new oak, one-third 1-year-old oak, and one-third neutral oak for barrel aging. She also spoke of vineyard management and the cycle of seasons, from early-spring bud break to the fall harvest.

For winemaking, Trium relies on veteran winemaker Peter Rosback of Sineann Cellars fame. With more than 20 years of experience making wine in the United States and New Zealand, Peter enjoys a stellar reputation in Oregon winemaking circles. He's also the winemaker for The Pines 1852 in Hood River and Medici Vineyards outside Newberg. You name the varietal, he's turned it into wine.

Outside Trium's ivy-covered English-cottage-style tasting room, visitors have an amazing view of the Bear Creek Valley below. As I watched a hawk circling in the summer sky, I knew I was deep in the heart of rich agricultural land. The quiet of the moment gave me the opportunity to reflect on the incredible knowledge that people like Laura bring to the Oregon wine industry.

TRIUM
winemaker(s): Peter Rosback
location: 7112 Rapp Lane, Talent, OR 97540
phone: 541-535-6093
web: www.triumwines.com
e-mail: info@triumwines.com
picnic area: Yes
wheelchair access: Yes
fee: $5 tasting fee refundable with purchase of 3 bottles
hours: Friday through Sunday 12–5:30, May through September, or by appointment

 **BEST Views**

DIRECTIONS: **Southbound on I-5** take exit 21 toward Talent. Turn right (west) onto Valley View Rd and go .5 miles. Turn left (east) onto SR-99 [S Pacific Hwy] and go left .4 miles. Turn right (southwest) onto Rapp Rd and go .6 miles. Turn left (south) onto Rapp Ln. and travel .5 miles. Arrive at Trium winery on the right.

From Ashland take SR-99 about 5 miles north to Talent. Turn left onto Rapp Rd and go .6 miles. Turn left (south) onto Rapp Ln., proceed .5 miles, and arrive at Trium winery on the right.

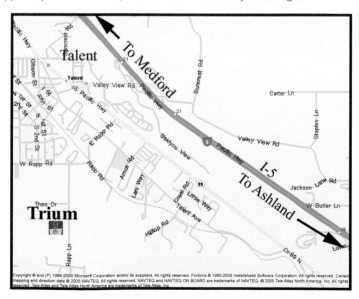

Ashland Vineyards & Winery 8

For nearly two decades, Phil and Kathy Kodak have been growing grapes and producing wine under their Ashland and more upscale Shakespeare labels. A bottle of their Midsummer's Night Dream Sauvignon Blanc even sports a picture of Will Shakespeare.

The Kodaks' vineyard and tasting room are located on the outskirts of Ashland near Southern Oregon University. A drive to the tasting room takes you past organically maintained vineyards where weeds grow freely between and among the vines. The tasting room itself is diminutive. Clearly, you are here to taste wines, not to stroll among manicured lawns and landscaped waterfalls. And leave the bocce balls at home. It's the wine that matters, and past accolades and awards speak to the winery's proud heritage.

Phil's professional background has contributed mightily to the winery's development. He has a long family history of winemaking, with origins dating to the 1800s in South Africa. And, as pointed out on the Ashland Vineyards & Winery website, he has several degrees in chemistry, taught chemistry at the university level, and took graduate-level enology classes at the University of California–Davis.

A visit to this winery will educate both the casual and the savvy wine tourist about the history of winemaking in the Rogue Valley, as taught by one of the founders.

ASHLAND VINEYARDS & WINERY
opened: 1990
winemaker(s): Phil Kodak
location: 2775 E Main Street, Ashland, OR 97520
phone: 541-488-0088
web: www.winenet.com
e-mail: wines@winenet.com
fee: $.50 per taste
hours: Tuesday through Sunday 11–5 March through December; by appointment only January and February; closed Mondays and holidays

DIRECTIONS: **Heading south on I-5 toward Ashland,** take exit 14 and turn left (east) onto SR-66 [Ashland St.] and go .5 miles. Turn left (north) onto E Main St. and go .4 miles. Arrive at 2775 E Main St.

From Ashland take SR-99 [N Main St.] southeast 1.6 miles. Bear left (east) onto SR-66 [Ashland St.] and go 1.7 miles. Turn left (north) onto E Main St. and arrive at destination in .4 miles.

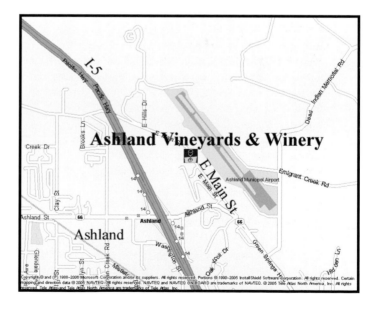

Weisinger's of Ashland 9

Just 14 miles north of the California border and four miles south of Ashland sits a special six-acre vineyard and winery — Weisinger's of Ashland. John Weisinger fulfilled a career dream by planting the vineyard back in 1978, making him an Oregon wine industry pioneer. Ten years later, with the completion of a production facility and tasting room, John launched the winery. He dubbed it Weisinger's of Ashland.

I arrived expecting a somewhat "tired" winery and tasting room — a place showing its age. After all, 20 years of winemaking wears on both staff and structures. I figured there

might be a little dust on the counter, a staff long in the tooth, and perhaps unsold wine from 2002. *Au contraire!*

Whatever preconceptions I had of a worn-down place evaporated quickly when the young staff greeted me with friendly vigor. The tasting room's valley-facing windows permit bright sunlight to stream through, creating a warm space. A door leads outside to a multilevel deck where stylish wrought iron furniture with umbrellas are arranged to ward off the noonday sun. During my visit, pods of visitors were gathered inside and out, laughing and enjoying wine. I was to learn that many guests were locals who routinely visited. The place was alive.

Reflecting Weisinger's openness to change was the hiring of Chanda (rhymes with "panda") Beeghley in 2007. In her 20s, Chanda is one of the youngest winemakers in Oregon, but her experience at RoxyAnn winery and studies at Southern Oregon University prepared her well. She follows in the footsteps of John's son Eric Weisinger, who had been Weisinger's winemaker since 1997.

Using estate and local fruit, Weisinger's of Ashland produces a wide variety of red and white wines. Likely choices for wine tourists to sample are gewürztraminer, pinot gris, sémillon, white blends, rosé, cabernet franc, cabernet sauvignon, claret, merlot, syrah, tempranillo, and a port-style wine. With this much variety, you're sure to find a wine you like. And, with the outside deck beckoning, it would be a shame not to heed it. Retreat with your purchased wine and enjoy the view.

Depending on whether you are coming from or going to California, Weisinger's of Ashland is either your first or last chance to discover Oregon wine. Whatever direction you're heading in, Weisinger's of Ashland stands ready to satisfy your wine palate with fresh vintages and vibrant energy.

BEST Lodging and views

WEISINGER'S OF ASHLAND
opened: 1988
winemaker(s): Chanda Beeghley
location: 3150 Siskiyou Blvd. (Highway 99),
Ashland, OR 97520
phone: 541-488-5989
web: www.weisingers.com
e-mail: wine@weisingers.com
picnic area: Yes
wheelchair access: Yes
fee: 1 free taste (excludes reserve) $3 white wines;
$7 for red wines and full tasting for $8. Refundable
with purchase of 3 or more bottles.
hours: Daily 11–5 May through September;
Wednesday through Sunday 11–5 October
through April

DIRECTIONS: **From Grants Pass heading south on I-5** take exit 14, turn right onto ramp toward SR-66 [Ashland St.]. Turn left (south) onto Tolman Creek Rd and go .7 miles. Turn left (east) onto SR-99 [Siskiyou Blvd.] and travel .9 miles. Arrive at 3150 Siskiyou Blvd.

If heading north on I-5 coming from California, take exit 11 onto SR-99 [Siskiyou Blvd] and go 1.4 miles.

From Ashland head southeast on SR-99 .5 miles. Keep straight onto SR-99 [Siskiyou Blvd] for 3.2 miles and arrive at winery.

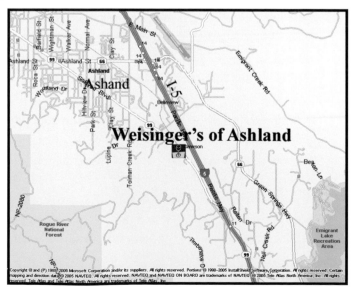

Applegate Valley
Wine Trail

Outside patio at Schmidt Family Vineyards

It can safely be said that Jacksonville is the gateway to the Applegate Valley. And rightly so. After all, it was pioneer Peter Britt himself who founded the Valley View Winery in 1873! Paying homage to Peter Britt, the Wisnovsky family named their winery Valley View Winery. Definitely budget time to visit this winery.

With a total of 13 wineries to visit (at the time of this writing), plan on a full three days of wine tasting if your goal is to visit all Applegate Valley WineTrail tasting rooms. Plus, there is an added bonus: if you don't have time to go to the Illinois Valley, Bridgeview Vineyards has a satellite tasting room on North Applegate Road.

A key message wine tourists will hear concerns sustainable wine-growing practices. Get ready to immerse yourself in organic and biodynamic farming discussions. It's all part of a movement by a majority of Oregon wineries to promote sustainable farming methods. After all, you want to taste the terroir associated with the vineyard — you should taste bottled sunshine, minerals, moonlit nights, groundwater and more. An excellent example of this practice is Cowhorn Garden & Vineyard. This is a pesticide-free zone to be sure. Somehow, I think Peter Britt would approve. He strikes me as a pretty organic guy.

Applegate Valley WineTrail

1. Applegate Red Winery
2. Rosella's Vineyard
3. Schmidt Family Vineyards
4. Troon Vineyard
5. Wooldridge Creek Winery
6. John Michael Champagne Cellars
7. Devitt Winery
8. Jacksonville Vineyards
9. Fiasco Winery
10. LongSword Vineyard
11. Valley View Winery
12. Cricket Hill Vineyard and Winery
13. Cowhorn Vineyard & Garden

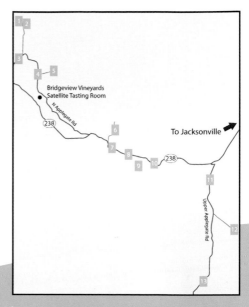

Region:	**Rogue Valley Wine Country**
# of tasting rooms on tour:	**13**
# of satellite tasting rooms:	**1**
Estimate # of days for tour:	**2 to 3**
Getting around:	**Car or bike**
Key Events:	❑ **Running from late February until early November, Ashland's Oregon Shakespeare Festival – see www.osfashland.org or contact 541-482-4331.**
	❑ **In May, Medford's Art in Bloom Festival – call 541-608-8524 or visit www.visitmedford.org.**
	❑ **From June to September, Jacksonville's Britt Festival – call 541-779-0847 or visit www.brittfest.org.**
Tips:	❑ **Bridgeview has a satellite tasting room in Applegate Valley.**
	❑ **Consider hiring a limousine service such as Ashland Wine Tours, 541-552-WINE (9463) or Jules of the Valley Wine Tours, 541-973-9699.**
	❑ **Many excellent restaurants to choose from – Monet, Chateaulin, Amuse, New Sammy's Cowboy Bistro (Talent) or Lela's Cafe to name some.**
	❑ **Excellent overnight accommodations including – Ashland Springs Hotel, Ashland's Inn and Garden Springs at Lithia Springs and the TouVelle House Bed and Breakfast in Jacksonville.**

 Best:

❑ **Eats: LongSword Vineyard.**
❑ **Gift shop: Valley View Winery.**
❑ **Views: Applegate Red Winery, Troon Vineyard, LongSword Vineyard, Valley View Winery.**

Applegate Red Winery

Frank Ferreira, the owner and vintner of Applegate Red Winery, states, "I'm a wine grower, not a wine maker." For him, it's all about the fruit in the vineyard, and in his case, it's a 20-acre vineyard situated in the spectacular Applegate Valley. The fact that he grows merlot, syrah, cabernet sauvignon, and cabernet franc tells you he is into reds. It is named Applegate Red Winery, after all.

His is the most eclectic winery in Oregon. Nowhere else would you find brilliantly colored parrots, a herd of miniature Sicilian donkeys, a picnic area to die for, a pond for waterfowl to enjoy, and a quaint scarlet-colored exterior tasting room complete with humorous plaques offering words to live by. It all reflects Frank's imaginative mind and attitude toward life. Born and bred on Maui, Frank moved to Oregon to "retire" but, ever the tinkerer, he started breeding parrots, raising miniature donkeys (because, as he puts it, "they're so damn cute"), and exercising his passion for growing wine.

Inside the friendly tasting room, Frank holds court while pouring samples of cabernet, syrah, merlot, and his signature blended wine, Applegate Red. While listening to Frank, be sure to check out the surrounding walls for those words to live by. Here are some of my favorites: "When in doubt, add wine," "Good wine and good friends, the perfect pairing," "Friends and wine get better with age," and "Wanted: Sugar Mama." When asked, Frank tells visitors that he uses organic practices in the vineyard and a minimalist approach to making wine: no sugar added while aging, and no fining or filtering before bottling.

You won't find another wine club in Oregon like that of Applegate Red Winery either. Membership to Frank's club is by invitation only. Named after the street number of his Missouri Flat Road address, the 222 Wine Club is limited to frequent visitors or those who have purchased a case or two of wine. The cost of membership is $222 and entitles you to an annual shipment of a case of wine. With the prices of his wines averaging in the mid-$20 range, that's a bargain.

As I drove toward the exit, past the miniature donkeys in the field, I reflected on one of Frank's wall quotations, "I hope my ship comes in before my dock rots!" Frank, trust me, your ship has arrived.

APPLEGATE RED WINERY
opened: 2001
winemaker(s): Frank Ferreira
location: 222 Missouri Flat Road,
Grants Pass, OR 97527
phone: 541-846-9422
web: www.applegatered.com
e-mail: applegatered@budget.net
picnic area: Yes
wheelchair access: Yes
tours: Yes
fee: Complimentary tasting for 3 wines
hours: Saturday, Sunday, and holidays 11–5

Frank Ferreira

 **BEST Views**

DIRECTIONS: **From Grants Pass** take US-199 [SR-99] 1.3 miles heading south. Keep left onto SR-238 [Williams Hwy] and proceed 6.1 miles. Turn left (east) onto N Applegate Rd and go 5.8 miles. Turn left (north) onto Kubli Rd and proceed .6 miles. Bear left (north) onto Missouri Flat Rd and look for signs to the winery.

From Jacksonville go west 15 miles on SR-238 [Jacksonville Hwy]. Bear right (west) onto N Applegate Rd for 4.5 miles. Keep straight onto Kubli Rd for 1.7 miles. Turn right (north) onto Missouri Flat Rd and go .1 miles and arrive at 222 Missouri Flat Rd.

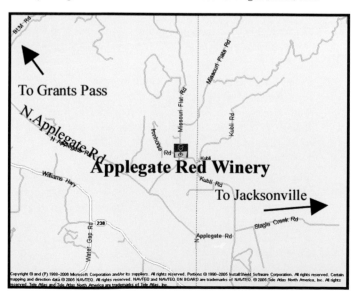

Rosella's Vineyard [2]

Rex Garoutte is blessed with the most amazing laugh; a laugh reflecting his positive attitude toward life and pure joy of living in Applegate Valley. Rex and his wife, Sandi, moved here in 1998 from the Bay Area, a return to Sandi's childhood home in Oregon. As Rex puts it, "It was a lifestyle decision. I just wanted to grow grapes." And growing grapes he does very well, on a 10-acre plot of land located off Missouri Flat Road in rural Grants Pass. He would not have it any other way.

The winery's name is homage to Rex's mother, Rosella, who died of cancer in 1998. He grew up in Washington's agricultural breadbasket, the Yakima Valley. Those agrarian roots serve him well. Producing only 600 cases of wine per year, Rex refers to himself the "garagiste" of the Applegate Valley. However, the fact that his winery is small adds to the intimacy and charm WineTrail trekkers experience at Rosella's Vineyard. His modest goal is to increase production to around 1,000 cases annually — a drop in the bucket by most winery standards.

While working in San Francisco, prior to the Garouttes' move north, Rex crafted homemade beer that friends and family found quite satisfying. His passion for fermenting things led to coursework in University of California–Davis' viticulture and enology program. After this, it was only fitting that the next step would be to grow premium grapes and make wine.

Along with Rex's good-natured demeanor, visitors get to experience a robust line-up of estate wines, including chardonnay, merlot, a merlot-zinfandel blend, and a "fun wine" blend of merlot and cabernet sauvignon called Ula Waina (Hawaiian for "red wine"). There is no tasting fee. What's more, with wines priced in the $15–$19 range, there are values galore at Rosella's Vineyard.

While it's easy to marvel at the surrounding beauty of the area as you sip Rosella's Vineyards complimentary wines, don't overlook the label on the bottle designed by local artist Morgan Johnson. The artist titled the painting "Picnic," and his carefree strokes and use of vibrant colors pair perfectly with the relaxed disposition of Rex and this personable winery. While you trek along the Applegate Valley WineTrail, be sure to budget time for this gem of a winery.

ROSELLA'S VINEYARD
winemaker(s): Rex Garoutte
location: 184 Missouri Flat Road,
Grants Pass, OR 97527
phone: 541-846-6372
web: www.rosellasvineyard.com
e-mail: sandig@peak.org
wheelchair access: Yes
tours: Yes
fee: Complimentary wine tasting
hours: Thursday through Monday 11–5; Tuesday and
Wednesday by appointment

DIRECTIONS: **From Grants Pass** head south on US-199 [SR-99] for 1.3 miles. Keep left onto SR-238 [Williams Hwy] for 6.1 miles. Turn left (east) onto N Applegate Rd and proceed 5.8 miles. Turn left (north) onto Kubli Rd and go .6 miles. Bear left (north) onto Missouri Flat Rd and arrive at Rosella's Vineyard.

From Jacksonville head west on SR-238 [Jacksonville Hwy] for 15 miles. Bear right (west) onto N Applegate Rd for 4.5 miles. Keep straight onto Kubli Rd and go 1.7 miles. Turn right (north) onto Missouri Flat Rd and arrive at the winery.

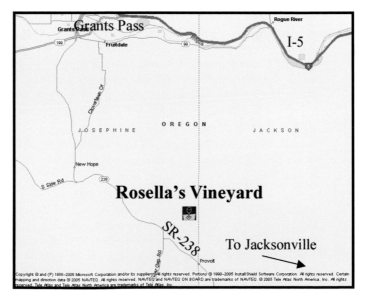

Schmidt Family Vineyards 3

Dateline Applegate Valley: *Cabinetmaker-Turned-Dirt-Guy Makes Wine*

You have to admire people who reinvent their lives and do something completely different. Such is the storyline behind the emergence of Schmidt Family Vineyards and its owners, Judy and Cal Schmidt. Though he owned a successful cabinetry business (Northwestern Design), Cal longed to farm the land and grow premium wine grapes. He began taking viticulture classes and in 2000, purchased a former ranch in the Missouri

Flat area of Applegate Valley. The Schmidts kept the cabinetry business, but there's no doubt that the demands of their successful winery consume most of their time.

Beginning in 2001, they converted a large chunk of the 12 acres into rows of cabernet sauvignon, merlot and syrah. Additional plantings of other varietals have since followed, including a Spanish-derived varietal called albarino. But the centerpiece of their property has to be the tasting room itself, where Craftsman style meets Northwest elegance and spills into an outdoor garden with inviting deck chairs and tables. (Note to WineTrail trekkers: Bring a picnic lunch.) Judy happens to be a Master Gardener, and this helps explain the winery's overall landscaping, including the flower and herb garden. Little wonder that their wine bottle label features a drawing of an herb, which gets me thinking about an herb-crusted rack of lamb to pair with their cabernet sauvignon.

The Schmidt Family Vineyards offers plenty of space to host events, including weddings, corporate meetings, and family reunions. In addition to the flower and herb garden, visitors can mill about, enjoying a large pond and taking in the views of the surrounding area.

To complete the transition from an abandoned ranch to a first-class winery, Cal and Judy turned to winemaker Bryan Wilson to transform their fruit into wine. In 2006, the winery released its first vintage and evidently it struck a cord with folks who like wine — the vintage sold out. Chief among the winery's early releases are merlot, cabernet sauvignon, and syrah, as well as a red blend with the cool name of Soulea. Greater production (but not to exceed 5,000 cases) and more varietals are in store for Schmidt Family Vineyards. However, the day that I happened upon the winery, it was the Soulea that appealed to my palate. I bought a bottle, retreated to the outside garden area, and gave myself a nice pour. What a perfect setting for a wine in full bloom.

SCHMIDT FAMILY VINEYARDS
opened: 2006
winemaker(s): Bryan Wilson
location: 320 Kubli Road, Grants Pass, OR 97527
phone: 541-846-1125
web: www.sfvineyards.com
e-mail: schmidt@sfvineyards.com
picnic area: Yes
weddings: Yes
fee: Complimentary wine tasting
hours: Friday through Sunday 12–5 from January through April; daily 12–5 from May through December, or by appointment

DIRECTIONS: **From Medford** take Jacksonvillle Hwy [SR-238] about 18 miles toward the west. Bear right (west) onto N Applegate Rd and proceed 4.5 miles. Turn left to stay on N Applegate Rd and go 1.5 miles. Turn right (north) onto Kubli Rd and continue .2 miles to the winery on your right.

From Ashland take SR-99 about 7 miles north. Turn left (west) onto Stage Rd S and go 3.4 miles. Road name changes to Griffin Creek Rd S. Turn left (west) onto Stage Rd S and go 2.8 miles. Road name changes to E California St. Continue on SR-238 [Jacksonville Hwy] for 15 miles. Bear right (west) onto N Applegate Rd and go 1.5 miles. Turn right (north) onto Kubli Rd and proceed .2 miles to Schmidt Family Vineyards on your right.

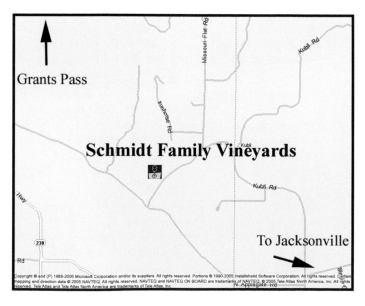

Troon Vineyard 4

I do believe that there is a direct correlation between attention to detail and fine wine. The wineries that are in shipshape condition and whose staff is professionally trained but not stuffy are the ones that get my palate's attention.

Such was the case when Kathleen and I pulled up to the French-villa-style compound of Troon Vineyard. The copper gutters reflected the noonday sun; the potted plants added elegance, and even the tasting room's door had a purposefully solid feel. Once inside I was stopped in my tracks by the panoramic vista of Applegate Valley, afforded by the huge pane-glass window behind the tasting room's wine bar. However, when I got

the "Welcome to Troon Vineyard" greeting from a staff member, the familiar automatic response was triggered — I began to salivate. It's an instinctual thing, but hardwood floors, granite countertops, and personalized wine-club member glasses stored behind the bar have a way of doing that to me.

I had already heard of Troon's signature wine, Druid's Fluid, and figured that any winery that bestows such a name on its top-selling wine must have a sense of humor. I wasn't disappointed. Despite all the elegant accouterments of the room, the staff makes you feel at ease. They pour from an extensive collection of fine wine, focusing primarily on five varietals: chardonnay, merlot, syrah, zinfandel, and cabernet sauvignon. There are also several blended wines to sample, including the popular River Guide White and River Guide Red, as well as a port-style wine with an audacious name of Insomnia Port.

Way back in 1972, the original owner of Troon Vineyard, Dick Troon, planted grapes that appealed to him, in particular, cabernet sauvignon and zinfandel. Dick continued to cultivate and make amazing wines, but somewhere in the process of producing one red-blend wine, he botched the mixture. The result tasted wonderful, and it quickly became Troon's number-one seller. Given his Celtic roots, Dick decided to name the wine Druid's Fluid.

The Martin family acquired Troon Vineyard in 2003 and have only added to its elegance, its vineyard holdings, and its winemaking capabilities. Stroll over the grounds (complete with bocce ball courts) and note the stylish lawn furniture and fountain-adorned gardens. Take time to enjoy a glass of wine on the patio, as we did. If the classiness of Troon Vineyards doesn't win you over, its award-winning wines will. It's clear that winemaker Herb Quady has all the new-fangled tools needed to create superb Old World wines. And you can bet he's got an eye for details.

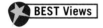

TROON VINEYARD
opened: 1993
winemaker(s): Herb Quady
location: 1475 Kubli Road, Grants Pass, OR 97527
phone: 541-846-9900
web: www.troonvineyard.com
e-mail: Lwan@troonvineyard.com
picnic area: Yes
wheelchair access: Yes
fee: $5 tasting fee waived on purchase of 6 or more bottles
hours: Daily 11–5 February to Memorial Day Weekend; Daily 11–6 Memorial Day Weekend through September; Daily 11–5 October through December; Closed July 4th, Thanksgiving Day, Christmas Day and January

DIRECTIONS: **From Medford** take Hwy 238 heading west 7 miles to Ruch. Continue on Hwy 238 7 more miles to Applegate, then turn right on N Applegate Road. Travel 5 miles to Kubli Road, bear right, and Troon Vineyard is located .25 miles ahead on left.

From Grants Pass take Hwy 199 to Hwy 238, travel 8 miles to Murphy, and then turn left on N Applegate Road. Continue 7 miles to second Kubli Road entrance and turn left. Vineyard is located on the left .25 miles ahead.

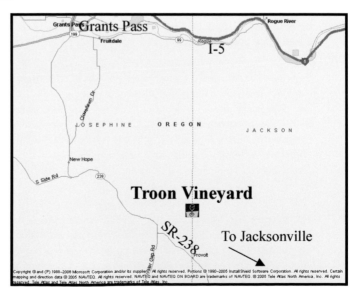

Wooldridge Creek Winery 5

Clichés exist for a reason — they express the truth. A prime example is the hackneyed phrase "The whole is greater than the sum of its parts." Such is the case with Wooldridge Creek Winery, where owners Ted Warrick, Mary Warrick, Greg Paneitz, and Kara Olmo come together to produce luscious wines in the heart of the Applegate Valley.

I suspected that I would be in for a treat. I had heard random comments by other wine tourists about their positive experiences at Wooldridge Creek Winery. One night at dinner, a couple next to me proudly noted that they were members of the Wooldridge

Creek Winery wine club. I was also aware that other wineries source grapes from Wooldridge. I figured it must be doing something right.

Kathleen and I hit the jackpot on the day of our visit to Wooldridge and got a guided tour from co-owner Ted Warrick. As he escorted us from crush pad to barrel room, Ted talked about the early days, back in the late 1970s, when he and his wife, Mary, and daughter Chrys moved to the Applegate Valley and began growing grapes. His piloting duties with United Airlines often took him away from the farm, but they persevered and the vineyard expanded to 56 acres. However, when it came time to make wine, Ted noted, he discovered that he should stay in the vineyard and leave the winemaking to someone else.

Enter into the equation the winemaking services of co-owners Greg and Kara. The two met while attending Fresno State University's enology program. Greg had an organic chemistry background, which included a stint with Pfizer pharmaceutical company as well as practical winemaking experience in France. Kara graduated from the San Francisco Culinary Institute and possessed an in-depth knowledge of food and wine pairing. Given their common passions but divergent backgrounds, the couple decided to pursue winemaking careers where they could indulge their shared interest in warm-weather grapes.

The union of Ted, Mary, Greg, and Kara has brought Wooldridge Creek Winery center stage among the other prestigious wineries of southern Oregon. Ted knew he could grow great grapes. Greg's and Kara's fields of expertise focus on the creation and pairing of great wine. Each person has a key role and each is dependent upon the others' abilities. It works. To borrow another *cliché*, "The proof is in the taste of the pudding" — and the fine wines of Wooldridge Creek Winery.

Greg Paneitz and Kara Olmo

WOOLDRIDGE CREEK WINERY
winemaker(s): Greg Paneitz and Kara Olmo
location: 818 Slagle Creek Road,
Grants Pass, OR 97527
phone: 541-846-6364
web: www.wcwinery.com
picnic area: Yes
wheelchair access: Yes
fee: Small tasting fee may apply
hours: Call for hours

DIRECTIONS: **From Grants Pass** head south on US-199 [SR-99] for 1.3 miles. Keep left onto SR-238 [Williams Hwy] and continue 6.1 miles. Turn left (east) onto N Applegate Rd and proceed 7.2 miles. Turn left (north) onto Kubli Rd, then immediately right (east) onto Slagle Creek Rd. Go .8 miles to 818 Slagle Creek Rd.

From Jacksonville take SR-238 [Jacksonville Hwy] 15 miles. Bear right (west) onto N Applegate Rd 4.5 miles and keep straight onto Kubli Rd. Turn right (east) onto Slagle Creek Rd and go .8 miles. Arrive at 818 Slagle Creek Rd.

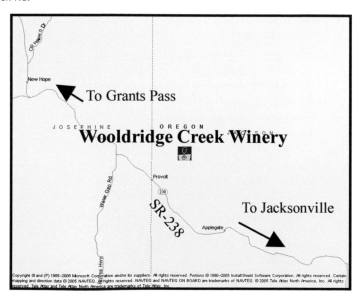

John Michael Champagne Cellars 6

John Michael Champagne Cellars is a boutique winery producing various champagnes and still wines. The tasting room is located on the vineyard side of the property, offering a spectacular view of Applegate Valley and Grayback Mountain. John Michael's specialty is "sparklers," and visitors can enjoy a number of sparkling surprises, including sparkling sake. Sparkling sake? Yep, and there's more. How about its sparkling Blanc de Blanc? Clearly, John Michael Champagne Cellars is a distinctive stop along the Applegate Valley WineTrail.

Situated on a bench bordering Humbug Creek Road (love that name), John Michael Champagne Cellars features a vineyard of neatly kept rows of premium grapes and the Giudici family home, which doubles as a winery/tasting room. Open 11 a.m. to 5 p.m. Friday through Sunday, the tasting room also features a hand-blown glass gallery. Check out the sconces gracing the walls.

Michael Giudici, John Michael Champagne Cellars' owner/winemaker, produces a full range of sparkling and still wines. But as his awards attest, he is most renowned for his wines of the sparkling variety. WineTrail enthusiasts can sample his product at a great price — for free.

The winery is available for weddings and special events. And, if you're lucky enough to host an event here, you won't have far to go to purchase your sparkling wine!

JOHN MICHAEL CHAMPAGNE CELLARS
winemaker(s): Michael Giudici
location: 1425 Humbug Creek Road,
Applegate, OR 97530
phone: 541-846-0810
web: None
picnic area: Yes
weddings: Yes
fee: Complimentary wine tasting
hours: Friday through Sunday 11–5

DIRECTIONS: **From Jacksonville** take SR-238 [Jacksonville Hwy] 13.8 miles heading west. Keep right onto Humbug Creek Rd and go 1 mile. Look for signs to the winery on your right.

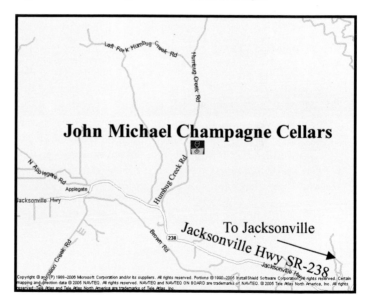

Devitt Winery 7

In early 2000, Jim and Sue Devitt came north from Napa to the Applegate Valley, following a successful winemaking career. They were looking for property with the intent to retire and found land in the spectacular Applegate Valley. They purchased some farm acreage where they could also grow grapes. Soon, with the acquisition of some nearby property, their initial 12-acre vineyard morphed into more than 20 acres. They just wanted to grow and sell grapes. However, in 2003, the market for selling grapes cooled, and they had a big problem: What were they to do with all those grapes? When Jim

approached Sue with the idea of making wine again, she retorted, "When pigs fly!"

Within a year, they got their license, built the winery and tasting room, and opened their doors in July 2004 with their first vintage, pinot gris. Of course, the "pigs fly" comment gave them a natural theme and brand to distinguish their winery. Outside the winery, a winged-pig statue and a pig windsock with rotating wings welcome visitors and loyal fans. Inside the tasting room, visitors taste wine from a full line-up of reds and whites, including some labeled with the image of flying pigs.

Using certified sustainable grapes, Jim makes small lots (usually fewer than 200 cases) of chardonnay, viognier, a syrah blush, merlot, cabernet franc, cabernet sauvignon, syrah, and a dessert wine with the name Le Petite Oink. At an annual production of 2,000 cases, most Devitt wines sell at the winery and select retail and restaurants in the Rogue Valley. In the friendly tasting room, Devitt wine samples are complimentary. My personal favorite was a red wine called Precipice — a blend of merlot and zinfandel from the Devitts' Old Stage Vineyards. Ready to drink, this red table wine would be a perfect match for pasta with marinara sauce, anything grilled or simply because it's Tuesday (or Thursday). At only $16 a bottle, it's a steal.

The phrase "If pigs could fly" reflects wishful thinking about something that can never happen. Fortunately, for us, in the case of Devitt Winery, pigs do fly. Oink!

DEVITT WINERY
opened: 2003
winemaker(s): Jim Devitt
location: 11412 Highway 238,
Jacksonville, OR 97530
phone: 541-899-7511
web: www.devittwinery.com
e-mail: james@devittwinery.com
picnic area: Yes
wheelchair access: Yes
tours: Yes
fee: Complimentary wine tasting
hours: Daily 11–7

DIRECTIONS: **From I-5 Grants Pass south**, take the old town exit and stay on this street through Grants Pass. Name changes to Hwy 238. Go 22 miles to the winery (between mile marker 21 & 22).

From Jacksonville take SR-238 [Jacksonville Hwy] west 11.4 miles, looking for signs to the winery. Arrive at 11412 Hwy 238.

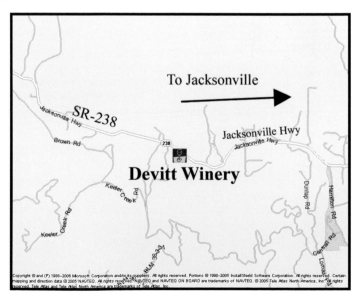

Jacksonville Vineyards 🔢

Two miles west of Ruch township in Applegate Valley lies Jacksonville Vineyards, where visitors find amazing gardens, great wine, one happy dog, and a property rich in Oregon history. Located off Highway 238, the gravel road ascends to the estate, where 100 years before, a man in his mid-20s homesteaded the property, building his home by hand. It still stands today. His name was William Matney — one of 17 children — and he must

David Palmer

have been a skilled craftsman and remarkable farmer. Today, the owners of the former homestead, David and Pamela Palmer, honor William Matney's legacy through their restoration and maintenance of the property.

Prior to acquiring the property some 20 years ago, David and Pamela traveled the world and visited the great wineries of France, Italy, and Australia. David's job as a pilot for FedEx certainly came in handy for traveling to distant lands. While touring, they picked up a serious wine bug and eventually found a cure for their wine fever in the Applegate Valley.

With blooming gardens and the home's classic architecture, the Palmers have succeeded in creating an Oregon-style winery villa. David happened to be there to greet us in the parking lot, and after an exchange of "hellos" it quickly became apparent that he's a jack of all trades — restoring the home, managing the vineyard, making wine, and keeping his energetic Australian shepherd, Brix, entertained. However, before you feel sorry for a guy who might appear overworked, understand that he wouldn't have it any other way.

When it comes to winemaking, David relies on extra aging (as long as two years) in 100 percent French oak barrels to create beautiful, full-bodied reds, including cabernet sauvignon, merlot, and a true Bordeaux-style blend of cabernet sauvignon, merlot, cabernet franc, and Malbec. He honors the past with an image of a Jacksonville pioneer on the label. Although Jacksonville Vineyards' focus is on reds, David also makes a silky chardonnay. Interestingly, the old-fashioned corset-dressed mannequin pictured on this wine's label actually resides in the tasting room!

Before leaving, don't forget to have your camera handy for some memorable shots. The massive tree on the side of property is one of the largest madrone trees in southern Oregon. Equally impressive is the set of gigantic handmade doors leading into the barrel room and winery. But be sure you snap a picture of David Palmer, whose passion for the vineyard and the history of this property is just as immense.

JACKSONVILLE VINEYARDS
opened: 2005
winemaker(s): David Palmer
location: 9730 Highway. 238,
Jacksonville, OR 97530
phone: 541-899-6923
web: www.jacksonvillevineyards.com
e-mail: wine@jacksonvillevineyards.com
picnic area: Yes
wheelchair access: Yes
weddings: Yes
fee: Complimentary wine tasting
hours: Wednesday through Monday 11–5; Closed
January and February

DIRECTIONS: **Heading southbound on I-5** at Grants Pass take exit 55 toward US-199/Redwood Hwy/
Oregon Caves. Proceed on US-199 [Grants Pass Pkwy.] 2.3 miles. Turn left (south) onto SR-238
[Williams Hwy] and go 13.3 miles. Road name changes to Jacksonville Hwy [SR-238]. Proceed 9.6
miles and arrive at Jacksonville Vineyards.

From downtown Jacksonville take Hwy 238 12 miles west toward the Applegate Valley. Follow the
blue signs marking the gravel lane entrance to Jacksonville Vineyards.

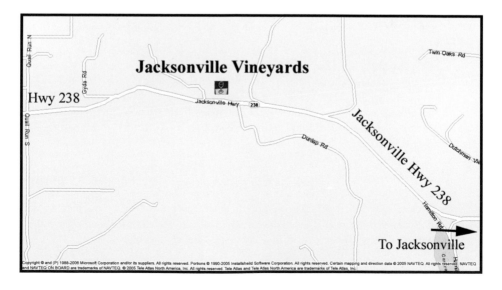

Fiasco Winery ⑨

Fiasco Winery is a second label winery of nearby Jacksonville Vineyards. However, don't mistake these wines for "second tier." Rather, think of Fiasco Winery's Italian-style wines as drinkable by themselves or paired with pasta or anything off the grill for that matter. Located right off Highway 238 in the Applegate Valley, the winery has some eye-catching signage and an attractive building that get your attention from the road. Fiasco is a convenient pit stop and a surprising find.

Owned by David and Pamela Palmer, Fiasco Winery is Pam's daily domain. You can find her pouring wine, entertaining guests, and probably explaining for the umpteenth time why they named the winery "Fiasco." **(WineTrail note:** As David explained to me, "fiasco" is a French term referring to a stage play gone bad. Of Italian origin, the word describes blown glass that easily breaks. We can only surmise that the Italian glass related to wine bottles.)

David, the human equivalent of the "Energizer Bunny", built the Fiasco Winery tasting room in less than a year. The stylish tasting room features plenty of light, a sand-covered floor, vintage posters, infused vinegars, and plenty of Fiasco wine to taste. Pam and David celebrate the fact that their 18 acres of vineyards produce cabernet sauvignon, merlot, cabernet franc, sangiovese, zinfandel, syrah, and a bit of nebbiolo, dolcetto, Malbec, tempranillo, and viognier. This full pallet of varietals gives David and Pam winemaking license to create wines specifically for Fiasco.

Prior to relocating to the Applegate Valley with David, Pam worked as a dental hygienist cleaning teeth. Now, she sees her role as staining teeth — but in the very best way. Her background includes considerable exposure to other wine-growing regions including France, Italy, and Australia. This experience gave her first-hand knowledge on what makes for a memorable winery visit — in addition to her naturally friendly self.

The winery offers picnic tables both inside and out for taking time to enjoy a glass (or two) of wine. In this amiable setting, fiasco is a good thing.

Pam Palmer

FIASCO WINERY
opened: 2008
winemaker(s): Pam and David Palmer
location: 8035 Highway 238, Ruch, OR 97530
phone: 541-899-6923
web: www.fiascowinery.com
e-mail: wine@fiascowinery.com
picnic area: Yes
wheelchair access: Yes
gift shop: Yes
fee: Complimentary wine tasting
hours: Tuesday through Sunday 11–5; closed January

DIRECTIONS: **From Grants Pass** take US-199 [SR-99] south 1.3 miles. Keep left onto SR-238 [Williams Hwy], go 7.5 miles, and arrive at Fiasco Winery.

From Jacksonville take SR-238 [Jacksonville Hwy] west 19.3 miles. Bear right (north) onto SR-238 [Williams Hwy], continue 5.8 miles, and look for signs to Fiasco Winery.

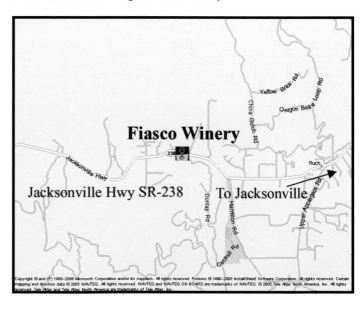

LongSword Vineyard

Located eight miles west of Jacksonville, right off Highway 238, LongSword Vineyard is one winery where visitors might end up with a stiff neck. At this remarkable winery, the "tasting room" is an outdoor patio, complete with deck furniture, nestled against the 22-acre LongSword vineyard. While drinking a glass of LongSword signature non-oaked chardonnay and noshing on the boxed-lunch special, I couldn't help but notice colorful objects gliding through the sky. As the objects came into focus, Maria Largaespada (co-owner and vintner of LongSword Vineyard, along with her husband, Matthew Sorensen) noted that they were paragliders coming off nearby Woodrat Mountain. Maria and Matthew came from Indianapolis in 1999 to pursue a dream. They had both worked in the pharmaceutical business most of their adult lives. One day Maria turned to Matthew and asked him what he would rather be doing. His response: growing grapes and making fine wine. After that, it was "goodbye, cubicle" and "hello, Applegate Valley."

While a guitarist played in the background I listened to Maria, and sensed a lively energy emanating from her smiling face. I concluded that the move to Applegate Valley must have rekindled her spirit and body. When you work 22 acres of vineyards, "you don't need a gym membership or a psychologist," she explained.

I asked about the origin of her last name, "Largaespada," and she replied that it is Spanish for "long" (*larga*) and "sword" (*espada*). Hence the name LongSword Vineyard. As I was finishing my crisp chardonnay, Matthew walked over with a sample of their Touché Rosé. Like Maria, he enjoys a very youthful appearance, yet both had punched the clock for more than 20 years in the pharmaceutical industry before relocating to Oregon. Perhaps Applegate has a fountain of youth… Whatever the reason for their youthfulness, it's clear that Maria and Matthew live by the motto "Life is too short to drink bad wine."

Both of them believe that fine wine is made in the vineyard. They and the other winery owners have plans to break ground soon on a new tasting room and to plant tempranillo to go along with the existing chardonnay, dolcetto, and syrah. However, I didn't get the sense that they wished to grow too big. They still want to take time to work the farm, greet visitors, and enjoy their hobbies — perhaps a parasailing flight or two off Woodrat Mountain?

LONGSWORD VINEYARD
winemaker(s): Matthew Sorensen and
Maria Largaespada
location: 8555 Highway 238, Jacksonville, OR 97530
phone: 541-899-1746
web: www.longswordvineyard.com
e-mail: info@longswordvineyard.com
picnic area: Yes;
wheelchair access: Yes
tours: Yes
fee: Complimentary wine tasting
hours: Daily 12-5 from May through October,
or by appointment

Maria Largaespada and Matthew Sorensen

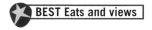

BEST Eats and views

DIRECTIONS: **LongSword Vineyard is located** 8 miles west of Jacksonville, and 1 mile west of Ruch on Hwy 238, between mile markers 25 and 26, on the south side of the highway. Look for the blue sign for LongSword Vineyard on Hwy 238.

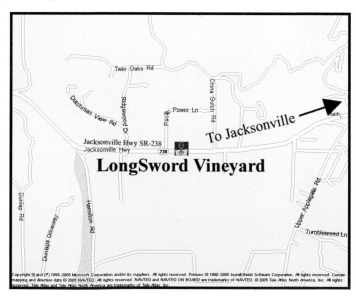

Valley View Winery 🔟🔟

Valley View Winery, in the Applegate Valley, defines tradition. The winery's name was retained from the original Valley View Winery, founded by pioneer Peter Britt in the mid-1800s. He's the same Peter Britt whom the hugely popular Britt Music Festival honors.

The father of current owners Ann, Mike, and Mark Wisnovsky moved west from the East Coast in the early 1970s. In 1972 he planted 12 acres of premium wine grapes, creating one of the earliest vineyards in Oregon. A few years later, the Wisnovsky family obtained a license to sell wine, and the tasting room officially opened in 1978. Now, 30 years

later, the remodeled tasting room offers plenty of space to accommodate wine tasters, a well-stocked gift shop, and lots of elbow room for guests attending the winery's many events; hence the room's name "The Pavilion."

Valley View Winery has the distinction of employing one of the longest-tenured winemakers in Oregon; John Guerrero has been at its winemaking helm since 1985. With its case production around 7,000 per year, it's interesting that the volume of Valley View wine produced is half that of the year 2000, when it produced 14,000 cases annually. However, consumer taste has moved toward finer wines, and the owners have adjusted to meet those demands. To this end, Valley View Winery produces a number of wines under its flagship label, Anna Maria Wines, named after the Wisnovskys' mother. Although the winery produces a number of different wines, including dessert and port-style wines, it concentrates on cabernet sauvignon, merlot, viognier, syrah, and tempranillo.

The spacious Pavilion provides an inviting place in which to pace yourself as you work through the many reds and whites. In between samples, take time to explore one of the finest winery gift shops in Oregon.

However, if you do escape the Pavilion to the great outdoors, consider grabbing a picnic table on the generous grounds. You'll find the perfect spot for viewing the surrounding hills and estate vineyard. It's also a great location to reflect on family and history. The current generation of Wisnovskys honors the history of the valley and the legacy of their parents. It's one thing to read about the concept of family roots on the Web or in a magazine article, but it's quite another to experience this tradition in person. There's much to gain by a visit to Valley View Winery; put it on your list of must-see wineries.

VALLEY VIEW WINERY
opened: 1978
winemaker(s): John F. Guerrero
location: 1000 Upper Applegate Road,
Jacksonville, OR 97530
phone: 541-899-8468
web: www.valleyviewwinery.com
e-mail: valleyviewwinery@charter.net
picnic area: Yes
weddings: Yes
gift shop: Yes
fee: Small tasting fee may apply
hours: Daily 11–5; closed Thanksgiving, Christmas,
and New Year's Day

BEST Gift shop and views

DIRECTIONS: The winery/tasting room at 1000 Upper Applegate Rd is 8 miles southwest of Jacksonville, just off Hwy 238.

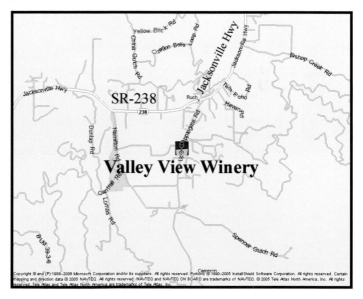

Cricket Hill Vineyard and Winery 🄬

"Great wines have special character — they're as different as a face. There's a bland sameness to large commercial wines that isn't in step with our philosophy of winemaking," responded Duane Bowman, Cricket Hill's winemaker, to my question about his winemaking style. "I want to make wine that expresses the unique attributes of this land and I want a vintage to mean something — to be different from the year before so it reflects Mother Nature's gift for that year," he concluded.

Duane and his wife, Kathy, the owners and entire operation staff, spent considerable time exploring Napa Valley in the 1980s — back before Napa became overcrowded. Then,

they could take the time to visit with the winemakers and develop an unabashed joy for wines. As payback, he does the same for visitors to Cricket Hill.

He learned winemaking through selected University of California–Davis classes plus trips to France. When the time came he and Kathy decided to jettison the academic and make the wines they had grown to love. They joined early area vineyard pioneers, choosing the Applegate Valley for its match against the soils and climate of Bordeaux, France — where they produced his personal favorite wines.

The couple chose the name "Cricket Hill" to underscore the fact that, although the vineyard is small, the grapes it produces have uniquely intense, full flavors, much like a small cricket with a loud chirp. "Struggling hillside vines are known to produce the best wines," Duane said.

On that special hillside they planted merlot and cabernet franc, clones of these grapes especially selected and imported from France because of the quality of the wines they make. He's installed birdhouses throughout the vineyard to attract "insectivore" populations saying that "the more work Mother Nature does, the less for me to do," so he farms the site with the help of the birds and beneficial insects — using no pesticides.

Duane practices the winemaker's art of blending wines, and notes, "Drinking straight varietals is like cooking without seasoning." His wines can be not only a blend of varietals, but even different vintages. Blends are done to his taste and like a chef he works around the particular attributes of the ingredients. Each Cricket Hill wine expresses a unique flavor profile. It gets back to that point about "sameness" that Duane first mentioned when I arrived. He wants you to swirl, sip and exclaim, "That's special!" To him, that's praise as melodic as a cricket's song.

Duane Bowman

CRICKET HILL VINEYARD AND WINERY
opened: 1991
winemaker(s): Duane Bowman
location: 2131 Little Applegate Road,
Jacksonville, OR 97530
phone: 541-899-7264
web: www.crickethillwinery.com
e-mail: DBowman@bmi.net
fee: Complimentary wine tasting
hours: Weekends 12–5 through September or
by appointment

DIRECTIONS: **From Jacksonville** take SR-238 [Jacksonville Hwy] west 7.5 miles. Turn left (south) onto Upper Applegate Rd and go 2.8 miles. Bear left (southeast) onto Little Applegate Rd and proceed 2.1 miles to the winery.

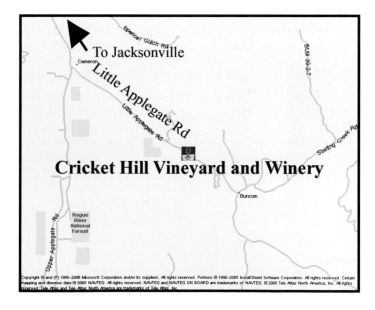

Cowhorn Vineyard & Garden ⒔

Cowhorn Vineyard & Garden is all about respect for the land and sustainability. From the use of multiple crops to a rejection of pesticides, herbicides and fertilizers owners Bill and Barbara Steele are earth-friendly to the core. Everything on the farm is recycled; there is no waste. This was the first winery in southern Oregon to achieve both biodynamic and organic certifications, which in the world of winegrowing means you've gone totally green.

Bill and Barbara Steele

It wasn't easy for the Steeles to get to this point. When they acquired the property in 2002, its 117 acres were in disarray, with weeds and blackberry bushes everywhere. All of it required clearing and the installation of three miles of fencing to keep out the deer, bears, cougars, and coyotes. The surrounding deer fence protects the grapes and keeps out animals that tend to menace dogs. It was hard work, but never for a minute have Bill and Barbara regretted leaving their corporate jobs: He was a Wall Street analyst, and she was a chief financial officer. From pinstripes to overalls, they made the transition.

The couple grows five grape varietals originating in France's Rhône region: syrah, grenache, viognier, roussanne, and marsanne. Bill noted that they would love to visit the Rhône region of France at some point. However, the daily demands of their farm require their attention now. In addition to 11 acres of grapes, they have planted asparagus, hazelnut and cherry trees, and black truffles, in keeping with their biodynamic philosophy of diversity. The "Garden" part of their establishment's name is well-considered. One plant just can't create a desired ecosystem; biodynamics takes a holistic approach to growing grapes and making wine.

For winemaking, Bill assumes the role as "assistant to the grape." To that end, the Steeles built an advanced wine production facility to control each step of the process and to ensure that their wines are organic. As they note on their website, "Habitat preservation, water conservation, and the well-being of the Earth factor in to each decision we make. We have stewardship of this landscape and consider it our responsibility and privilege to foster its health and strength."

They take their cues from the wisdom of nature, a sageness evident in the soul-nurturing wines they produce.

COWHORN VINEYARD & GARDEN
opened: 2008
winemaker(s): Bill Steele
location: 1665 Eastside Road, Jacksonville, OR 97530
phone: 541-899-6876
web: www.cowhornwine.com
e-mail: Bill@cowhornwine.com
picnic area: Yes
fee: $5 tasting fee for 5 wines waived with the purchase of 6 bottles
hours: Daily 11–4

DIRECTIONS: **From Jacksonville** take SR-238 [Jacksonville Hwy] 7.1 miles heading west. Turn left (south) onto Upper Applegate Rd and continue 4.4 miles. Keep straight onto Eastside Rd and proceed 1.2 miles to Cowhorn Vineyard & Garden on the left.

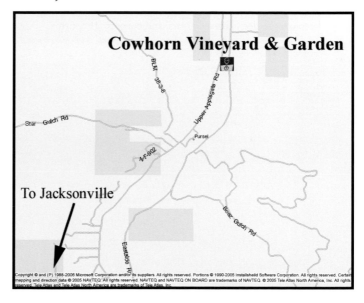

Illinois Valley
Wine Trail

Deer Creek Vineyards

Pluck out the map before venturing to the Illinois Valley Wine Trail. Yes, you need to know that the quickest way there is through Grants Pass, but Wine Trail adventurers also need to see the proximity of the Illinois Valley to the Pacific Ocean. Of the Rogue's wine-growing valleys, the Illinois Valley is the coolest in temperature. Translation: get ready to enjoy cool-weather grapes.

Given the cool climes and the size of their vineyards, it's little wonder that Bridgeview Vineyards is one of the state's largest producers of pinot noir, pinot gris, and riesling. But it would be a mistake for visitors to believe that all the wines they will experience are of the cool weather variety. Both Bridgeview Vineyards and Foris Vineyards Winery produce a host of other Bordeaux and Rhone style varieties. However, all four wineries that are part of the Illinois Valley Wine Trail (the three aforementioned plus Windridge Vineyard) produce pinot noir. Your challenge, dear Wine Trail trekker, is to sample their pinot noir and compare it to those of the Willamette Valley or other wine-growing regions of the world that your tongue is familiar with.

Illinois Valley WineTrail

1 Deer Creek Vineyards
2 Windridge Vineyard

3 Bridgeview Vineyards & Winery
4 Foris Vineyards Winery

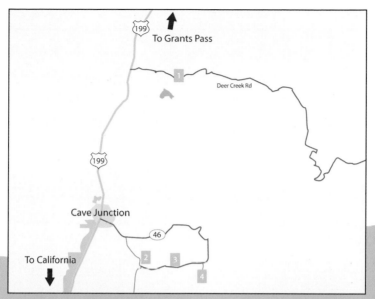

Region:	**Rogue Valley Wine Country**
# of tasting rooms on tour:	**4**
Estimate # of days for tour:	**1**
Getting around:	**Car or bike**
Key Events:	❑ **Running from late February until early November, Ashland's Oregon Shakespeare Festival – see www.osfashland.org or call 541-482-4331.**
	❑ **In May, Medford's Art in Bloom Festival – call 541-608-8524 or visit www.visitmedford.org.**
	❑ **From June to September, Jacksonville's Britt Festival – call 541-779-0847 or visit www.brittfest.org.**
Tips:	❑ **Visit nearby Oregon Caves National Monument.**
	❑ **Drive into California and check out the Redwoods – must see.**
	❑ **Consider hiring a limousine service such as Ashland Wine Tours, 541-552-WINE (9463) or Jules of the Valley Wine Tours, 541-973-9699.**
	❑ **Many excellent restaurants to choose from – Monet, Chateaulin, Amuse, New Sammy's Cowboy Bistro (Talent) or Lela's Cafe to name some.**
	❑ **Excellent overnight accommodations including – Ashland Springs Hotel, Ashland's Inn and Garden Springs at Lithia Springs and the TouVelle House Bed and Breakfast in Jacksonville.**

 Best: ❑ **Lodging: Bridgeview Vineyards & Winery.**

Deer Creek Vineyards **1**

For Sale — *70.47 acres in southern Oregon's Illinois Valley; 3-bedroom home; 30 acres of vineyards; 1,024-square-foot tasting room; large winery facility; shop or barn; water rights; 2 ponds; 2 wells and beautiful panoramic view. Property also includes grazing pastures and hay production. Asking $2.25 million.*

Every once in a while, I come across a winery on the selling block. Typically, it's the other way around: The wineries I visit often have new owners — many of them recent immigrants to Oregon — who have brought a renewed energy to the business. However, my visit to Deer Creek Vineyard uncovered the opposite situation. In this case, the current owners, Gary and Ann Garnett, were hoping to sell the vineyard and move to their existing residence in Arizona.

The lucky buyer will inherit a turnkey operation. After considerable work, Gary and Ann converted a derelict farm into prime real estate, complete with well-manicured grounds, 30 acres of chardonnay, pinot gris, and pinot noir vines, a large production facility, and a view to die for. Not only that, the new owner will also acquire an established brand — the Deer Creek Vineyards label — in the deal. At 8,000 cases annually, the new proprietor won't be starting from scratch. He or she can join in the bottling line on day one.

When asked about making wine in Arizona, Ann laughed and remarked that their goal is to retire. They have places to see and friends to visit. They wish to fill their days having time to relax, rather than working sunup to sundown. I suspect that they will maintain a private stash of Deer Creek Vineyard wine for an evening glass or two in the Arizona desert.

DEER CREEK VINEYARDS
winemaker(s): Steve Harriman
location: 2680 Deer Creek Road, Selma, OR 97583
phone: 541-597-4226
web: www.deercreekvineyards.com
picnic area: Yes
wheelchair access: Yes
gift shop: Yes
fee: Complimentary wine tasting
hours: Daily 11–5

DIRECTIONS: **From Grants Pass**, take US-199 [Redwood Hwy] south about 20 miles to Selma. Turn left (east) onto Deer Creek Rd and travel 2.7 mile to Deer Creek Vineyards on your left.

From Cave Junction, take US-199 [Redwood Hwy] north for 8.6 miles. Turn right (east) onto Deer Creek Rd and go 2.7 miles to the winery on your left.

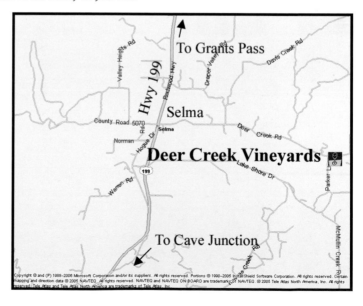

435

Windridge Vineyard 2

Terry and Cate Bendock came from Alaska to southern Oregon to retire. However, the decision to move to Oregon's Illinois Valley was two years in the making. During that time, the Bendocks looked from British Columbia to northern California for a place that met their relocation criteria. In Alaska, Terry worked as a fisherman biologist, and Cate was a public school teacher. They were ready for a warmer clime with plenty of space to

garden and give their chocolate Chesapeake Bay retriever, Willow, room to run. Luck was with them.

They purchased a 50-acre former thoroughbred farm in 1998. Located near the California border, the area is warmer than the Willamette Valley, yet at 1,400 feet in elevation, it cools off significantly at night. With Cate's penchant for growing things and Terry's biological background, it wasn't long before they converted 8 acres of land into pinot noir plantings; more recently they added pinot blanc. Visitors this far south might be a little surprised to see pinot noir, but the marine air and cool nights result in perfect growing conditions.

At Windridge Vineyard, visitors experience pinot noir under the Bendock label. For convenience, the Bendocks make their wine at nearby Foris Vineyards Winery. However, visitors to Windridge Vineyard are also treated to other local wines such as Daisy Creek and Madrone Mountains. Carrying the spirit of cooperation further, Terry and Cate also are members of the renegade Rogue Appellation Garagiste Society (RAGS) — a not-so-secret gathering of small wineries and visitors who celebrate life, wine, and good food. Please visit www.windridgevineyard.com for event information.

This part of the Siskiyou Mountains offers unusual geology and flora. Here, for example, you will find unique serpentine soil and carnivorous pitcher plants that you won't find anywhere else. It's a biologist's dream, and goes a long way toward explaining Terry's tagging of many of Windridge Vineyard property's trees, each sporting a label with its biological name. Just like a scientist. Now, he has something else to label — genus Bendock Pinot Noir.

WINDRIDGE VINEYARD
opened: 2001
winemaker(s): Terry and Cate Bendock
location: 2789 Holland Loop Road,
Cave Junction, OR 97523
phone: 541-592-5333
web: www.windridgevineyard.com
e-mail: bendock@frontiernet.net
picnic area: Yes
fee: Complimentary wine tasting
hours: Saturday and Sunday 11–5 February through
April; Wednesday through Sunday 11–5 April through
October; Saturday and Sunday 11–5 in November;
closed December and January

Cate Bendock

DIRECTIONS: **From Grants Pass** take US-199 [Redwood Hwy] about 30 miles traveling south. Turn left (east) onto SR-46 [Caves Hwy] and proceed 1.8 miles. Turn right (south) onto Holland Loop Rd and proceed 1 mile to Windridge Vineyard on left.

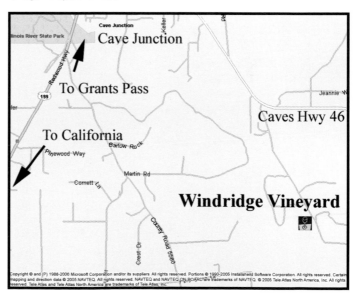

Bridgeview Vineyards & Winery 3

Bridgeview Vineyards & Winery's famed Blue Moon Riesling speaks volumes about this remarkable winery near Cave Junction. The fact that this wine comes in a blue bottle reflects some of the maverick character of founders and owners Bob and Lelo Kerivan. They do things differently. Bob and Lelo moved from Miami in the 1980s and converted a 75-acre parcel into vineyards of chardonnay, pinot noir, pinot gris, riesling, and gewürztraminer. People thought Bob was crazy for growing premium wine grapes in

Illinois Valley, but years later Bridgeview's significant number of awards and accolades have proven the naysayers wrong.

The Blue Moon Riesling is less than $10 a bottle. In fact, all of their Blue Moon collection of wines — including chardonnay, pinot gris, cabernet sauvignon, and merlot — are priced around $10; the one exception is the pinot noir, which still goes for less than $20. The Kerivans laugh at the idea that some people spend $100 for a bottle of wine. Their reasoning is that they wouldn't spend such exorbitant amounts, so why would they charge that much for their wines.

They also produce cabernet sauvignon, merlot, syrah, and a red-blend wine under their Black Beauty label. In addition, they make other premium and specialty wines, such as dessert, port-style and sparkling wines. Under the winemaking direction of Lelo's son René Eichmann, Bridgeview's production has grown to more than 85,000 cases per year, putting the winery in the top echelon of Oregon winery producers.

Today, Bridgeview Vineyards & Winery manages roughly 200 acres of grapes in Illinois Valley, in addition to 80 acres in Applegate Valley. Whereas Illinois Valley produces cool-weather grapes such as riesling and pinot noir, the Applegate vineyards generate Bordeaux-style grapes such as merlot and cabernet sauvignon. Because of the high numbers of wine tourists visiting the Applegate WineTrail, in 2004 Bridgeview opened a satellite tasting room in a distinguished red barn on North Applegate Road. **WineTrail tip:** If visiting Illinois Valley, consider staying at the Kerbyville Inn. Owned by the Kerivans, it has four wine-themed suites, two with spas, and a guest room, all with private entrances and bathrooms.

Despite the fact that Bridgeview Vineyards & Winery is off the beaten wine tour path, thousands of visitors stop at the Kerivans' Cave Junction tasting room every year. Drawn by the winery's manicured grounds and pristine lake, wine tourists come for the great values and, of course, those beautiful blue bottles.

BRIDGEVIEW VINEYARDS & WINERY
opened: 1986
winemaker(s): René Eichmann
location: 4210 Holland Loop Road, Cave Junction, OR 97523
phone: 541-592-4688
web: www.bridgeviewwine.com
e-mail: bvw@bridgeviewwine.com
picnic area: Yes
wheelchair access: Yes
gift shop: Yes
fee: Complimentary wine tasting
hours: Daily 11–5

 **BEST Lodging**

DIRECTIONS: **From the Coast** travel north on Hwy 199 east to Cave Junction. Turn right on Caves Highway [Hwy 46] toward the Oregon Caves. Follow Caves Highway east 1.7 miles. Turn right on Holland Loop Rd and continue approximately 2 miles. Bridgeview is located at 4210 Holland Loop Rd.

From I-5, exit at Grants Pass exit 55 or 58 and take the 199 Redwood Hwy west to Cave Junction. Turn left onto Caves Highway [Hwy 46] towards the Oregon Caves. Follow Caves Highway East 1.7 miles and turn right on Holland Loop Rd. Continue 2 miles to destination.

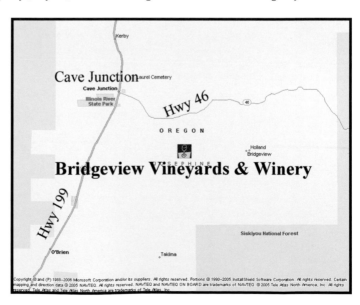

Foris Vineyards Winery 4

Ted Gerber had a great reason for choosing the name Foris Vineyards Winery for his enterprise. Foris is Latin for "outdoors," and a visit to this part of Illinois Valley, close to the Siskiyou mountain range, reveals why. It's beautiful. Being the southernmost winery in

Oregon, Foris is a short drive to California's redwood forests, Oregon's coast, and the amazing Oregon Caves National Monument — all very scenic destinations.

Foris Vineyards Winery boasts three individual vineyards: Gerber, Maple Ranch, and Three Creeks Ranch vineyards. Together these three vineyards comprise 115 acres of premium wine grapes. The westernmost Gerber Vineyard is just 25 miles due east of the Oregon coast. Here, the rainfall is close to 60 inches per year, but during the growing season, it's relatively dry. The *terroir* is ideal for pinot noir, gewürztraminer, pinot gris, chardonnay, pinot blanc, early muscat, and gamay noir.

In my research prior to my visit, I uncovered the fact that Foris Vineyards Winery produces a host of wines under the direction of experienced winemaker Bryan Wilson. I was eager to try Foris' number-one seller, Fly Over Red, a blend of cabernet sauvignon, merlot and cabernet franc. I skipped over the whites and went right to this popular red blend. While relishing my sip of Fly Over Red, our tasting room host explained that Ted named the wine after California wine snobs who fly over his winery to get to the Willamette Valley. This tongue-in-cheek name reflects the joyful spirits of Ted and his wife, Teresa. They like to have fun, and their many celebratory wine events throughout the year reflect this.

In keeping with the outdoor theme, a couple of wine bottles sporting cougar- and cave-bear-adorned labels caught my eye. They are part of the Wildlife series produced at Foris Vineyards Winery. Proceeds from these wine sales benefit Wildlife Images Rehabilitation Center, located in Grants Pass. A worthy cause.

Since 1986, Ted has made wine under the Foris Vineyards Winery label. Year after year, vintage after vintage, he has seen it all. Throughout the years, his commitment to the spirit of the land comes through in the taste of his wines. We think of wine as a complement to food and music, but he's proven that it pairs wonderfully with the beauty of the outdoors. It's just too bad that those flying over are blowing their chance to experience this great wine.

FORIS VINEYARDS WINERY
opened: 1987
winemaker(s): Bryan Wilson
location: 654 Kendall Road, Cave Junction, OR 97523
phone: 541-592-3752
web: www.foriswine.com
e-mail: foris@foriswine.com
picnic area: Yes
wheelchair access: Yes
tours: Yes
fee: Complimentary wine tasting
hours: Daily 11–5 except some holidays

DIRECTIONS: **From Cave Junction** go east on SR-46 [Caves Hwy] for 1.8 miles. Turn right (south) onto Holland Loop Rd and proceed 5.3 miles. Turn right (south) onto Kendall Rd and go 1.8 miles. Arrive at 654 Kendall Rd.

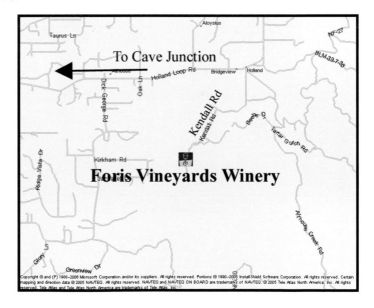

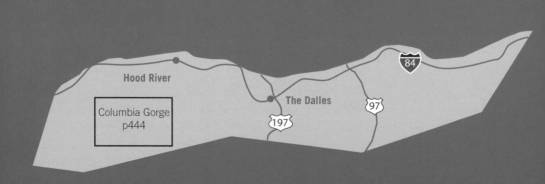

Hood River

Columbia Gorge
p444

The Dalles

84

197

97

Columbia Gorge
WINE COUNTRY

Columbia Gorge
WineTrail

Hood River Area

Going east from Portland, the Columbia Gorge WineTrail takes you through the territory made famous by Lewis and Clark. However, the Columbia River is far tamer now than what they experienced in the fall of 1805. Today, we have plenty of windsurfers, destination resorts, vineyards, and wineries to experience. Your tour will introduce you to wineries with names like Springhouse Cellar Winery, Naked Winery, Cathedral Ridge Winery, Phelps Creek Vineyards, Bolton Cellars, and Erin Glenn Winery. For the most part the wineries are located in Hood River, with a few residing to the east in The Dalles.

WineTrail Tip #1: there are four tasting rooms in Hood River's town center. Simply park the car and plan on stretching your legs.

In between wine tasting, there are inviting spots for sleeping, such as the Columbia Gorge Hotel, the Hood River Hotel, the Oak Street Hotel, and the Inn at the Gorge B&B. For eats, Hood River offers plenty of tummy-filling choices. Check out Brian's Pourhouse, Stonehedge Gardens, The North Oak Brasserie, or Celilo Restaurant & Bar. All offer great fare with select wines.

WineTrail Tip #2: limited time? Go to the Gorge White House to sample and purchase wine from throughout the Columbia Gorge — both Washington and Oregon. See www.thegorgewhitehouse.com.

Columbia Gorge WineTrail

1 Naked Winery
2 Springhouse Cellar Winery
3 Quenett Winery
4 The Pines 1852
5 Cathedral Ridge Winery

6 Hood River Vineyards
7 Phelps Creek Vineyards
8 Pheasant Valley Winery
9 Wy'East Vineyards
10 Mt. Hood Winery

11 Bolton Cellars
12 Erin Glenn Winery
13 Wheatridge in the Nook

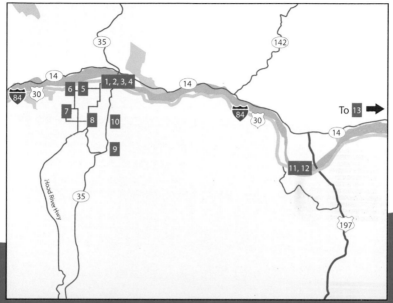

Region:	**Columbia Gorge Wine Country**
# of tasting rooms on tour:	**13**
Estimate # of days for tour:	**3**
Getting around:	**Car, bike and foot**
Key Events:	❑ **Memorial Day Weekend Open House – call 1-866-413-WINE or see columbiagorgewine.com.**
	❑ **In August, Columbia Gorge Wine Celebration – See www.columbiagorgewine.com for details.**
	❑ **Thanksgiving Weekend Open House – call 1-866-413-WINE or see columbiagorgewine.com.**
Tips:	❑ **Enjoy live music Friday nights at Erin Glenn Winery.**
	❑ **Cross over the bridge to Washington and check out Maryhill Museum and Stonehedge Replica near Maryhill Winery.**
	❑ **Limited time? Visit The Gorge White House outside Hood River and Hwy 35 where wines of the Columbia Gorge await your tasting.**
	❑ **Consider using a limousine service – My Chauffeur Wine Tours – 877-692-4283, winetour@winetouroregon.com, www.winetouroregon.com and Oregon Wine Tours 503-681-WINE (9463) www.orwinetours.com.**

 Best: ❑ **Eats: Erin Glenn Winery.**
❑ **Gift shop, lodging and views: Pheasant Valley Winery.**

445

Naked Winery ■

Clothing's optional figuratively speaking of course.

It wasn't a chance encounter that brought Dave Michalec and David and Jody Barringer together around the turn of the millennium. Turns out the Barringers, with children in tow, escaped the big city for the more bucolic setting of the Hood River area and they needed a real estate agent. Enter Dave, a local real estate agent who showed them a property that became the Barringers' new home. The fact that the property had some neglected premium grape vines got them talking about their love for the fruit of the vine,

one thing led to another and eventually Naked Winery was born.

"Why the name Naked Winery?"
I asked.

"Because we aim to tease," responded Dave. At this point, David chimed in with a philosophical point about putting romance back into wine. Indeed, we think of pairing wine with food, music, and good friends, but wine pairing with sex? Absolutely! There are probably a fair number of babies born every day that are conceived with the help of cabernet sauvignon. Dave noted that they will be adding dancing poles in the tasting room and giving away T-shirts to those brave women who dare to do a pole dance. Imagine the reaction of Hood River's salty founders if they saw "Do you want to get naked?" on the back of T-shirts worn by the women of Hood River.

But aside from the winery's rather *risqué* trappings, the two Davids produce some serious vino. Not surprisingly, given their Columbia Gorge location and easy access to cool climate and hot-weather grapes, they make a full line-up of reds and whites. But it's the names that carry on the brand theme. How's this for reds: Dominatrix Pinot Noir, Penetration Cabernet Sauvignon, and Missionary Cabernet Sauvignon? Not to be outdone, the whites check in with names like Tease Riesling, Foreplay Chardonnay and Sugar Daddy Muscat.

Naked's tasting room location in Hood River provides the perfect venue to host gatherings, including small weddings, winemaker dinners and, of course, bachelorette parties. Coincidently, the day I visited Naked Winery, the staff was preparing for an "industry party" for that evening. The community associated with the burgeoning wine industry, from growing grapes to slapping the labels on the bottles, was invited to stop by and enjoy nibbles and wine. I hear tell it was an orgasmic experience.

NAKED WINERY
opened: 2005
winemaker(s): Naked Nymphs
location: 102 2nd Street, Hood River, OR 97031
phone: 800-666-9303
web: www.nakedwinery.com
e-mail: dave@nakedwinery.com
weddings: Yes
fee: $5 for 14 wines refundable with purchase
hours: Sunday through Thursday 12–6; Friday and
Saturday 12–8, or by appointment

Dave Michalec and David Barringer, Director of Affairs, with tasting room staff Mego and Anna (l to r)

DIRECTIONS: Heading east on I-84 take exit 63 to Hood River/City Center. Turn right (south) onto 2nd St. and go .1 miles. Arrive at the Naked Winery tasting room at 102 2nd St. on the right.

Heading west on I-84 take exit 63 to Hood River/City Center. Turn left (south) onto 2nd St. and go .1 miles. The tasting room is on the right at the corner of 2nd and Cascade.

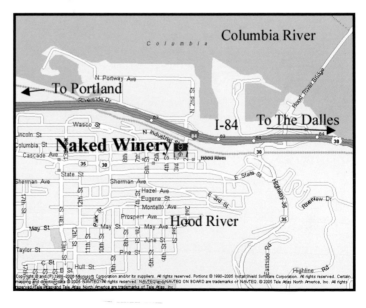

Springhouse Cellar Winery 2

He looked up from his laptop, and we gave each other that "I know you from somewhere" look. It was James Matthisen. "What the hell are you doing here?" I asked.

"Well," replied James, "this is my winery." It had been at least 15 years since our last get-together in Seattle. We both have our roots in the healthcare field: James, an actuary, and me, a sales and marketing representative for different insurers. After a minute, James smiled and recalled that we had met several times in Anchorage, where he was working

for Alyeska Pipeline in its benefits department. Who knew that these two turbo-charged, briefcase-carrying dudes would meet years later in a Hood River winery?

While James and his wife, Lisa, continue to work as actuaries, he increasingly devotes time, energy and his Visa card to growing Springhouse Cellar. His new tasting winery at the back end of the Mount Hood Railroad lot is testimony to his passion. It has plenty of light, room to spread out, and a wine bar that invites tourists and locals alike to imbibe. (**WineTrail Tip:** Ask James if you can check out the "ruins" on the side of the building and imagine this as a wedding or reception site.)

As I sampled his Perpetual Merlotion (which recently received a silver medal at the Northwest Wine Summit), James noted that the winery has outgrown its production area and storage at his 1875 homesteaded property east of the town of Hood River in Mosier. A "springhouse" on the property served as the barrel room and is also the inspiration for his wine labels. But to take Springhouse Cellar to the next level, he's had to think bigger. Hence, the relocation of his winemaking and barrel storage to a Hood River facility.

While tasting his cabernet franc, I was compelled to read the back label, which states, "Smooth as frog's fur, this bright, fruity, medium-bodied cabernet franc will make your toes curl." Yes, dear wine trekker, even actuaries have a sense of humor. Although James makes wines that you can cellar for years, I found this cabernet franc ready to be opened and enjoyed that day.

When I asked about his one-man operation, James corrected me, saying that he gets help from his family and friends. It even appears that his two kids are winemakers in training. Five-year-old Erica can smell the difference between syrah and merlot during punch-down, and 3-year-old Dylan can say "gewürztraminer."

James Matthisen

SPRINGHOUSE CELLAR WINERY
opened: 2004
winemaker(s): James Matthisen
location: 13 Railroad Avenue,
(1st Street and Cascade),
Hood River, OR 97031
phone: 541-478-3237
web: www.springhousecellar.com
e-mail: whomever@springhousecellar.com
picnic area: Yes
wheelchair access: Yes
fee: Complimentary wine tasting
hours: Thursday through Sunday 12–6

DIRECTIONS: Heading east or west on I-84 take exit 63 to Hood River/City Center. Turn right (south) onto 2nd St. and go .1 miles. Turn left onto Cascade Avenue and travel 1 block to the entrance of the Hood River Railroad lot. Continue to the end of the lot and find the Springhouse Cellar tasting room on the right.

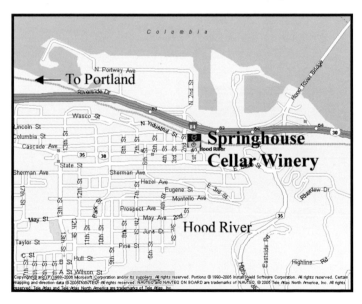

Quenett Winery 3

If you're in the town of Hood River and you just want to relax, sit back, and enjoy the experience of one tasting room, Quenett Winery fits the bill. Even hardcore WineTrail trekkers need a day to recharge and find a peaceful space to enjoy good wine and company.

I went there expecting to snap some pictures, pepper the wine-pouring staff with my usual assortment of oddball questions, and exit within 30 minutes. However, Quenett Winery proved to be the quicksand of tasting rooms for me. Here's why.

First, you need to know that there are 10 wines to sample. Not that you need to swirl and sip all 10 wines, but curiosity got the better of me and I ended up sampling most of them. The wine list includes a healthy dose of Mediterranean varietals, such as barbera, pinot gris, and Sangiovese, which helps explain the Italian flag outside. Second, the ambiance is intentionally cozy. The owners strove for a relaxed ambiance and they nailed it. It's a refuge for contemplating your navel armed with a glass of wine. Opened in late 2006, the downtown tasting-room location of Quenett Winery is the pride and joy of James and Molli Martin.

Finally, I couldn't make my exit until I learned the origin of the name Quenett. Fortunately for me (and the Martins), I found some literature noting that the word "quenett" is derived from a Native American word for steelhead trout, which happened to be a main staple of the native diet. Too bad they didn't have pinot noir to pair with their quenett.

Like other winemakers in the Columbia Gorge, the Martins are descendants of pioneer orchardists who settled here a gazillion years ago. Time marches on, and the Martins have replaced cherry trees with premium wine grapes in response to consumer demand and economic realities. But it is clear that they are passionate about their wines, given the herculean energy needed to launch the tasting room, invest in top-quality French wine barrels, and open their own production facility in their hometown, The Dalles. Put Quenett Winery on the top of your "ones to watch" list!

QUENETT WINERY
opened: 2003
winemaker(s): James and Molli Martin
location: 111 Oak Street, Hood River, OR 97031
phone: 541-386-2229
web: www.quenett.com
e-mail: info@quenett.com
fee: $5 to taste 6 wines refundable with purchase
hours: Daily 12–6; Friday and Saturday twilight until 8 during summer

DIRECTIONS: **Heading east on I-84** take exit 63 to Hood River/City Center. Turn right (south) onto 2nd St. and go .1 miles. Turn left (east) onto US-30 [SR-35] a short distance and arrive at 111 Oak St.

Heading west on I-84 take exit 64 toward US-30/OR-35/Mt. Hood Hwy/White Salmon/Govt. Camp. Turn left (south) onto US-30 [Button Bridge Rd] and go a short distance. Turn right (west) onto US-30 [SR-35] and go .3 miles. Turn right (west) onto US-30 [E Mt. Hood Hwy] and go .2 miles. Turn right (west) onto US-30 [SR-35] and go .2 miles. Turn right to stay on US-30 [SR-35] and arrive at Quenett Winery.

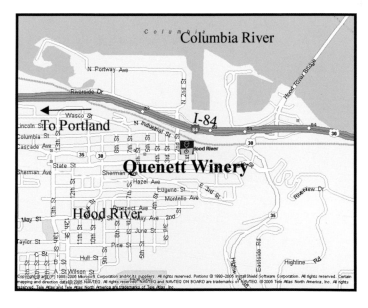

The Pines 1852 4

"He's called the grape guru of the Gorge," noted The Pines tasting-room pourer. She was referring to Lonnie Wright, owner of The Pines. I was sniffing my sample of their white blend called Satin (a 50/50 blend of pinot gris and gewürztraminer), which the pourer referred to as "summer in a bottle." I entertained the notion of Lonnie as the modern-day viticultural version of Johnny Appleseed. Perhaps he is. As owner of Columbia Country Vineyards, Lonnie is responsible for about 200 acres of grapes throughout the region. That's in addition to his vineyard, which features old zinfandel vines originally planted in — you guessed it — 1852.

Indeed, many of the labels that define the Oregon wine industry rely on grapes from vineyards created by Lonnie. Next time you are in a bottle shop, check out the labels of Sineann, Pheasant Valley, Cathedral Ridge, Mystic, Eola Hills and Owen Roe wines, to name a few. Chances are the grapes were sourced from the Columbia Gorge viticultural area.

The owner/winemaker of Sineann, Peter Rosback, continues as the winemaker for The Pines 1852. Peter and Lonnie's grape-growing/winemaking relationship began years ago in the 1980s and continues today with Lonnie's own label. At The Pines' Hood River tasting room, visitors have a *chance* to sample a lineup of regionally grown varietals, including pinot gris, viognier, pinot noir, merlot, syrah, a port-style zinfandel called Sweet Sierra, and of course old-vine zinfandel. I emphasize "chance," because many of their wines sell out during the year. So please remember, my wine-trekking friend, to call ahead if you have a hankering for Sweet Sierra or one of Lonnie's ever-popular zins.

Have you noticed how wine pairs wonderfully with art? At The Pines 1852, visitors have the pleasure of checking out contemporary photographs with a decidedly viticultural theme. An art gallery shares space with the tasting room. The one drawback is that you can't take your wine glass with you to the gallery area — it's just not allowed. Still, take the time to visit the art gallery, and as you look at the art, say a silent thank-you to that Italian settler who planted zinfandel vines in the Gorge. *Grazie*, dear immigrant!

THE PINES 1852
opened: 2001
winemaker(s): Peter Rosback
location: 202 State Street, Hood River, OR 97031
phone: 541-993-8301
web: www.thepinesvineyard.com
e-mail: sierra@thepinesvineyard.com
gift shop: Yes – onsite art gallery
tours: Yes
fee: $5 refundable with purchase
hours: Wednesday through Friday 12–9; Saturday through Monday 12–5; closed Tuesdays

DIRECTIONS: Heading east on I-84 take exit 63 to Hood River/City Center. Turn right (south) onto 2nd St. and go .2 miles. Arrive at The Pines winery at 202 State St. The Pines is on the right-hand side, on the corner of 2nd and State with Westwind Frame & Gallery.

Heading west on I-84 take exit 63 to Hood River/City Center. Turn left (south) onto 2nd St. and go .2 miles. Arrive at 202 State St. The Pines is on the right-hand side on the corner of 2nd and State with Westwind Frame & Gallery.

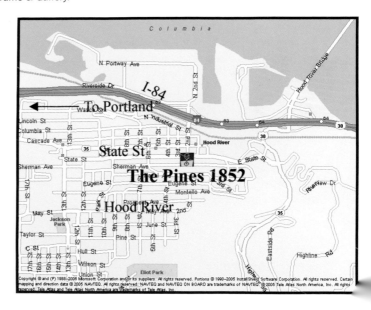

Cathedral Ridge Winery 🖸

Columbia Gorge wineries face a major challenge when competing for the attention of tourists and locals. You've got wind surfing, bicycling, hiking, great restaurants, roadside fruit stands, unique shopping ops, and lots more. But that's just half the problem. WineTrail trekkers have dozens of other wineries they can visit within a stone's throw (or a river crossing) of each other! As a winery owner, your challenge is twofold. Getting folks to come by and getting them to come back — often.

Enter Cathedral Ridge Winery. Named after the outcropping on the northwest summit of Mount Hood, Cathedral Ridge Winery has succeeded in getting a steady stream of repeat customers, for a number of reasons.

Owner Robb Bell knows full well that it is the fruit that matters. In his mind, you would have to be a pretty bad winemaker to ruin the premium grapes that come from the Gorge appellation. From zinfandel to syrah, Robb either grows or selects grapes from the best vineyards to create a full lineup of wines, dominated by reds. What's more, he has the talents of grape-growing experts such as The Pines' Lonnie Wright to tap into. It's a collaboration of sorts, something the vintners in these parts do with great regularity.

Speaking of syrah, can you say "Double Platinum"? That was the award given by *Wine Press Northwest* for Cathedral Ridge Winery's 2004 syrah. Double latte, double airline miles, double scoops of ice cream are all good in my book, but a Double Platinum! Kudos. But Robb Bell would be quick to point out that it is the talented Sonoma-based winemaker Michael Sebastiani who deserves the credit. Besides Bordeaux- and Rhône-style reds, Sebastiani also crafts wines of the white persuasion, including gewürztraminer, riesling, pinot gris, and chardonnay.

Another key reason for Cathedral Ridge's success lies outdoors. Visitors can saunter outside its tasting room, wine in hand, to one of a dozen comfy chairs and benches. Here you can take in the garden and the sculpture dotting the landscape, but it is the views of Mount Adams and Mount Hood that get our attention.

Finally, if you are looking for another reason to visit Cathedral Ridge Winery, try this one on for size. It is the recipient of *Wine Press Northwest's* prestigious Oregon Winery of the Year for 2007. Certainly, Robb Bell and his team must be doing something right. I'll be ᴐming back, for sure.

CATHEDRAL RIDGE WINERY
winemaker(s): Michael Sebastiani
location: 4200 Post Canyon Drive,
Hood River, OR 97031
phone: 541-386-2882
web: www.cathedralridgewinery.com
e-mail: crw@cathedralridgewinery.com
picnic area: Yes
wheelchair access: Yes
weddings: Yes
tours: Yes
fee: Complimentary wine tasting
hours: Daily 11–5 November through May;
Daily 11–6 June through October

DIRECTIONS: From Portland take I-84 [US-30] about 60 miles east to exit 62. Bear right (east) onto US-30 [SR-35], then an immediate right (southwest) onto Country Club Rd and go 1.5 miles. Turn left (east) onto Post Canyon Dr. and proceed .3 miles to the winery.

From Hood River take US-30 [SR-35] west 1.9 miles. Turn left (southwest) onto Country Club Rd and go 1.4 miles. Turn left (east) onto Post Canyon Dr. and go .3 miles to Cathedral Ridge Winery.

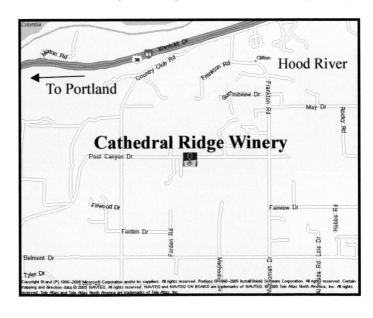

Hood River Vineyards 6

If you visit this winery in the summer, you're likely to see purple vetch growing between the vineyard rows. While purple vetch is pretty, it serves a more practical purpose, according to Anne Lerch, co-owner of Hood River Vineyards & Winery. "It's a good nitrogen fixer," she notes.

Before there were premium grapes in the Hood River Valley, there were fruit orchards. Miles of them — cherry, peach, pear, apple, plum — along with strawberry fields and raspberry farms. There's a reason this area is called Oregon's Fruit Loop. Thus, it's no surprise that the early wineries developed a reputation for their fruit wines, such as pear, peach, cherry, and others. As did Hood River Vineyards & Winery.

Anne Lerch on the right

Originally started in 1981, Hood River rightfully claims the title of the oldest winery in the Gorge. And, true to their roots, Bernard and Anne Lerch continue the tradition of making fine fruit wines, along with an assortment of premium grape wines. Anne works the quaint tasting room, while Bernard tends to the myriad vineyard and winemaking chores.

For those wine lovers who have a sweet tooth, you won't be disappointed. Included in the list of wines are late-harvest riesling, pear wine, black muscat, zinfandel port, black cherry wine, and raspberry wine. Bernard's Ph.D. in biochemistry certainly must come in handy when he's concocting these dessert beauties.

Although the glasses are small, the tastes are big. If you do manage to exercise your palate through their full array of wines, you will have gotten your tasting fee's worth. Take time to look around the tasting room and note Anne's "mission statement" on the wall: "We do not do weddings or big events, nor do we blow glass or make cheese, chocolates, jellies, or sauces. We simply grow and make wine." It is this matter-of-fact statement that defines the winery. If you're seeking glorious landscaped grounds, complete with a bocce ball court, and the name "Domaine" or "Chateau" in the branding, you won't find it at Hood River Vineyards & Winery. Instead, you will stumble onto some fines wines, discover more about the region's winemaking history, and gain insight into the people who define the Gorge.

HOOD RIVER VINEYARDS
opened: 1981
winemaker(s): Bernard Lerch
location: 4693 Westwood Drive,
Hood River, OR 97031
phone: 541-386-3772
web: www.hoodrivervineyards.us
e-mail: hoodriverwines@gorge.net
wheelchair access: Yes
fee: $5 tasting fee refundable with purchase
hours: Daily 11–5 March through October; Wednesday
to Sunday 11–5 November through March

DIRECTIONS: Traveling eastbound on I-84 from Portland take exit 62 toward US-30/W. Hood River. Bear right (east) onto US-30 [SR-35] then immediately turn right (southwest) onto Country Club Rd and go 1.5 miles. Turn right (west) onto Post Canyon Dr. and go .4 miles. Turn right (west) onto Westwood Dr. (gravel road) for .5 miles and arrive at Hood River Vineyards on the left.

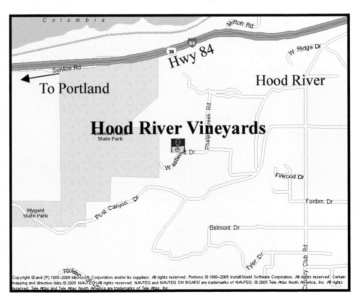

Phelps Creek Vineyards 🟦

South of Hood River and a dogleg to the right lies Phelps Creek Vineyards. How Phelps Creek Vineyards' tasting room ended up in the middle of Hood River Golf Course is a question for Phelps Creek owner Bob Morus to answer. However, we do have him to thank for its gorgeous setting and inviting ambiance. By design, the tasting room has a lot of windows for easy viewing of the greens and the fairway tees just an easy 9-iron shot

away. Another marvelous surprise is the Phelps Creek tasting room's location right next door to the Oak Grove Restaurant. It's a perfect spot for satisfying the appetite you'll work up while touring wine country.

Those who bicycle here from the town of Hood River appreciate more than most the fact that Phelps Creek is at a higher elevation — around 900 to 1,000 feet. In the wintertime, the area often gets snow, which, for the tasting-room staff, can make for an interesting drive just getting to work. But when you visit in the summer, snow is the furthest thing from your mind, and the sight of nearby Phelps Creek Vineyards is a beautiful spectacle. Snap a picture or two of the vineyards, of which about 30 acres are under production.

Make a point of tasting winemaker Rich Cushman's red and white blends, called Brimstone and Hellfire, respectively. These wines are named for local "celebrity" Billy Sunday, who maintained an orchard in Hood River in the early 1900s. Sunday is best known for his storied evangelical career (following a professional baseball career in the National League), during which he toured the country spreading the gospel to throngs of people coming to the "kerosene lamp tour." Check out the labels for Brimstone and Hellfire, with their caricatures of an animated Billy Sunday.

Besides Hellfire and Brimstone, visitors have the opportunity to sample Phelps Creek's other beauties, such as Le Petit Pinot Noir, Becky's Cuvée, and Judith's Reserve Pinot Noir. The philosophy at Phelps Creek Vineyards is "quality over quantity." The fact that they harvest a relatively low tonnage of premium wine grapes per acre translates into intense flavor. (**WineTrail tip:** While you're visiting, ask if any wines made by a guest winemaker are available to taste. In 2007, for example, Bob Morus invited Alexandrine Roy from France-based Domaine Marc Roy to produce pinot noir cuvée.) Don't resist this temptation to experience the wines of the Colmbia Gorge!

PHELPS CREEK VINEYARDS
winemaker(s): Rich Cushman
location: 1850 Country Club Road,
Hood River, OR 97031
phone: 541-386-2607
web: www.phelpscreekvineyards.com
e-mail: info@phelpscreekvineyards.com
picnic area: Yes
wheelchair access: Yes
tours: Yes
fee: $5 tasting fee refundable with purchase
hours: Friday through Sunday 11–5 March, April and
November; Thursday through Monday 11–5 May and
June; daily 11–5 July through October

DIRECTIONS: Traveling east or west on I-84 take exit 62 toward US-30/W. Hood River/Westcliff Dr. Go east onto US-30 [SR-35], then immediately turn right (southwest) onto Country Club Rd. Drive 3 miles. Turn right to stay on Country Club Rd and go .2 miles. Turn left to stay on Country Club Rd proceed 1 mile. Turn left to stay on Country Club Road and arrive at 1850 Country Club Rd. The tasting room is on your right on the Hood River Golf Course.

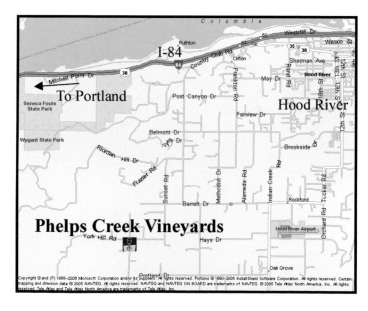

Pheasant Valley Winery 8

For Scott and Gail Hagee, owners of Pheasant Valley Winery, it's all about relationships. Their lives center on their relationships with family and friends, a nearby mountain, a thriving winery, and a dog named Lulu. It's the bounty of the land that fuels their way of life, with acres of pear and apple orchards, thriving vineyards, and fields of lavender. With

a straight-on view of spectacular Mount Hood, visitors catch a glimpse of Scott and Gail's "earth-rich" lives, matched only by the taste of their earth-rich wines.

For years, Pheasant Valley orchards produced signature organic pear and apple crops. They still do. However, with the emergence of the Columbia Gorge wine country, it didn't take long for Scott to replace some fruit trees with pinot gris, pinot noir, tempranillo, zinfandel, and gewürztraminer vines. Until the tasting room opened in 2004, fans of Pheasant Valley Winery were only familiar with the winery's delectable off-dry pear wines. With the opening of the tasting room, however, they discovered Pheasant Valley's portfolio of award-winning white and red wines.

Once inside Pheasant Hill's spacious tasting room, be sure to admire the historic back bar (which traveled around Cape Horn to get here), the large rock fireplace with comfy furniture, wine-related merchandise, art on the wall, and breathtaking views. The Brittany spaniel vying for your attention is Lulu, and the original oil painting on the wall is by their good friend and local artist Dennis Wentworth Porter. His painting of Mount Hood with fall vineyards and flying pheasants in the foreground graces the wine bottles of Pheasant Valley Winery. (**WineTrail tip:** While vacationing in Hood River, consider staying at the Hagees' roomy guesthouse, located on the winery's property. Visit www.pheasantvalleyorchards.com for details.)

Because of its great variety of warm- and cool-weather grapes, Hood River provides the ultimate in convenient wine touring. To that end, Pheasant Valley Winery delights the taste buds, with samples of a wide assortment of reds and whites, from its award-winning pinot noir to its riesling. Yet, despite the many Old World wines to taste, I couldn't help but relieve Scott and Gail of a bottle of their spicy semi-sweet pear wine. I had the perfect pasta chicken dish to "pear" with this beauty.

Lulu and Scott Hagee

PHEASANT VALLEY WINERY
winemaker(s): John Hall (Consultant winemaker)
location: 3890 Acree Drive, Hood River, OR 97031
phone: 541-387-3040
web: www.pheasantvalleywinery.com
e-mail: wine@pheasantvalleywinery.com
picnic area: Yes
weddings: Yes
gift shop: Yes
fee: Tasting fee applies
hours: Daily 11–5 October through March; daily 11–6
April through September; closed January

⭐ **BEST Lodging, views and gift shop**

DIRECTIONS: If traveling eastbound on I-84 take exit 62 toward US-30/W. Hood River. Bear right (east) onto US-30 [SR-35] and proceed 1.2 miles. Turn right (south) onto 13th St. and go .7 miles. Bear right (south) onto 12th St. and travel .4 miles. Road name changes to Tucker Rd. Continue on Tucker Rd for 2 miles. Turn left to stay on Tucker Rd and go 1.2 miles. Turn right (southwest) onto Acree Dr. and drive .2 miles to the winery on your right.

If heading westbound on I-84 take exit 63 toward Hood River/City Center. Turn left (south) onto 2nd St. and proceed .2 miles. Turn left (south) onto 13th St. and go .7 miles. Bear right (south) onto 12th St. and proceed .4 miles. Road name changes to Tucker Rd. Continue on Tucker Rd for 2 miles. Turn left to stay on Tucker Rd and travel 1.2 miles. Turn right (southwest) onto Acree Dr. and go .2 miles to the winery on your right.

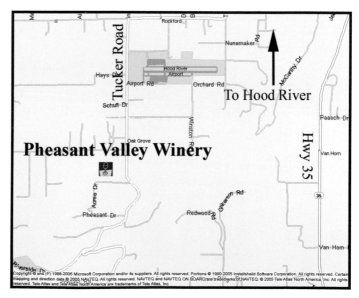

Wy'East Vineyards

Wy'East is a popular name around Hood River. The high school bears this name; there's a road called Wy'East; and, for cycling fans, there's even the Wy'East Road Race. Turns out, the local Native Americans referred to Mount Hood as Wy'East. It's also the name Dick and Christie Reed chose for their vineyard when they arrived in the area in the early 1980s.

The Wy'East Vineyards tasting room may be 5.5 miles south of Hood River, but it is a million miles away from the Reeds' former lives. Prior to moving to Oregon, Dick and Christie were floor traders at the Chicago Board Options Exchange. They enjoyed the hustle and bustle of the stock exchange, but two catalysts brought about a change.

First, they fell in love with wine (when it comes to fermented juice, Chicago is a sophisticated town). Second, they wanted a more rural setting to raise their three young children. Hood River, Oregon, filled the bill.

Still, if you told Christie then that she would be moving to a farm, she would have told you that you are out of your mind. But the Reeds succeeded in transforming their lives. Perhaps it was their love of the outdoors (both are avid skiers and own a place in New Mexico where they ski) or simply satisfying Christie's love of horses that made Hood River a good fit. But it was establishing Wy'East Vineyards and growing premium grapes that really cemented the decision for them.

Together with Steve Bickford, the couple launched Mt. Hood Winery. This gave them the opportunity to move beyond growing grapes to learn the wine industry trade. In 2007 the partners realized that they had developed different visions for the winery. As a result, the Reeds made the decision to amicably split from Mt. Hood Winery and start their own label using the vineyard's name.

The Reeds' goals for Wy'East Vineyards are to produce small-lot batches of premium wine, to be economically sustainable, and to have fun while they do it. Following the "small is beautiful" paradigm, they work with winemaker Alexis Pouillon, focusing on pinot noir, pinot gris, chardonnay, syrah, and cabernet sauvignon. When you visit the tasting room, budget time to purchase a glass of their Reserve Pinot Noir and mosey outside to the patio. There, as you enjoy the splendor of their gardens and the sound of a nearby waterfall, indulge your taste buds in the intense berry flavors of their reserve pinot. *C'est bon la vie!*

WY'EAST VINEYARDS
opened: 2008
winemaker(s): Alexis Pouillon
location: 3189 Highway 35, Mount Hood, OR 97031
phone: 541-386-1277
web: www.wyeastvineyards.com
e-mail: info@wyeastvineyards.com
picnic area: Yes
wheelchair access: Yes
weddings: Yes
tours: Yes
fee: Tasting fee may apply
hours: Daily 11–5; mid-April through October;
open weekends early spring and November

DIRECTIONS: Traveling east or west on I-84 take exit 64 toward OR-35/Mt. Hood Hwy/White Salmon/ Govt. Camp. Turn right (west) onto US-30 [SR-35] and go .3 miles. Keep straight onto SR-35 for about 5.5 miles, and arrive at Wy'East Vineyards tasting room on the left.

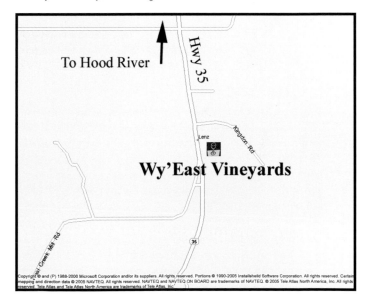

Mt. Hood Winery 🔟

This is a little awkward. I usually report on what visitors can expect when they come by a winery. However, in the case of Mt. Hood Winery, I am at a loss. The tasting room I went to in the summer of 2008 will be toast by the time this book lands in your hands. In August 2008, the proprietors of Mt. Hood Winery broke ground on the new winery and tasting room. During my visit, though, I was able to view architectural drawings of the

winery's new location at Vanhorn Drive on Highway 35. The renderings were impressive. Visitors to the Mt. Hood Winery will experience the real thing in the summer of 2009.

Since 2002, family-owned Mt. Hood Winery has produced exceptional wines under the winemaking direction of Steve Bickford. As co-owners, his brother Don and Don's wife, Libby, are part of the Bickford contingent, involved in pruning, harvesting, and bottling. It's a family affair to be sure — especially when you add Steve's daughter and son-in-law to the mix of cellar and vineyard assistants.

Visitors to Mt. Hood Winery take pleasure in tasting pinot gris, chardonnay, riesling, pinot noir (from its own Barking Dog Vineyard), merlot, and its signature port-style wine with the name Puerto Montaña. In total, the winery produces nearly 2,000 cases annually. To supplement the winery's own grape production, the Bickfords source their grapes from other nearby vineyards as well as Washington's Columbia Valley. However, as their 22-acre vineyard — composed of pinot noir, pinot gris, riesling, and tempranillo — matures, we can expect more estate wines.

There is little doubt that the new 8,000-square-foot tasting room will be grander and provide plenty of space in which to experience Mt. Hood wines, view the vineyard, and take in Mount Hood in the distance — to say nothing of plentiful space for weddings and other events. Ironically, in 2009 the Bickfords will mark 100 years of growing fruit in the Hood River Valley. However, during my visit to the soon-to-be-demolished tasting room, my mind was on my wine. For $5, I took a glass of their Mt. Hood Winery pinot noir to the great outdoors, kicked back, and enjoyed.

Steve Bickford

MT. HOOD WINERY
opened: 2002
winemaker(s): Steve Bickford
location: 2265 Highway 35, Hood River, OR 97031
phone: 541-386-8333
web: www.mthoodwinery.com
e-mail: sales@mthoodwinery.com
picnic area: Yes
wheelchair access: Yes
weddings: Yes
fee: Complimentary wine tasting
hours: Daily 12–5

DIRECTIONS: Traveling east or west on I-84 take exit 64 toward OR-35/Mt. Hood Hwy/White Salmon/ Govt. Camp. Turn right (west) onto US-30 [SR-35] and go .3 miles. Keep straight onto SR-35 for about 4 miles and arrive at Mt. Hood Winery.

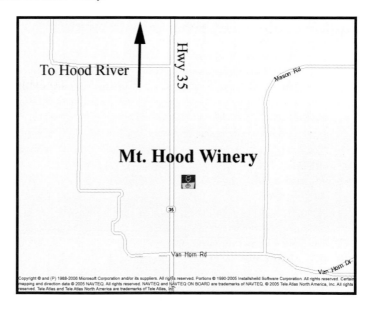

Bolton Cellars 🔟🔟

Dan Bolton's 6-foot-4-inch frame belies his gentle nature. But the owner of Bolton Cellars has a contagious smile, a caring attitude, and a great sense of fun. As Patty Rolen, the manager of his The Dalles tasting room, puts it, "Dan wants the tasting room to be an enjoyable experience. If we're not having fun sharing our wine with folks, then why bother?" In keeping with this philosophy, Bolton Cellars hosts Cinco de Vino in May and

cosponsors events with the local chamber of commerce and other organizations to raise funds and help causes.

It was Dan Bolton's distant relative, Absalom Bolton, who homesteaded the family farm in 1858. Dan himself is the fourth generation of Boltons to work the farm. We suspect, however, that Absalom would be surprised to find that, instead of wheat, the Bolton farm is producing premium varietals such as merlot and pinot noir. But take a good look at the Bolton Cellars wine labels. Sporting images of wheat, weather vanes and tractors, the labels pay homage to the farm. My personal favorite is the picture of the Great Southern Railroad train on the Bolton Cellars' pinot noir. The railroad once went through this property and must have made for some fitful, sleep-depriving nights.

Bolton Cellars produces 100 percent estate wines from two vineyards. The main vineyard and family farm is located on the northeast edge of Dufur Valley near The Dalles; the other vineyard is located in Washington, across the Columbia River at Horsethief Lake. Growing grapes for Bolton Cellars is in itself, a huge commitment, but Dan also manages to squeeze in a full-time job working for The Dalles Iron Works. Fortunately, he has excellent staff and volunteers to assist in creating wine and happy customers. The actual winemaking is left to Tim Schechtel, co-owner/winemaker of Erin Glenn Winery, which ironically is located next door to the The Dalles Iron Works.

Volunteer staff for Bolton Cellars get to sell their wares at the tasting room. You can find wallets, sunglasses cases, jewelry, note cards, and wine bags to purchase. You may want to splurge and get both the Beaver- and the Duck-adorned wine bags — to keep the family peace.

Tradition. Hard work. Fun. Great wine. These words come to mind when I think of Bolton Cellars.

Dan Bolton

BOLTON CELLARS
opened: 2006
winemaker(s): Tim Schechtel
location: 306 Court Street, The Dalles, OR 97058
phone: 541-296-7139
web: www.boltoncellars.com
e-mail: sales@boltoncellars.com
gift shop: Yes
fee: Complimentary wine tasting
hours: Winter hours: Thursday and Friday 3 to close; Saturday and Sunday 2 until close. Summer hours: Monday through Friday 3 to close; Saturday and Sunday 2 until close

DIRECTIONS: From Portland take I-84 about 80 miles to the east toward The Dalles. Take exit 84 toward City Center/The Dalles. Keep straight onto US-30 for .5 miles. Bear right (southeast) onto US-30 [E 3rd St.] and then immediately turn left (north) onto Court St. Arrive at 306 Court St.

If traveling east on I-84 take exit 85 toward City Center/The Dalles. Keep straight onto US-30 continuing on E 2nd St. Arrive at 306 Court St., where the tasting room is located.

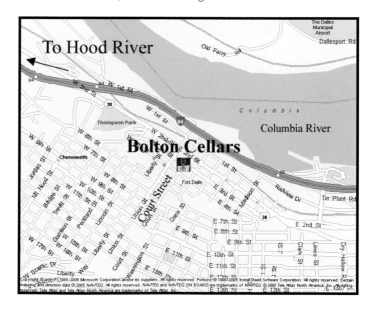

Erin Glenn Winery 🔢

History buffs are in for a treat when they visit Erin Glenn Winery in The Dalles. Originally commissioned by President Abraham Lincoln in 1864, the winery's Mint building was intended to be a fortress-like structure to house gold. Unfortunately, the gold rush failed to materialize, which left an unfinished building that was used for various purposes over the years.

Tim and Erin Schechtel

Erin Glenn Winery is the brainchild of owners Erin and Tim Schechtel. In 1997, they succeeded in making gewürztraminer in their Hood River garage, and because of that positive experience, decided to grow grapes and make wine. They subsequently moved to The Dalles and rehabbed The Mint to house their winery and tasting room. Their addition of such interesting touches as a candelabra in the brick-walled tasting room enriches the room's historic charm. A tour of the thick-walled facility takes visitors to the downstairs catacombs, where wine barrels reside rather than stacks of gold bars.

When I inquired what the number-one question asked by visitors is, Tim and Erin both exclaimed, "Our name!" Erin Glenn reflects their Irish heritage with Erin's first name meaning "Ireland" in the old Gaelic language, and the word "glenn" meaning a secret valley. Erin Glenn's logo further reinforces the Celtic branding. Inspired by one of artist Margaret Mackintosh's drawings, the logo consists of a large Celtic knot at its top with four smaller knots representing the Schechtels' four daughters making up the rest of the image.

At Erin Glenn's large tasting bar, WineTrail trekkers can sample Bordeaux-style blends, cabernet sauvignon, dolcetto, gewürztraminer, sauvignon blanc, syrah, viognier, tempranillo, rosé, and dessert wines. While swirling and sipping, note the names of the wines; someone fueled by a quad latte and a healthy dose of imagination came up with these terrific names. For example, the most popular red blend, named in honor of Tim and Erin's daughters, is Tantrum Red. Other names include Power Block Bordeaux Blend, Threemile Cabernet Sauvignon, and Blind Dog Estate Syrah. But my personal favorite is Velvet Ass Rosé. Nice.

If possible, time your visit for a Friday evening, when live music fills the air and light fare is served up from the downstairs kitchen. However, if a Friday-night visit isn't in the cards, any time is perfect for experiencing this unique setting and tasting Erin Glenn wines — which are true expressions of the Columbia Gorge. I think this is the kind of place ol' Abe would appreciate.

Tim Schechtel

ERIN GLENN WINERY
opened: 2005
winemaker(s): Tim Schechtel
location: 710 East 2nd Street, The Dalles, OR 97058
phone: 541-296-4707
web: www.eringlenn.com
picnic area: Yes
wheelchair access: Yes
tours: Yes
fee: Complimentary wine tasting
hours: Friday 12–9; Saturday through Monday 12–5;
live music Friday nights

 BEST Eats

DIRECTIONS: From Portland, take I-84 east to exit 85 (City Center/The Dalles exit). Turn right off the exit and another right at the first stop sign (E Second St.). Follow E Second St. 2 blocks into town and the winery will be on the left in The Mint building.

From Bend/Madras, take Hwy 97 north to Hwy 197 towards The Dalles. Continue on Hwy 197 to Hwy 30. Merge onto Hwy 30. Hwy 30 becomes E Second St. Follow E Second St. 2 blocks into town and find the winery on the left in The Mint building.

From Pendleton, take I-84 west to exit 85 (City Center/The Dalles exit). Turn left off the exit and then take a right at the first stop sign (E Second St.). Follow E Second St. 2 blocks into town the winery on the left.

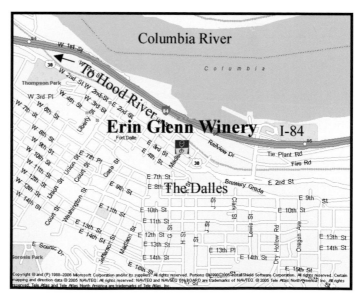

Wheatridge in the Nook 🔢

I paced around the tasting room and looked at the open wine bottles on the counter. I was the only one there. I contemplated grabbing a wineglass and giving myself a healthy pour, but resisted the temptation. I walked outside, gave the winery dog a few pats, and looked around. No one in sight. That was my experience at Wheatridge in the Nook... but not quite.

The information I had for Wheatridge in the Nook noted that it was open daily from 11 a.m. to 6 p.m., but requested that visitors "please call ahead." So I called and left a message that I would be there later. Without confirming it would be open, I hit the road,

mistakenly thinking someone would be there when I arrived.

Once you get off I-84 and head up the hill toward Philippi Canyon, the rolling wheatfields of eastern Oregon take over. After a few miles, I pulled the car over and got out, camera in hand. It was amazingly quiet and at the same time, breathtaking. I realized that Wheatridge in the Nook's literature had come to life: "Hidden in the gentle folds of 'The Nook' between the John Day and Columbia rivers, the golden rows of wheat lay next to acres of lush green grape vines."

I didn't taste any Wheatridge in the Nook wines that day, but I did witness the hard work Larry Bartlemay invested to create his winery. There was dedicated space for winemaking, and equipment spread across the grounds. On the porch, an Adirondack chair beckoned visitors to relax and enjoy a glass of wine. I was aware that Larry's farm had been in the family for more than 100 years. I wanted to get his take on that history; stories of the Depression, paralyzing winter storms, droughts, that sort of thing. I figured the next time I would get my chance to meet Larry.

I know some folks say things happen for a reason. In this case, I can vouch for that. Later that day, I was at The Gorge White House wine shop outside Hood River on Highway 35. I spotted among the other local wines a bottle of Wheatridge in the Nook's 2005 Cabernet Sauvignon, with its distinctive black and gold label. I sprung for it and took it home. Several weeks later, I paired this cabernet sauvignon with some baby back ribs fresh off the barbecue. I *can* tell you this about Wheatridge in the Nook: Larry Bartlemay makes mighty fine wine!

WHEATRIDGE IN THE NOOK
opened: 2005
winemaker(s): Larry Bartlemay
location: 11102 Philippi Canyon Lane,
Arlington, OR 97812
phone: 541-454-2585
web: www.wheatridgeinthenook.com
e-mail: wheatridge@hughes.net
picnic area: Yes
wheelchair access: Yes
weddings: Yes
tours: Yes
fee: Complimentary wine tasting
hours: Daily 11–6 but call ahead

DIRECTIONS: Heading east on I-84 take exit 123 toward Philippi Canyon. Turn right (south) onto Quinton Canyon Rd and go 1.3 miles. Road name changes to Philippi Canyon Ln. Proceed to Wheatridge in the Nook at 11102 Philippi Canyon Lane following signs to the winery.

Heading west on I-84 take exit 123 toward Philippi Canyon. Turn left (south) onto Quinton Canyon Rd and go 1.3 miles. Road name changes to Philippi Canyon Ln. Proceed to Wheatridge in the Nook at 11102 Philippi Canyon Lane looking for winery signs.

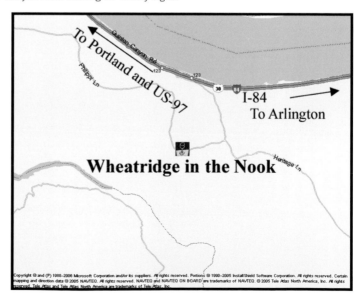

Central &
Eastern Oregon
p474

Central & Eastern Oregon
WINE COUNTRY

Central and Eastern Oregon
Wine Trail

Maragas Winery

Few wineries in Oregon reside east of the Cascades. In fact, a full 68% of Oregon's wineries call the Willamette Valley home. Ironically, it is reversed up north in Washington where the biggest chunk of wineries exists in eastern Washington. But even in Washington, Walla Walla's wineries rely on fruit made in Oregon's Umatilla County where a large percentage of the Walla Walla AVA thrives. The newly designated Snake River Valley AVA extends into eastern Oregon's Baker and Malheur Counties. No doubt we will witness a significant growth of vineyards on the Snake River Valley.

So it is most surprising that the Central and Eastern Oregon WineTrail is comprised of only four wineries — Maragas Winery and Volcano Vineyards in Bend and Zerba Cellars and Watermill Winery in Milton-Freewater. Of course a trip to Bend also entails plenty of time for exploring nature's wonders — rock climbing, skiing, and hiking and biking. You'll need to work off some calories. There are just too many good restaurants around! Ditto for Walla Walla (Milton-Freewater). But for a real surprise and experience, try the fine chocolates available at Petits Noirs (622 S Main St.) in Milton-Freewater. Petits Noirs has designed chocolates that pair beautifully with specific wines produced by local wineries in Walla Walla. Yummy!

Central and Eastern Oregon WineTrail

1 Maragas Winery
2 Volcano Vineyards
3 Zerba Cellars
4 Watermill Winery & Blue Mountain Cider Company

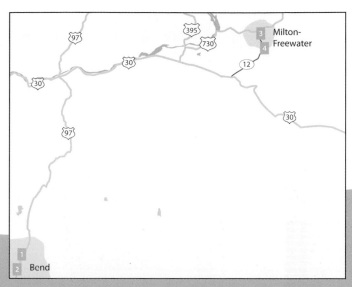

Region:	**Central and Eastern Oregon Wine Country**
# of tasting rooms on tour:	**4**
# of satellite tasting rooms:	**1**
Estimate # of days for tour:	**2 to 3**
Getting around:	**Car**
Key Events:	❏ **In May, Walla Walla-Milton-Freewater's Spring Release Weekend – contact the Walla Walla Valley Wine Alliance at 509-526-3117.**
	❏ **In June, Bend's Wine by the River – call 541-383-3910 or go online to www.winebytheriver.com.**
	❏ **In December, Walla Walla-Milton Freewater's Holiday Barrel Tasting – call 509-526-3117 or visit www.wallawallawine.com.**
Tips:	❏ **Explore wine country on horseback at Muscat-Dun Vineyard and Ranch – call 541-571-3640.**
	❏ **Pair wine with chocolate at Milton-Freewater's Petit Noirs – it's the best! Located at 622 Main Street in a beautifully restored bungalow. Visit http://petitsnoirs.com.**
	❏ **Depending on season pack skis, bikes, golf clubs, climbing gear, hiking boots – you will need them for outdoorsy Bend.**
	❏ **Bend features a number of restaurants – personal favorite is Cork – call 541-382-6881 for reservations.**
	❏ **Need a place to stay? Consider McMenamin's Old St. Francis School – call 877-661-4228.**

 Best: ❏ **Views: Maragas Winery.**

Maragas Winery

You could say that three females shaped Doug Maragas' life, leading him to central Oregon to grow grapes and make wine. Their names are Anna, Joanne, and Gina.

Back in the 1940s and 1950s, Doug's grandmother Anna Maragas established a grape brokerage business in Ohio. Being a female grape broker 60 years ago was rare indeed. Anna always managed to set aside grapes each year to make wine for the family, and this tradition allowed her young grandson Doug the opportunity to learn how to make and appreciate fine wine. While most kids were playing Davy Crockett, Doug was swirling and picking up the "nose" of cabernet.

Doug's artistic mother, Joanne Lattavo, nurtured in him an appreciation for fine art of the kooky, offbeat kind. Her "beatnik" sketches adorn his wine labels,

Maragas Winery's mascot Cloé

including those of Kool Kat Muscat, Pinot Riche Pinot Gris, and his signature Legal Zin (Doug is a former trial lawyer). His mother's artistic talent evidently rubbed off on Doug. His drawing of his laid-back American Bulldog, Cloé, became the winery's logo.

With his wife, Gina, Doug moved west to Bend in the late '90s to pursue his passion for winemaking. They chose Bend for its high desert climate, proximity to great hiking and biking, and the opportunity to purchase grapes from vineyards in southern Oregon and California. The 72-hour round trip Doug makes to Ukiah, Calif., to pick up zinfandel grapes for the winery is a sleep-depriving ordeal, but he wouldn't trade the experience for anything. It's all part of the adrenaline-filled fall crush. However, as the Maragases' vineyard matures, the family plans to produce more wine with their own grapes.

The winery is located north of Bend, right off Highway 97. Inside its spacious tasting room and production area, visitors can taste exceptional wines for a nominal tasting fee of $5, which includes a complimentary Maragas wineglass. As you pull into the winery complex, it's easy to see why Doug and Gina chose this part of the world to call home. The views of the surrounding Cascade Mountains, in particular, the Three Sisters (Faith, Hope, and Charity), are nothing short of spectacular.

WineTrail note: Maragas Winery has a second tasting room, located in Bend in a charming Craftsman-style home on Colorado Street. It's a relaxing space in which to enjoy a glass of Legal Zin, and contemplate the beauty of Bend and the emergence of this wine-growing region.

MARAGAS WINERY
opened: 1999
winemaker(s): Doug Maragas
location: 15523 S Highway 97, Bend, OR 97734
phone: 541-330-0919
web: www.maragaswinery.com
e-mail: info@maragaswinery.com
picnic area: Yes
wheelchair access: Yes
gift shop: Yes
fee: $5 tasting fee includes wineglass
hours: Wednesday to Sunday 12–5 May through September; Friday to Sunday 11–4 October through December

Doug Maragas

 **BEST Views**

DIRECTIONS: **From Sisters** take US-20 [SR-126] east 20 miles. Take ramp (right) onto US-97 [Bend Hwy] and go 1.7 miles toward US-97/Mt. Bachelor. At exit 138 keep right onto ramp and turn right (west) onto NW Colorado Ave. Go .3 miles to arrive at Maragas Winery.

From Redmond go south onto SR-126 [S Canal Blvd] for .3 miles. Turn left (south) onto US-97 [SW 6th St.] and go 16.6 miles. At exit 138 keep right onto ramp toward downtown Bend/Mt. Bachelor. Turn right (west) onto NW Colorado and proceed .3 miles to Maragas Winery.

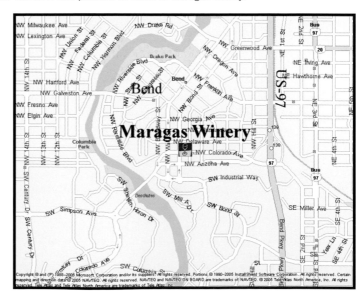

Volcano Vineyards 2

The attractive Volcano Vineyards "tasting lounge" is located in Bend's Brooks Street pedestrian alley by the Pine Tavern. Upon entering, the child-sized furniture out front clearly communicated that this is a kid-friendly tasting room. That's unusual in the winery world. Kathleen and I arrived under the impression that the proprietors of Volcano Vineyards, Scott and Liz Ratcliff, created a winery in name only. That is, they simply slapped their label on the bottle and relied on others for grapes and winemaking. Within a few minutes, however, that notion was dispelled.

We had hoped to visit with Scott and Liz in the friendly confines of the tasting room, but discovered that they were busy with the harvest in Rogue Valley. There went myth number one; they don't just sit and wait for the grapes to roll in. They are out there harvesting and sorting grapes with their grape-growing partners. Beginning in September and through most of October, they are racking up the miles on the family vehicle making the three-hour trek from Bend to the Medford area where the grapes grow.

The second myth to go concerns the actual winemaking. While it's true that they saved big bucks by not purchasing their own equipment, that doesn't mean they aren't intimately involved in the winemaking. Scott's amateur winemaking forays have come in handy while collaborating with RoxyAnn's chief winemaker, Gus Janeway. Don't be surprised in a few years to find Scott making wine on his own. For right now, however, Scott appreciates the experience and mentoring that Gus brings.

With the virtual-winery misconception behind us, we could then focus on the real purpose of our visit — tasting Volcano Vineyard's Rogue Valley Bordeaux Blend, a second red blend with the name Lava Blend, and their Fortmiller Vineyard Syrah. As I sipped these delicious wines, I recalled thinking earlier that the name Volcano for a winery sounded funny. Now, however, I see that the name is fitting: Volcanic mountains lie to the west of Bend, and red lava rock dominates the area's landscape. It's little wonder that the winery's slogan is, "Inspired by the volcanic peaks of the Cascades."

For Scott and Liz Ratcliff, transplants from the Bay Area, their relocation is proving to be the right move. Here they can exercise their entrepreneurial spirit, make award-winning wines, and imagine a future in which they exchange destemmers for Christmas!

VOLCANO VINEYARDS
winemaker(s): Gus Janeway and Scott Ratcliff
location: 930 NW Brooks Street, Bend, OR 97701
phone: 541-647-1102
web: www.volcanovineyards.com
e-mail: info@volcanovineyards.com
picnic area: Yes
fee: Fee refundable with purchase
hours: Tuesday through Sunday 11–6

DIRECTIONS: **From Sisters** take US-20 [SR-126] east about 20 miles. Take ramp (right) onto US-97 [Bend Pkwy] and go .5 miles. At exit 137 keep right onto ramp toward Revere Ave./Downtown. Road name changes to NW Hill St. and then NW Wall St. Continue for .6 miles. Turn right (northwest) onto NW Oregon Ave., then immediately left (southwest) onto NW Brooks St. Arrive at Volcano Vineyards.

From Redmond take US-97 south for about 16 miles. At exit 137 keep right onto ramp toward Revere Ave/Downtown. Road name changes to NW Hill St. and then NW Wall St. Continue for .6 miles. Turn right (northwest) onto NW Oregon Ave., then immediately left (southwest) onto NW Brooks St. and arrive at Volcano Vineyards.

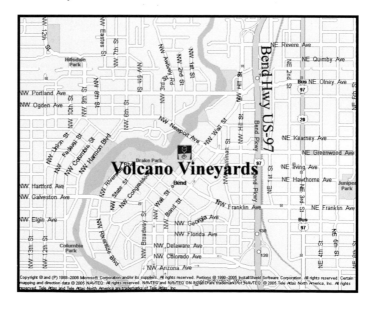

Zerba Cellars 3

Prior to launching their winery, Cecil and Marilyn Zerba had a successful nursery business that served the Walla Walla Valley. However, their love of wine and the economics of growing premium cabernet sauvignon and other varieties convinced the couple to plant grapes in three vineyards: Dad's Place, Cockburn Hills, and Winesap Road. In 2004, Cecil and Marilyn opened Zerba Cellars with their estate-bottled 2002 wines. It was a slow start — their 2004 release checking in at a paltry 200 cases. But production is on a roll now,

Zerba Cellars tasting room

with more than 6,000 cases released in 2008. This growth and other recent accolades have confirmed Cecil's mantra, "It's about the vines in the wines."

When I first met Marilyn at the tasting room, I made the same mistake that nine out of 10 visitors make. Dyslexia must have hit me, because I referred to her winery as "Zebra Cellars." The confusion is due, in part, to a drawing of a zebra prominently displayed on Zerba's Wild Z Red Wine label. Marilyn explained that the zebra-adorned label was "tongue in cheek," because so many people make the mistake of referring to the Zerbas' winery as Zebra Cellars. I wasn't the first, nor will I be the last.

The winery's log-cabin-inspired tasting room was built with western juniper from central Oregon. This knotty tree consumes 40 to 50 gallons of water per day; consequently, vegetation is scarce surrounding a western juniper. The trees used to build the tasting room laid on the forest floor for years, allowing worms to attack and eat their way between bark and wood. The results are amazing patterns of etched wood — as you sample Zerba's finest, study the wood to see nature's artwork. No two patterns are the same; just like the distinctive reds and whites of Zerba Cellars.

One of the real joys visitors experience at Zerba is its tasting extravaganza — especially if they like Walla Walla's big reds. Anticipate tastes of cabernet sauvignon, merlot, cabernet franc, Malbec, sangiovese, chardonnay, viognier, semillon, port, and red and white blends. With this bounty, it's little wonder that the zebra on Zerba's Wild Z label is smiling.

ZERBA CELLARS
opened: 2004
winemaker(s): Cecil Zerba
location: 85530 Highway 11,
Milton-Freewater, OR 97862
phone: 541-938-9463
web: www.zerbacellars.com
e-mail: info@zerbacellars.com
picnic area: Yes
fee: Complimentary wine tasting
hours: Daily 12–5

DIRECTIONS: **From Walla Walla** take Hwy 125 south. After you cross the State Line Rd, Hwy 125 becomes Hwy 11 in Oregon. When you cross State Line Rd, stay right, and Zerba Cellars is one block south on the right-hand side.

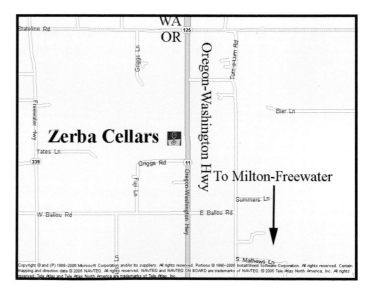

Watermill Winery &
Blue Mountain Cider Company 4

Just like the old Doublemint gum jingle "Double your pleasure, Double your fun…," Watermill Winery & Blue Mountain Cider Company offers twice the tasting pleasure with two tasting rooms in one. Here, you can savor noble wine varietals while also sampling refreshing hard cider. It's all under one roof in a renovated tasting room, complete with a private dining area and a full-service kitchen.

Watermill Winery is located just 10 miles south of Walla Walla in the historic town of Milton-Freewater. The tasting room is actually a diminutive structure near the front of

the property with the many-storied Watermill Building dominating the property in the back. With plenty of space for wine production and storage, capacity is clearly not an issue here.

Perhaps the Brown family, who owns the winery and cider house, will elect to ramp up production in the future, but right now they seem content to rack up awards. Their 2005 Midnight Red Walla Walla Valley Bordeaux blend just took home the double gold from the 2008 San Francisco Wine Competition. I took one sip and a sale was made. Their 2005 Reserve Syrah also received 90 points from *Wine Enthusiast*.

Watermill Winery's future looks promising, because it has the three essential ingredients for success: exceptional vineyards, advanced winemaking equipment and facilities, and a skilled and experienced winemaker, Richard Funk (of nearby Saviah Cellars). But perhaps the most important ingredient is this family's sense of unity and their devotion to the land and history of this unique part of the Walla Walla Valley. You feel this passion at the winery. The Browns also have a strong sense of responsibility toward the environment, paying strict attention to eco-friendly, organic practices in managing Anna Marie Vineyard, McClellen Estate Vineyard, and Watermill Estate Vineyard.

The Blue Mountain Cider was a surprise find when I visited on a hot August day. Though a hardship to walk the six feet from the wine-tasting bar to the cider-tasting bar, I somehow managed. The hard cider has less alcohol than its wine counterpart and clearly delivers on taste and refreshment. It's perfect by itself or paired with a summer salad or barbecue. My favorite was the carbonated Cherry Hard Apple Cider, created from a blending process of five types of local apples and a splash of tart cherry freshness. A sip of this and I was reaching for my wallet a second time!

482   WineTrails NW   www.winetrailsnw.com/wineries/watermill_winery_and_blue_
                                              mountain_cider_company

WATERMILL WINERY & BLUE MOUNTAIN CIDER COMPANY
opened: 2005
winemaker(s): Richard Funk
location: 235 E Broadway Avenue,
Milton-Freewater, OR 97862
phone: 541-938-5575
web: www.watermillwinery.com
e-mail: info@watermillwinery.com
picnic area: Yes
wheelchair access: Yes
fee: Complimentary wine tasting
hours: Monday through Saturday 11–4, or
by appointment

DIRECTIONS: **From Walla Walla** take SR-125 [S 9th Ave.] 5.2 miles and enter Oregon. Keep straight onto SR-11 [Oregon-Washington Hwy] for 4.4 miles. Turn right (west) onto E Broadway Ave. and go .2 miles to the Watermill Winery & Blue Mountain Cider Company.

From Pendleton take SR-11 [Oregon-Washington Hwy] 27.6 miles north to Milton-Freewater. Bear left (northwest) onto SR-11 [S Main St.], keep straight onto S Main St. for .4 miles, and arrive at destination.

Appendix A - Practical Information
Wine Tasting 101

The key to tasting wine is to slow down and concentrate.

Beyond that, you just need to swirl, smell, and taste. A visual check of the wine simply informs your brain what you are about to taste. Red wine ranges

in color from purple, ruby red, deep red, red brown, mahogany, to brown. White wine hues range from yellow green through straw, gold, yellow-brown, and amber brown to brown. It's a good idea to hold your glass up to a white background (a wall or a napkin) to judge the color of the wine. Where the wine is on the color palette

Oak Knoll Winery's tasting room

gives your taste buds a heads-up for what they are about to experience.

Once the wine is poured, some folks like to tilt the glass and observe how the wine flows down the inside of the glass. However, there is no correlation between the "legs" or "tears" on the inside of the glass and the taste itself.

Swirling
A wine just poured needs to stretch its legs and aerate. Swirling lets the wine release aromas. Up to this point, oxygen has been a bad thing; now, oxygen is the wine's best friend. It allows the wine to open up and create a bouquet. Most tasting rooms provide wine glasses roomy enough to swirl the wine without spillage. You need that space between the wine and your nose to smell the aroma. If you chance upon a winery that uses little plastic cups, or tiny "orange juice glasses," you might consider shortening your visit and moving on to the next winery.

Smelling
The aroma given off by a wine is its "nose." Right after a vigorous swirl, quickly smell the wine by sticking your nose into the glass. Get your nose as far down as possible. Concentrate and let your imagination run wild as you attempt to describe what you smell. In time, descriptions such as sweaty saddle, cat pee (no kidding), tar, kerosene, burnt match, and asparagus may enter your

smelling lexicon. Researchers say that flavor is 75 percent smell and 25 percent taste. No wonder food tastes bland when you have a cold: you can't smell it. Merlot, pinot noir, and cabernet sauvignon all have distinctive smells.

Tasting

Most of us grew up with the understanding that the tongue has certain regions that taste salt, bitter, sweet, and sour. Have you ever seen those drawings of the tongue that depict which part of the tongue tastes what?

Gewürztraminer

But according to current research, all taste buds can taste salt, bitter, sweet and sour to varying degrees. Taste buds are on the front of the tongue and the back. That's why you see sommeliers and wine connoisseurs vigorously swishing the wine around their mouths; they are getting the maximum exposure throughout their mouths to taste the wine. While you swish, your brain is also registering other sensations, such as heaviness, roundness, finish, and astringency from the tannins found in the wine. Concentrate for a few seconds while the wine is in your mouth. Swirl it around your mouth and attempt to suck a little air in — without committing a faux pas such as gagging — to pick up the wine's full flavors.

Remember, slow down and concentrate.

Tasting Room Etiquette

There are definite rules of the road when it comes to visiting tasting rooms, and most involve common sense. Moderation is a good thing. Those little ounces add up. So have a strategy ahead of time and try to stick to it. Here's some WineTrail do's and don'ts:

Do's:

- Drink responsibly — designate a driver or hire a limo.
- Spit or dump as much as you want — that's what those buckets are for!
- Have patience with the wine pourer — don't poodle your way forward with outstretched hand begging for another fill; they'll get to you.
- Have a tasting strategy — choose which wines you would like to sample. If you are only interested in the reds, let your pourer know.

- Ask questions — tasting room staff are passionate about their wines and anxious to tell you why.
- Purchase wine if you want to — assuming it is in your budget and you like it, spring for it.
- Be open to wines that you believe you will not like — reds, whites, port wines. You might be surprised to learn how delicious chardonnay from Idaho's Snake River Valley can be, or how perfect an accompaniment blackberry wine might be to the pound cake you plan to serve.
- Let them know if you like their wine — there's a reason that the pourer is staring at you with an expectant look in their eyes. If you like it, tell them. Winemakers live for such moments.

Don'ts:

- Ask for a second helping — unless you are contemplating purchasing a bottle, or you need a second helping to clarify what you just tasted.
- Feel that you have to purchase a bottle of wine — the winery's primary goal is to provide you with a positive experience so you'll tell your friends and family about it.
- Wear perfume or cologne — your nose needs to smell the wine.
- Attempt to engage the tasting room staff in esoteric debates — save the Hungarian versus American oak debate for a conversation with the winemaker, not the poor pourer.
- Take anything — the wine glasses are theirs, not yours (unless the tasting fee includes a glass).
- Drink excessively — keep your wits; spit often and pace yourself.

Wooldridge Creek Winery

Decoding an Oregon Wine Label

(Front)

1 **Winery Name**

2 **Vintage:** at least 95 percent of the grapes used were harvested in the year shown on the label.

3 **Vineyard designation:** a subsection of the vineyard. Identifies where the grapes were grown.

4 **Varietal:** In Oregon, a varietal designation (e.g., pinot noir, chardonnay, or pinot blanc) means that 90 percent of the grapes are of this varietal. Oregon Liquor Control Commission allows select varietals an exception to this rule. For the following varietals, only 75 percent of the volume must be composed of the grape variety named: cabernet franc, cabernet sauvignon, carmenère, petite sirah, grenache, malbec, marsanne, merlot, mourvèdre, petit verdot, roussanne, sangiovese, sauvignon blanc (fumé blanc), sémillon, syrah, tannat, tempranillo and zinfandel.

5 **Appellation:** 95 percent of the grapes in this wine must come from the named appellation (e.g., Willamette Valley).

Additional Terms:

Estate wine denotes that the grapes were grown and the wine bottled at the winery, with both winery and vineyard in the same appellation.

Reserve wine is a term given to a specific wine to imply that is of a higher quality than usual, or a wine that has been aged before being sold, or both. Traditionally winemakers would "reserve" some of their best wine rather than sell it immediately, thus the term.

(Back)

6 **Produced and bottled by:** Denotes who actually made and bottled the wine and their location.

7 **Contents:** Presence of sulfites, volume (e.g., 750 ml), and alcohol content by volume.

8 **Government warning:** Notice to pregnant women that wine may cause health problems and the ability to drive a car or operate machinery may be impaired by drinking alcohol.

9 **Growing green designations:** Oregon wineries understand the importance of sustainable farming. Encouraged by the Oregon Wine Board, wineries self-report select designations such as Salmon Safe, LIVE (Low Input Viticulture and Enology), Demeter Certified Biodynamic, and Oregon Tilth Certified Organic.

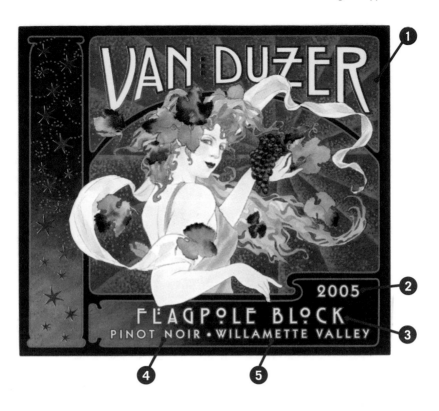

Bicycling in Wine Country

Looking to minimize your carbon footprint in wine country? How about forgoing the car in favor of your bike? Sipping and cycling in wine country is more than wishful thinking. Choices abound in the Pacific Northwest to ride alongside lush vineyards and sample amazing wines. What better way to work off some calories while taking in some much needed refreshment in the form of reds and whites. It's the ol' input and output equation — by the end of the day you break even calorie-wise but gain immeasurably in life's pleasures.

Elk Cove Winery

A great regional resource for planning your bike tours is found at www.bicyclepaper.com. Here's "everything biking" with respect to news and event information, including a number of rides that take you through the heart of wine country. If you're looking for an experienced touring company that provides fully supported bike touring (i.e., from boxed lunches to overnight accommodations) check out www.bicycleadventures.com.

Oregon offers a plethora of bike trails via undulating back roads surrounded by well-mannered rows of grapes. In the mid-Willamette Valley of Oregon, Tom Huggins, founder and general manager of Eola Hills winery, is also an avid cyclist. Every Sunday morning in August, a large group of cyclists gathers at Eola Hills Wine Cellars in Rickreall for a 45- or 52-mile group ride led by Tom Huggins and other guides. It's a superb way to explore the back roads of the Eola Hills and make pit stops at seven wineries, with a salmon barbecue and wine tasting at the end. Although the magnificent scenery is free, there's a nominal fee to pay for the cost of the support vehicle, lunch, and post-ride barbecue. For more information, contact Eola Hills at 800-291-6730, or visit www.eolahillswinery.com.

For cycling enthusiasts, there's the annual Vine Ride in August that features wine country tours of 35-, 50-, 65-, and 100-mile routes. This is a fully supported bicycle event with plenty of food, helpful volunteers, and music to boot. The ride begins at Newberg High School. Routes include charming villages, century-old farms, berry groves, and vineyards, with proceeds from the event going toward Children's Cancer Association. For more information including itinerary, registration, and maps, see www.vineride.com or call 866-262-8339.

Beyond the Willamette Valley, Oregon offers a variety of other great places to bring along your bike and experience the charm of wine country. Whether you travel to the Oregon Coast, the Rogue River Valley, or the Columbia Gorge, you have the opportunity to swirl, sip, and spin through miles of vineyards.

To plan such an adventure, there are a number of resources you can tap into. For starters, check out:

- Oregon's Park and Recreation website at www.oregon.gov/OPRD/PARKS/ BIKE/bike_links.shtml for maps and touring information

- The Bicycle Transportation Alliance at www.bta4bikes.org for tips and links to statewide bicycle clubs

- ORbike at www.orbike.com for event information registration and member advice

Washington is also a bicycler's paradise for weekend getaway wine touring. Think Walla Walla, Yakima Valley, San Juan Island, and the Columbia Gorge, and pairing biking with wine touring gets the heart pumping. Throughout the year, you can find bicycling events to combine sipping and cycling. For example, Skagit Valley's Tulip Pedal in April takes you through miles of tulips and nearby wineries; the Walla Walla Wine Tour in June includes rolling hills and vineyards; and Yakima Valley's Wine Country Trek in September are great opportunities to pair pedaling with amazing wines.

David Lowe, owner and winemaker of Wineglass Cellars in Zillah, is an avid cyclist when he's not making great wine. Lowe has developed a 60-miler for WineTrail biking enthusiasts. Combining rolling hills and the Valley's beauty, this tour immerses you in America's heartland. At the end of the day, your legs will know you've travelled far, and that lamb shank will be a perfect accompaniment to a bottle of Wineglass Cellars' red blend Capizimo at a nearby restaurant. Learn more about Lowe's 60-miler at www.wineglasscellars.com.

Cyclists at Kramer Vineyards

If you are planning a Washington state bike tour with swirling and sipping included, here are some online resources:

- The state's Department of Transportation's website at www.wsdot.wa.gov/ Bike/ for tour and map information

- The Bicycle Alliance of Washington's site at www.bicyclealliance.org for events, clubs, and resources

Idaho offers many a bike touring treasures including the Snake River Valley viticultural area. For additional information, check out the state's transportation website at www.itd.idaho.gov/bike_ped.

A word of caution is in order here. Riding a bicycle is potentially dangerous. It's often not the cyclist's riding behavior, but the car driver's inability to either see the cyclist or exercise appropriate caution. Adding alcohol only compounds the danger. Riders need to have a tasting strategy - either sip and spit with great frequency, or sample only one or two wines at each winery and limit the number of tasting rooms you visit. Alternatively, plan your biking for the morning and leave the wine tasting for the afternoon. Drink responsibly; ride responsibly.

Wine Touring with Kids

As a general rule wineries are not set up to handle little tykes — after all this is a "no whining zone." The stacked bottles of wine and Riedel Crystal are easy targets for a wandering three-year old. Few wineries offer a play area as part

of the tasting room or a playground for kids to enjoy. When they do, it is often more of a distraction to allow parents to sip and swirl and experience the wine. However, if you do have your children along and insist on checking out a winery or two, here are a few tips to make it family friendly in wine country.

Playground at Henry Estate Winery

First, make it informational, and choose wineries that feature a tour. Treat it like a field trip and discover how wine is made. At harvest time it is not unusual to see kids stomping grapes (talk about cheap labor). The smiles on their faces are testimony to their glee.

Try and combine wine tasting with family activities such as picnicking at the winery, checking out a hands-on museum, or going on a nature hike. Involve the kids in the planning. Sure, you're picking up the tab, but if you give in to their needs it's easier for them to accommodate you.

Don't attempt more than a couple of wineries in a day. Dragging kids to more than one or two wineries is a surefire way to squash a good day.

Finally, if your focus really is wine tasting throughout the day, consider splitting up. Dad takes the kids the first day and enjoys kid-friendly activities, while mom checks out three or four must-see wineries. Perhaps on day two, it's dad's turn to sample his favorite wineries while mom has the kids. Divide and conquer!

There's plenty to do in wine country for families. However, to make it truly memorable you need to plan ahead and create a win-win situation for both kids and parents.

Wine Touring with Pets

"Pets welcome" signs are seldom seen at wineries. In fact, it is quite the opposite. Wineries, by and large, don't welcome dogs into the tasting room. There are simply too many things that can go wrong — wine bottles crashing, a counter-surfing dog that attacks the crackers and cheese, or a scrap with the winery cat.

Ironically, a large percentage of wineries do have dogs of their own, which has led to an explosion of coffee-table books featuring mug shots of winery pooches. But even though the winery might be dog-friendly with their pooch, it's bound to create territorial issues if you introduce your dog into the tasting room.

However, if you do bring Fido along on your next wine tour, you will find a number of hotels and quaint country inns that welcome pets. Some may charge an additional fee, but it's typically a nominal amount. If you do bring along your dog in the car, be sure to pack doggy snacks and water and allow for pit stops along the way. Always keep the window open, especially in hot weather, to avoid

Cathedral Ridge Winery

baking your dog, and park in the shade. In the summertime, it's especially dangerous to keep a dog in a car even with windows open in wine country regions such as Walla Walla, Columbia Gorge, and Rogue River Valley. Bottom line... take your dog to the park, but not to the winery.

Wine Touring and Wheelchair Access

Increasingly wine tasting rooms throughout the Pacific Northwest are wheelchair accessible. Being wheelchair friendly means that the winery designates special parking spaces for cars bearing wheelchair placards, has no stairs that wheelchairs can't bypass, wide doors for easy access, and restrooms meeting ADA standards.

Oregon wineries in particular are sensitive to this issue, and a big chunk of them design or re-design their wineries to accommodate disabled travelers. Throughout *Wine Trails of Oregon* we have identified wineries that are wheelchair friendly.

Still, even if the winery indicates that they are wheelchair accessible, we believe it is a good idea to call ahead if you have concerns. For example, if you have a van that is specially equipped for wheelchair loading and unloading, you might be concerned about room in the parking lot to accommodate this. There also might be a concern if you are attending a special event such as a winemaker dinner or a wedding - you might have wheelchair access to the tasting room, but what about the rest of the winery, the bathroom facilities, or outdoors among the vineyards? Call ahead or email the winery to find out.

For general information to assist disabled travelers, check out these websites:

- Access-Able Travel Source (www.access-able.com)

- Global Access Disabled Travel Network (www.globalaccessnews.com)

- Mobility International (www.miusa.org)

Picnickers at Tyee Wine Cellars

Appendix B – Wine Tour Planning

Resources for Oregon Wine Country Touring

Statewide Resources

AAA of Oregon/Idaho
Serving members in Oregon and
Southern Idaho
800-444-8091
www.aaaorid.com

Alaska Airlines – City Guides
800-ALASKAAIR
www.alaskaair.com

Oregon Wine Board
info@oregonwine.org
www.oregonwine.org

Oregon Bed and Breakfast Guild
P.O. Box 12702
Salem, OR 97309
800-944-6196
stay@obbg.org
www.obbg.org

Travel Oregon
800-547-7842
www.traveloregon.com

WineTrails Northwest
Companion website to this guidebook
– get event and latest winery
information
800-533-6165
info@winetrailsnw.com
www.winetrailsnw.com

Oregon Coast Wine Country

Oregon Coast Visitors Association
Pioneer Courthouse Square
137 NE First Street
Newport, OR 97365
541-574-2679 or 888-628-2101
www.visittheoregoncoast.com

Rose City Wine Country

Portland Oregon Information Center
Pioneer Courthouse Square
701 SW Sixth Avenue, Suite 1
Portland, OR 97204
877-678-5263
www.travelportland.com

**Willamette Valley (Including North,
Mid, South and East Wine Countries)**

Benton County
553 NW Harrison Blvd.
Corvallis, OR 97330
541-757-1544 or 800-334-8118
info@visitcorvallis.com
www.VisitCorvallis.com

Benton County Wineries
P.O. Box 1565
Philomath, OR 97370
contact@bentoncountywineries.com
www.bentoncountywineries.com

Chehalem Valley
415 E Sheridan
Newberg, OR 97132
503-538-2014
info@newberg.org
www.chehalemvalley.org

Convention and Visitors Association of Lane County, Oregon
754 Olive Street
Eugene, OR 97401
800-547-5445
info@cvalco.org
www.VisitLaneCounty.org

Dundee Hills Winegrowers Association
P.O. Box 2
Dundee, OR 97115
503-864-2700
info@dundeehills.org
www.dundeehills.org

East Valley Winery Tour
info@eastvalleywine.com
www.eastvalleywine.com

International Pinot Noir Celebration
P.O. Box 1310
McMinnville, OR 97128
503-472-8964 or 800-775-4762
info@ipnc.org
www.ipnc.org

Linn County
www.AlbanyVisitors.com

McMinnville Area
417 NW Adams Street
McMinnville, OR 97128
503-472-6196
www.mcminnville.org

Salem Convention & Visitors Association
1313 Mill Street SE
Salem, OR 97301
800-874-7012
information@travelsalem.com
www.TravelSalem.com

Washington County Visitors Association
11000 SW Stratus Street, #170
Beaverton, OR 97008
800-537-3149
www.wcva.org and www.ComePlayYourWay.com

Willamette Valley Visitors Association
553 NW Harrison Blvd.
Corvallis, OR 97330
866-548-5018
info@oregonwinecountry.org
www.oregonwinecountry.org

Willamette Valley Wine Country
P.O. Box 25162
Portland, OR 97298
503-646-2985
info@willamettewines.com
www.willamettewines.com

Yamhill Valley Visitors Association
P.O. Box 774
McMinnville, OR 97128
503-883-7770
info@yamhillvalley.org
www.yamhillvalley.org

Umpqua Valley Wine Country

Roseburg Visitors & Convention Bureau
410 SE Spruce Street
Roseburg, OR 97470
800-444-9584
info@visitroseburg.com
www.visitroseburg.com

Southern Oregon Winery Association
www.sorwa.org

Umpqua Valley Wineries Association
P.O. Box 367
Roseburg, OR 97470
541-673-5323
info@umpquavalleywineries.org
www.umpquavalleywineries.org

Rogue Valley Wine Country

Southern Oregon Visitors Association
1512 E Main Street
Ashland, OR 97520
office@sova.org
www.southernoregon.org

Southern Oregon Winery Association
www.sorwa.org

Columbia Gorge Wine Country

Columbia Gorge Winegrowers' Association
P.O. Box 665
Hood River, OR 97031
866-413-WINE
info@columbiagorgewine.com
www.ColumbiaGorgeWine.com

Dalles Area Chamber of Commerce
404 W Second Street
The Dalles, OR 97058
800-255-3385
www.thedalleschamber.com

Hood River County Chamber of Commerce & Visitors Center
405 Portway Avenue
Hood River, OR 97031
541-386-2000 or 800-366-3530
hrccc@hoodriver.org
www.hoodriver.org

Mt. Hood Territory
2051 Kaen Road, Suite 427
Oregon City, OR 97045
503-655-8490 or 800-424-3002
www.MtHoodTerritory.com

Central and Eastern Oregon Wine Country

Bend Visitor & Convention Bureau
917 NW Harriman
Bend, OR 97701
877-245-8484
www.visitbend.com

Central Oregon Visitors Association
661 SW Powerhouse Drive, Suite 1301
Bend, OR 97702
800-800-8334
www.visitcentraloregon.com

Milton-Freewater Chamber of Commerce
157 S Columbia
Milton-Freewater, OR 97862
541-938-5563
mfmdfrog@oregontrail.net
www.mfchamber.com

Tourism Walla Walla
877-WW-VISIT
www.wallawalla.org

Walla Walla Valley Wine Alliance
13½ E Main Street, Suite 214
Walla Walla, WA 99362
509-526-3117
info@wallawallawine.com
www.wallawallawine.com;

Touring Companies – Getting Around

Serving Willamette Valley & Columbia Gorge (where noted)

Eagle Towncar Corp.
Portland, OR
503-222-2763
800-565-2783

EcoTours of Oregon
Portland, OR
503-245-1428
888-TOURS-33 (888-868-7733)

Executive Touch Limousine, Inc.
Portland, OR
503-310-7776

Five Star Limousine Service
503-585-8533
800-517-9555

Grape Escape Winery Tours, Inc.
Portland, OR
503-283-3380
grrrape@GrapeEscapeTours.com
www.grapeescapetours.com

My Chauffeur Wine Tours –
also serving Columbia Gorge
Portland, OR
503-969-4370
877-692-4283
winetour@winetouroregon.com
www.winetouroregon.com

Northwest Limousine & Wine Tours –
also serving Columbia Gorge
Portland, OR
503-282-5414
503-650-3885
nwlimousine@aol.com
www.nwlimousine.com

Off the Beaten Path Tours
Junction City, OR
541-998-2450
offthebeatenpathtransport@yahoo.com
www.junctioncity.com

Oregon Wine Tours
Portland, OR
503-681-WINE (9463)
ron@orwinetours.com
www.orwinetours.com

Premiere Tours, LLC
Portland, OR
503-244-4653
800-778-6214
info@premierewinetours.com
www.premierewinetours.com

Pro Limo
Salem, OR
503-391-2900
877-800-LIMO (5466)

Sea to Summit Outdoor Adventures –
also serving Columbia Gorge
Portland, OR
503-286-9333
seatosummit@qwest.net
www.seatosummit.net

Sunshine Limo Service
Eugene, OR
541-344-LIMO (5466)
info@sunshinelimoservice.com
www.sunshinelimoservice.com

Willamette Tours
Portland, OR
877-868-7295 or 360-904-1402
www.willamettetours.com

Serving Umpqua Valley

Oregon Wine Country Tours
Roseburg, OR
800-704-2943
www.oregonwinecountrytours.com

Serving Rogue Valley

Ashland Wine Tours
Ashland, OR
541-552-WINE (9463)

Jules of the Valley Wine Tours
Ashland, OR
541-973-9699
877-215-7676
julesofthevalley@smartwire.net
www.julesvalley.com

Serving Columbia River Gorge

Columbia Gorge Limousine
Hood River, OR
541-386-2384
800-899-5676
cg_limo@yahoo.com
www.explorethegorge.com

Hood River Tours
Hood River, OR
541-350-9850
info@hoodrivertours.com
www.hoodrivertours.com

Serving Central & Eastern Oregon

**Muscat-Dun – Vineyard and Ranch
Tours on Horseback**
Echo, OR
541-571-3640
MuscatDun@aol.com
www.muscatdun.com

Domaine Serene

Events

Every effort is made to ensure the accuracy of these events; however, WineTrails Northwest cannot be responsible for date and venue changes or cancellations. Please contact individual events to confirm information. Most individual wineries host events of their own: spring release parties, winemaker dinners, grape-stomping bashes and more. **WineTrail Tip:** Go online to www.winetrailsnw.com for winery-specific events or call the winery you have in mind for details.

January
Oregon Wine & Food Festival — Salem
Held at the Oregon State Fairgrounds, this annual wine and food event features more than 100 booths of Oregon wineries, microbreweries, eateries, arts and crafts, celebrity cooks and authors, and live music. Call 503-580-2509 or go online to www.oregonstatefair.org for event information, including tickets and schedule.

February
Newport Seafood & Wine Festival — Newport
It wouldn't be winter on the coast without the Newport Seafood & Wine Festival. Since 1978, the Newport Seafood & Wine Festival has attracted visitors from around the world to the central Oregon coast. Packed with great food and wine, this event puts a stopper in any WineTrail enthusiast's winter blues. See www.newportchamber.org. Call 541-265-8801 or 800-COAST44 (800-262-7844).

View from Penner-Ash Wine Cellars

Oregon Shakespeare Festival — Ashland
The celebrated drama festival runs from late February until early November. There are great places to stay and eat in and around Ashland. Have you noticed that there is nothing here about wine? Take heart, my fellow trekker — you're in Rogue River Valley and therefore surrounded by vineyards and great wine. As Shakespeare scribed in Othello (Act II, scene iii), "Good wine is a good familiar creature if it be well used." Visit www.osfashland.org or contact 541-482-4331 or boxoffice@oshashland.org for more information.

March
Annual Greatest of the Grape — Canyonville
Sponsored by the Umpqua Valley Winegrowers Association, this is Oregon's oldest winery event. Nearly 30 wineries from around Oregon participate in

the annual event with top restaurants pairing culinary treasures with wine. The event includes wine tasting, dinner with great wine, entertainment, more great wine and a fine-arts auction. Tickets are limited. Call 541-673-7575 or go online to www.umpquavalleywineries.org to order tickets.

McMinnville Wine & Food Classic — McMinnville

This event is open to all ages and features cooking demonstrations, wine tasting 101, music, and plenty of great food and wine. Visit with the artisans and view their work, which also is available for purchase. Call 503-472-4033 or email info@macwfc.org. Visit www.macwfc.org for event schedule and ticketing.

April

Astoria-Warrenton Crab and Seafood Festival — Astoria

The Crab and Seafood Festival brings together more than 200 regional vendors.

Enjoy crab dinners and other culinary delights, live music, wine from more than 40 wineries, and more at this classic event. For more information, contact the Astoria-Warrenton Area Chamber of Commerce at 503-325-6311 or 800-875-6807, or visit www.oldoregon.com.

Dundee Hills Passport Weekend — Dundee

Hosted by Sokol Blosser Winery, this annual event offers the opportunity to sample a variety of Dundee Hills wines and get a dose of vineyard education organic style. Advance tickets are not required; pay at the door. Contact Sokol Blosser Winery for more

Phelps Creek Vineyards

information at 503-864-2282, 800-582-6668 or by email, info@sokolblosser.com. You can also visit www.sokolblosser.com for event information.

Umpqua Valley Barrel Tasting Bus Tour — Roseburg

Jump on the tour bus and experience Umpqua Valley wineries. Check out some of Umpqua Valley's 100 valleys and snap pictures of covered bridges. This barrel tasting tour requires reservations. For details, call 541-672-5701, 800-444-9584, or email info@umpquavalleywineries.org. Also visit www.umpquavalleywineries.org or www.visitroseburg.com for more event-specific information.

May

Art in Bloom Festival — Medford

This annual Mother's Day weekend bash in downtown Medford showcases fine artists from the West Coast, floral workshops, local food, and wine. Call 541-608-8524 or visit www.visitmedford.org for more information.

Memorial Weekend in Wine Country — Willamette Valley

Imagine springtime in wine country and wine from more than 120 wineries to sample. This is the opportunity to visit (and taste wines from) a number of small, family-owned wineries not usually open to the public. In addition, Memorial Day weekend in wine country offers WineTrail trekkers the chance to sample new releases, taste barrel samples, and nosh on gourmet foods. For more information, send an email to info@willamettevines.com or visit www.willamettewines.com.

Seaside Downtown Wine Walk — Seaside

Seaside Downtown Development Association sponsors the Seaside Downtown Wine Walk showcasing Oregon wineries and downtown businesses. Oregon wineries and Seaside downtown businesses partner to offer fine wine and complimentary nibbles. Some wineries charge a nominal tasting fee. Call 503-717-1914 or email director@seasidedowntown.com.

Spring Release Weekend — Walla Walla/Milton-Freewater

During the first full weekend in May, more than 50 of the Walla Walla Valley's wineries, including wineries on the Oregon side of the valley, open their doors and present their new wines. Visitors can talk to the winemakers and take away bottles of the new vintage. For more information, contact the Walla Walla Valley Wine Alliance at 509-526-3117 or info@wallawallawine.com. Another option is to go online to www.wallawallawine.com for more information.

Umpqua Winery Association sponsors Memorial Day Open House — Umpqua Valley Wineries

Wineries of the Umpqua Valley Winegrowers Association invite WineTrail enthusiasts to come check out their wines, including newly released vintages. Call 541-679-6642 or email wine@abacela.com for more information, or visit www.umpquavalleywineries.org.

June
Britt Festival — Jacksonville

This is the Pacific Northwest's premier outdoor summer performing-arts festival running from June to September. It features dozens of summer concerts showcasing classical music, dance, jazz, blues, folk, bluegrass, pop and country music. The outdoor venue is an amazing natural amphitheater situated on the Peter Britt estate (among other remarkable achievements, Peter Britt also cultivated wine grapes in the 19th century). Although this event is not about wine, guests are welcomed to throw down a blanket and uncork some wine. With all the nearby wineries, it's likely that the wine will be fresh from the Applegate Valley. For details call 541-779-0847 or visit www.brittfest.org.

Wine by the River — Bend

Bend's premier wine event, Wine by the River, offers superb chocolates, excellent cuisine, fine arts, evening musicals, and premium wines. Held at the Les Schwab Amphitheater, Wine by the River is presented by Hospice Center Bend with proceeds benefiting terminally ill children in central Oregon. Call 541-383-3910 or go online to www.winebytheriver.com for more information.

Wineries of Lane County Summer Barrel Tour — Eugene Area

Six wineries per day via a deluxe chartered bus — now that's livin'! The wineries of Lane County open their doors for this once-a-year special event. Each winery features appetizers paired with three wine tastings. Tickets are limited, with reservations required. Call 800-992-8499 for more information and tickets.

July
Art and the Vineyard — Eugene

Art and the Vineyard is one of the Northwest's top art, wine, and music festivals, staged along the banks of the Willamette River in scenic Alton Baker Park. For this three-day event, tickets are available at the festival gate or in advance at Maude Kerns Art Center. Call 541-485-2221 or go online to www.artandthevineyard.org.

International Pinot Noir Celebration — McMinnville

Every year since 1987 pinot lovers from around the world gather in McMinnville to celebrate pinot noir. This is a gathering of pinot noir aficionados enjoying a weekend of wine, food and giving it up for a singular grape: pinot noir. The IPNC hosts grand tastings in the afternoons at which

Stoller Vineyard and Winery

winemakers pour their featured pinots. Tickets are hard to come by, but give it a try by calling 800-775-4762 or visiting www.ipnc.org.

August
Carlton's Walk in the Park — Carlton

Carlton's Walk in the Park, a benefit for local charities, combines fabulous artists and musicians with outstanding local restaurants and wineries for a self-described "one magical August weekend in Yamhill County's beautiful wine country." For details, contact 503-852-6572, info@carltonswalkinthepark.com, or visit www.carltonswalkinthepark.com.

September
Rhapsody in the Vineyard — Corvallis

Sponsored by the Downtown Corvallis Association, the Rhapsody in the Vineyard highlights some of Oregon's premier wineries. Downtown businesses provide a variety of yummy appetizers along with music and/or artwork by local artists, and you get a chance to walk off some of those calories as you saunter from one retailer to another. Wine is available for purchase, by the bottle or the case. Call 541-754-6624 or check out www.downtowncorvallis.org.

November
Lane County Wineries Thanksgiving — Eugene Area

"Thanksgiving in wine country" evokes a sense of warm indulgence, and the wineries of Lane County epitomize this feeling. Most wineries are open to the

Paschal Winery

public over Thanksgiving weekend and invite WineTrail trekkers to sample wine (often right out of the barrel), enjoy music and partake in tasty appetizers. A keepsake wine glass is included as you sip and swirl your way through Lane County wine country. Call 541-484-5307 or visit www.visitlanecounty.org for more information.

NW Food and Wine Festival — Portland

Benefiting Camp Fire USA, this event fills the main floor of the Memorial Coliseum — former home of the Portland Trail Blazers. Using the catch phrase "Prepare to meet your Maker... your wine maker that is!" this event features more than 600 wines and more than 50 gourmet and epicurean offerings. What's more, there is a "wine down" cigar bar area where you can experience some terrific ports. Surrounded by live music and friendly pourers, this is the chance to discover your favorite wines while contributing to a good cause. For event information and tickets, call 800-422-0251 or visit www.nwfoodandwinefestival.com

¡Salud! Oregon's Pinot Noir Auction — Portland

¡Salud! is a unique collaboration between Oregon winemakers and healthcare professionals to provide access to healthcare services for Oregon's seasonal vineyard workers and their families. Since its inception in the early '90s, ¡Salud! has raised more than $6 million to provide healthcare to seasonal vineyard workers. Picture a pinot-noir-meets-black-tie event with luscious Northwest cuisine and you have one of Oregon's premier auction events. Call 503-681-1850 or go online to www.saludauction.org and discover how you can be a part of this important event.

Wine Country Thanksgiving – Willamette Valley

Sponsored by the Willamette Valley Wineries Association, this is the premier Thanksgiving event in wine country, featuring dozens of wineries from throughout the valley, including many small family-owned wineries not typically open to the public. For more than 25 years, this event has drawn crowds on the first weekend after Thanksgiving. Each winery serves up special treats to pair with its wines, be it music, wreaths made with vines from the vineyard, or delectable cheeses and other appetizers. Contact 503-646-2985 or info@willamettewines.com for more information. You can also visit www.willamettewines.com.

December
Holiday Barrel Tasting – Walla Walla/Milton-Freewater

Block off the first full weekend in December on your calendar and head east. Taste future releases straight from the barrel amidst the festive spirit of the season in the Walla Walla Valley. For further information, contact Walla Walla Valley Wine Alliance at 509-526-3117 or visit www.wallawallawine.com.

Carlo & Julian Winery

Wineries to Visit By Appointment Only

Wine Trails of Oregon features wineries that are open to the public and have regular tasting room hours. However, there are a number of wineries that are open to the public yet do not have regular tasting room hours. These wineries welcome visitors "by appointment only." Listed by wine country region are wineries that you can visit by calling ahead and scheduling a visit. Enjoy!

Rose City Wine Country

Beran Vineyards
30088 SW Egger Road
Hillsboro, OR 97123
www.beranvineyards.com
info@beranvineyards.com
503-628-1298

Christopher Bridge Cellars and Satori Springs Vineyard
12770 S Casto Road
Oregon City, OR 97045
www.christopherbridgewines.com
info@christopherbridgewines.com
503-263-6267

Cloudrest Vineyards
34780 SW Cloudrest Lane
Hillsboro, OR 97123
www.gardenaesthetics.com/grapeharvest.htm
lengstro@teleport.com
503-628-2552

Dimmick Cellars
7401 SW Corbett Avenue
Portland, OR 97219
dimmickcellars@attbi.com
503-246-0659

Holloran Vineyard Wines
2636 SW Shaeffer Road
West Linn, OR 97068
www.holloranvineyardwines.com
bill@holloranvineyardwines.com
503-638-6224

J. Albin Winery
19495 Vista Hill Drive
Hillsboro, OR 97123
jalbin@mindspring.com
503-628-2986

King's Raven Winery
11625 S New Era Road
Oregon City, OR
503-784-6298

North Willamette Valley Wine Country

ADEA Wine Company
26421 NW Hwy 47
Gaston, OR 97119
www.adeawine.com
info@adeawine.com
503-662-4509

Alloro Vineyard
22075 SW Lebeau Road
Sherwood, OR 97140
www.allorovineyard.com
winemaker@allorovineyard.com
503-625-1978

Anam Cara Cellars
P.O. Box 475
Newberg, OR 97132
www.anamcaracellars.com
info@anamcaracellars.com
503-537-9150

Anderson Family Vineyard
20120 NE Herring Lane
Newberg, OR 97132
cliffanderson@mindspring.com
503-554-5541

Atticus Wine
Russell Creek Road
Yamhill, OR 97148
www.atticuswine.com
503-662-3485

Ayoub Vineyard
9650 NE Keyes Lane
Dundee, OR 97115
www.ayoubwines.com
mo@ayoubwines.com
503-554-9583

Ayres Vineyard & Winery
17971 NE Lewis Rogers Lane
Newberg, OR 97132
www.ayresvineyard.com
503-538-7450

Barbara Thomas Wines
8663 NE Blackburn Road
Yamhill, OR 97148
www.barbarathomaswines.com
info@barabarathomaswines.com
503-662-4585

Beaux Freres
15155 NE North Valley Road
Newberg, OR 97132
www.beauxfreres.com
infor@beauxfreres.com
503-537-1137

Belle Pente Vineyards and Winery
12470 NE Rowland Road
Carlton, OR 97111
www.bellepente.com
wine@bellepente.com
503-852-9500

Black Cap of Oregon
935 NE 10th Avenue
McMinnville, OR 97128
www.blackcapwine.com
971-237-0626

Brick House Wine Company
18200 Lewis Rogers Lane
Newberg, OR 97132
www.brickhousewines.com
info@brickhousewines.com
503-538-5136

Brooks
1043 NE 4th Street
McMinnville, OR 97128
www.brookswine.com
info@brookswine.com
503-435-1278

Cameron Winery
8200 Worden Hill Road
Dundee, OR 97115
www.cameronwines.com
cameronwinery@earthlink.com
503-538-0336

Carlton Cellars
P.O. Box 974
Carlton, OR 97111
www.carltoncellars.com
dave@carltoncellars.com
503-852-7888

Coeur de Terre Vineyard
21000 SE Eagle Point Road
McMinnville, OR 97128
503-472-3976

Coleman Vineyard
22734 SW Latham Road (at Redhawk)
McMinnville, OR 97128
www.colemanwine.com
colemanvineyard@msn.com
503-843-2707

de Lancellotti Family Vineyards
18405 NE Calkins Lane
Newberg, OR 97132
www.deLancellottiFamilyVineyards.com
paul@lancellottifamilyvineyards.com
503-554-6802

ElvenGlade Vineyards
3500 Bridgefarmer Road
Gaston, OR 97119
www.elvenglade.com
bill@elvenglade.com
503-662-9960

Hatcher Wine Works
990 N Hwy 99W
Dundee, OR 97115
503-864-4489

J.K. Carriere Wines
30295 Hwy 99W
Newberg, OR 97132
www.jkcarriere.com
jim@jkcarriere.com
503-554-0721

Ken Wright Cellars
236 N Kutch Street
Carlton, OR 97111
www.kenwrightcellars.com
info@kenwrightcellars.com
503-852-7070

La Dolce Vita Vineyards
6223 SW Old Highway 47
Gaston, OR 97119
www.ladolcevitavineyards.net
brentfree@msn.com
503-992-7195

Lachini Vineyards
18225 Calkins Lane
Newberg, OR 97132
www.lachinivineyards.com
info@lachinivineyards.com
503-864-4553

Laura Volkman Vineyards
14000 NE Quarry Road
Newberg, OR 97132
www.volkmanvineyards.com
Customers@lauravolkman.com
503-806-4047

Lawton Winery
20990 NE Kings Grade
Newberg, OR 97132
www.lawtonwinery.com
keith@lawtonwinery.com
503-538-6509

Le Bête Wines
845 NE 5th Street, Ste. 400
McMinnville, OR 97128
503-977-1493

Le Cadeau Vineyard
P.O. Box 268
Dundee, OR 97115
www.LeCadeauVineyard.com
503-625-2777

Lemelson Vineyards
12020 NE Stag Hollow Road
Carlton, OR 97111
www.lemelsonvineyards.com
info@lemelsonvineyards.com
503-852-6619

McKinlay Vineyards
7120 Earlwood Road
Newberg, OR 97132
mckwine@aol.com
503-625-2534

Medici Vineyards at Dark Horse Wine Bar
1505 Portland Road
Newberg, OR 97132
halmedici@aol.com
503-538-9668

Monks Gate Vineyard
9500 NE Oak Springs Farm Road
Carlton, OR 97111
www.monksgate.com
503-852-6521

Natalie's Estate Winery
16825 NE Chehalem Drive
Newberg, OR 97132
www.nataliesestatewinery.com
contact@nataliesestatewinery.com
503-554-9350

Owen Roe
31590 NE Schaad Road
Newberg, OR 97132
www.owenroe.com
info@owenroe.com
503-678-5058

Quailhurst Vineyard Estate
16031 SE Pleasant Hill Road
Sherwood, OR 97140
www.quailhurstwines.com
info@quailhurstwines.com
503-936-3633

Ransom Cellars
845 NE 5th Street
McMinnville, OR 97128
www.ransomspirits.com
tad@ransomspirits.com
541-738-1565

Raptor Ridge Winery
29090 SW Wildhaven Lane
Scholls, OR 97123
www.raptoridge.com
info@raptoridge.com
503-628-3534

Redman Vineyard & Winery
18975 NE Ribbon Ridge Road
Newberg, OR 97132
www.redmanwines.com
Info.redmanwines.com
503-554-1290

Remy Wines
3500 NW Bridgefarmer Road
Gaston, OR 97119
www.remywines.com
503-560-2003

RR
21080 NE Ribbon Ridge Road
Newberg, OR 97232
503-706-9277

Soter Vineyards
10880 NE Mineral Springs Road
Carlton, OR 97111
www.sotervineyards.com
james@sotervineyards.com
503-662-5600

Stag Hollow Wines
7930 NE Blackburn Road
Yamhill, OR 97148
www.staghollow.com
staghollow@staghollow.com
503-662-5609

Stony Mountain Vineyard
27734 SW Latham Road
McMinnville, OR 97128
smurayama@stonymountain.com
503-550-6317

Styring Vineyards
19960 NE Ribbon Ridge Road
Newberg, OR 97132
503-866-6741

Twelve Wine
12401 NW Fir Crest Road
Carlton, OR 97111
www.twelvewine.com
staff@twelvewine.com
503-358-6707

Utopia Vineyard and Cellars
116 W Main Street
Carlton, OR 97111
www.utopiawine.com
info@utopiawine.com
503-852-7546

Vidon Vineyard, LLC
17425 NE Hillside Drive
Newberg, OR 97132
www.vidonvineyard.com
Info@vidonvineyards.com
503-538-4092

Westrey Wine Co.
1065 NE Alpine Street
McMinnville, OR 97218
www.westrey.com
westrey@easystreet.com
503-224-7360

Whistling Ridge Vineyard
15025 NE North Valley Road
Newberg, OR 97132
www.whistlingridgevineyard.com
patgus@teleport.com
503-538-6641

Youngberg Hill Vineyards
10660 SW Youngberg Hill Road
McMinnville, OR 97126
www.youngberghill.com
Info@youngberghill.com
503-472-2727

Mid Willamette Valley Wine Country

Amalie Robert Estate
13531 Bursell Road
Dallas, OR 97338
www.amalierobert.com
amalierobert@msn.com
503-831-4703

Evesham Wood Vineyard & Winery
3795 Wallace Road NW
Salem, OR 97304
www.eveshamwood.com
info@eveshamwood.com
503-371-8478

Francis Tannahill
9360 Eola Hills Road
Amity, OR 97101
www.francistannahill.com
sam@francitannahill.com
503-835-9010

Patricia Green Cellars
15225 NE North Valley Road
Newberg, OR 97132
www.patriciagreencellars.com
winery@patriciagreencellars.com
503-554-0821

Sass Winery/Wild Winds Winery
9092 Jackson Hill Road SE
Salem, OR 97306
Sasswinery@aol.com
503-391-9991

Viridian Wines
8930 Suver Road
Monmouth, OR 97361

South Willamette Valley Wine Country

Belle Vallee Cellars, LLC
804 NW Buchanan Avenue
Corvallis, OR 97330
www.bellevallee.com
info@bellevallee.com
541-757-9463

Broadley Vineyards
265 S Fifth Street
Monroe, OR 97456
www.broadleyvineyards.com
broadley@peak.org
541-847-5934

Houston Vineyards
86187 Hoya Lane
Eugene, OR 97405
www.houstonvineyards.com
mailbox@houstonvineyards.com
541-747-4681

Lumos Wine Company
24000 Cardwell Hill Drive
Philomath, OR 97370
www.lumoswine.com
lumos@lumoswine.com
541-929-3519

RainSong Vineyard
92989 Templeton Road
Cheshire, OR 97419
503-998-1786

East Willamette Valley Wine Country

Abiqua Wind Vineyard
19822 McKillop Road NE
Scotts Mills, OR 97375
www.abiquawind.com
ckbuffi@attg.net
503-874-9818

Saga Vineyards
30815 S Wall Street
Colton, OR 97017
saga@mollala.net
503-824-4600

Umpqua Valley Wine Country

Freed Estate Vineyard
555 Hooten Road
Winston, OR 97496
541-679-9342

Rogue Valley Wine Country

12 Ranch Wines
4550 Burgdorf Road
Bonanza, OR 97623
www.12ranchwines.com
wine@12ranchwines.com
541-545-1204

Academy of Wine
18200 Highway 238
Grants Pass, OR 97527
www.academyofwine.com
academy@internetcds.com
541-846-6817

Daisy Creek Vineyard
675 Shafer Lane
Jacksonville, OR 97530
www.daisycreekwine.com
daisycreek@clearwire.net
541-899-8329

Madrone Mountain Vineyard
540 Tumbleweed Trail
Jacksonville, OR 97530
www.madronemountain.com
winery@madronemountain.com
541-899-9642

Columbia Gorge Wine Country

Marchesi Vineyards
3955 Belmont Drive
Hood River, OR 97031
marchesif@aol.com
541-386-1800

Central and Eastern Oregon Wine Country

Gilstrap Brothers
69789 Antles Lane
Cove, OR 97824
www.gilstrapbrothers.com
info@gilstrapbrothers.com
541-568-4450

Appendix C
Glossary of Oregon Grape Varieties

I love diversity — diversity of mind, food, and grape. In Oregon, WineTrail enthusiasts have a cornucopia of grape varieties to taste — dozens and dozens. And that doesn't take into account the many dessert-style wines, ports, sparkling wines, and blends. The 2007 Oregon Vineyard and Winery Report, sponsored by the Oregon Wine Board, found that Oregon grape growers harvested 13,800 acres of premium wine grapes. That's harvested — there's

Summer Grapes — Willamette Valley

a total of 17,400 premium wine grapes in production and the number is growing. Following is a glossary of the most popular white and red grapes cultivated in Oregon.

White Grapes

The cooler climes of the Willamette Valley provide excellent conditions for growing premium white grapes. However, the warmer regions of southern Oregon's Umpqua and Rogue River valleys are not to be outdone. Following is a list of the most popular white wine grapes cultivated in Oregon. Keep in mind, that there are a variety of obscure whites to sample along Oregon's WineTrails. Don't pass up the chance to experience the amazing flavors of albariño, arneis, Auxerrois, grüner veltliner, pinot meunier (used in the production of champagne), seyval, and tocai friulano (say that ten times). See www.winetrailsnw.com to learn which wineries feature these hard-to-find white varieties.

Chardonnay
This French grape is widely planted throughout the Willamette Valley, where the introduction of Dijon clones from Burgundy has helped this grape to adapt to the Oregon climate and soils. Chardonnay varies with climate and fermentation methods, with a fruitiness that can comprise apple, pear, lemon, peach, mango, and grapefruit; a buttery creaminess is its most common characteristic. It is also used in many blended white wines.

Gewürztraminer
Gewürztraminer (pronounced guh-VOORTS-truh-MEE-ner) is a German-Alsatian grape variety. "Gewürz," which is German for "spicy," is the main characteristic of gewürztraminer. "Traminer" means "coming from Tramin," a small city in Austria's Tyrol region, where the grape originated. The wine is delicious and fruity, with strong aromas; a very perfumed and flowery bouquet.

511

Gewürztraminer is sweeter than riesling, which is a dry wine. A thick, rich wine that can be aged, gewürztraminer is better with sauerkraut, sausages, the Alsatian cheese muenster, curry-seasoned dishes, Chinese and Mexican cuisine, and other spicy dishes. A gewürztraminer can even be served as a dessert wine. A little over 200 acres of gewürztraminer is cultivated in Oregon.

Müller-Thurgau

Müller-Thurgau was developed in Germany in the late 19th century by a Dr. Müller from the Swiss town of Thurgau. The wine's name is pronounced something like "MEW-lehr toor-gow." Müller-Thurgau is widely grown in the Willamette Valley AVA. Müller-Thurgau is a pleasantly scented wine with good acidity and a flavor that resembles riesling.

Pinot blanc

Pinot blanc is a white grape genetic mutation of pinot gris, which is itself a mutation of pinot noir. More than 200 acres of pinot blanc grow in Oregon, primarily in the Willamette Valley, although a few vineyards in the Southern Oregon appellation include pinot blanc. This is a grape that thrives in cooler climes devoid of excessive heat. Pinot blanc reminds most wine enthusiasts of chardonnay and goes wonderfully with seafood and chicken dishes.

Pinot gris

Pinot gris is a white grape variety of the species Vitis vinifera. A variant clone of the pinot noir grape, it normally has a grayish-blue fruit, accounting for its name ("gris" meaning "gray" in French). The name "pinot," which is the French

word for "pinecone," may have been given to it because the grapes grow in small, pinecone-shaped clusters. (And in case you were wondering, "pinot grigio" and "pinot gris" are one and the same, the former being the Italian name for the grape variety.) The wines produced from this grape also vary in color, from a

Late July grapes at Eola Hills Wine Cellars

deep golden yellow to copper and even a light shade of pink. Oregon boasts more than 2,500 acres of pinot gris in production; pinot gris is the second-most-planted premium wine grape in Oregon, behind pinot noir. Like its red cousin, pinot gris grows primarily in the Willamette Valley, where grapes avoid getting sunburned. This wine pairs exceptionally well with Northwest seafood or chicken dishes, or drink it by itself as you take in the sight of Haystack Rock off Cannon Beach.

Sauvignon blanc

Sauvignon blanc is a green-skinned grape variety that originated in the Bordeaux region of France. The grape gets it name from the French words sauvage ("wild") and blanc ("white") because of its early origins as an indigenous grape in southwestern France. It is now planted in many of the world's wine regions, producing a crisp, dry, and refreshing white varietal wine. Depending on climate, its flavor can range from aggressively grassy to sweetly tropical. Wine experts have used the phrase "crisp, elegant, and

Maysara Winery

fresh" as a favorable description of sauvignon blanc of the Loire Valley and New Zealand. When fermented in oak, sauvignon blanc is referred to as fumé blanc. Sauvignon blanc, when slightly chilled, pairs well with fish or cheese.

Riesling

Riesling is a German white grape originating in the Rhine River valley region of Germany, Austria, and France, as far back as the mid-1400s. Its popularity has waxed and waned over the centuries. Today, more than 700 acres of riesling grapes are cultivated in Oregon. (**WineTrail trivia:** More than 50,000 acres of riesling are planted in Germany!) As a general rule, rieslings balance on a fine line between acidity and delicacy. They are very "terroir expressive," meaning their flavors are heavily influenced by the region in which they're grown; peach, green apple, quince and citrus are among the flavors most often expressed when describing riesling. Riesling is usually included in the "top three" white wine varieties, together with chardonnay and sauvignon blanc.

Viognier

Viognier is a white grape believed to have been brought to the Rhône region of France from Dalmatia by the Romans way back in A.D. 281. The wine itself is golden colored and has a fruity bouquet. Viognier grows in Willamette, Umpqua, and Rogue River Valley vineyards.

Red Grapes

Pinot lovers, take heart: A full 58 percent of the grapes grown in the Willamette Valley are of the pinot noir persuasion. However, WineTrail trekkers would be remiss in not traveling to Walla Walla, the Columbia Gorge, Umpqua, and the Rogue Valley to experience warm-weather varietals. In these viticulture areas, get ready to taste Bordeaux-style wines such as cabernet sauvignon, cabernet franc, and merlot. In addition, zinfandel and syrah thrive in these warmer climes and are not to be missed. Other red grapes grown in Oregon — including baco noir, dolcetto, gamay noir, and marechal foch — account for a small percentage of total production, yet are a delight to discover. Tasting rooms that feature these hard-to-find varietals are highlighted elsewhere in this book, and trekkers should swirl and sample. Our personal favorite: baco noir.

Cabernet franc

This black-skinned Bordeaux grape dates back to the end of the 18th century and is thought to be a parent of the cabernet sauvignon grape. It is softer than cabernet sauvignon, and therefore is often used in blends. However, a number

Torii Mor Vineyard and Winery

of wineries produce cabernet franc by itself with great results. Cabernet franc is primarily grown in the Columbia Gorge, and to a lesser extent, in Oregon's Rogue River Valley.

Cabernet sauvignon

Cabernet sauvignon is a cross between cabernet franc and sauvignon blanc grapes, and is thought to have originated in the fields of Bordeaux. This noble grape is one of the world's most renowned red grapes, with the flavor of black currant and aromas of cherry and plum. Cabernet sauvignon grows well in Oregon's Rogue and Umpqua valleys.

Merlot

Merlot is a popular French noble grape with origins dating back to the late 1700s. Merlot-based wines usually have medium body with hints of berry, plum, and currant. Its softness and "fleshiness," combined with its earlier ripening, make merlot an ideal grape to blend with the sterner, later-ripening cabernet sauvignon. This grape has complex and varying flavors, most consistently described as smooth. It is lighter in color, acid, and tannins than cabernet sauvignon, and is often combined with cabernet sauvignon and cabernet franc to make a Bordeaux blend. Merlot grows throughout Oregon's warmer climes, including the Walla Walla Valley, the Columbia Gorge, Umpqua Valley, and Rogue River Valley.

Pinot noir

Pinot noir is the signature grape of Oregon's Willamette Valley, where more than 20,000 tons are produced annually. Food was invented to pair with this wine! Of Oregon's roughly 17,000 acres under premium wine grape production, nearly 10,000 are planted with pinot noir. This noble grape has its origins in France's east-central Burgundy region and is believed to date from the fourth century. At its best, pinot noir is described as sensual and transparent, with a fruit-forward sweetness and a relatively low tannin level.

Syrah

Syrah is a noble black grape variety indigenous to the Rhône region of France since the time of the Roman Empire. This grape is called "shiraz" in Australia. Syrah is big-bodied, complex, and capable of aging for decades. Syrah is often blended with cabernet sauvignon or grenache to extend its aging ability. It is grown in hot, arid climates in austere soils such as those found in Oregon's Umpqua Valley and Rogue River Valley appellations.

Tempranillo

Tempranillo is a variety of black grape widely grown in its native Spain to make full-bodied red wines. It is the main grape used in Rioja, and is often referred to as Spain's "noble grape"; it is as common in Spain as cabernet sauvignon is in France. Its name is derived from the Spanish word temprano ("early"), a reference to the fact that it ripens several weeks earlier than most Spanish red grapes. Tempranillo wines can be consumed young, but the most expensive ones are aged for several years in oak barrels. The wines are ruby red in color, with aromas and flavors of berries, plum, tobacco, vanilla, leather, and herbs. Tempranillo is grown in southern Oregon's appellations, including the Rogue River and Umpqua valleys, as well as the Columbia Gorge.

Zinfandel

Zinfandel is a hot-weather grape that is cultivated in the Columbia Gorge and Rogue River Valley. Its origins are somewhat murky, but its California clones rival other wine grapes in terms of complexity and balance. With less than 100 acres of zinfandel grapes growing in the Pacific Northwest, California zinfandel growers have nothing to sweat from their competition to the north.

Late October in the Columbia Gorge

Winery	Chardonnay	Gewürztraminer	Grüner Veltliner	Melon de Bourgogne	Müller-Thurgau	Pinot Blanc	Pinot Gris	Riesling	Sauvignon Blanc	Viognier
A to Z Wineworks	●				●	●	●			
Abacela Vineyards & Winery									●	
Adelsheim Vineyard	●					●	●			
Agate Ridge Vineyard							●	●	●	
Airlie Winery	●			●			●			
Alexeli Vineyard & Winery	●	●		●		●	●			
Amity Vineyards		●				●	●			
Anindor Vineyards		●				●	●			
Ankeny Vineyard							●			
Anne Amie Vineyards				●	●	●	●			
Anthony Dell Cellars							●			
Apolloni Vineyards	●					●	●			
Applegate Red Winery										
Aramenta Cellars	●									
ArborBrook Vineyards							●			
Arcane Cellars	●						●		●	
Archery Summit										
Argyle Winery	●						●	●		
Ashland Vineyards							●	●		
August Cellars	●	●				●	●			
Barking Frog Winery										
Becker Vineyard				●			●			
Bella Vida Vineyard							●	●		
Benton-Lane Winery						●	●			
Bethel Heights Vineyard	●					●	●			
Bolton Cellars		●								
Bradley Vineyards							●			
Brandborg Winery		●				●	●	●		
Brandy Peak Distillery										
Bridgeview Vineyards	●	●					●	●		
Bryn Mawr Vineyards	●									
Cana's Feast Winery										
Cardwell Hill Cellars							●			
Carlo & Julian Winery										
Carlton Winemakers Studio	●						●	●	●	
Cathedral Ridge Winery	●	●					●	●		
Chateau Bianca Winery	●	●				●	●			

Baco noir	Cabernet Franc	Cabernet Sauvignon	Dolcetto	Maréchal Foch	Merlot	Petite Sirah	Pinot Noir	Syrah	Tempranillo	Zinfandel	Wine Country	Pg #
						•						144
	•	•		•			•	•		•		374
						•	•					118
	•	•			•	•	•		•			390
			•			•						274
		•				•						326
						•						216
						•						342
			•			•						268
						•						182
	•	•		•		•	•					192
						•						60
	•	•		•		•	•					406
						•						122
						•						120
		•		•		•						224
						•						164
						•						142
•				•		•						400
			•			•						112
		•				•		•				94
		•				•		•				360
						•						154
						•						294
						•						234
				•		•						466
•						•						346
	•					•		•				344
						•						28
		•		•		•	•					438
						•			•			236
	•	•				•	•					84
						•						288
						•			•			106
•						•	•					82
		•		•		•	•			•		454
			•			•						258

Winery	Chardonnay	Gewürztraminer	Grüner Veltliner	Melon de Bourgogne	Müller-Thurgau	Pinot Blanc	Pinot Gris	Riesling	Sauvignon Blanc	Viognier
Chateau Lorane	●	●		●			●	●	●	
Chehalem	●				●	●	●			
Cherry Hill Winery							●			
Clear Creek Distillery										
Cliff Creek Cellars										
Coelho Winery of Amity	●						●			
Cooper Mountain Vineyards	●						●			
Cowhorn Vineyard & Garden										●
Crater Lake Cellars	●	●			●		●			
Cricket Hill Vineyard										
Cristom Vineyards	●						●			●
Cubanisimo Vineyards							●			
David Hill Vineyard	●	●				●		●		
De Ponte Cellars				●						
Deer Creek Vineyards	●						●			
Del Rio Vineyards & Winery	●						●			●
Devitt Winery	●									●
Dobbes Family Estate					●		●			●
Domaine Coteau										
Domaine Drouhin Oregon	●									
Domaine Serene	●									
Duck Pond Cellars	●	●					●			●
EdenVale Winery	●						●			●
Edgefield Winery	●						●	●		●
EIEIO & Company										
Elk Cove Vineyards						●	●	●		●
Emerson Vineyards	●						●			
Eola Hills Wine Cellars	●	●					●		●	
Erath Vineyards		●			●	●	●			
Erin Glenn Wincry		●						●		●
Evergreen Vineyards	●						●			
Fiasco Winery	●									
Firesteed Cellars	●						●	●		
Flying Dutchman Winery								●		
Folin Cellars										●
Foris Vineyards Winery	●	●			●		●	●		
Girardet Wine Cellars	●	●					●	●		

REDS

Winery	Chardonnay	Gewürztraminer	Grüner Veltliner	Melon de Bourgogne	Müller-Thurgau	Pinot Blanc	Pinot Gris	Riesling	Sauvignon Blanc	Viognier
Harris Bridge Vineyard										
Hauer of the Dauen	●	●				●	●			
Helvetia Vineyards	●					●	●		●	
Henry Estate Winery	●	●		●		●	●		●	
High Pass Winery						●				
HillCrest Vineyard	●						●	●	●	
Hip Chicks Do Wine	●	●					●			
Honeywood Winery	●	●		●		●	●			
Hood River Vineyards	●	●				●	●			
Jacksonville Vineyards	●									
John Michael					●	●				
Julianna Vineyards								●		
Kathken Vineyards						●	●			
King Estate Winery	●	●				●				●
Kramer Vineyards	●			●		●				
Kristin Hill Winery	●	●				●				
Lange Estate Winery	●									
Laurel Hood										
Laurel Ridge Winery	●	●				●	●	●		
LaVelle Vineyards	●					●	●			
Left Coast Cellars	●					●				
Lenné Estate										
LongSword Vineyard	●									
Maragas Winery						●				
Maresh Red Barn					●	●	●			
MarshAnne Landing	●									●
Maysara Winery					●	●	●			
Melrose Vineyard	●					●				●
Methven Family Vineyards	●					●	●			
Misty Oaks Vineyard		●			●					
Montinore Estate		●		●		●	●			
Mt. Hood Winery	●	●				●	●			
Mystic Wines	●									
Naked Winery	●					●	●			
Namasté Vineyards	●	●					●			
Nehalem Bay Wine Co.										
Noble Estate Vineyard	●					●	●			

WHITES

Baco noir	Cabernet Franc	Cabernet Sauvignon	Dolcetto	Maréchal Foch	Merlot	Petite Sirah	Pinot Noir	Syrah	Tempranillo	Zinfandel	Wine Country	Pg #
												290
						•						210
						•						38
				•		•	•					356
						•						302
	•			•		•			•			368
•	•			•		•	•					48
	•		•	•		•						264
	•			•		•	•		•			456
	•			•								420
				•		•			•			416
•	•		•	•								362
						•						244
	•			•				•				314
						•						78
						•						218
						•						150
						•						22
						•						108
	•			•		•	•					304
						•						252
						•						128
			•				•					424
				•					•			476
						•						156
	•			•								350
						•						202
•				•		•	•					366
						•						212
	•					•						354
						•						70
				•		•						464
	•			•			•		•			214
	•			•		•	•					446
						•						256
												24
	•			•		•						308

Winery	Chardonnay	Gewürztraminer	Grüner Veltliner	Melon de Bourgogne	Müller-Thurgau	Pinot Blanc	Pinot Gris	Riesling	Sauvignon Blanc	Viognier
Oak Knoll Winery	•	•		•			•	•		
Old Bridge Winery	•							•		
Orchard Heights Winery		•					•			
Oswego Hills							•		•	
Palotai Vineyard & Winery	•									
Panther Creek Cellars	•									
Paschal Winery	•						•			
Patton Valley Vineyard										
Penner-Ash Wine Cellars								•	•	
Pfeiffer Vineyards	•						•			
Pheasant Court Winery	•						•			
Pheasant Valley Winery	•	•					•	•		
Phelps Creek Vineyards	•	•								
Piluso Vineyard & Winery										
Pioneer Hopyard Vineyard	•						•			
Plum Hill Vineyards					•		•	•		
Ponzi Vineyard	•				•		•	•		
Pudding River Wine Cellars	•						•		•	
Purple Cow Vineyards	•									
Quenett Winery	•						•		•	
R. Stuart & Co.							•			
Redhawk Winery	•						•	•		
Reustle-Prayer			•				•	•	•	•
Rex Hill Vineyards	•						•			
River's Edge Winery		•					•			
Rosella's Vineyard	•									
RoxyAnn Winery							•		•	
Saginaw Vineyard	•			•			•			
SakéOne										
Schmidt Family Vineyards	•	•					•		•	
Scott Paul Wines										
Secret House Winery	•			•			•	•		
Seufert Winery								•		
Shafer Vineyard Cellars	•	•		•			•	•		
Shallon Winery										
Sienna Ridge Estate	•	•			•		•	•		
Silvan Ridge-Hinman	•						•			•

WHITES

REDS

Winery	Chardonnay	Gewürztraminer	Grüner Veltliner	Melon de Bourgogne	Müller-Thurgau	Pinot Blanc	Pinot Gris	Riesling	Sauvignon Blanc	Viognier
Silver Falls Vineyards	•					•	•			
Sineann Cellars	•	•				•	•	•		
Sokol Blosser						•	•			
Soléna Cellars						•				
Spangler Vineyards	•								•	•
Spindrift Cellars					•	•				
Springhill Cellars						•				
Springhouse Cellar Winery	•	•				•				
St. Innocent Winery	•				•	•				
St. Josef's Winery	•	•				•	•			
Stangeland Vineyards	•	•				•				
Stoller Vineyard and Winery	•									
Stone Wolf Vineyards	•			•		•				
Sweet Cheeks Winery	•					•	•			
Terra Vina Wines	•									
Territorial Vineyards	•					•	•			
The Eyrie Vineyards	•				•	•				
The Four Graces					•	•				
The Pines 1852						•				•
Torii Mor Vineyard & Winery					•	•				
Trium						•				•
Troon Vineyard	•	•						•	•	•
Tualatin Estate Vineyards	•	•				•	•			
Tyee Wine Cellars	•	•			•	•				
Tyrus Evan										•
Urban Wineworks						•				
Valley View Winery	•									•
Van Duzer Vineyards						•		•		
Vista Hills Vineyard & Winery						•				
Vitae Springs Vineyard		•	•	•			•			
Vitis Ridge	•	•				•	•			
Volcano Vineyards										
VX (Vercingetorix)					•	•				
Walnut City WineWorks						•				•
Wasson Brothers Winery	•							•		
Watermill Winery									•	•
Weisinger's of Ashland	•	•				•				

Winery	Chardonnay	Gewürztraminer	Grüner Veltliner	Melon de Bourgogne	Müller-Thurgau	Pinot Blanc	Pinot Gris	Riesling	Sauvignon Blanc	Viognier
Wheatridge in the Nook	●									
White Rose Wines										
Wild Rose Vineyard						●				
WillaKenzie Estate					●	●				
Willamette Valley Vineyards	●						●	●	●	
Winderlea Vineyard	●									
Windridge Vineyard										
Wine Country Farm Cellars	●			●			●			
Winter's Hill Vineyard					●	●				
Witness Tree Vineyard	●				●				●	
Wooldridge Creek Winery	●	●							●	
Wy'East Vineyards	●					●				
Yamhill Valley Vineyards					●		●			
Zenas Wines								●		
Zerba Cellars	●								●	

Please note that the information for the above chart was collected during 2008 and is subject to change in the future.

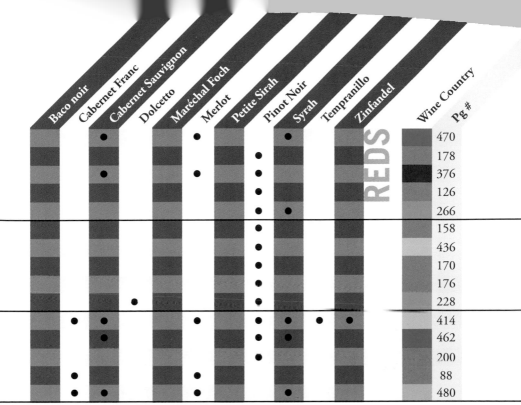

Baco noir	Cabernet Franc	Cabernet Sauvignon	Dolcetto	Maréchal Foch	Merlot	Petite Sirah	Pinot Noir	Syrah	Tempranillo	Zinfandel	Wine Country	Pg #
	●			●			●					470
						●						178
	●			●		●						376
						●						126
						●	●					266
						●						158
						●						436
							●					170
						●						176
			●			●						228
●	●			●		●	●	●	●			414
	●						●	●				462
						●						200
●				●								88
●	●			●			●					480

Please note that the information for the above chart was collected during 2008 and is subject to change in the future.

Get the Complete WineTrails Northwest Series!

WineTrails OF WASHINGTON
First Edition
Published December 2007
608-full color pages; 32 WineTrails;
    228 wineries; 1 book
Only $19.95 plus S&H while the
    First Edition lasts!

WineTrails OF OREGON
First Edition
Published 2009
Your guide to all things great about
    Oregon wine – travel, taste and experience.
Only $24.95 plus S&H!

TO ORDER:
Call **800-533-6165** or order online at
www.winetrailsnw.com/shop

It's easy, it's convenient and the books are signed
and personalized with your message. Hey, why waste
gas when you can order via phone or Internet and
have it delivered to your home? How cool is that!

VISIT. TASTE. EXPERIENCE.

Index

This index covers cities and wineries. Cities are listed in bold. Wineries can be found individually in alphabetical order or under the city in which they belong.

Tasting Notes